Elections, Voting, Technology

Series Editor
Kathleen Hale
Department of Political Science
Auburn University
Auburn, AL, USA

This series examines the relationships between people, electoral processes and technologies, and democracy. Elections are a fundamental aspect of a free and democratic society and, at their core, they involve a citizenry making selections for who will represent them. This series examines the ways in which citizens select their candidates—the voting technologies used, the rules of the game that govern the process—and considers how changes in processes and technologies affect the voter and the democratic process.

More information about this series at
http://www.palgrave.com/gp/series/14965

Mitchell Brown · Kathleen Hale ·
Bridgett A. King
Editors

The Future of Election Administration

palgrave
macmillan

Editors
Mitchell Brown
Auburn University
Auburn, AL, USA

Kathleen Hale
Auburn University
Auburn, AL, USA

Bridgett A. King
Auburn University
Auburn, AL, USA

Elections, Voting, Technology
ISBN 978-3-030-14946-8   ISBN 978-3-030-14947-5 (eBook)
https://doi.org/10.1007/978-3-030-14947-5

© The Editor(s) (if applicable) and The Author(s), under exclusive license to Springer Nature Switzerland AG 2020
This work is subject to copyright. All rights are solely and exclusively licensed by the Publisher, whether the whole or part of the material is concerned, specifically the rights of translation, reprinting, reuse of illustrations, recitation, broadcasting, reproduction on microfilms or in any other physical way, and transmission or information storage and retrieval, electronic adaptation, computer software, or by similar or dissimilar methodology now known or hereafter developed.
The use of general descriptive names, registered names, trademarks, service marks, etc. in this publication does not imply, even in the absence of a specific statement, that such names are exempt from the relevant protective laws and regulations and therefore free for general use.
The publisher, the authors and the editors are safe to assume that the advice and information in this book are believed to be true and accurate at the date of publication. Neither the publisher nor the authors or the editors give a warranty, expressed or implied, with respect to the material contained herein or for any errors or omissions that may have been made. The publisher remains neutral with regard to jurisdictional claims in published maps and institutional affiliations.

Cover design by Frido Steinen-Broo/eStudio Calamar

This Palgrave Macmillan imprint is published by the registered company Springer Nature Switzerland AG
The registered company address is: Gewerbestrasse 11, 6330 Cham, Switzerland

Foreword

Everyone should have a voice in improving election administration. There are some who see competition—negative competition—and try to maneuver territories for control. I don't see it that way—I think everyone should have a voice in the process. But this approach takes time.

Shortly after the US Election Assistance Commission (EAC) first opened in 2005, I walked in the door as their new Executive Director. They had been working for eight months without many employees—the ones there were people who came from the old Federal Election Commission (FEC) Clearinghouse and from a few other federal agencies. The EAC hired the general counsel first, and looking back, this was a wise decision. We had a lot of federal regulations to deal with. For a number of years, there were many rules about compliance that we had to deal with in order to become a federal agency. Achieving full compliance was a challenge, and Alice Miller in particular helped us get through our first federal audit. The auditors came and lived in our office for over six months, went through every sheet of paper, and made sure we complied with every regulation out there.

In addition to the audit, the other major work of our office at the time was developing the voting system certification program. We received a lot of criticism from Congress and some advocacy groups because it was slow work—but that slowness was necessary. This kind of work cannot be done overnight. Working with our partner organization the National Institute for Standards and Technology (NIST), Commissioner Donetta Davidson served as the designated federal officer and tirelessly worked with our staff and other stakeholders from around the country for a long time to develop the program. The result is that today we have a set of protocols with involvement and buy-in from all sectors. Standards and processes change and evolve, but the approach and infrastructure is there and it took almost ten years to build. This type of work is murky, takes a long time, and involves a lot of blood, sweat, and tears. It involves trial and error. It means working with vendors and advocacy groups. But ultimately the outcome is worth a process like this, one that is multifaceted, complicated, involves many people, and takes time.

It's like that in all aspects of our business. This year, I will celebrate my 50th anniversary in elections, and none of the changes I've been a part of happened overnight. They happened because someone had an idea and worked for years to make it work.

There are many other examples. When Washington state first had the idea of moving to voting by mail, the naysayers said it wouldn't work, that the United States Postal Service (USPS) couldn't handle the load, that voters wouldn't accept it, and that there would be fraud. But today the voters in Washington, Oregon, and Colorado love vote-by-mail and if it went away they would be upset. Electronic pollbooks (EPBs) are another example of this—voters were wary at first, jurisdictions were reluctant to purchase them because of the kinks that need to be worked out when adopting first-generation technology, but today EPBs help the process. Another is early voting. Texas was the first state to adopt this, and many people were reluctant, afraid of how hard it would be to manage. But early voting has been a success there and spread around the country.

To improve election administration systems, you need cooperation between local election officials, state legislatures, and county boards.

You need to work with other stakeholders. And you need to take the time to work things out. There is nothing that has happened in our business in the last 50 years that was an instantaneous success. Change takes time and cooperation among officials, voters, legislators, vendors, and community groups. People need to work together to make positive change happen.

The next generation of positive reform is coming. There are new ways for people to transmit ballots from overseas and sophisticated tracking programs for absentee ballots. These are big services for voters, but their development and spread require vendors, USPS, local election offices, and other groups, all to cooperate and to support voter experiences and consequently to enhance the confidence of voters.

There is also no crystal ball to know what's going to happen 10 years from now. But we can get there by including a plurality of voices to help identify, prepare for, and address gaps. There are other issues that we need to pay attention to and determine whether they are consistent problems and concerns around the country—provisional voting (particularly poll workers who make the process uneven across jurisdictions); ballot layout; signature requirements and signature verification rules that no longer make any sense; short periods for canvassing; and so on. There are situations all around the country right now that need greater scrutiny, and these things need to be examined by outside parties who won't make a buck off of the results of the research.

The Election Administration Program at Auburn University filled a critical space when they helped to create the Certified Elections/Registration Administrator (CERA) program with the Election Center and later created the Election Administration Symposium Series. The entrance of the academic community into election administration after 2000 was a good thing. But some parts of the election administration community have been more reluctant about this research in part because they didn't understand the value of good research and in part because they were wary of bad research. It is important that we study practical topics surrounding election administration so long as there is feedback from practitioners. Academics who do this work in a vacuum produce useless research. This is where Auburn University researchers have done a good job in comparison with many other academic researchers in this area. And this is the value of their Symposium Series and this volume—bridging the gap between practitioners and researchers.

If you look at a crossword puzzle and you call it the election process, and then take some pieces out and lay them to the side, these pieces become, or represent, the problems and issues in election administration today. These include things like ballot design, security, equipment, provisional voting, and so on. Then you have to find people to help you pick up the pieces and fill in the holes. When this is done, you have a beautiful picture.

I know there are a lot of election officials who express concern that other people are in their business, and others who feel that people are stepping on their toes or encroaching on their territory. But no one election official, advocacy group, or researcher owns this topic—there is no single individual or organization who can solve this topic. Bringing election officials at all levels together with researchers and other stakeholders, like Brown, Hale, and King do in these volumes, pushes the conversation forward and only helps in the long run. The Auburn University Symposium Series is designed around panels with a great mix of stakeholders—practitioners, academics, vendors, and advocates—talking about important topics. These books put those conversations on paper to help move conversation, policy, practice, and research in election administration forward.

Loudonville, New York

Tom Wilkey
Executive Director, United States
Election Assistance Commission (Retd.)
Executive Director, New York State Board of Elections (Retd.)

Tom Wilkey is a founding member of the Election Center and joined the Erie County Board of Elections in Buffalo, New York. He joined the New York State Board of Elections in 1979 serving as director of communications and voter education, where he was responsible for the oversight of New York's 62 county election offices. Wilkey has served as executive director of the New York Board of Elections, and as both a member and participant in numerous national committees involved in developing the National Voter Registration Act and the Help America Vote Act. Wilkey served as president of the National Association of State Election Directors and is a proud life member of the New York State Election Commissioners Association. Most recently, Wilkey served as the first executive director of the US Election Assistance Commission.

Acknowledgements

We extend our deep appreciation to the election administrators, academics, and advocacy professionals who took time out of their busy schedules to attend the Inclusion and Integrity Symposium at Auburn University in 2017 and to subsequently contribute to *The Future of Election Administration* and *The Future of Election Administration: Cases and Conversations*. We know that we asked you to contribute to this volume during an election year. Your willingness to openly accept our invitation, first to the Symposium and then to write for these volumes, is but another indication of your commitment to the profession and to scholarship for and about the field.

Because of your collective efforts, we are able to contribute two volumes to the literature that include voices and perspectives from the range of stakeholder groups who contribute to and play integral roles in the evolving field of election administration. It is our hope that the expertise reflected in this collection of chapters and case studies will serve as a resource that facilitates better understanding of the complexity of voting and election processes in the USA and the profession of election administration.

We would also thank Auburn University for its support of our efforts. The Department of Political Science and the College of Liberal Arts supported this work, as did the Master of Public Administration (MPA) and Ph.D. in Public Administration and Policy Programs, and the Graduate Program in Election Administration. Special thanks are due to the Charles Wesley Edwards, Jr. Endowment for supporting the Symposiums. And in particular we thank our graduate students—M.P.A. Election Center Fellow Tyler St. Clair, M.P.A. graduate research assistant Emily Hale, and Ph.D. students Lindsey Forson and Shaniqua Williams. We are always learning about this field, and it has been a pleasure to have you learn along with us.

Research about public programs is not possible without open access to data—and not just numbers, but also observations, interviews, and more. The transparency provided by election officials and other election community stakeholders has been essential to this project specifically and the field of election sciences more generally, and we are grateful for that. The openness of federal, state, and local officials, and vendors and advocates along with their interest in advancing the profession is encouraging and something for us all to celebrate and continue.

And not least, we are grateful for the support of the Election Center, also known as the National Association of Election Officials, both for its support for the symposium and its partnership with Auburn University. We believe our partnership and joint efforts over the past several decades to professionalize the field through CERA, the national certification for election professionals, has helped develop the field, and we look forward to future collaboration.

Contents

1 **Introduction** 1
   Bridgett A. King, Mitchell Brown and Kathleen Hale

Part I Current Challenges and the Future of Access and Participation

2 **The Federal Response and New Considerations for Election Administration** 17
   Bridgett A. King

3 **Parties and Politics: The Evolution of Election Administration** 31
   Doug Lewis

4 **Accessible and Secure: Improving Voter Confidence by Protecting the Right to Vote** 49
   Thomas Hicks

5   Challenges in Voter Registration   59
    Thessalia Merivaki and Daniel A. Smith

6   Polling Place Quality and Access   83
    Robert Stein, Christopher Mann and Charles Stewart III

Part II Meeting the Challenges of Professionalism

7   The Evolution of Professionalism in the Field
    of Election Administration   103
    Mitchell Brown and Kathleen Hale

8   The Elections Performance Index: Past, Present,
    and Future   119
    Charles Stewart III

9   Building Terminology in the Field   155
    Katy Owens Hubler and Tammy Patrick

10 Diversity and Descriptive Representation in Election
    Administration   169
    Bridgett A. King

11 Election Costs: A Study of North Carolina   185
    Martha Kropf and JoEllen V. Pope

Part III Emerging and Future Issues in Election Administration

12 The Role of Election Vendors in Election Administration   201
    Peter Lichtenheld

13 Election Integrity in Ensuring Accuracy   213
    Christy McCormick

| 14 | Election Security: Increasing Election Integrity by Improving Cybersecurity
Marian K. Schneider | 243 |

| 15 | Election Audits
Jennifer Morrell | 261 |

| 16 | Election Cybersecurity
Judd Choate and Robert Smith | 279 |

| 17 | Special Elections Costs: Filling Legislative and Congressional Vacancies
Dean C. Logan | 301 |

| 18 | Increasing Confidence in International Elections
Kelly Ann Krawczyk and Avery Davis-Roberts | 317 |

| 19 | Conclusion
Kathleen Hale, Mitchell Brown and Bridgett A. King | 345 |

Appendix: The Future of Election Administration: Cases and Conversations — 351

Index — 355

Contributors

Mitchell Brown Auburn University, Auburn, AL, USA

Judd Choate Colorado Department of State, Denver, CO, USA

Avery Davis-Roberts The Carter Center, Atlanta, GA, USA

Kathleen Hale Auburn University, Auburn, AL, USA

Thomas Hicks United States Election Assistance Commission, Silver Spring, MD, USA

Katy Owens Hubler Democracy Research, Park City, UT, USA

Bridgett A. King Auburn University, Auburn, AL, USA

Kelly Ann Krawczyk Auburn University, Auburn, AL, USA

Martha Kropf University of North Carolina at Charlotte, Charlotte, NC, USA

Doug Lewis Election Center (Retd.), Katy, TX, USA

Peter Lichtenheld Hart InterCivic, Austin, TX, USA

Dean C. Logan Los Angeles County Registrar-Recorder/County Clerk, Los Angeles County, CA, USA

Christopher Mann Skidmore College, Saratoga Springs, NY, USA

Christy McCormick United States Election Assistance Commission, Silver Spring, MD, USA

Thessalia Merivaki Mississippi State University, Starkville, MS, USA

Jennifer Morrell Democracy Fund, Washington, DC, USA

Tammy Patrick Democracy Fund, Washington, DC, USA

JoEllen V. Pope University of North Carolina at Charlotte, Charlotte, NC, USA

Marian K. Schneider Verified Voting, Philadelphia, PA, USA

Daniel A. Smith University of Florida, Gainesville, FL, USA

Robert Smith National Intelligence University, Bethesda, MD, USA

Robert Stein Rice University, Houston, TX, USA

Charles Stewart III Massachusetts Institute of Technology, Cambridge, MA, USA

List of Figures

Fig. 5.1	Rates of accepted provisional ballots cast by "Previously Removed" voters in North Carolina in 2016	75
Fig. 5.2	Likelihood of casting a valid provisional ballot in North Carolina 2016 general election, by race	76
Fig. 8.1	Election Performance Index scores for the 2016 election	125
Fig. 8.2	Comparison of index values in 2016 with values in 2008	128
Fig. 8.3	Change in normalized EPI indicator scores for each state, 2008–2016	140
Fig. 10.1	Racial distribution of poll workers and voting age population in the United States	179
Fig. 11.1	Spending per registered voter in 100 North Carolina counties	193
Fig. 12.1	Voting systems as part of the election system	202
Fig. 16.1	The 21 states who learned they were targeted by Russian hackers during the 2016 general election	285
Fig. 16.2	Distribution of 2018 Help America Vote Act (HAVA) funds	292
Fig. 17.1	Election costs compared to voter turnout for special vacancy elections, 2000–2009	303

List of Tables

Table 5.1	Voter registration reforms across the United States	64
Table 5.2	State data-sharing membership and VRD systems	70
Table 5.3	Reasons for Election Day provisional ballots cast in the North Carolina 2016 general election	73
Table 6.1	Jurisdictions and polling places	86
Table 6.2	Demographics of study jurisdictions and 2016 national exit poll	87
Table 6.3	Polling place accessibility	90
Table 6.4	Polling place quality	91
Table 6.5	Polling place barriers to voting	92
Table 6.6	Descriptive statistics: polling place scores	92
Table 6.7	Regression coefficient for 2016 polling place attributes	96
Table 7.1	Distribution of states across Election Administration Professionalism Index v 1.0	111
Table 8.1	Indicators in the Elections Performance Index	123
Table 8.2	Comparison of three state profiles in the EPI	126
Table 8.3	Comparison of raw turnout rates in 2016 with normalized rates that take into account political competition and educational attainment	148
Table 10.1	Descriptive statistics of poll voter/workers interactions in 2016	179

Table 11.1	Descriptive statistics for election administration expenditures versus Colorado election cost 2013–2015	192
Table 13.1	Select list of NVRA cases from the most recent decade	218
Table 13.2	Ballot design requirements	225
Table 15.1	Example calculation of diluted margin	267
Table 17.1	Summary of ranked choice voting impact	310
Table 17.2	Comparison of alternatives and impact	313

1

Introduction

Bridgett A. King, Mitchell Brown and Kathleen Hale

At 6:00 a.m. on election day 2018 in Maricopa County, an election official reported that one of the polling locations used by the county was foreclosed overnight and locked with the voting equipment inside. Voters were advised to go to an emergency voting center. At 6:30 a.m., five of the 503 polling location had technology-related problems. At 7:00 a.m., long lines were reported before the polls opened. At 9:00 a.m., the locked polling location was accessible, and at 10:40 a.m., the building was accessible for voters. At 11:48 a.m., long lines were reported at Arizona State University (ASU). At 2:30 p.m., a man entered a polling location with a BB gun on his hip and was arrested.

B. A. King (✉) · M. Brown · K. Hale
Auburn University, Auburn, AL, USA
e-mail: bak0020@auburn.edu

M. Brown
e-mail: brown11@auburn.edu

K. Hale
e-mail: halekat@auburn.edu

© The Author(s) 2020
M. Brown et al. (eds.), *The Future of Election Administration*, Elections, Voting, Technology, https://doi.org/10.1007/978-3-030-14947-5_1

At 6:00 p.m., there was an estimated three hour wait at ASU—no problems were reported, just more people than expected. An order to extend polling hours was denied by the Maricopa County Superior Court. To combat the lines at ASU, voting booths were set up outside. Officials described the midterm election in Maricopa County as typical, with ordinary issues that crop up.

In many ways, this description of events encapsulates the nature of election administration. The field is rife with challenges that require immediate remedy. Before, during and after Election Day, administrators plan for and adjust to unexpected challenges and irregularities. In any given election cycle, there can be any number of unexpected challenges that arise. National, state, and local election officials have to defend their actions to the public and elected officials.

The American election administration landscape has changed dramatically since the passage of the Help America Vote Act (HAVA) in 2002, and the voting experience has improved in many ways. When registering to vote or casting ballots, voters in many states have a plethora of options that vary across the states, including online registration, automatic voter registration when obtaining a drivers' license, early voting, no-fault absentee voting, and expanded opportunities to vote by mail or vote centers. Mechanical equipment has been replaced with electronic voting systems, and in many places paper books of voter rolls have been replaced with electronic poll books to facilitate the use of registration data in the voting process. Local and state election offices are increasingly sophisticated in the use of election data for process improvement. Voters with disabilities are now guaranteed access to equipment and processes that allow them to vote privately and independently, and polling locations are accessible to all voters.

The work of election officials today is both more complicated and more important than ever before. The heartbeat of the American election systems that operate in more than (roughly) 8000 election jurisdictions around the country rests on process improvement and technological modernization, the details of which remain, for the most part, behind the scenes.[1] Not surprising, it has been increasingly apparent in recent years that the policy conversations, media reports, and research conducted about election administration do not always align with the complexities on the ground. This has downsides. As election administration practices continue to advance, public confidence in the electoral process has been severely challenged. At the most fundamental level, prominent media outlets widely and frequently report competing claims from candidates, elected officials, and advocacy groups that elections are rigged, that voter fraud abounds, that equipment and databases have been manipulated, and that voter participation is suppressed in record numbers by administrative or political decisions. Elections are the way we measure American democracy—access, participation, equity, transparency, accountability—and the future efforts of election administrators are essential if we are to continue to uphold these values and maintain confidence in our public institutions.

The Future of Election Administration tackles the critical dimensions of elections from the perspectives of some of the country's most forward-thinking practitioner, policy, advocacy, and research experts and leaders in these areas today. The theoretical framework of the book is grounded in the systems perspective of elections (Hale et al. 2015), which establishes election operations within the context of complex, interdependent organizational arrangements. We identify the most critical current and upcoming aspects of election administration systems, and these experts and leaders lend their experiences, understanding, and analysis about what is happening now and what we need to focus on in the future. Our goal is to describe, analyze, and anticipate the key areas of election administration systems on which students, researchers, advocates, policymakers, and practitioners should focus. Along with its companion volume, *The Future of Election Administration: Cases and*

---

[1] No census of local election jurisdictions has been taken; estimates range from 6000 to more than 10,000 and depend upon which local jurisdictions (towns, townships, cities, etc.) are included in addition to the nation's 3100 counties. Crawford et al. (2019) have recently initiated efforts in this direction, extending the work of Kimball and Baybeck (2013); future progress in this direction will be a welcome addition to the field.

Conversations, this book adds to an emerging body of literature that is part of the election sciences community with an emphasis on analyses of practical aspects of administration.

The Auburn University Election Administration Symposium Series

This project is the culmination of nearly five years of dialogue that began with a series of conversations between public administration and political science faculty at Auburn University and election officials around the country (including the leadership of the Election Center, the national professional association for election officials) about how to gather these perspectives and present them collectively to critical audiences. The most obvious of these audiences of course includes election administration professionals in the field and the researchers who study it. But we also hope to reach the policy arena, where local county and township commissions, state legislatures, and policy advisors at all levels of government propose ideas and make decisions that affect election operations, as well as the media who cover this critical aspect of American democratic functioning.

The Auburn Symposium on Election Administration was conceived as the vehicle to convene an initial set of conversations between leading academics, practitioners, and advocacy groups in the field. The first gathering was held at Auburn University on September 14–15, 2015. Titled *The Evolution of Election Administration Since the Voting Rights Act: 1965–2015*, the symposium brought together a diverse set of more than 60 voices through plenary sessions, panels, and informal gatherings to examine how the field has developed over the past-half century, the challenges that remain, and future trends. The Auburn University symposium series expanded in 2017, and faculty hosted *Inclusion and Integrity in Election Administration* on October 15–17, which featured the US Election Assistance Commissioners and data-driven conversations around the Election Assistance Commission's Election Administration and Voting Survey (EAVS) and featured the Election

Assistance Commission members. The goals of *Inclusion and Integrity* were to foster conversation about critical issues that impact American democratic institutions, support the development of common language across diverse professional communities engaged in the practice of election administration, and promote dialogue between those who conduct elections and those who study the way elections operate. Drawing more than 200 participants over 2 days, *Inclusion and Integrity* advanced the conversation with cutting-edge (and controversial) topics including the lack of diversity in the election workforce, the difficulties in untangling financial aspects of election operations, and presentations by representatives of leading equipment and service providers in the field about security concerns and the future of voting equipment. Through 64 separate panels and plenaries, participants discussed data and measurement issues around national surveys, voter access and participation, diversity, voting system vendor concerns, election professionalism, technology and security, costs and resources, measuring success, and emerging research in the field.

The Future of Election Administration and its companion case study volume result directly from the 2017 symposium; together they bring forward the voices and dialogue of election officials, advocates, and scholars at the event and the continuing conversations that were fostered there. These contributions hold great promise for the future of American election administration. The Auburn Symposium on Election Administration convenes again in the fall of 2019, where participants consider lessons learned in the 2018 election cycle, reflect on preparations for the 2020 presidential election, and better understand how to invest in innovation for the field.

The Context of Election Administration

Election administration is complicated. It involves many systems and subsystems, national and state laws and legal challenges, state and local procedures, contracting with private vendors, challenging interactions with the media, and pressures from citizens and third-party organizations. And after the 2016 presidential election, it also requires consideration of bad actors from other countries. Simultaneously, people's sense of what election administration should provide has also solidified around a straightforward series of steps: People should show up at the polls on election day and receive a ballot (or get a ballot in the mail in advance of the election), mark that ballot, return it, have it counted, and know who won the election by the end of election day. And likely what they really want now is to vote online or through an app. The disconnect between the public perception of elections and the reality of them is vast, and this disconnect is exacerbated by widespread disinformation, be it unintentional or malicious, spread by word of mouth, through social media, or through traditional media sources. Where elections and election administrators have been—and where they are now—provide information about where we are going. And to the extent that we can, knowing where we are going helps us develop the policies, practices, and training for a vibrant future.

No election runs perfectly, but the fears that many people expressed about 2018 were misplaced. Instead, most of the problems around the country that grabbed national headlines revolved around nuances related to election rules and practices. Lines in some places, malfunctioning machines in others, confusion over when ballots had to be counted, and when recounts were necessary are a few examples.

Between 2014 and 2018, we asked hundreds of election administrators to think about the future of their work with a target of the 2032 presidential election—far enough in the future that real change is possible, but close enough that they hopefully would not be tempted to imagine vastly unrealistic scenarios (though some did anyway). We asked about voter registration, balloting, equipment, turnout, and election administration itself. Their answers changed over the years, starting in 2014 with imaginative and daring ideas about internet-based voting that would make the process so convenient that all or most would want to be involved. By 2017, the tide had shifted completely, likely in response to the 2016 cyber hacking attempts: most administrators were convinced that paper ballots were here to stay.

In general, though, the administrators whom we asked were and remain optimistic about the future of their field. Simultaneously they were, as a group, certain that despite the importance of paper audit trails (essentially, paper records) of ballots cast, the field will become more and more reliant on technology, particularly ballot-on-demand systems or adaptations of current commercial off-the-shelf (COTS) technology. Although at present most states do not permit within state portability (in which voters can cast ballots outside the particular precinct to which they are assigned), they also believe that we will move to 50-state portability for registration, and likely automatic registration in most places across the country. If so, this portends the formation of a federal election administration system, with more robust federal authority that is significantly different than the one we have now.

With reliance on technology comes increasingly complex administrative demands. These demands will mean a more educated and sophisticated workforce. Combining a more sophisticated workforce with the new technology envisioned (which almost no one believes will be funded by the federal government) is expensive. Where the resources for the elections of the future will come from is a critical and often overlooked consideration, and one that is fundamental to the capacity of government to conduct elections.

Plan of the Book and Companion Book

Our publisher encouraged us to develop two companion books to capture the range of issues and voices in election administration today. The chapters in this volume reflect panels at the October 2017 Auburn symposium, and the book is designed around three themes. The first addresses current challenges and the future of access and participation. The second addresses the challenges of professionalizing the field of election administration. And the third part focuses on emerging and future issues in the field of election administration. The authors of these chapters represent election officials at local, state, and national levels, as well as vendors, researchers, and advocates.

The companion volume tracks these three parts and is comprised of accessible case studies written primarily by practitioners and from their first-person perspectives. These volumes can be read jointly or separately as stand-alone books, but our intent (and our hope) is that they are used together. The illustrative case studies lift up particular issues addressed in this volume through first-hand accounts of often complicated and compelling issues.

In this volume, Part I presents a historical lens through which the evolution of access and participation can be understood, while also focusing on new and emerging issues in the field, current responses, and opportunities for innovation. Part II examines the professionalism of the field of election administration as an area of public service and emerging concerns. The chapters include perspectives from the administrative professionals who run elections, professionals who work in the field as academics, and those who work as members of professional associations and other nonprofit organizations. Part III addresses issues that have emerged recently as either challenges or opportunities (or both), the ways in which election administrators have responded, and how they are preparing to address foreseeable challenges in the future.

Part I: Current Challenges and the Future of Access and Participation

In Chapter 2, Bridgett A. King provides a historical and contextual discussion of the major issues in access and participation and lays out concurrent challenges, innovations, and opportunities.

In Chapter 3, Doug Lewis more explicitly addresses the evolution of democratic inclusion and political interplay that shaped elections and voting in the United States. The chapter provides an overview of the history of voting in the United States and discusses the most critical issues related to electoral inclusion since the passage of the Help America Vote Act in 2002.

In Chapter 4, Election Assistance Commissioner Thomas Hicks discusses current controversies and initiatives related to proof of eligibility, overseas voters, and language minority voters. Drawing primarily from existing issues and initiatives, he provides a practical discussion of the current dimensions of voter access.

Thessalia Merivaki and Daniel A. Smith examine current issues relating to voter registration in Chapter 5 and address current changes to registration from automatic registration to online registration as well as more traditional methods. The authors focus on current controversies about purging or cleaning state voter registration lists and national efforts to aid in these efforts.

In Chapter 6, Robert Stein, Christopher Mann, Charles Stewart III, and their co-authors discuss the roles that polling location and poll worker quality play in the voter decision to participate in elections.

Part II: Meeting the Challenges of Professionalism

In Chapter 7, Mitchell Brown and Kathleen Hale discuss the development of public service professionalism generally, and the professionalism of election administration specifically. They identify the critical elements of professionalism in election administration, focusing on the influence of national and state associations in professionalizing the field. They compare levels of professionalism across the country at the state level and conclude with a discussion of the critical elements of a professionalized election administration workforce for today and the future.

In Chapter 8, Charles Stewart III details the Election Performance Index (EPI) as a central method of comparing election performance across the states. The chapter chronicles the creation of the index and the underlying framework of the national Election Administration and Voting Survey (EAVS). The chapter discusses the challenges that EAVS has faced since its inception in terms of motivations for data collection and local and state compliance with this voluntary initiative. The author concludes with a discussion of the potential value and uses of EAVS data as reflected through the EPI.

In Chapter 9, Katy Owens Hubler and Tammy Patrick tackle the importance of common language across the field of election systems, and specifically, the challenges in building common terminology and data formats. They focus on the impetus for several tools currently in development for the field including election process models, a glossary, and the common data format. They present points of current agreement about the utility of these tools and the anticipated implications for election administration, as well as the challenges to finding common languages across and within states for election administration purposes.

In Chapter 10, Bridgett A. King discusses the history and development of diversity in public administration and public service generally, and then diversity in election administration specifically. Based on a review of extant academic literature and secondary data, the chapter addresses critical concerns around various dimensions of diversity in election administration.

In Chapter 11, Martha Kropf and JoEllen V. Pope present a framework of costs and resources related to election administrative expenses, and then discuss complexities and interdependencies that make the study of election administration budgets and costs particularly challenging. The chapter reviews current practice initiatives to attempt to measure cost per voter and the strengths and weaknesses of those approaches. They then consider cost data from North Carolina's 100 counties as a way to address cost issues across the country.

Part III: Emerging and Future Issues in Election Administration

In Chapter 12, Peter Lichtenheld discusses the context of the election equipment environment and the role of vendors in the election administration environment today and in the future. From the vendor's perspective, he illustrates the vendor role as an election solution provider (ESP). He details the intricacies that election jurisdictions present, the approach that vendors take in understanding issues and generating solutions with their customers, and the essential nature of the contributions that vendors provide.

Election Administration Commissioner Christy McCormick takes up election integrity in Chapter 13. She details an approach to understanding integrity based on the principles of democracy and political equality, recent history including key judicial determinations, and the practical aspects of running an election. McCormick identifies possible best practices for state officials to increase election integrity through approaches to list maintenance, ballot design, balloting practices, security, and other election practices.

In Chapter 14, Marian Schneider continues the discussion of election integrity. She lays out principles of election integrity and applies them to the US context. She pursues an in-depth discussion of integrity in the 2016 American election including secure computer processes, the conduct of elections, and tabulation. Schneider concludes with a discussion of incorrect narratives about integrity and security that increase distrust in American democracy.

Jennifer Morrell discusses the use of election audits in Chapter 15. She provides the rationale for using audits as well as a compendium of different types of audits and procedures. She discusses the utility of various approaches and the challenges that election administrators face in implementing them.

In Chapter 16, Judd Choate and Robert Smith take on cybersecurity in elections. They begin with a broad overview of cybersecurity and cyber threats writ large, detail the federal infrastructure that has emerged around cyber threats, and then discuss the infrastructure around election administration specifically. Choate and Smith detail the work of the Department of Homeland Security, state coordination, and examine the case of one state's work in this area.

In Chapter 17, Dean Logan addresses innovations in voting methods that address dual concerns, including the costs associated with smaller and infrequent elections and the voter experience.

Finally, in Chapter 18, Kelly Ann Krawczyk and Avery Davis Roberts synthesize the literature on comparative elections, capturing the different approaches to registration and casting and counting ballots around the world today. This is juxtaposed against the American election administration system, and the authors make suggestions for lessons that can be gleaned from other countries for improving and modernizing the US election system.

The book concludes with a synthesis of major themes throughout. The authors first reinforce major themes and linkages, and then examine the implications of these moving forward. They conclude by laying out the key issues that policymakers, administrators, students, and the general public should be paying attention to in upcoming elections.

References

Crawford, Evan, Paul Gronke, and Paul Manson. "Surveying Local Election Officials in the United States: Methodological Considerations." Presented at the Southern Political Science Association in Austin, TX, January 19, 2019.

Hale, Kathleen, Robert Montjoy, and Mitchell Brown. *Administering Elections: How American Elections Work*. New York, NY: Palgrave, 2015.

Kimball, David C., and Brady Baybeck. "Are All Jurisdictions Equal? Size Disparity in Election Administration." *Election Law Journal*, 12, no. 2 (2013): 130–145.

Bridgett A. King Ph.D., is an assistant professor and Director of the Master of Public Administration Program at Auburn University. She teaches graduate and undergraduate courses in state institutions and policy, public policy, and diversity in public administration. Her research focuses on political participation, voter disenfranchisement, and citizen perceptions of the electoral system. Formerly a voting rights researcher in the Democracy Program at the Brennan Center for Justice at New York University, she contributes regularly to the Election Center Certified Election/Registration Administrator Program (CERA).

Mitchell Brown Ph.D., is a Professor in the Department of Political Science at Auburn University and is an Associate Editor of the Journal of Political Science Education (2016–2020). Her broader research agenda focuses on the empowerment efforts of marginalized communities, which she pursues through applied research. She is the author of numerous books, research articles, and reports, in related areas. In addition to her work at the university, she serves as a researcher, evaluator, trainer, and consultant on applied projects around the country focusing on election administration, community building, and community-based problem-solving.

Kathleen Hale JD, Ph.D., is Professor of Political Science at Auburn University where she directs its Graduate Program in Election Administration. She is the Series Editor for Palgrave Macmillan's Elections, Voting, and Technology series. Her research examines how to improve government capacity, and particularly in the area of election administration operations.

Kathleen serves on the Board of Directors of the Election Center and directs faculty involvement in the Certified Elections/Registration Administrator (CERA) Program. She is an active instructor in the CERA Program and frequent speaker on election matters around the country. She serves as an active reviewer for journals and book manuscripts and is a member of the advisory board for the MIT Election Data Sciences Lab.

Part I

Current Challenges and the Future of Access and Participation

2

The Federal Response and New Considerations for Election Administration

Bridgett A. King

The 10th amendment of the United States Constitution provides states and the citizens therein with authority to determine the time, manner, and place of elections. This, coupled with our federalist structure of government, has contributed to a system of election administration where states choose to structure access and address challenges associated with voting and registration in a variety of different ways. For many states, addressing the challenges associated with voting has involved policy innovations ranging from all-mail elections, early in-person voting, curbside voting for voters with physical challenges, and online applications that allow voters to determine the length of the line at their polling location. While some of the state policy and administrative innovations have had demonstrably positive effects on voter participation, others have not yielded the same positive effect; even though they remain highly favorable among voters. In addition to ensuring eligible citizens can register and vote, the current political environment has required election officials to operate in an environment of diminished

---

B. A. King (✉)
Auburn University, Auburn, AL, USA
e-mail: bak0020@auburn.edu

public confidence in which the narrative surrounding elections and election administration is fractured and not guided by the expertise of the administrative professionals who are responsible processing voting and registration in the United States.

The Costs of Voting

Since the early twentieth century, many of the challenges and solutions related to access and participation have centered on the costs and benefits of voting. Downs (1957) suggested that the decision to vote is the result of a cost-benefit calculus in which potential voters weight the cost of voting against the benefit. In instances, when the cost outweighs the benefit, voters abstain. Conversely, when the benefit outweighs the cost, voters participate. The costs and benefits of voting are not distributed equally across demographic groups in the population of the United States. The cost for an individual voter is directly related to the resources they have at their disposal to gather information, the rules associated with voting and registration, and the administrative procedures that determine the manner in which a voter may register and cast a ballot. Although the ability of states to address the personal resources that potential voters have is limited, policies have been introduced to lessen the administrative and procedural costs associated with voter registration and turnout.

Throughout the nation, many of the costs associated with voting and registration have been directly addressed by federal legislation and decisions made by the Supreme Court of the United States. The 1964 Civil Rights Act, for example, invalidated the unequal application of voter registration requirements. The 1965 Voting Rights Act made the use of tests or devices in federal elections to determine voter eligibility unlawful. While pieces of mid-century federal legislation had the explicit goal of providing access for racial and ethnic minorities, most notably African Americans, more recent legislation has tried to increase access to voting and registration and improve the administration of elections. The 1993 National Voter Registration Act (NVRA or Motor Voter) created increased opportunities for voter registration by requiring public agencies to provide potential voters with voter registration forms (in some states, the voter registration information is transmitted electronically). The provision had the express intention of removing registration barriers that existed for individuals who are economically disadvantaged. NVRA mandates that states without Election Day Registration establish mail-in and agency-based registration programs and eliminate the purging of registrants from the voting rolls solely on the basis of not voting. The primary feature of NVRA that was expected to have the most positive impact on turnout was the provision of voter registration for driver license applicants (Knack 1999). The provision requires "each state [to] include a voter registration application form for election for Federal office as part of an application for state motor vehicle driver's license."

The 2002 Help America Vote Act (HAVA) provided states with resources to purchase new voting equipment, required each state to identify a chief election official, and established the Election Assistance Commission (EAC), a bipartisan executive branch agency charged with providing states and local jurisdictions with guidance on equipment, technology, and administrative procedures. The implementation of these new policies was not without challenges. While NVRA lowered the cost of voter registration for low-income voters (Highton 1997) and increased the number of registered voters, it did little to increase voter turnout. Following the purchase of new voting machines, many states experienced machine malfunctions during the 2004 election, forcing states to purchase new voting equipment shortly after the election.

Most recently, in 2018 the EAC again distributed resources to states to address current challenges in election administration related to security, technology, and the accuracy of election results. States were additionally able to use the money to replace voting machines, implement a post-election audit system, upgrade election-related computer systems to address cyber vulnerabilities identified through the Department of Homeland Security, or similar scans or assessments of, existing election systems, facilitate cybersecurity training for the state chief election official's office and local election officials; implement established cybersecurity best practices for election systems; and fund other activities that will improve the security of elections for Federal office (Election Assistance Commission 2018). While we are still waiting to see the effect of these new resources on election administration, as new challenges emerge and old challenges persist, election administrations will continually need access to financial resources.

Although the aforementioned pieces of federal legislation may be the most salient, the federal government has also taken steps to reduce the costs of voting for military and overseas citizens and the disabled.

Accessibility for Citizens Overseas

The Uniformed and Overseas Citizen Absentee Voting Act (UOCAVA) was enacted by Congress in 1986. UOCAVA requires that states and territories allow certain groups of citizens to register and vote absentee in elections for federal offices. In 2009, the Military and Overseas Voter Empowerment Act (MOVE Act) amended UOCAVA to establish new voter registration and absentee ballot procedures. The MOVE Act requires states to send requested ballots to UOCAVA voters 45 days prior to the election. This assures adequate time to vote from abroad. Another key provision of the MOVE Act is that UOCAVA voters have the option to request and receive voter registration and absentee ballot applications by electronic transmissions and establish electronic transmission options for the delivery of blank absentee ballots (Title 42 Chapter 20§1973ff). For military voters, their eligible family members, and other citizens who are located overseas, the process of voting and registration is coordinated by the Federal Voting Assistance Program (FVAP).

During the 2016 presidential election, there were an estimated 3 million US citizens of voting age living abroad. These individuals cast approximately 208,000 ballots. Overseas voter turnout is approximately 7% whereas domestic turnout is 72% (Federal Voting Assistance Program 2018a). FVAP suggests that the turnout gap between overseas and domestic voters is the result of unique obstacles that are faced by overseas voters. These obstacles include the time it takes the election materials to travel overseas and the voter's local election office (Federal Voting Assistance Program 2018b) and vary relative to the country and region in which the voter resides. FVAP estimates that if the obstacles that overseas voters encounter were eliminated, turnout would increase from 7 to 37.5% (Federal Voting Assistance Program 2018a).

Ensuring that military and overseas citizens have access to the franchise is a coordinated effort on the part of the Department of Defense, FVAP, the United States Postal Service (USPS), and state and local election officials. Third-party organizations like the US Vote Foundation and the Council of State Governments also contribute to identifying ways to improve the voting and registration process for military and civilian citizens who are overseas.

Accessibility for Elderly and Disabled Voters

The Americans with Disabilities Act (ADA) requires "state and local governments ('public entities') to ensure that people with disabilities have a full and equal opportunity to vote. The ADA's provisions apply to all aspects of voting, including voter registration, polling site selection, and the casting of ballots, whether on election day or during an early voting process" (United States Department of Justice 2014). Provisions for the disabled are also included in the Voting Rights Act (1965), NVRA (1993), and HAVA (2002). The VRA requires election officials to allow a voter who is blind or has another disability to receive assistance from a person of the voter's choice (other than the voter's employer or its agent or an officer or agent of the voter's union). The VRA also prohibits conditioning the right to vote on a citizen being able to read or write, attaining a particular level of education, or passing an interpretation "test." NVRA requires all offices that provide public assistance or state-funded programs that primarily serve persons with disabilities to also provide the opportunity to register to vote in federal elections. Both HAVA and the 1984 Voting Accessibility for the Elderly and Handicapped (VAEHA) require jurisdictions responsible for conducting federal elections to provide at least one accessible voting system for persons with disabilities at each polling place in federal elections. The accessible voting system must provide the same opportunity for access and participation, including privacy and independence that other voters receive (United States Department of Justice 2014). In spite of these federal rules, a participation gap between people with and without disabilities remains.

Bergman and Sylvester-Tran (2016) report many disabled voters do not know how to find their polling place, find out if the polling place is accessible, or identify the requirements of federal laws for disabled voters, including the requirement for accessible voting machines in polling locations (p. 88). Further, they find that many disabled voters do not have access to accessible voting machines. While there is limited data to explain this, they suggest that it may be the result of voter ignorance, voter choice, poll worker failure, machine failure, or administrator failure. Regardless of the reason, without investment in accessible voting machines and practices that lower the cost of political participation for elderly and disabled voters, the participation gap will persist. Identifying administrative remedies for low participation among the disabled will continue to be a challenge as the population in the United States continues to age.

Accessibility for Language Minorities

Section 203 of the Voting Rights Act provides, "Whenever any state or political subdivision provides registration or voting notices, forms, instructions, assistance, or other materials or information relating to the electoral process, including ballots, it shall provide them in the language of the applicable minority group as well as in the English language." Section 203 specifically focuses on language minorities that have suffered a history of exclusion from the political process: Spanish, Asian, Native American, and Alaskan Native. In some jurisdictions, two or more language minority groups are present in a number sufficient to trigger the Section 203 requirements. The law applies to primary and general elections, bond elections, and referenda and to elections of each municipality, school district, or special purpose district within the designated jurisdiction (Department of Justice 2018). There are a variety of challenges that election officials must overcome to ensure that the needs of citizens who are language minorities covered by Section 203 are met.

In 2013, approximately 61.6 million individuals, foreign and US born, spoke a language other than English at home. While the majority of these individuals also spoke English with native fluency or very well, about 41% (25.1 million) were considered Limited English Proficient (LEP) (Zhong and Batalova 2015). The ability of election administrators to effectively reach individuals who are language minorities and conduct a successful voting and registration program for language minorities can be compounded by the resources available to facilitate an outreach campaign, hire bilingual election personnel, and ensure the accurate translation and distribution of materials (Department of Justice 2018). Beyond logistic challenges, English only advocates have continually introduced bills to repeal the language minority provisions of the VRA. In spite of these challenges, in the initial 30 years after the implementation of Section 203, among American Indians, registration and turnout increased between 50 and 150% in many places. Increased enforcement of Section 203 contributed to the increase of registered Hispanic voters from 7.6 million to 9.3 million between 2000 and 2004 (Tucker 2006). As the non-white population in the United States is expected to be the majority by 2045 (Frey 2018), the need to expand resources for eligible voters who speak languages other than English will continue to be a challenge faced by election administrators.

In addition to the federal government, states continue to identify new and innovative ways to address challenges faced by voters when trying to register or vote. The innovation of states has created significant literature on the variation in state rules regulating voting, some arguing that election rules matter and affect turnout (Fitzgerald 2005) and others not (Berinsky 2005). While federal laws have limited states' ability to regulate access to voting, there remains tremendous variation in state laws. States regulate how and if individuals are required to register, in some instances requiring that voters register as many as 30 days before the election. States regulate how individuals vote (polling place or from home via mail, before the election or only on election day), whether citizens with felony convictions can vote, and whether one must obtain an excuse for an absentee mail ballot. While changes in the structure of voting have been shown to affect turnout, the literature suggests that the effects are not equally beneficial for all voters across racial and socioeconomic divisions (e.g., Neeley and Richardson 2001).

The Role of Administrative Decision-Making at the Local Level

In recent elections, considerable attention has been given to long lines as part of the political landscape of American elections. Although scholarship has suggested that the extent to which voters across the nation wait is minimal (Ansolabehere and Shaw 2016) and there is no consensus among election administrators regarding what constitutes a wait that is *too* long (Government Accountability Office 2014), for voters, wait times and lines are seen as the greatest barrier to an efficient and enjoyable voting experience (Smith et al. 2015). Because of this, scholars have sought to understand better who experiences long lines when voting in person and the consequences for political participation. They find that neighborhood composition is strongly associated with how long a voter will wait on election day, noting that neighborhoods that are more population dense and non-white experience longer wait times (Stewart and Ansolabehere 2013; Kimball 2013; Pettigrew 2017). Pettigrew (2017) also finds that, for citizens who wait, long lines reduce confidence in elections and the likelihood of voting in future elections. Investigating how administrative decision-making contributes to long lines on election day, Famaghetti et al. (2014), suggests that the way in which poll workers and voting machines are distributed across polling locations relative to the number of voters can contribute to delays on election day. As election officials operate in an environment of limited resources, in response to long lines, many jurisdictions have implemented polling location wait time estimators that are available for voters online. Although those do not solve the problem, they do provide voters with an additional resource to plan their election day.

Election administrators have also come under scrutiny for decisions regarding precinct boundaries and the selection of polling location sites. Before the 2018 election, state election officials created a plan to eliminate seven of nine polling locations in Randolph County, Georgia, a predominately rural black county in the southern part of the state. Following the announcement of the decision, there was an immediate backlash from civil rights and voting rights advocates and citizens in the county. Their primary concern was that the closure of the seven polling locations was an act of voter suppression meant to diminish the political participation of black Democrats who would have to drive long distances to vote during a highly contested race for governor in which then Secretary of State, Brian Kemp, was the Republican Party candidate. The consequences of polling location placement have not gone unnoticed by scholars. Haspell and Knotts (2005) find that small differences in the distance to a polling location from a voter's residence and moving a polling location can have a negative effect on voter turnout.

The way in which voters understand the role of election administration has been shaped by the political and administrative context in which recent American elections have occurred (Nunnally 2011). Increased mistrust in election outcomes stemming from the 2000 and 2004 elections have created an environment in which the public perceives election administrators as both facilitator and barrier to democratic participation. Given this, the decisions made by election officials not only have consequences for political participation, but also confidence in election administration and electoral outcomes.

Citizen Confidence in Election Administration

Citizens perceiving elections and the results they generate as legitimate is essential for democracy. For democracies to be effective, citizens must trust the administrative rules and procedures that determine who wins and who loses elections (Norris 2014). Confidence serves as a necessary resource that allows voters to accept that election results are fair and give deference to those who are elected (Norris 2014) and the policy and administrative decisions that they make. When specifically addressing confidence in election administration, the concept also serves as a measure of electoral system performance (Alvarez et al. 2008a; Atkeson et al. 2015; Atkeson and Saunders 2007; Hall et al. 2009).

Scholars have argued that confidence in elections or electoral processes is unique and different from general evaluations of trust in government. Assessments of trust in government often require citizens to evaluate specific elected officials and their policy decisions. This approach, however, does not capture the nuance of citizen evaluation of different aspects of government and government decision-making. As an example, a voter may not be confident in the voting machines or technology, but they may trust their elected officials and representatives (Alvarez et al. 2008b). It is also plausible that voters may believe that all elected officials are corrupt while trusting the processes and procedures that produce election outcomes (755). Measures of trust in election administration capture this nuance by requiring voters to articulate their confidence in administrative processes and procedures as opposed to government or individuals in government (Citrin and Luks 2001). Measures of confidence in election administration are also unique because they ask voters about a "very specific additive component (confidence) and a very specific objective component (whether a voter's ballot was counted correctly)" (Atkeson et al. 2015, 209). Given that elections are the primary way that citizens express their preferences for representation and policy (Montjoy and Slaton 2002), understating how an individual experiences the voting process and identifying ways to enhance confidence is of particular importance, not only for elections and democratic functioning but also because if voters do not believe that ballots are counted accurately and outcomes are legitimate, they may be less likely to participate and also have lower levels of trust in other government institutions (Atkeson et al. 2015, 210).

Directly related to election administration, the perception of legitimacy can be undermined when a voter's preferred candidate loses, problems that the voter did not directly experience are made public (Avery 2009), voters directly experience problems at the polling place (Atkeson and Saunders 2007; Hale et al. 2015; King 2017), and voters perceive electoral malpractice (Norris 2014). When political legitimacy is undermined, the authority of elected officials is diminished.

In addition to policy changes and administrative decisions, there are other challenges to access and participation that lie outside the scope of election administration. These include general attitudes about the government and participation, campaigns and candidates, third-party organizations and voter mobilization efforts. Where these may lessen the information costs, in many instances efforts are focused on highlighting the benefits of political participation and consequences of supporting an alternative candidate or position.

As the field of election administration is rapidly changing, election administration must evolve to be responsive to the administrative needs of the American public and the election system. The solutions to these issues will involve a highly networked and collaborative effort (Hale 2011) between federal, state, and local agencies who work together to address challenges for access and participation in the present and consider innovations that will shape election administration in the future.

References

Alvarez, R. Michael, Thad E. Hall, and Morgan H. Llewellyn. "Are Americans Confident Their Ballots Are Counted?" *The Journal of Politics*, 70, no. 3 (2008a): 754–766.

Alvarez, R. Michael, Stephen Ansolabehere, Adam Berinksky, Gabriel Lenz, Charles Stewart III, and Thad Hall. Survey of the Performance of American Elections Final Report, 2008b. https://dataverse.harvard.edu/dataset.xhtml?persistentId=hdl:1902.1/20580.

Ansolabehere, Stephen, and Daron Shaw. "Assessing (and Fixing) Election Day Lines: Evidence from a Survey of Local Election Officials." *Electoral Studies*, 4 (2016): 1–11.

Atkeson, Lonna Rae, and Kyle L. Saunders. "The Effect of Election Administration on Voter Confidence: A Local Matter?" *PS: Political Science & Politics*, 40, no. 4 (2007): 655–660.

Atkeson, Lonna Rae, Alvarez, R. Michael, and Hall, Thad E. "Trust in Elections and Trust in Government: Why Voter Confidence Differs from Other Measures of System Support." *Election Law Journal*, 14, no. 3 (2015): 207–219.

Avery, James M. "Political Mistrust Among African Americans and Support for the Political System." *Political Research Quarterly*, 62, no. 1 (2009): 132–145.

Bergman, Elizabeth, and Dari Sylvester-Tran. "Logistical Barriers to Voting." In *Why Don't American Vote? Causes and Consequences*, edited by Bridgett King and Kathleen Hale, 86–93. Santa Barbara, CA: ABC-CLIO, 2016.

Berinsky, Adam. "The Perverse Consequences of Electoral Reform in the United States." *American Politics Research*, 33, no. 4 (2005): 471–491.

Citrin, Jack, and Samantha Luks. "Political Trust Revisited: Déjà vu All Over Again?" In *What Is It About Government That Americans Dislike?* edited by John R. Hibbing and Elizabeth Theiss-Morse, 456–532. New York: Cambridge University Press, 2001.

Department of Justice. "The Americans with Disabilities Act and Other Federal Laws Protecting the Right of Voters with Disabilities." 2014. https://www.ada.gov/ada_voting/ada_voting_ta.htm.

Department of Justice. "Language Minority Citizens." 2018. https://www.justice.gov/crt/language-minority-citizens.

Downs, Anthony. *An Economic Theory of Democracy.* New York: Harper & Row, 1957.

Election Assistance Commission. "State & Territories Plan to Spend Majority of HAVA Grant Funds on Election Security, System Upgrades." Press Release, 2018. https://www.eac.gov/news/2018/08/21/state–territories-plan-to-spend-majority-of-hava-grant-funds-on-election-security-system-upgrades/.

Famaghetti, Christopher, Amanda Melillo, and Myrna Peréz. "Election Day Long Lines: Resource Allocation." *Brennan Center for Justice at New York University School of Law*, 2014. https://www.brennancenter.org/publication/election-day-long-lines-resource-allocation.

Federal Voting Assistance Program. "DOD Releases Study of U.S. Voters Abroad." Press Release, 2018a. https://www.fvap.gov/info/news/2018/9/12/dod-releases-biennial-study-of-us-voters-abroad.

Federal Voting Assistance Program. "2016 Overseas Citizen Population Analysis Report." 2018b. https://www.fvap.gov/uploads/FVAP/Reports/FVAP-2016-OCPA-FINAL-Report.pdf.

Fitzgerald, Mary. "Greater Confidence but Not Greater Turnout: The Impact of Alternative Voting Methods on Electoral Participation in the United States." *American Politics Research*, 33, no. 6 (2005): 842–867.

Frey, William. "The US Will Become 'Minority White' in 2045, Census Projects." *Brookings Institute*, 2018. https://www.brookings.edu/blog/the-avenue/2018/03/14/the-us-will-become-minority-white-in-2045-census-projects/.

Government Accountability Office. "Elections: Observations on Wait Times for Voters on Election Day 2012." 2014. https://www.gao.gov/products/GAO-14-850.

Hale, Kathleen. *How Information Matters: Networks and Public Policy Innovation.* New York: Georgetown University Press, 2011.

Hale, Kathleen, Mitchell Brown, and Robert Montjoy. *Administering Elections: How American Elections Work.* New York: Palgrave, 2015.

Hall, Thad E., J. Quin Monson, and Kelly D. Patterson. "The Human Dimension of Elections: How Poll Workers Shape Public Confidence in Elections." *Political Research Quarterly*, 62, no. 3 (2009): 507–522.

Haspell, M., and H. Gibbs Knotts. "Location, Location, Location: Precinct Placement and the Costs of Voting." *The Journal of Politics*, 67 (2005): 560–573.

Highton, Benjamin. "Easy Registration and Voter Turnout." *The Journal of Politics*, 59, no. 7 (1997): 565–575.

Kimball, David. "Why Are Voting Lines Longer for Urban Voters." Paper Presented at the Southwestern Social Science Association Conference: New Orleans, LA, 2013.

King, Bridgett A. "Policy and Precinct: Citizen Evaluations and Electoral Confidence." *Social Science Quarterly*, 98, no. 2 (2017): 672–689.

Knack, Stephen. "Drivers Wanted: Motor Voter and the Election of 1996." *PS: Political Science and Politics*, 32, no. 2 (1999): 237–243.

Montjoy, Robert S., and Christa Daryl Slaton. "Interdependence and Ethics in Election Systems: The Case of the Butterfly Ballot." *Public Integrity*, 4 (Summer, 2002), 195–210.

Neely, Grant, and Lilliard Richardson. "Who is Early Voting? An Individual Level Examination." *The Social Science Journal*, 38 (2001): 381–392.

Norris, Pippa. "Why Mass Perceptions of Electoral Integrity Matter." *The Election Integrity Project*, 2014. http://hcvictoria.clubs.harvard.edu/images.html?file_id=lVQdfqms8RU%3D.

Nunnally, Shayla C. "(Dis)counting on Democracy to Work: Perceptions of Electoral Fairness in the 2008 Presidential Election." *Journal of Black Studies*, 42, no. 6 (2011): 923–942.

Pettigrew, Stephen. "The Racial Gap in Wait Times: Why Minority Precincts Are Underserved by Local Election Officials." *Political Science Quarterly*, 132 (2017): 527–547.

Smith, Melissa, Samuel S. Monfort, and Eric J. Blumberg. "Improving Voter Experience Through User Testing and Interactive Design." *Journal of Usability Studies*, 10 (2015): 116–128.

Stewart III, Charles, and Stephen Ansolabehere. "Waiting in Line to Vote." White Paper (2013). https://www.eac.gov/documents/2017/02/24/waiting-in-line-to-vote-white-paper-stewart-ansolabehere/.

Tolbert, Caroline, Todd Donovan, Bridgett King, and Shawn Bowler. "Election Day Registration, Competition and Voter Turnout." In *Democracy in the States: Experiments in Election Reform*, edited by Bruce Cain, Todd Donovan, and Caroline Tolbert, 83–98. Washington, DC: Brookings Institute Press, 2008.

Tucker, James. "Enfranchising Language Minority Citizens: The Bilingual Election Provisions of the Voting Rights Act." *Legislation and Public Policy*, 10 (2006): 195–260.

Zhong, Jie, and Jeanne Batalova. The Limited English Proficient Population in the United States. Migration Policy Institute, 2015. https://www.migration-policy.org/article/limited-english-proficient-population-united-states.

Bridgett A. King Ph.D., is an assistant professor and Director of the Master of Public Administration Program at Auburn University. She teaches graduate and undergraduate courses in state institutions and policy, public policy, and diversity in public administration. Her research focuses on political participation, voter disenfranchisement, and citizen perceptions of the electoral system. Formerly a voting rights researcher in the Democracy Program at the Brennan Center for Justice at New York University, she contributes regularly to the Election Center Certified Election/Registration Administrator Program (CERA).

3

Parties and Politics: The Evolution of Election Administration

Doug Lewis

How does any democracy survive in a period of hyper-partisanship? Especially when voters themselves are so divided as to who should govern? Can the process remain fair for all segments of the population or will partisans structure it in such a way that democracy is no longer democracy but is shaped by laws or rules or administration that manipulate the process to favor "more of us and less of them"?

And with potential outside influence from foreign governments and nation-states trying to manipulate elections in the United States, is the process robust enough to withstand bad actors who probe for weaknesses in the process and exploit those, or can our elections be determined by the actions of other countries? Do outside actors pose the biggest risk to American elections or are there other influences that can thwart democracy by interference in election administration?

The lessons that America learns in seeking answers to these questions are the fundamental foundations for maintaining voter faith in the democratic process. Finding methods of election administration that

D. Lewis (✉)
Houston, TX, USA
e-mail: doug.lewis@apramerica.net

© The Author(s) 2020
M. Brown et al. (eds.), *The Future of Election Administration*, Elections, Voting, Technology, https://doi.org/10.1007/978-3-030-14947-5_3

allow legal participation by the widest range of voters, and that equally assure the election process itself has safeguarded election integrity so that results are an accurate reflection of the public will, and in accordance with the Constitution and laws governing the election process, is tantamount to ensuring that voters believe the resulting elected government is legitimate.

This fundamental foundation was questioned following the 2000 election in the United States, the closest presidential election of the modern political era; George W. Bush prevailed over Al Gore by 537 votes in a process litigated in state and federal courts before it was resolved by the US Supreme Court in Bush's favor. No matter who had been declared the winner of the *Bush v. Gore* election (and in any of the litigation that surrounded that election), half of the country was certain that their candidate should have been the victor and the other half was equally certain their candidate should have been the eventual winner.

Faith in election administration suffered greatly during that intense period of self-examination and partisans of very differing viewpoints wanted to reshape election administration to force rules and laws to favor their ideas about elections. When it became apparent that neither the Democrats nor the Republicans (or even the liberals or conservatives) could gain the upper hand in shaping the rules through legislation, bipartisanship ensued and resulted in a new emphasis on election administration practices and procedures designed to improve the process for all. The resulting passage of the Help America Vote Act of 2002 (HAVA) meant that both sides had to agree to address election administration throughout the nation, and it became a truly bipartisan law.

HAVA likely would have been considerably different if not for the input of state and local election officials. Because neither of the two major parties could gain the upper hand in negotiations, the resulting law relied on state and local governments to design the best solutions to serve their own voters. Legislators engaged 8000 plus local election jurisdictions and the 50 states, the District of Columbia and the US territories in fashioning the framework for accomplishing both the broad goals and specific objectives of Congress. At each stage of legislative development, the Congressional staff of each party met with election administrators at the state and local levels to float ideas, concerns, and mandates, and to discuss how best to achieve legislative goals. It is perhaps the first piece of major federal election legislation to have had significant input from the people who would have to administer the specific legislative mandates. It is highly likely that doing so meant that changes came more quickly and got implemented more efficiently because local governments were more committed to their own administrative solutions than they would have been under federally controlled mandates.

It was through this continuous development process that many changes occurred in the legislation to avoid unintended consequences. Congressional leaders were committed to assuring that future election changes would add to the confidence in the system rather than pandering to concerns of political activists. HAVA also differed significantly from most federal legislation in that it left the design of the solutions to state and local governments rather than mandating specific procedures. Most federal election legislation attempts to mandate ways to administer the election process with a one-size fits all approach. HAVA took an entirely different approach that resulted in states finding solutions to quickly repair problems that they discovered and rebuilding voter confidence that the process itself is fair.

US elections survived that period of intense distrust by partisans, and the Congress acted to infuse almost $4 billion in federal money into election administration at the state and local levels. Concurrently, through HAVA, Congress created the US Election Assistance Commission (EAC) to assist the nation's election administrators and voters in assuring better elections and a bipartisan commission to develop an information clearinghouse in EAC and gather data affecting elections among other roles. HAVA essentially provided the impetus to modernize elections and to improve election administration throughout the nation.

The result was that Americans once again developed considerable faith in the fairness and integrity of the election process. Since HAVA's passage in 2002, many federal bills governing elections and mandating stronger federal controls have failed to pass even with one-party control of the Presidency and the Congress. And during that period of 2002 up to Election 2016, voters' faith in the process returned to pre-Election 2000 levels.

Allegations of Russian interference in elections have brought new concerns about whether the election administration process can be secure when foreign nation-states are dedicating significant foreign government resources to try to manipulate the outcomes of US elections or, failing that, to then shake the foundation of faith in the democratic process so that Americans distrust the outcomes and feel that eventual winners are "tainted" and unfairly elected. If this interference were to be successful, then voters would no longer trust the politicians or the government because they have little or no faith in the voting process that elected the government leaders.

Collectively, Congress, national security agencies, and election administration officials at all levels of government cannot ignore the attempts by nation-states to influence elections in the United States. It is paramount that all take those threats seriously and, to the extent possible, protect democracy from outside influences.

The genius of the American election process, however, is that it not a top-down, centralized, election process. America is the only developed democracy where election administration is not controlled by the national government. The entire American election process is organized from the local and state level upward. As a result, election manipulation at a national level requires the ability to penetrate more than 8000 local governments and 50 states plus the District of Columbia; it is unlikely that effective control of outcomes could be executed in a presidential election by impacting either the voting or counting of ballots. To be able to do so undetected is highly improbable. Since ballots are counted locally and vote totals recorded locally before they are sent onto the state governments, it is easy to recheck totals and see that they match. While it would not take a foreign government penetrating all 8000 or more local jurisdictions for election administration, it would require a significant number of diverse districts in swing states to change vote totals and declare a different winner from what the election process determined in the election. Those multiple jurisdictions use different voting equipment and have different procedures for counting and transmitting results; this gives us a fairly high degree of confidence that attempts to manipulate the outcome cannot be done in a practical sense. However, that is different from being able to make voters believe the process is "tainted" or to undermine confidence in electoral outcomes. That undermining can occur and is an intentional practice used not just by foreign nation-states but also by partisans in the United States.

"We Have Met the Enemy and He Is Us"

A quote from the now-defunct newspaper comic strip "Pogo" authored by Walt Kelly is an apt description of what happens in campaigns from the two major US political parties during virtually every election cycle. One side alleges there is significant voter fraud and the other side alleges voter intimidation and voter suppression. The constant use of these campaigns, designed to energize their base voters, has deep acceptance within the party faithful and activists and even permeates media outlets to accept the allegations as fact (depending on the viewpoint of the media outlets).

Originally thought to be a purely callous political strategy by each side to exhort the party stalwarts for more diligence because the other side is trying to steal the election through unfair tactics, it appears that these fundamental tenets of the Republicans (fraud) and the Democrats (suppression) have deep-seated acceptance by rank and file party members. The belief structure appears to carry a weight similar to a sacred tenet in the sense that the positions are accepted as universal truths and no amount of factual information or concepts contrary to the "truth" will be accepted by the partisans and their media supporters.

All who engage in these continuing allegations are not recognizing that they are undermining American's faith in the democratic process as fair and not acknowledging that the process has any integrity beyond political expediency. It is important to think about which is more likely to have a lasting impact on believing in the US democratic process—Russia (or some other nation-state) or US groups that have credibility with many voters? The answer is likely that both can damage faith in the process, but to have Americans repeatedly and intentionally whipping the frenzy, election-after-election, builds in distrust by voters. Voters end up questioning whether they should participate at all if the system is rigged to elect only certain people or that the process itself has no integrity concerning the inclusion or exclusion of voters. "We have met the enemy, and he is us" becomes not an observation but becomes a reality in an intensely destructive way.

From an election administration standpoint, what are the factual observations about these allegations? There is provable, demonstrable fraud in some elections and it happens frequently enough that it remains fresh as a threat. But does it constitute a major systemic threat to democracy and the outcome of elections on a regular basis? The answer to that appears to be no if those making the allegations are held to a proof standard. Equally unsettling are the allegations of voter intimidation or voter suppression. There are also provable, real-world examples in some elections where partisans are trying to keep some from voting or even intimidating voters. But does it constitute a major systemic threat to democracy and the outcome of elections on a regular basis? Not likely if you force proof of harm rather than rely on anecdotal stories.

So how does the process, or how do election administrators, foster a solution that accommodates the fears of both viewpoints and structure a method that allows maximum participation while supporting voter confidence in the process? It is unlikely that the legislators of the two political parties can take on the dogmatic fervor of their party and intellectual stalwarts in finding a solution to the issue. Doing so can imperil their standing within their own parties as either Dino (Democrat in name only) or Rino (Republican in name only).

Some Republicans believe in their core that fraud is a major issue and operate from the theory that no one should oppose a voter identification requirement unless they want (as the Republicans state) "to cheat by allowing ineligible voters." They take the position of "trust but verify." Some Democrats believe in their core that voter suppression is the major issue in elections and that the opposition is trying to make sure that voters don't participate in elections. For them, it is alleged that the other side only wants some (but not all) voters to have access. They operate on the theory that to deny any citizen the right to vote is a fundamental right and that it is un-American to restrict that participation.

According to a YouGov poll conducted May 17–20, 2018 by the Huffington Post and YouGov, both sides find agreement from the public with members of the opposite party showing support for each concept. Overall, the poll indicates that 63% of the public is either very concerned or somewhat concerned about fraud in elections. At the same time, 62% of the public is either very concerned or somewhat concerned about making sure that eligible voters not be prevented from voting. When the pollsters queried about which is more important, the public decided 38% on fraud concerns and 33% on voter suppression concerns. Readers will want to look at the poll tables to see the extent to which each of the political parties believes the dogma as espoused by their party ("YouGov" 2018).

What this tells election administrators (as well as legislators and policymakers) is that the issues are of concern to the general public as well as the political partisans and that election administration needs to ensure that the processes address those concerns to allay fears. Handling the problem from either administrative or legislative perspectives, however, is far more difficult. The issue tends to engage political warfare when handling fraud concerns translates to showing a government-issued ID (Republicans) versus unfettered access to voting either through Election Day Registration (EDR) or vote by mail (Democrats). This political warfare results in allegations from both political sides that continue to do damage to the public's faith that the election process is fair. Equally important is that voters feel a high degree of confidence that the process protects against fraud to the extent possible and that it also assures eligible voters have access to the system.

Finding a path forward that pleases both sides of the political equation has escaped election administration for several decades due to the dogmatic acceptance by each side of its own animosity toward the opposition's fears; facts seem not to matter to either side. Democratic activists detest the notion of forcing positive ID on voters with the supposition that it only discourages some segments of the population from voting. And yet, the United States is perhaps the only major democracy that does not require some form of positive identification in order to vote. Republican activists detest the notion of some form of either automatic voter registration or allowing late-stage registration for all potential eligible voters, so they can participate when they are motivated to do so. Yet, other advanced democracies treat registration as an automatic function rather than requiring individuals to act on their own.

The tragedy for US election processes is the lack of a path to reach common ground on the fears and concerns of each side of these arguments that would end the political warfare. The damage is to the full faith that democracy works in the United States. Each side is so willing to argue that the process is unfair that public confidence in fairness is always in question. Given the actions of nation-states trying to damage Americans confidence in the system, can the activists be allowed to continue to allege such confidence-destroying tactics?

Additional Challenges Affecting Confidence in Elections and Their Outcomes

Lawsuits to Manipulate Election Processes

A more recent trend in the last 20–30 years in US democracy is the increased use of partisan lawsuits designed to override laws passed by state legislatures to force new procedures favoring the voters of a desired party or movement. Partisan activists indicate such suits are necessary to assure that voters are given the greatest opportunity to participate and to eliminate laws or practices that a court could deem as impacting the right to vote. Yet it becomes far more likely to assume that the interest is not so much concern for the rights of voters as the possibility that court-mandated changes can influence election outcomes favorable to the plaintiff's political interest. If real concern for righting legislative "wrongs" were the order of the day, far more of those lawsuits would occur in non-election years, and judicial decisions could be implemented over many months rather than in very short-time frames closer to the election.

Any interested observer or participant in election administration processes wants the election to serve the interests of any eligible voter. The problem arises when lawsuits and courts interact with the current election process to change the rules mid-stream. The US Supreme Court has noticed such impacts and their potential for damage to the process by application of the Purcell rule (*Purcell v. Gonzalez* 2006) whereby changes are delayed past the current election and can affect elections going forward rather than influencing the one currently adjudicated. State and local courts should begin the process of indicating that any lawsuits affecting elections must have final decisions rendered a minimum of 180 days before the general election.

Suits filed too late to have such a decision rendered would then have implementation applied to future elections but not the current one. The impact of adopting such judicial practices would likely result in fewer "game the system" lawsuits but still allow suits which deal with genuine issues of voters' rights or to correct egregious wrongs. Systemic problems that infringe on participation as a matter of civil liberty or system integrity are still worthy goals and their pursuit can still occur with the necessity of not adversely affecting the current election if they fall within the minimum days mandate.

Legislative Action to Changes Processes in the Current Election Year

Generally speaking, election legislation generated by competitive state legislatures (i.e., where the political parties are about of equal strength in numbers) tends either to produce legislation that is truly bipartisan and therefore necessary to serve voters, or renders election law changes unlikely because there is not enough agreement to be able to pass these. When legislative bodies have enough votes to control the legislation, it becomes far more likely to foster changes that favor one political interest over another. In such instances, legislators seem to want immediate change while they are in control and want to force those changes to occur in the then current election year. However, election administrators need time to study legislative changes and time to structure administrative practices and procedures. Time is needed to train election administrators, full-time and part-time election workers, and voters. In some cases, such as when buying different voting equipment, additional time may be needed to provide sufficient lead time to meet government purchasing determinations and other requirements.

It is likely that legislative bodies also need to follow the 180 day minimum for changes to election laws which affect current year elections. Major changes to the election process generally require learning acquired from experience and sorting out unintended consequences that inevitably occur when implementation plans meet legislative mandates. Experience suggests that it takes three elections (not three general elections but three sizable elections) to figure out whether and how new practices can be adjusted to assure that voters have a higher degree of success in casting countable ballots. Having political strength to change the process immediately is not necessarily the same thing as having an election process that leads to high confidence of voters and assures the integrity of the process while protecting the rights of the voters.

Political Influence in Election Administration—Civil Rights Era

Dealing with political influences has long been problematic for election administrators. Since the civil rights era of the 1960s, election administration changed greatly in the United States. The most impactful (for election administration purposes) is the Voting Rights Act of 1965 (VRA). Following on the heels of the Civil Rights Act of 1964 (CRA), the VRA moved election administration beyond previous constitutional provisions or other federal laws. The VRA ushered in the modern era of election administration by forcing new types of election administration and reshaping how voter registration and minority access to the polling place would be enforced.

At points in America's election history, political leaders found it useful to control the elections office and the staff therein. This was not always about denying minorities access to the system or abuses of the election process in Southern states. It was also useful to any government leader at the local level who wanted to assure political power for them and their allies. Big cities (e.g., Chicago, New York, Kansas City, and Philadelphia) are examples of where the election administration offices were under the control of strong political types who assured that only "friends" got to vote or have their votes counted. The abuses of similar systems grew significantly in the Southern United States to make sure that those in power stayed in power and worked systemically to thwart participation from "unwanted" persons.

But in the aftermath of the VRA in 1965, election administration began to change dramatically to have a far more neutral stance, and city and county governments began to prize more even-handed approaches. With strong enforcement provisions available to the federal government through the US Department of Justice, it became abundantly clear there were consequences to denying the civil rights of voters. Not only did enforcement change the bad behaviors of Southern governments, but it also changed the worst of the violations of local governments throughout the nation.

During the 1970s, it became far more common practice to have the election administration functions operate more independently with a focus on ensuring the rights of citizens rather than rights of office holders. By the mid-1980s, non-governmental organizations (NGOs) were offering programs and conferences showing local governments how to apply better nonpartisan or at least bipartisan administration to both voter registration and election administration issues. Organizations such as National Association of Counties (NACo), National Association of Secretaries of State (NASS) and International Institute of Municipal Clerks (IIMC) and the International Association of Clerks, Recorders and Election Officials and Treasurers (IACREOT and now named the International Association of Government Officials or iGO), the National Association of State Election Directors (NASED), and The Election Center (aka National Association of Election Officials) were all offering best practices practical training for state and local election officials.

The Election Center developed the first national certification program to professionalize all parts of voter registration and election administration. By 1994, the Election Center launched a new national certification program with academic instruction provided by Auburn University's political science and public administration faculty and which is certified by Auburn University for continuing education credit. The result of this structured and demanding instruction is that it formalized the need for election and voter registration to operate professionally (not politically) and to assure that the needs of democracy and its voters became paramount rather political favoritism. Essentially, election and voter registration administrators serve as referees of the process rather than as partisan participants in the process. That professionalization has led to ever-increasing confidence in the fairness of elections. Those who obtain the Certified Election/Registration Administrator (CERA) status from the Election Center and Auburn University commit to a code of ethics that focuses on professionalism and fairness of the process to serve voters and to protect the process itself.

Political Influence in Election Administration—Post Election 2000 Era

Perhaps one of the most dangerous prospects of having election administration serving political interests rather than democracy has been the renewed emphasis of political partisans on controlling election administrators. Partisans began to run for Chief Election Official (CEO) of the state (typically but not always the office of Secretary of State), with the idea that they would politically mandate policies and practices designed to favor their party or their ideology and force election administrators to follow their mandates. The hyper-partisanship that followed Election 2000 brought with it a new wave of office seekers aiming to use those CEO positions in their states first to control the policies and practices related to election administration at the local level and, second, as stepping stones to higher state and federal offices for themselves. The aftershocks of those political influences are still being felt within state governments and have the potential to shape outcomes. How to structure the state administrative apparatus so that it is at least bipartisan rather than principally partisan is the new concern for serious policymakers. A return to the days of assuring voters that the only votes that count are those desired by the parties hardly builds confidence that elections can remain fair and equitable.

Policy debates will be needed to find solutions that favor a healthy democracy rather than structured favoritism of partisan interests. It will be difficult to get partisans to see the interest in a more neutral administration, but the question remains: Is it truly democracy if the process is manipulated to favor some voters?

Accessibility Issues Loom Large for the Foreseeable Future

For many years, groups working on behalf of voters with disabilities have sought to provide a method that allows all voters to vote privately and independently. HAVA established this concept in federal law as a compliance requirement for elections within the United States. According to information provided by the Research Alliance for Accessible Voting, there are approximately 54 million voters with disabilities out of approximately 242 million people of voting age population out of a total population of 317 million (Election Assistance Commission 2017). Of that potential fewer than 134 million voted in 2012 and roughly 140 million in 2016. It has been difficult to achieve voter privacy and independence because of the requirement in many states that all voters vote on paper ballots. A survey of 3022 voters in 2012 (2000 voters with disabilities and 1022 voters with no disabilities) conducted for RAAV by the Rutgers School of Management and Labor Relations[1] showed that 49% of voters with disabilities voted on paper, compared to 52% of voters with no disabilities (Election Assistance Commission 2017). Due to the wide disparity of problems for voters with accessibility needs, 36% of voters with disabilities had difficulty voting on paper compared to only 2.6% of those with no disability according to the RAAV survey.

The problems of voting accessibility are likely to grow at a geometric progression as the nation's voters age. The "baby boomer" population, defined by the Census Bureau as those born between 1946 and 1964, participate in elections in much higher numbers than any other age

---

[1] Part of a grant from the US Election Assistance Commission on Accessible Voting and conducted by Lisa Schur and Doug Kruse of Rutgers and Meera Adya at the Burlington Blatt Institute at Syracuse University.

group. Older voters are now living longer than any previous generation, and their higher participation rate as voters means that much about election administration will change for the next two to three decades. Data from the Census Bureau show this group growing by more than 50% in the period from 1998 to 2012 (United States Census Bureau, n.d.).[2] It is expected that those numbers will continue to increase for the foreseeable future as the wave of baby boomers swells the numbers of voters with accessibility needs over the next 25–35 years.

What this means for elections in America is that more voters will have mobility issues, more will have sight or limited vision problems, more will have difficulty standing in lines waiting to vote, more will have some cognitive difficulties, and a higher percentage will have hearing difficulties. It means that election jurisdictions will need to rethink how to process voters, how to provide seating for those with difficulty standing, and how to provide voting assistance. The Rutgers survey indicated that 29.5% of voters with disabilities need assistance in voting compared to 10.7% of voters with no disabilities (Election Assistance Commission 2017).

What this means for policymakers and for election administrators is that the cost of serving voters will increase to cover the variety of methods and equipment and personnel to serve a vastly increased segment of voters with accessibility needs. It also means significant shifts in methods of voting such as growth in curbside voting and greater use of facilities that can accommodate a variety of disabilities. It also means greater investment in voting equipment that can handle a wide spectrum of disability needs. The survey indicates that these voters also will need almost three times as much assistance as voters with no disabilities; the result will be a greater investment in polling place personnel and more time spent with each voter. Ultimately that means greater resources in voting equipment, in accessible polling places, and in tools that can assist the voters. The explosion of accessibility needs likely to accompany the growth of the baby boomers suggests that accessibility accommodations will be needed for 35% of the voting public, compared to roughly 15% today.

---

[2]The number of voters aged 45 or older in 1998 was 80 million. By 2012 the number of voters increased to 120 million (United States Census Bureau, n.d.).

Final Concerns for the Future of Election Administration

Continuing to professionalize election and voter registration administration will be healthy for American elections. As long as the courses of instruction and the shaping of administrative ideas are process-oriented and provide awareness of the concerns of the various political ideologies, there is a long-term future for democracy and democratic elections. Acceptance by policymakers that professionalization is not only desirable but a necessity to neutral administration becomes paramount. Election administrators cannot favor one team if America is to have a fair and trusted process that voters believe in. Encouraging election administrators to serve as neutral referees of the process needs to be reinforced. Mandates that local and state governments pay for training and travel and certification costs for election officials at all levels will help to assure confidence in the process.

Related, resources must be enhanced and new resources must be developed for elections to survive in the modern era. It is now a fact of life that technology expertise has to be funded and created within each state and with local jurisdictions to protect democracy from manipulation by bad actors whether they are foreign nation-states or domestic groups or organizations. Voting equipment must be funded by state and local governments with the understanding that life cycle issues cannot reasonably be stretched for years on end. The life cycle of modern era voting equipment and software is likely to be limited to 10 years maximum and perhaps less than that considering the rapidly changing software and hardware technology cycles.

Good elections are likely to cost more in the near term—but the cost of bad elections is likely to far outweigh the advantages of delay. Solving the appropriate funding of elections is achievable and may be one of the less thorny issues confronting policymakers related to elections within the states. Good elections are not simply the result of administrative excellence, although that is necessary; good elections also result from the proper mix of policies, politics, practices, and procedures.

Aristotle's Advice

And a final note and as a call for fairness: we should be reminded of Aristotle's concerns when he laid out the tenets for democracy. He noted that for democracy to survive and to be accepted by the voters, it necessitates a large middle class. A situation where too many voters are at the wealthy end of the spectrum dooms acceptance from the other segments of society. A situation where too many voters are at the poorer end of the spectrum means that voters then prefer systems of government other than democracy so that their lives will improve. For democracy to survive and do well, Aristotle reminds us that we must have a large middle class who believe in the essential worth of democracy to govern their lives and who give self-governance credibility. Because voters believe in the processes, they also believe in the governments that result from those elections. Whether Democrats or Republicans are elected, it is wise to structure society to assure a very broad middle class in order for democracy to remain a desirable form of government.

References

Election Assistance Commission. "RAAV-Seminars-Overview Doug Lewis." Last Modified February 27, 2017. https://www.eac.gov/documents/2017/02/27/raav-seminars-overview-doug-lewis/.

Purcell v. Gonzalez, 549 U.S. 1 (2006).

United States Census Bureau. "Table 399. Voting-Age Population—Reported Registration and Voting by Selected Characteristics: 1996 to 2010." 2012 Statistical Study Table 399 of Voting Age Population. Accessed January 13, 2019. https://www.census.gov/prod/2011pubs/12statab/election.pdf.

"Voter Fraud." *Huffington Post/YouGov*. Last Modified May 25, 2018. https://big.assets.huffingtonpost.com/athena/files/2018/05/25/5b084adbe-4b0568a880b4571.pdf.

Doug Lewis served for 20 years as executive director of the Election Center (The National Association of Election Officials), a national nonprofit dedicated to improving election administration in America. He also served as executive director of National Association of State Election Directors (NASED). A National Hall of Fame for Election Administration inductee, Lewis received the Distinguished Service Award from NASED, the organization's highest award. He served as the first chairman of the Board of Advisors to the US Election Assistance Commission, serving on the panel for more than 10 years.

4

Accessible and Secure: Improving Voter Confidence by Protecting the Right to Vote

Thomas Hicks

Introduction

Much of the public discourse around elections during and since the 2016 federal election has focused on security—and for good reason. While election officials have prioritized election security for a long time, 2016 changed the threat environment, pitting state and local officials against nation-state actors who scanned for vulnerabilities and were reportedly successful in accessing at least one state's voter rolls. These same actors made additional attempts to penetrate election systems ahead of the 2018 midterms and, by all accounts, will be back again in 2020. Election officials are taking this threat extremely seriously and have gone to great lengths since the 2016 federal election to increase both the security and resiliency of their systems. However, election administrators must ensure that these increased protections do not come at the expense of limiting accessibility.

T. Hicks (✉)
United States Election Assistance Commission, Silver Spring, MD, USA
e-mail: thicks@eac.gov

© The Author(s) 2020
M. Brown et al. (eds.), *The Future of Election Administration*, Elections, Voting, Technology, https://doi.org/10.1007/978-3-030-14947-5_4

The right to vote is one of the most fundamental, and hard-won, principles of our democracy. Yet, the work to ensure its promise extends to all eligible citizens is still unfinished. I learned this lesson at an early age from my parents, who grew up in the Jim Crow-era American South where there were considerable obstacles in place which restricted their access to the ballot, and in some cases, prevented them from casting a vote all together. Today, as a two-time Chairman of the US Election Assistance Commission (EAC), I have seen firsthand the progress that has been made to not only secure the vote, but also to expand the institution so it is accessible to all eligible voters. However, obstacles still exist for many who have historically faced issues when they go to vote.

In the work to secure our elections, we shouldn't choose between heightened security and expanded access, and we don't have to. At its heart, the debate over greater security is about the accuracy and integrity of our elections. One of the greatest ways to ensure voter confidence is to ensure the process in place can work for everyone, regardless of ability.

In this chapter, I will cover three areas of accessibility at the polls that need improvement: provisions for voters with disabilities, those who need language assistance, and military and overseas voters. Each of these issues represents a significant portion of the electorate whose right to vote must be protected and advanced through solutions that are both accessible and secure.

Voters with Disabilities

More than 35 million Americans with disabilities—roughly one-sixth of the total electorate—are eligible to vote in the United States. This accounts for a broad range of disabilities, including mobility, communicative, physical, and cognitive impairments. This ever-growing population of voters also faces educational, cultural, and political barriers that can make participating in elections difficult.

The Help America Vote Act (HAVA) of 2002, the EAC's founding legislation, charged the Commission with helping election officials administer accurate, accessible, and secure elections that provide the opportunity for all voters to vote privately and independently. Since our establishment, the EAC has committed to this principle by providing resources, promoting best practices, educating voters with disabilities about their rights, and testing and certifying voting systems to ensure they are accessible to all.

The EAC also hosts public forums and gathers feedback to share with election officials about challenges voters with disabilities can face when they go to the polls. For instance, the Commission received feedback from a voter in a wheelchair that, when she went to use the only accessible voting machine at the polling place during a recent election, she was told the machine did not work and was "just for show."

Voters with disabilities often find themselves in the position of having to advocate for polling place provisions required by law, as this voter had to. Many election officials, however, already realize that full accessibility should be at the top of their list of priorities and actively pursue ways to improve the election process for voters with disabilities.

For example, in 2016, the Office of the Secretary of State in Washington developed the MyVote portal, one of the nation's leading elections Web sites for people with disabilities. MyVote gives voters information, including registration details, contact information for their elected officials, an online voter guide, location of ballot drop boxes and voting centers, and their ballot status. Through a partnership with the Statewide Disability Advisory Committee and other stakeholders, the Secretary of State's office was able to ensure the tool was more accessible than previous tools and easy to use for all voters across the state, specifically those with disabilities.

Technological advances such as this have made the process of voting easier for voters with disabilities; however, many election officials around the country do not have the manpower or budgets to allow for large-scale technology upgrades. In such cases, one of the best ways to ensure barriers are eliminated for voters with disabilities is to better train election workers. Election workers can often make or break a voter's experience, particularly if a voter needs assistance. The EAC received feedback from one voter with mobility challenges that, after the location of her polling place was changed, she was unable to access the polling place using her manual chair. Instead of receiving help when she asked, this voter was told by a poll worker, "Why can't you push yourself?" This voter went on to say, "That day, I fought for my voting rights and was able to vote with assistance. But other people, this stops them from voting. If you have a bad experience like this, you are not going to want to go back."

If a voter who needs special provisions cannot cast a ballot privately and independently, this not only breaks the law, it sends a message to this voter that they are not valued in the democratic process—an outcome no election official wants.

Often, this issue can be attributed to lack of understanding on the part of an election worker of what it is like to have an accessibility issue at the polls. Some jurisdictions have addressed this disconnect through specialized training, such as the Accessible Polling Place Location and Equipment (APPLE) class launched in Contra Costa County, California. This program places election workers in the shoes of voters who need assistance to give them a new perspective and provides real-life examples of situations that can occur at a polling place on election day. In just over six months, 700 poll workers (about half of the county's total number of election day volunteers) completed the class and during the June 2018 primary, there was at least one APPLE-trained election worker at each of the county's 269 polling places.

Other jurisdictions, such as El Paso County, Colorado, have partnered with disability rights groups and resource centers to create universally accessible polling places. Seeking out partners and building relationships in the community can help election officials make the most of their often limited resources and benefit from additional expertise. While jurisdictions have made advances in providing access to disabled voters, more work needs to be done and election officials should be continuously reminded to do all they can to ensure accessibility.

Voters with Language Access Needs

According to US Census Bureau data, there are more than 25 million people in the United States with limited English proficiency and more than 60 million who speak a language other than English at home. Such individuals can face challenges when attempting to register to vote and cast a ballot. From translated materials to bilingual assistance at the polls, election officials across the country take a number of steps to help such voters overcome language barriers and participate meaningfully in the elections process. In certain jurisdictions, such assistance is required by language provisions outlined in Section 203 in the federal Voting Rights Act.

Section 203 of the Voting Rights Act has fostered language assistance for many language minority voters over the last forty-plus years. However, as effective as it has been, Section 203 is limited to specific jurisdictions that meet certain coverage thresholds and then, only in certain languages. The most recent round of determinations in 2016 identified just 263 jurisdictions that met such thresholds, including statewide coverage California, Florida, and Texas.

Many election officials go above and beyond the requirements of Section 203 to support language minority voters. These activities include jurisdictions that provide assistance in languages that are not covered by Section 203, as well as jurisdictions that provide language assistance on a voluntary basis. Other smaller and medium-sized jurisdictions are open to providing language assistance but must do so without additional funds from state and local budget authorities.

Election officials know better than most the importance of adopting strategies to spend their limited resources as effectively as possible and are constantly finding ways to be more efficient and cost-effective in their work. Providing assistance to voters with language needs is no different. For example, if given no additional budget for language assistance, election officials can leverage existing translation glossaries of election terminology, collaborate on translation needs with neighboring jurisdictions or their state elections offices and partner with language community organizations to support recruitment of bilingual poll workers.

At times, the best solution can lie in increasing the ethnic and age diversity of election judges and poll workers to better reflect the face of the community. For example, the City of Minneapolis created the Student Election Judge Program to recruit more young people as election workers and ensure there would not be a shortage of poll workers on election day. As with many other jurisdictions, they also found that recruiting more young people also increased the number of bilingual election workers and increased the diversity of their election workforce.

Cost-effective practices for providing language assistance will continue to be a priority for many of the nation's election officials, particularly as shifting demographics increase the need for language assistance and potentially increase the number of jurisdictions covered by Section 203 requirements.

At the EAC's most recent Language Access Summit, Alberto Olivas, Founding Executive Director of the Pastor Center for Politics and Public Service at Arizona State University effectively stressed the stakes involved in ensuring citizens are provided with language assistance at the polls.

> Voting is what happens when we've done a good job at helping people understand their rights and their roles as citizens, but it is also the front door to citizenship. Especially when we think about our newest citizens, it is critical we get it right for our newest citizens, those turning eighteen and voting for the first time, those who have gone through the naturalization process and newly have the right to vote, it is so important that their first experience with our election system goes well because we know that if it doesn't go well, we've significantly impinged on their likelihood to vote in the future.

Military and Overseas Voters

Another group which faces unique challenges in registering to vote and in requesting, receiving, and returning their ballots are military and overseas personnel and their families. Our country's active duty service members, their families, and Americans living overseas are charged with taking on significantly more responsibility than the average voter if they want to cast a ballot on election day. These citizens move often. They do not have the benefit of going to a physical polling place and often must make their voting plans months in advance if they are going to cast a ballot.

Such citizens are covered through the Uniformed and Overseas Citizens Absentee Voting Act (UOCAVA). Because of issues that can arise with the timely and accurate delivery of election materials, however, the voting process can be an arduous one for voters and election officials alike.

Compounding these issues is the fact that all countries do not have the same high level of postal service delivery that we enjoy here in the United States. To counter these obstacles for UOCAVA voters, the Military and Overseas Voter Empowerment (MOVE) Act currently allows for the electronic distribution and receipt of ballots, and this is a practice that must continue.

West Virginia Secretary of State Mac Warner knows all too well the difficulties that can arise when UOCAVA voters attempt to cast a ballot. When the EAC hosted an Election Readiness Summit on Capitol Hill one month before the 2018 midterm elections, he described his and his family's experience with voting while serving overseas, and how those experiences led West Virginia to establish a blockchain-based Mobile Voting App Pilot Project ahead of the 2018 midterms to help UOCAVA voters cast their ballots.

> My wife and I have raised four children, all of whom served in the military. I had a military career. My wife and I served all over the world, and we had difficulty voting throughout that time. It wasn't because we didn't want to. It was because it was difficult to get through obstacles in the process. Each of my children have [also] had trouble voting [while overseas]. My oldest, Stephen, served a year in Afghanistan…. He went through a number of harrowing experiences. I asked him what his toughest time was, and he said, 'Dad, it was election day.'
>
> He went into quite a bit of detail, but he was required to secure one polling place, and in the [course] of the day, long days, they dug up five IEDs. Five. So think of the amount of effort the Taliban went through, and the risk that American soldiers put their lives into secure that polling place so people could vote in the first election in Afghanistan's history, democracy at work in a foreign land that soldiers put their lives on the line to protect. Keep that image in your mind and multiply it times soldiers in 120 countries through the world today on a daily basis, the State

Department, and people putting in their years of service in 170 countries around the world. They have as much right to vote as we do, and we owe it to them to give them the opportunity.

With its Secure Military Mobile Voting pilot project, West Virginia became the first state in the nation to attempt a blockchain-run election at such a scale. The state received criticism from some who felt the process would not be secure. There are valid security concerns which can arise from the electronic transfer of ballots. However, technology solutions can often be the difference between a UOCAVA voter's ballot being counted and not. No voter should be disenfranchised because of an ability not to be able to send their ballot back to the United States while we continue to bolster safeguards to ensure that their vote is not compromised.

Beyond blockchain technology, there are other proactive measures both parties can take to help ease the burden on UOCAVA voters. Election officials should make sure their staff is knowledgeable about the postal requirements of election mail, meet with regional postmaster generals early and coordinate mailings with the local post office. Forming relationships with federal offices as well, including the United States Postal Service (USPS) and the Department of Defense's Federal Voting Assistance Program (FVAP) can also be beneficial. Many of these agents provide invaluable resources, such as FVAP's UOCAVA Election Official Online Training Course or USPS Election Officials' Mailing Resource Site, Election Mail Kit and guidance on designing election mail.

Other productive partnerships can be made with local military establishments and military base personnel who are Voting Assistance Officers. These relationships will be particularly beneficial for outreach efforts to UOCAVA voters.

Communication with UOCAVA voters themselves is also key. Election officials should publish election year calendars with clearly marked deadlines for registration, ballot requests, and ballot return. Mailing lists should be current, envelopes addressed properly and UOCAVA voters should know what their backup options are in case mail ballots are not received in a timely manner. Many UOCAVA voters also prefer e-mail communication, since many move frequently, and find notification of their registration status, confirmation of their current mailing address, and the receipt of their voted ballot, as well as whether their ballot was accepted or rejected, helpful.

Election officials should also provide state election offices with UOCAVA data for the EAC Election Administration and Voting Survey (EAVS) and examine past data to identify ways to better manage the process for transmitting ballots and understand what may lead some ballots to not be counted.

For UOCAVA voters themselves, one of the biggest factors in the military and overseas voting process is the timely delivery of election materials to the correct address. Many overseas voters have contacted the EAC because they have not received requested ballots. When a number of states blocked foreign IP addresses to prevent mischief, the EAC and FVAP worked with several states to find solutions so that affected UOCAVA voters could still receive election mail.

The most important thing is for voters and election officials to act early. Be aware of the latest USPS guidelines and delivery windows to ensure that blank ballots will be delivered to election officials on time. Check with your state Election Official for the most current processes and procedures for UOCAVA voters and know the resources available to help UOCAVA voters through the voting process, including federal partners at FVAP.

Conclusion

Much has been said in this chapter about the role of election officials in easing burdens for communities that have historically faced accessibility issues when attempting to cast a ballot. There is a significant role for private citizens to play, particularly those who have a disability, are multilingual, or are a veteran member of the US Armed Forces. All have a specific experience when they go to cast their ballot, and all could provide valuable assistance to others who may encounter similar challenges when going to vote.

There is also a great need to have more young people as election workers. By leveraging the talents of an eager, tech-savvy generation, election officials can foster the next generation of poll workers and civic leaders, relieve current poll worker shortages, and increase the diversity of their election workforce. Engaging young people in the election process early also encourages lifelong participation in democracy and helps young people form deeper connections with their communities.

Many jurisdictions struggle with recruiting enough poll workers to serve at physical polling places on election day—particularly poll workers who reflect the diversity of the electorate they are serving. All citizens should feel compelled to serve their communities as election workers because there is an overwhelming need for them.

Increasing citizen engagement will also help us confront the biggest risk to our elections: decreased voter confidence. Secure election systems mean nothing if voters are not confident in the process as a whole. Ensuring accessibility at the polls will go a long way toward reinstating voter confidence, and it is my hope that public interest in election security continues and results in more citizens becoming involved in the voting process outside of casting a ballot. Election officials encourage such involvement. Not only is it indicative of an engaged electorate, but when voters become educated about the process, the security measures in place, and the lengths to which election officials and poll workers go to ensure elections are accurate and have integrity, the result is almost always a deeper appreciation for election administration and a desire to continue contributing to it.

Thomas Hicks has served as Chairman of the US Election Assistance Commission for two terms and as Vice Chairman for an additional two terms. During his time with the Commission, Mr. Hicks has focused his efforts on voting accessibility, including developing a guide to voters rights for voters with disabilities and creating a help desk to address ballot delivery issues for overseas voters. Prior to his appointment with EAC, Mr. Hicks served as a senior elections counsel and minority elections counsel on the US House of Representatives Committee on House Administration, a senior lobbyist and policy analyst for Common Cause, and as a special assistant and legislative assistant in the Office of Congressional Relations for the Office of Personnel Management during the Clinton administration.

5

Challenges in Voter Registration

Thessalia Merivaki and Daniel A. Smith

A panoply of issues concerning voter registration in the United States is generating considerable attention among lawmakers, election officials, academics, and lawyers, largely because of the increasing politicization of what should be a routine, noncontroversial administrative task of state and local elections officials—the registration of eligible citizens to vote. Across the country, battles are being waged in state legislatures, with state and local election officials, and in the courts over what have become competing goals of easing (and increasing) access to voter registration for eligible citizens and the maintenance and integrity of voter rolls to ensure fair elections. Reports of outdated voter registration lists, high rates of provisional ballots cast and rejected, absentee ballot requests that fail to reach voters due to address errors, and eligible voters removed from voter rolls are all representative of a complex administrative process that has significant implications for the ability voters to cast a ballot.

T. Merivaki (✉)
Mississippi State University, Starkville, MS, USA

D. A. Smith
University of Florida, Gainesville, FL, USA

With very few exceptions, casting a ballot in the United States is not possible unless a voter is first registered to vote.

Although Congress and federal courts provide broad guidelines for the voter registration process, state and local officials have considerable latitude regarding the ease of voter registration and the structures of list maintenance. Many states have adopted voter registration reforms—such as pre-registration for those under 18 years of age, Election Day and Same Day Registration, and Online and Automatic Voter Registration—but others have made it more difficult for voters to register, limiting the availability of registration locations or requiring proof of citizenship when applying. For their part, local election officials are generally responsible for ensuring that eligible voters are properly entered on the voter rolls in time for an upcoming election and maintaining a clean and up-to-date voter registry. In evaluating how administrative voter registration and list maintenance procedures impact citizens who want to register to vote, update their voter registration, or remain on the voter rolls, scholars rely on official voter registration data whose availability and reliability vary dramatically across states and localities.

Increasing Access to Voter Registration

The National Voter Registration Act (NVRA) of 1993 stands as one the most significant legislative interventions at the federal level (besides the Voting Rights Act of 1965) when it comes to the protection, and expansion, of eligible citizens' access to voter registration. States are required to offer access to voter registration at local motor vehicle offices, public and state agencies, as well as at state and local election officials' offices. Under the law, prospective registrants are also permitted to submit their voter registration application by mail or via groups conducting voter registration drives up to 30 days prior to a federal election.[1] Despite

---

[1] The National Voter Registration Act (NVRA) of 1993. Available at https://www.justice.gov/crt/title-42-public-health-and-welfare-chapter-20-elective-franchise-subchapter-i-h-national-voter#anchor_1973gg.

the maximum threshold of 30 days set by the NVRA, states vary in the length of time they allow prospective voters to register prior to an upcoming election—anywhere from the maximum of 30 days prior to Election Day or on Election Day itself (Hanmer 2009). There are other anomalies, too. States that had already implemented or adopted Election Day Registration (EDR) when the NVRA was signed into law by President Bill Clinton in 1993 are exempt from the Act, under the expectation that eliminating voter registration prior to Election Day would positively impact voter turnout.

Scholars have documented extensively the success of the NVRA in increasing the rates of registered voters (Crocker 2013; FEC 1997, 1999; Hess and Novakowski 2008). However, challenges remain as to how well state agencies and local election officials comply with the federal law. Advocacy groups and researchers report that eligible voters are not always offered the option to register to vote in public assistance offices (Hess and Novakowski 2008) or motor vehicle offices (Naifeh 2015), resulting in litigation against many states, including Louisiana, Massachusetts, New York, Rhode Island, and Tennessee.[2] Such litigation often uncovers the difficulties that non-election officials experience when trying to register eligible citizens to vote, particularly due to lack of training and familiarity with the requirements of the NVRA (Crocker 2013) or restrictions placed on individuals or groups engaged in voter registration efforts (Herron and Smith 2013).

Despite the relative success of the NVRA in increasing the pool of registered voters, millions of eligible citizens remain unregistered. Many of these Americans report that their failure to participate in an election was because they were not registered to vote, attributing their neglect to do so to voter registration deadlines or a lack of knowledge about their state's voter registration requirements. According to the 2012 US Census' Current Population Survey, approximately 21% of Americans reported that they did not vote due to these reasons in 2012, with the majority claiming that they did not meet the voter registration deadline

---

[2]U.S. Department of Justice. "Cases Raising Claims Under the National Voter Registration Act." Available at https://www.justice.gov/crt/cases-raising-claims-under-national-voter-registration-act.

within their state (Merivaki 2016). According to the Pew Charitable Trusts (2017), in 2016 more than 60% of eligible Americans who are unregistered said they were "never asked to register to vote," by either a political campaign, a civic organization, or an official at a motor vehicle office or other government offices.[3]

The discussion over increasing access to the electoral process is often framed in terms of how actively the federal and state governments should be involved in lowering barriers to voter registration, within an electoral structure where voter registration is inherently passive and voluntary (Alvarez and Hall 2014). To be sure, the NVRA liberalized access to voter registration by increasing the opportunities citizens have when interacting with motor vehicle officials, public service officials, and non-governmental actors. But the NVRA did not explicitly address many of the persistent problems citizens experience when trying to register, most notably having to meet a state's voter registration deadline. Innovations by states, including Same Day and Election Day Registration (SDR and EDR), directly resolve the voter registration deadline problem, allowing eligible citizens to register to vote on the same day they turn out in person at the polls, either at an early voting facility or on Election Day at their local precinct. Since 2002, beyond the five NVRA-exempt states (Idaho, New Hampshire, Minnesota, Wisconsin, and Wyoming), 13 states have adopted SDR/EDR.[4]

Aside from EDR, states have experimented with additional reforms in effort to modernize the process of registering to vote and encourage youth voter participation. Half of the states allow for the pre-registration of 16- and 17-year-olds, and at least 37 states have adopted Online Voter Registration (OVR) since Arizona adopted it in 2002 (Hicks et al. 2016). Between 2015 and 2018, 12 states including Washington, DC have adopted Automatic Voter Registration (AVR), and at least 20 states

---

[3]Pew Research Brief. June 21, 2017. "Why Are Millions of Citizens Not Registered to Vote?" Available at http://www.pewtrusts.org/en/research-and-analysis/issue-briefs/2017/06/why-are-millions-of-citizens-not-registered-to-vote#0-overview.

[4]National Conference of State Legislatures. "Same Day Registration." Available at http://www.ncsl.org/research/elections-and-campaigns/same-day-registration.aspx.

are considering legislation to adopt it (Merivaki 2019).[5] California, Colorado, Washington, DC, and Oregon are leading accessible voter registration.[6]

As Table 5.1 shows, states vary in which reforms they adopt, with many having already adopted OVR or EDR and youth pre-registration. The only outliers are Arkansas, Ohio, and South Dakota, which only have adopted the minimal requirements of the NVRA.[7] North Carolina adopted a new law in 2013 repealing its youth pre-registration policy in 2013, but the 4th US Court of Appeals struck it down, rendering the policy again in effect. There is little systematic evidence suggesting that states with more voter registration reforms have higher rates of registered voters (Merivaki 2019). However, evidence from Oregon, the first state to adopt AVR, suggests that automatically registering voters when registering their vehicles has a positive effect on turnout among first-time voters (McElwee et al. 2016).

The Challenge of Successfully Registering to Vote

In order to become a registered voter, most eligible Americans are first required to submit a voter registration application. The NVRA requires that election officials process complete and valid applications, without providing a clear definition of the meaning of either "complete" or "valid" (Merivaki 2018). Whereas at a first glance these terms appear very straightforward, how states and localities interpret them varies for two reasons. First, what is the necessary information for an application to be complete? Is an application valid if it is missing the

---

[5] Brennan Center for Justice. "Automatic Voter Registration and Modernization in the States." Available at https://www.brennancenter.org/analysis/automatic-voter-registration.
[6] Oregon does not have SDR/EDR, as it conducts elections exclusively by mail.
[7] Ohio in 2014 eliminated its "Golden Week" of registration, when voters could register to vote and cast an early in-person ballot the week prior to the voter registration deadline. https://www.nytimes.com/2016/09/14/us/politics/supreme-court-wont-restore-golden-week-voting-in-ohio.html.

Table 5.1 Voter registration reforms across the United States

	OVR	Pre-reg. +OVR	EDR +OVR +AVR	Pre-reg. +EDR +OVR	Pre-reg. +OVR +AVR	Pre-reg. +EDR	Pre-reg. +OVR +AVR
NVRA states	Alabama Indiana Kentucky Massachusetts New Mexico	Alaska Arizona Delaware Florida Georgia	Vermont	Hawaii Iowa Maryland	California Colorado DC		Oregon
	New York Oklahoma Pennsylvania South Carolina Tennessee Virginia	Kansas Louisiana Missouri Nebraska Nevada Utah West Virginia	EDR Montana	EDR+OVR Connecticut Illinois	Pre-reg. Texas Maine Mississippi Michigan North Carolina		No reform Arkansas Ohio South Dakota
			AVR New Jersey				
NVRA-exempt states	EDR New Hampshire	EDR +OVR Idaho Wisconsin		Pre-reg. +EDR Wyoming	Pre-reg. +EDR +OVR Minnesota		

applicant's driver's license, or date of birth? Second, if the applicant's address has an error, is the application incomplete or invalid? These seemingly trivial questions often determine whether an eligible voter will successfully enter the state's voter rolls and thus be able to cast a ballot on Election Day, or be placed on a list of pending or suspended registrations.

According to the Election Assistance Commission's (EAC) Election Administration and Voting Survey (EAVS), 37.3% of all voter registration forms received in 2016 were new applications that were initially accepted as valid. Another 53% were duplicate registrations or updates to existing voter registrations. Only 3% of all these forms were rejected as invalid, which is a negligible amount.[8] However, when comparing across and within states, there are notable discrepancies in the voter registration rejection rates. Texas, for instance, reported to the EAC in the 2012 EAVS survey that it rejected 25.4% of all voter registration applications, the highest rejection rate that election cycle (EAC 2013). In 2016, Texas reported rejecting 2.52% of all voter registration applications submitted, a notable decrease.

These estimates should be taken with a grain of salt due to the extensive underreporting and non-reporting by states and localities. Indicatively, Kentucky reported rejecting 32% of all voter registration applications submitted in 2016 but provided no information on invalid voter registration applications in 2012 (EAC 2013). As Pew's Election Performance Index (EPI) explains, the EAVS does not collect information on why voter registrations are rejected.[9] This is a limitation for researchers trying to understand variances in rates of rejected applications, as well as determine which part of the voter registration process increases the risk of invalid applications.

Institutional, seasonal, and administrative factors often explain variation in voter registration rejections, especially at the local level. As a

---

[8]The remaining 6.7% is categorized as "Other" or "Not Categorized" (EAC 2017).
[9]Pew Charitable Trusts. "Election Performance Index: Data Visualization." August 9, 2016. http://www.pewtrusts.org/en/research-and-analysis/data-visualizations/2014/elections-performance-index#indicatorProfile-RR.

state's voter registration deadline approaches prior to Election Day, popular interest and accompanying voter registration and mobilization efforts rise, posing challenges for both prospective voters and election administrators. Applications submitted very close to a state's voter registration deadline that are incomplete or contain erroneous information may be more likely to be rejected as local election administrators have a smaller window of time to reach out to the applicants to assist them in properly completing their registration form. Evidence from Florida's 67 counties in the 2012 presidential election suggests that when voter registration submissions peak, so do the rates of rejected registrations. Densely populated counties rejected more voter registration applications on average that election cycle, likely due to the higher volume of applications that local election officials had to process very close to, or on the day of, Florida's 29-day registration book closing prior to Election Day (Merivaki 2018).

While a voter registration application may be rejected because an applicant is not eligible to vote due to a disenfranchising crime or lack of US citizenship, incomplete and missing information such as a driver's license number or a missing address is frequently the given reason why applications are rejected. Yet there is considerable variation across the states in how new voter registrations are processed. As Merivaki and Conner (2018) note, Mississippi local election officials mark incomplete applications as pending until they contact the prospective voter to complete the voter registration process. Interestingly, some county election officials claim to "never reject" voter registration applications, but retain them as pending, offering the prospective voter the opportunity to cast a ballot on Election Day if she provides documentation of voter eligibility. In Florida, however, applications that remain incomplete after the state's book closing deadline are rejected; prospective voters have the option to vote provisionally, as per the Help America Vote Act (HAVA) of 2002, but those ballots will be rejected as invalid (Merivaki 2018). These differences across the states indicate the existence of local practices that are most likely non-uniform even within the same state but have important implications about prospective voters' capacity to vote on Election Day.

Maintaining Accurate Voter Records

Maintaining voter records constitutes one of the most challenging tasks for state and local election officials (Ansolabehere and Hersh 2014). Newly registered voters enter the voter rolls every day, voters move from one county or state to another, while many Americans need to be removed from the list of registered voters because they are deceased or became ineligible due to a disenfranchising crime. At the same time, not every registered voter turns out to vote regularly and even those who do often experience problems with casting a ballot. According to the NVRA, election officials are required to maintain voter lists of eligible registered voters and remove those who are no longer eligible in a manner that is "non-discriminatory and uniform" and no later than 90 days prior to an upcoming federal election.[10] This process is very complex, as it involves meticulous record keeping of newly registered voters, voters who vote regularly, as well as voters who have not been actively participating, and contacting them to confirm that they are still eligible voters and reside in the jurisdiction in which they originally registered to vote.

Because the voter registration process is predominantly paper-based, voter records often contain errors. Duplicate records, missing dates of birth, phone numbers, and typographical errors in the voter's last name are likely to be entered and retained as such in a jurisdiction's voter list and may cause trouble for voters because when they turn out to vote, their information will not match the voter records. Errors in voter lists may also affect voters who vote by mail or cast absentee mail ballots. If, for instance, a voter's address contains errors, her mail ballot will not be delivered, and as a result, she will not be able to vote. This is particularly significant in states that conduct elections exclusively by mail, such as Oregon, Colorado, and Washington.[11]

---

[10] The National Voter Registration Act (NVRA) of 1993. https://www.justice.gov/crt/title-42-public-health-and-welfare-chapter-20-elective-franchise-subchapter-i-h-national-voter#anchor_1973gg.

[11] The National Conference of State Legislatures. August 17, 2017. "Absentee and Early Voting." http://www.ncsl.org/research/elections-and-campaigns/absentee-and-early-voting.aspx.

While a missing birthdate may appear less influential than a missing or erroneous address insofar as prohibiting a voter from casting a vote, it can pose a challenge for local election administrators, who are responsible for removing ineligible voters from the rolls, particularly those who are deceased. If a birthdate is missing, the most common default date is 01/01/1900. Such errors pose additional administrative burden for local election officials, because they determine whether the record is erroneous and correct it without risking removing eligible voters from the rolls. On another note, it is not clear why records with missing data are even included in the states' voter lists, considering that a voter registration application would be technically incomplete if it is missing any of the requested information. The existence of such records, therefore, suggests that election officials might use more relaxed "completeness" criteria when processing voter registration applications.

Prior to 2004, voters whose registration status could not be verified were turned away from the polls. Recognizing that many voters were disenfranchised due to errors in the voter registration process, the US Congress adopted HAVA, which improved the voting process in two meaningful ways. First, it added a failsafe by allowing voters whose voter registration status could not be verified at the polls to cast a provisional ballot. Second, it required that states adopt and maintain statewide, centralized voter registration databases, so as to facilitate the voter list maintenance process and minimize errors in voter records (Alvarez and Hall 2014; Merivaki and Conner 2018). There is limited research indicating that adopting centralized databases has increased the accuracy of voter records. This is because states have adopted different voter registration database structures, which the EAC calls "VRD Systems" (Table 5.2). Most states have opted for top-down or bottom-up structures, with nine states defining themselves as "hybrids." In top-down structures, the state maintains voter records and any changes are immediately accessible by localities. In bottom-up structures, localities maintain the records and share them with the state at regular intervals. According to the EAC, hybrids are a combination of the two.

The adoption of these statewide management structures has facilitated information sharing between states and various governmental agencies. Until 2012, all but a few states were participating in the Interstate Crosscheck program, which matches voter lists from all participating states and identifies duplicates which suggest the possibility of voters who are registered to vote in more than one state. Crosscheck has been extensively criticized for the high rates of "false positive" matches that may result in erroneously removing eligible voters from states' voter records.[12] Since 2012, 24 states have joined the Electronic Registration Information Center (ERIC), which supplements this process by comparing data from state agencies, as well as governmental agencies, such as the US Post Office (USPS) and the Social Security Death records (Table 5.2).

ERIC states share voter registration data and import lists of deceased voters and voters who changed their mailing address through the US Postal Services' National Change of Address (NCOA), and flag voter records that match across the states as potential duplicates. A few states are currently members of both, although some of the states that joined ERIC since 2015, such as Alaska, Florida, Kentucky, Massachusetts, New York, Oregon, Pennsylvania, and Washington, were former Crosscheck members. Of the 25 ERIC states, 18 are top-down states, which suggest that there is a relationship between the states' database structure and the decision to switch from Crosscheck to ERIC.

The pressure to maintain accurate voter records may have led election officials to follow more aggressive voter list maintenance practices in the name of accuracy that appear to conform with the NVRA's "non-discriminatory" and "uniform" mandate. As per the NVRA, voters who have not participated in two consecutive federal elections and have not responded to election officials' requests to confirm their status may be removed from the lists of registered voters and explicitly

---

[12]Ingraham, Christopher. July 20, 2017. "This Anti-Voter-Fraud-Program Gets It Wrong Over 99% of the Time: The GOP Wants to Take It Nationwide." *The Washington Post*. https://www.washingtonpost.com/news/wonk/wp/2017/07/20/this-anti-voter-fraud-program-gets-it-wrong-over-99-of-the-time-the-gop-wants-to-take-it-nationwide/?noredirect=on&utm_term=.a15224206514.

Table 5.2 State data-sharing membership and VRD systems

State	Crosscheck	ERIC	Database structure
California	N	N	Bottom-up
Illinois	Y	Y	Bottom-up
Nevada	Y	Y	Bottom-up
New York	N	N	Bottom-up
Ohio	Y	Y	Bottom-up
Tennessee	Y	N	Bottom-up
Arizona	Y	Y	Hybrid
Mississippi	Y	N	Hybrid
Oklahoma	Y	N	Hybrid
Rhode Island	N	Y	Hybrid
Texas	Y	N	Hybrid
Washington	N	Y	Hybrid
Wisconsin	Y	Y	Hybrid
Alaska	N	Y	Top-down
Connecticut	N	Y	Top-down
Delaware	N	Y	Top-down
DC	N	Y	Top-down
Florida	N	Y[a]	Top-down
Hawaii	N	N	Top-down
Kentucky	N	N	Top-down
Maryland	N	Y	Top-down
Massachusetts	N	N	Top-down
Minnesota	N	Y	Top-down
Montana	N	N	Top-down
New Jersey	N	N	Top-down
New Mexico	N	Y	Top-down
Oregon	N	Y	Top-down
Pennsylvania	N	Y	Top-down
South Carolina	N	Y	Top-down
Utah	N	Y	Top-down
Vermont	N	N	Top-down
West Virginia	N	Y	Top-down
Wyoming	N	N	Top-down
Alabama	Y	Y	Top-down
Arkansas	Y	N	Top-down
Colorado	Y	Y	Top-down
Georgia	Y	N	Top-down
Idaho	Y	N	Top-down
Indiana	Y	N	Top-down
Iowa	Y	N	Top-down
Kansas	Y	N	Top-down
Louisiana	Y	Y	Top-down
Maine	Y	N	Top-down

(continued)

Table 5.2 (continued)

State	Crosscheck	ERIC	Database structure
Michigan	Y	N	Top-down
Missouri	Y	Y	Top-down
Nebraska	Y	N	Top-down
New Hampshire	Y	N	Top-down
North Carolina	Y	N	Top-down
South Dakota	Y	N	Top-down
Virginia	Y	Y	Top-down
North Dakota	–	–	Top-down

[a]Florida adopted ERIC in the Spring of 2018 and is scheduled to implement it in 2019

states that "failure to vote" does not constitute a reason to remove a voter from the rolls.[13] Ohio's voter removal practices were recently challenged in *Husted v. A. Phillip Randolph Institute*. According to Herron and Smith (2018), Ohio began the removal process once a voter failed to vote in one federal election, essentially treating non-voting as a trigger for removal. Ohio contacted the voters who did not vote in the 2010 federal election by mailing a voter confirmation card. If no response was received, and these voters did not vote in 2012 and 2014, they were removed from the state's list of registered voters. The US Supreme upheld Ohio's voter removal approach on the grounds that it does not violate the NVRA. While it is too early to tell, researchers argue that this decision may motivate other states to pursue similar practices to remove inactive voters from their lists.[14] According to the Brennan Center for Justice, some states have been removing voters by not following the procedures laid out in the NVRA and there has been an increase in litigation as a result of high voter removal rates and questionable purging practices in the post-*Shelby v. Holder* era (Brater et al. 2018).

---

[13]Section 1973gg-6(b)(2) of the National Voter Registration Act.

[14]Michael C. Herron and Daniel A. Smith. "If More States Start Using Ohio's System, How Many Voters Will Be Purged?" *The Washington Post*. June 17, 2018. https://www.washingtonpost.com/news/monkey-cage/wp/2018/06/17/if-every-u-s-state-used-ohios-system-how-many-voters-would-be-purged/?noredirect=on&utm_term=.1957a41079c0.

Voter Registration and the Challenges for Voters

Whereas a voter cannot cast a ballot if she is not registered to vote, many eligible and registered voters often face challenges in casting a vote. Verifying voter information at the registration check-in may be time consuming if there is a high influx of voters showing up at the polls on Election Day, or if poll workers have trouble verifying voters' information. Researchers note that such events increase the wait time at the polls and significantly impact the voting experience (Herron and Smith 2016a; Spencer and Markovits 2010; Stewart 2015).

The rates of provisional ballots cast and rejected across states and localities are key indicators of how issues with voter registration may deter voters from having their ballot counted (Hanmer and Herrnson 2014; Kimball et al. 2006; Merivaki and Smith 2018). Since 2006, when provisional voting was implemented for the first time, the rates of provisional ballots cast and rejected were unusually high, particularly in some jurisdictions. In 2008, for instance, Hillsborough and Broward Counties in Florida rejected more than 90% of all provisional ballots cast (Merivaki and Smith 2016; Smith et al. 2018). In the 2016 presidential election, less than 3% of voters voted provisionally, and even fewer had their provisional ballot rejected. In that context, high acceptance rates strongly suggest that provisional ballots are a failsafe to voting, as HAVA intended (Merivaki and Smith 2018). However, the fact that voters had to cast a provisional ballot also suggests that issues with maintaining voter records or successfully registering to vote remain.

There are various reasons why a voter may vote provisionally, which fall under the broad definition of "eligibility" to vote in an election and voting location. We use North Carolina as a case study to investigate why voters voted provisionally in the 2016 presidential election. Approximately 1.3% of all Election Day voters cast a provisional vote, a total of 58,100. As Table 5.3 shows, 56% of all provisional ballots cast were rejected in North Carolina in 2016.

Many provisional voters in North Carolina had trouble casting a regular ballot for three reasons: Because there was no record of their voter registration in their precinct's voter list (35,883 voters), they

Table 5.3 Reasons for Election Day provisional ballots cast in the North Carolina 2016 general election

Reason for provisional ballot	Full approval	Rejected	Partial approval	Total
Incorrect party	19	6	2	27
	70.37	22.22	7.41	100
Incorrect precinct	3336	421	3790	7547
	44.2	5.58	50.22	100
Jurisdiction dispute	179	181	51	411
	43.55	44.04	12.41	100
No acceptable ID	60	177	11	248
	24.19	71.37	4.44	100
No record of registration	7158	28,093	632	35,883
	19.95	78.29	1.76	100
Non-reasonable resemblance	3	4	0	7
	42.86	57.14	0	100
Previously removed	2642	2600	124	5366
	49.24	48.45	2.31	100
Unrecognized address	160	321	34	515
	31.07	62.33	6.6	100
Unreported move	6697	641	429	7767
	86.22	8.25	5.52	100
Voted extended hours	19	2	13	34
	55.88	5.88	38.24	100
Already voted	203	80	12	295
	68.81	27.12	4.07	100
Total	20,476	32,526	5098	58,100
	35.24	55.98	8.77	100

turned out to vote in the wrong precinct or moved to a new jurisdiction without updating their address prior to voting (15,314), or they were previously removed from the voter rolls (5366). "No record of registration" here does not necessarily mean that these individuals were not registered to vote. In fact, 21.7% had their ballot accepted either partially or in full. Among the remaining "no record of registration" voters, approximately 88% had their ballot rejected because they were deemed "not registered" by county election officials. Only about 6% of provisional votes cast in the wrong precinct were rejected, as well as 8.3% of voters who moved in a new jurisdiction but did not update their address before the election. These patterns of accepting and rejecting provisional ballots demonstrate the dynamics of voting provisionally, which extend beyond determining whether a voter is registered to vote.

These patterns show that provisional voting is also contextual. In North Carolina, provisional ballots cast in the wrong precinct are to be at least partially counted due to ongoing litigation against North Carolina's VIVA Act, which was adopted in 2013 (Herron and Smith 2016b; Merivaki and Smith 2018).[15] This explains the low rejection rates for "incorrect precinct" and "unreported move" voters, although it is not clear why even a small percentage of those provisional ballots were rejected. However, 54 out of 100 counties reported rejecting provisional ballots cast in the wrong precinct, and 59 counties reported rejecting provisional ballots cast by "unreported move" voters. It is possible that these discrepancies reflect variation in administrative practices at the local level insofar as processing provisional voters. Local elections officials, for instance, may choose to redirect those voters to their correct precinct instead of issuing a provisional ballot.

A look at the "previously removed" voters also merits attention insofar as the impact of purging on voters. About 52% of all "previously removed" provisional voters (5366 in total, or 9.23%) in North Carolina had their provisional vote accepted partially or in full. Were it not for the option to vote provisionally, these voters would have been turned away from the polls on Election Day. Interestingly, eight counties had zero provisional ballots cast for that reason.[16] As Fig. 5.1 shows, there is significant variation in the acceptance rates, partial or full, of provisional ballots cast by voters that were marked as "previously removed." Mecklenburg and Wake Counties are the notable outliers, because they are North Carolina's largest counties, yet the latter accepted 6.5% of those provisional ballots, while Mecklenburg accepted

---

[15]2016 Statutory Overview Individual State Responses. https://www.eac.gov/research-and-data/2016-election-administration-voting-survey/.

[16]Burke, Cleveland, Franklin, Gates, Granville, Harnett, Jones, Sampson, Swain, Warren Counties.

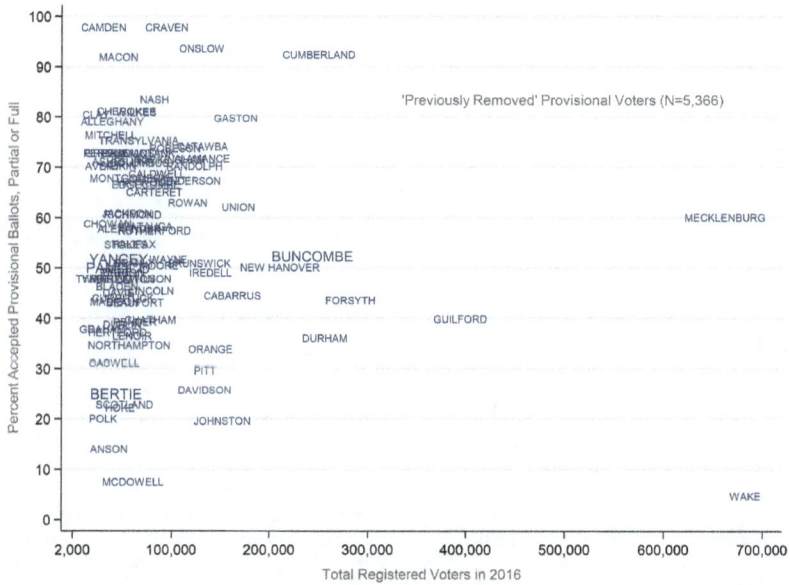

Fig. 5.1 Rates of accepted provisional ballots cast by "Previously Removed" voters in North Carolina in 2016

65.3%. There does not seem to be an association between the number of registered voters and the county's acceptance rates of "previously removed" provisional ballots. This may be another indication of variation in administrative practices at the local level in processing provisional ballots.

Whether or not certain voters, or groups of voters, are more prone than others to cast a provisional ballot is an important issue, as it raises questions of equity. Since scholars have limited knowledge of who casts provisional ballots, and whether these voters are representative of the broader electorate, it is difficult to determine whether there might be a violation of equal treatment under the law. As such, understanding which voters are more likely to cast provisional ballots is more than just of interest to those who strive to improve election administration or ensure that the candidate with the most votes actually wins in a close election contest.

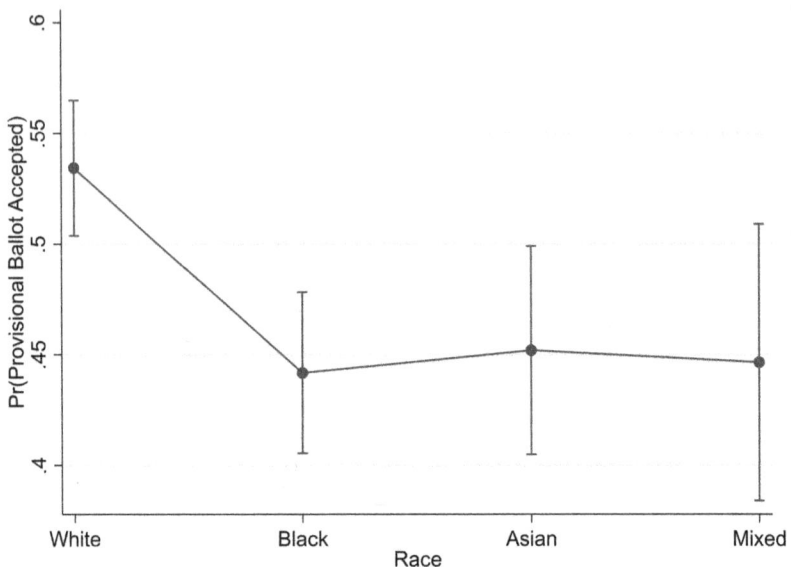

Fig. 5.2 Likelihood of casting a valid provisional ballot in North Carolina 2016 general election, by race

As a hypothetical example, we determine the likelihood that a provisional ballot is accepted if it is cast by a non-Hispanic, Democratic female voter who is alternatively white, black, Asian, or of mixed race. Setting all the reasons why a voter cast a provisional ballot in North Carolina at their mean value, we find that the hypothetical white, non-Hispanic, Democratic female provisional voter has a 53.4% likelihood of having her ballot accepted as valid; the comparable black, non-Hispanic, Democratic female provisional voter has just a 44.2% chance of having her ballot accepted, a statistically significant difference. As Fig. 5.2 shows, our hypothetical Asian and mixed-race non-Hispanic, Democratic female voters are also significantly less likely to cast valid provisional ballots than comparable white voters. The disproportionate impact of provisional ballots on minority voters is an important finding, which raises concerns about the equal treatment under the law of provisional voters.

Challenges to Studying Voter Registration

The systematic study of voter registration has traditionally involved research on implementation of the NVRA across the states (Crocker 2013; Hess and Novakowski 2008; Highton and Wolfinger 1998; Knack 1995; Martinez and Hill 1999; Rogers 2009; Rugeley and Jackson 2009), and the increase of voter registration rates and turnout over time, especially among states that adopted Election Day Registration (Brians and Grofman 2001; Hanmer 2009; Knack 2001; Neiheisel and Burden 2012). Over the last decade, the scope of research has expanded and is now a part of the growing field of election sciences, which brings together researchers and practitioners, and thus effectively incorporating the study of election administration into the study of voter registration. Extant research demonstrates how existing variation in administrative practices result in discrepancies in voter registration rates and turnout among many voting groups, such as racial and ethnic minorities (Hess et al. 2016; Merivaki 2018; Merivaki and Smith 2016). In addition, the accuracy of voter lists constitutes a fast-growing field of research insofar as assessing issues in the process of registering to vote, but also the ability of eligible voters to cast a valid vote (Ansolabehere and Hersh 2014; Ansolabehere et al. 2010; Herron and Smith 2018; Merivaki and Conner 2018).

Studying the conduct of elections, broadly defined, as well as voter registration would not be possible without the EAC's Election Administration and Voting bi-annual Surveys (EAVS), which are the most comprehensive source of election administration and voting data across the states at the local jurisdiction level. Localities report to the EAVS a vast array of data, from the total number of ballots cast in-person before or on Election Day, absentee by mail, to the number of poll workers and voting machines in every jurisdiction for every federal election since HAVA came into effect in 2004. Regarding voter registration, the EAVS collects information that is essential for determining if states comply with the NVRA, such as the number of voter registration applications received every election cycle by various voter registration agencies (DMV, public assistance offices, registration drives, etc.), total number of removed registrations, and duplicate, valid and invalid voter registrations.

The EAVS comes with several caveats, however. As noted previously, much of the information is often non-reported by jurisdictions and states. Merivaki and Smith (2015) demonstrate that several jurisdictions have been repeatedly non-reporting to the EAVS data that are necessary for the study of voter registration, such as the number of rejected voter registrations, as well as the numbers of provisional ballots cast and rejected. Missing data hinder our capacity to systematically and comprehensively evaluate how states and localities conduct elections, as the EPI reports, but also limit our ability to meaningfully discuss reforms that improve voter registration and the voting experience.

The next best source of such data, although not as centralized and comprehensive as the EAVS, is the individual state. There is notable variation, however, in which data states are reporting on their statewide election Web sites and whether these data are not only available, but also affordable to the public. The cost of individual voter registration lists for example, which are useful for researchers who study voter list maintenance, is prohibitive in many states, such as Arizona and Alabama and Kentucky, among others.[17] Estimates of voter registration from local jurisdictions such as those collected by the EAVS are not equally available either. Indicatively, Colorado, Florida, and North Carolina report monthly voter registration statistics on their statewide election Web site, whereas Mississippi does not. Given the hyper-federalized nature of election administration in the United States, where localities essentially run elections, it is not sufficient to report statewide estimates of registered voters and turnout. Unfortunately, many states do not make readily available such data at the local jurisdiction level. Such discrepancies suggest that states and localities may not uniformly collect the data: this raises important issues about data availability and transparency, and potential non-compliance with the NVRA's disclosure provision.

---

[17]Michael P. McDonald, Peter Licari, and Thessalia Merivaki. "The Cost of Using Big Data in Elections," *The Washington Post*. October 18, 2015. https://www.washingtonpost.com/opinions/the-big-cost-of-using-big-data-in-elections/2015/10/18/cb7bdf6c-7443-11e5-8248-98e0f5a2e830_story.html?utm_term=.1e2332ed9f92.

References

Alvarez, Michael R., and Thad E. Hall. "Resolving Voter Registration Problems: Making Registration Easier, Less Costly, and More Accurate." In *Election Administration in the United States: The State of Reform After Bush V. Gore*, edited by R. Michael Alvarez and Bernard Grofman, 186–198. New York: Cambridge University Press, 2014.

Ansolabehere, Stephen, and Eitan Hersh. "Voter Registration: The Process and Quality of Lists." In *The Measure of American Elections*, edited by Barry C. Burden and Charles Stewart III, 61–90. New York: Cambridge University Press, 2014.

Ansolabehere, Stephen, Eitan Hersh, Alan Gerber, and David Doherty. *Voter Registration List Quality Pilot Studies: Report on Methodology*. Washington, DC: The Pew Center on the States, 2010.

Brater, Jonathan, Kevin Morris, Myrna Pérez, and Christopher Deluzio. "Purges: A Growing Threat to the Right to Vote." *Brennan Center for Justice* (2018): 1–26.

Brians, Craig Leonard, and Bernard Grofman. "Election Day Registration's Effect on US Voter Turnout." *Social Science Quarterly*, 82, no. 1 (2001): 170–183.

Crocker, Royce. "The National Voter Registration Act of 1993: History, Implementation, and Effects." *Congressional Research Service* (2013): 1–36.

Election Assistance Commission. 2012 Election Administration and Voting Survey Comprehensive Report, 2013. https://www.eac.gov/assets/1/6/2012ElectionAdministrationandVoterSurvey.pdf.

———. 2016 Election Administration and Voting Survey Comprehensive Report, 2017. https://www.eac.gov/assets/1/6/2016_EAVS_Comprehensive_Report.pdf.

Federal Election Commission. "The Impact of the National Voter Registration Act of 1993 on the Administration of Elections for Federal Office 1995–1996." 1997. https://www.eac.gov/assets/1/6/The%20Impact%20of%20the%20National%20Voter%20Registration%20Act%20on%20Federal%20Elections%201995-1996.pdf.

———. "The Impact of the National Voter Registration Act of 1993 on the Administration of Elections for Federal Office 1997–1998." 1999. https://www.eac.gov/assets/1/6/The%20Impact%20of%20the%20National%20Voter%20Registration%20Act%20on%20Federal%20Elections%201997-1998.pdf.

Hanmer, Michael J. *Discount Voting: Voter Registration Reforms and Their Effects*. New York: Cambridge University Press, 2009.

Hanmer, Michael J., and Paul S. Herrnson. 2014. "Provisional Ballots." In *The Measure of American Elections*, edited by Barry C. Burden and Charles Stewart III, 91–112. New York: Cambridge University Press, 2014.

Herron, Michael C., and Daniel A. Smith. "The Effects of House Bill 1355 on Voter Registration in Florida." *State Politics and Policy Quarterly*, 13 (2013): 279–305.

———. "Precinct Resources and Voter Wait Times." *Electoral Studies*, 42 (2016a): 249–263.

———. "Race, Shelby County, and the Voter Information Verification Act in North Carolina." *Florida State University Law Review*, 43 (2016b): 465–506.

———. "Estimating the Differential Effects of Purging Inactive Registered Voters." Conference Paper Presentation, Election Sciences, Reform and Administration (ESRA), Madison, Wisconsin, July 2018.

Hess, Douglas R., and Scott Novakowski. *Neglecting the National Voter Registration Act, 1995–2007*. Washington, DC: Project Vote and Demos, 2008.

Hess, Douglas R., Michael J. Hanmer, and David W. Nickerson. "Encouraging Local Compliance with Federal Civil Rights Laws: Field Experiments with the National Voter Registration Act." *Public Administration Review*, 76 (2016): 165–174.

Hicks, William D., Seth C. McKee, and Daniel A. Smith. "A Bipartisan Election Reform? Explaining Support for Online Voter Registration in the American States." *American Politics Research*, 44, no. 6 (2016): 1008–1036.

Highton, Benjamin, and Raymond E. Wolfinger. "Estimating the Effects of the National Voter Registration Act of 1993." *Political Behavior*, 20 (1998): 79–104.

Kimball, David C., Martha Kropf, and Lindsay Battles. "Helping America Vote? Election Administration, Partisanship, and Provisional Voting in the 2004 Election." *Election Law Journal*, 5, no. 4 (2006): 447–461.

Knack, Stephen. "Does 'Motor Voter' Work? Evidence from State-Level Data." *The Journal of Politics*, 57 (1995): 796–811.

———. "Election-Day Registration: The Second Wave." *American Politics Research*, 29 (2001): 65–78.

Martinez, Michael D., and David Hill. "Did Motor Voter Work?" *American Politics Quarterly*, 27 (1999): 296–315.

McElwee, Sean, Brian Schaffner, and Jesse Rhodes. "Automatic Voter Registration in Oregon." *Demos* (2016): 1–6.

Merivaki, Thessalia. "Investigating Voter Registration Rejections in Florida." *State Politics and Policy Quarterly* (2018). https://doi.org/10.1177/1532440018800334.

———. *The Administration of Voter Registration: Patterns and Variation Across and Within the American States*. New York: Palgrave Macmillan, 2019.

Merivaki, Thessalia, and Daniel A. Smith. "The Contributions and Conundrums of Technology: The Election Administration and Voting Survey and Data Reporting Consistency." The Evolution of Election Administration Since the VRA 1965–2015 Symposium, Auburn, September 15, 2015.

———. "Casting and Verifying Provisional Ballots in Florida." *Social Science Quarterly*, 97, no. 3 (2016): 729–747.

———. "Who Casts Provisional Ballots?" 2 May 2018 (Blog). https://medium.com/mit-election-lab/who-votes-provisionally-and-why-4dd413c02fa9.

Merivaki, Thessalia, and Sean Conner. "Managing Voter Rolls the Hybrid Way: The Case of Mississippi." Conference Paper Presentation, Election Sciences, Reform and Administration (ESRA), Madison, Wisconsin, July 2018.

Naifeh, Stuart. "Driving the Vote: Are States Complying with the Motor Voter Requirements of the National Voter Registration Act?" *Demos* (2015): 1–33.

Neiheisel, Jacob R., and Barry C. Burden. "The Impact of Election Day Registration on Voter Turnout and Election Outcomes." *American Politics Research*, 40, no. 4 (2012): 636–664.

Rogers, Estelle H. "The National Voter Registration Act: Fifteen Years On." *American Constitution Society for Law and Policy Issue Brief* (2009): 1–16.

Rugeley, Cynthia, and Robert A. Jackson. "Getting on the Rolls: Analyzing the Effects of Lowered Barriers on Voter Registration." *State Politics and Policy Quarterly*, 9, no. 1 (2009): 56–78.

Smith, Daniel A., Dillon Boatner, Caitlin Ostroff, Pedro Otálora, and Laura Uribe. "Early Bird Special: Convenience Voting in Florida's 2016 General Election." In *Florida 2016: Ground Zero for America's New Political Revolt*, edited by Matthew Corrigan and Michael Binder. Gainesville: University of Florida Press, 2018.

Spencer, Douglas M., and Zachary S. Markovits. "Long Lines at Polling Stations? Observations from an Election Day Field Study." *Election Law Journal*, 9, no.1 (2010): 3–17.

Stewart III, Charles. "Waiting to Vote." *Election Law Journal: Rules, Politics and Policy*, 14, no. 1 (2015): 47–53.

Thessalia Merivaki is an assistant professor in American politics at Mississippi State University. Her research focuses on the empirical assessment of election reforms on the administration of elections across the United States. Currently, she is collaborating with the Stennis Institute of Government at MSU to thoroughly document election administrative practices across Mississippi's 82 counties and investigate the quality of voter list maintenance, a project funded by the MIT Election Sciences and Data lab.

Daniel A. Smith is University of Florida Research Foundation (2010–2012) Professor and Chair of Political Science at the University of Florida. Smith's research examines how political institutions affect political behavior across and within the American states. He has written extensively on the politics of direct democracy, elections, and voting rights in the United States.

6

Polling Place Quality and Access

Robert Stein, Christopher Mann and Charles Stewart III

Introduction

Polling places, their location, staff, equipment, and operations are thought to be consequential to the voting experience, including voter turnout and voter confidence that their vote will be counted as they intended (Alvarez et al. 2008; Akteson and Saunders 2007; Barreto et al. 2009;

Additional co-authors Zachary Birenbaum (Rice), Anson Fung (Rice), Jeb Greenberg (Rice), Farhan Kawsar (Rice), Lonna Atkeson (Universit of New Mexico), Gayle Alberda (Fairfield University), R. Michael Alvarez (Caltech), Emily Beaulieu (Kentucky), Nathaniel A. Birkhead (Kansas State), Frederick J. Boehmke (Iowa), Joshua Boston (Washington University), Barry C. Burden (Wisconsin), Francisco Cantu (Houston), Rachael Cobb (Suffolk University), David Darmofal (University of South Carolina), Thomas C. Ellington (Wesleyan College),

---

R. Stein (✉)
Rice University, Houston, TX, USA
e-mail: stein@rice.edu

C. Mann
Skidmore College, Saratoga Springs, NY, USA

C. Stewart III
Massachusetts Institute of Technology, Cambridge, MA, USA

© The Author(s) 2020
M. Brown et al. (eds.), *The Future of Election Administration*, Elections, Voting, Technology, https://doi.org/10.1007/978-3-030-14947-5_6

Bowler et al. 2015; Herron and Smith 2016; Spencer and Markovits 2010). This assessment is based on studies of voting place locations in single jurisdictions. To date, there have been no multi-jurisdictional studies of polling place practices, although some data about polling places are collected in the Survey of the Performance of American Elections (Stewart 2017).

This chapter reports the findings from a national study of polling places and polling place practices in 26 election jurisdictions and 17 states across the United States during the 2016 presidential election. We evaluate polling places on three dimensions including their accessibility to voters, the quality of the facility/location, and barriers to voting. We measure the variation on these characteristics between and within jurisdictions in order to determine the origin of variance in polling place attributes and practices. We find that polling place operations, facilities, and practices in 2016 exhibit an overall high quality. Contrary to prior research on these characteristics in a case study of Los Angeles County in 2004 (Barreto et al. 2009), we do not find that polling place quality varies by race, ethnicity, or the socioeconomic composition of voters at each polling location. Variation in polling place operations, facilities, and practices in 2016 appears to be a function of county and state level factors.

Previous Research

Previous research on polling places has identified access to the polling place, the quality of polling place facilities, and polling place operations as consequential to the voting experience (Barreto et al. 2009; Spencer

---

Terri Susan Fine (University of Central Florida), Charles J. Finocchiaro (South Carolina), Michael Gilbert (University of Virginia), Victor Haynes (Claremont Graduate University), Brian Janssen (University of Iowa), David Kimball (University of Missouri, St. Louis), Charles Kromkowski (University of Virginia), Elena Llaudet (Suffolk University), Kenneth R. Mayer (Wisconsin), Matthew R. Miles (BYU-Idaho), David Miller (Washington University), Lindsay Nielson (Bucknell), Yu Ouyang (Purdue University Northwest), Costas Panagopoulos (Northeastern), Andrew Reeves (Washington University), Min Hee Seo (Washington University), Haley Simmons (University of Mississippi), Corwin Smidt (Michigan State), Rachel VanSickle-Ward (Pitzer College), Jennifer Nicoll Victor (George Mason University), Abby Wood (USC, Gould School of Law), Julie Wronski (University of Mississippi).

and Markovits 2010) and penultimate to voter participation. The Barreto et al. (2009) study of Los Angeles (L.A.) County, CA polling places during the 2004 primary election serves as the touchstone for our own national study. They report significant variation in polling place access, quality, and operations within Los Angeles County. Their principal finding was that ["L]ow-income and minority communities tend to have 'lower quality' precincts, which tended to depress voter turnout" (2009, 445). We ask what variation, if any, is observed in polling places across, rather than just within voting jurisdictions (here, counties) and whether this variation is attributable to conditions within or between voting jurisdictions and their respective states.

Reliance on polling place studies in single jurisdictions risks confounding the effects of polling attributes with differences in other factors across counties and states. Studying polling places across states and jurisdictions allows us to apportion the variance in polling place attributes and performance to state and county effects that might be omitted and unobserved in studies of just one voting jurisdiction. Accurately attributing the source of variation in polling place attributes and operations is important to identify where policy interventions might be adopted to enhance the quality and performance of polling places.

Overview of the Project

Research teams recruited from local colleges and universities and located in over 26 election jurisdictions and 17 states across the US observed polling place operations and voters as they entered the queue at their respective polling places on November 8, 2016.[1] A common set of protocols was used across all jurisdictions participating in the data collection (Mann et al. 2018). The jurisdictions that comprise our data set constitute a sample of convenience, because they depend on who

---

[1] In addition to studying polling place attributes and operations, students observed and timed voters as they waited to vote, voted or left, i.e., abandoned the voting line. These data are reported elsewhere (Stein et al. 2019).

Table 6.1 Jurisdictions and polling places

Jurisdiction	Polling places
Los Angeles, CA	38
Fairfield, CT	11
Orange, FL	20
Bibb, GA	8
Madison, ID	9
Johnson, IA	28
Riley, KS	16
Fayette, KY	43
Suffolk, MA	25
Ingham, MI	25
St Louis, MO	94
Albany, NY	30
Bronx, NY	3
Kings, NY	5
New York, NY	18
Rensselaer, NY	19
Saratoga, NY	16
Sullivan, NY	1
Westchester, NY	8
Union, PA	7
Richland, SC	14
Harris, TX	18
Albemarle, VA	7
Henrico, VA	21
Fairfax, VA	35
Dane, WI	9
Total	528

responded to the call to participate in the study. The obvious bias induced by this sampling method, compared to drawing a representative sample of voters or polling places, is that jurisdictions without a college or university are unlikely to be included in the study. However, as the list of jurisdictions in Table 6.1 makes clear, the jurisdictions that were in the study were distributed geographically across the country and across urban, suburban, and rural locations. Thus, while not representative, the collection of precincts is varied enough that important empirical insights can perhaps be gleaned from the data. The jurisdictions studied closely approximate the demographic makeup of the 2016 electorate, as illustrated in Table 6.2.

Table 6.2 Demographics of study jurisdictions and 2016 national exit poll

Variable	National[a] (%)	Study jurisdictions (%)
65+	16	20
White	72	76
African-American	12	15
Hispanic	11	6
Other	4	4
College graduate	50	42

[a]National exit poll, 2016 presidential election https://www.cnn.com/election/2016/results/exit-polls

Within jurisdictions, polling places were selected randomly by participating faculty. The unit of random sampling was the polling place rather than physical location, since multiple polling places may be physically located in a single facility (e.g., library, school, community center). In some cases, multiple polling places were selected at a single location. There were instances where local conditions necessitated deviating from random selection; this was most often due to difficulty traveling to voting location or wanting to observe campus voting locations. When such circumstances occurred, the teams were instructed not to select locations expected to have problems or lines (to ensure that selection did not constitute sampling on the dependent variable).

The protocol for observing polling place attributes and operations was based on previous research (Barreto et al. 2009; Herron and Smith 2016; Spencer and Markovits 2010; Stewart 2015). Pairs of student-researchers were assigned to observe election day polling places for two-hour periods. Researchers were tasked with collecting several pieces of information about voters' experience including length of lines, time waiting to vote, and time to cast a ballot. Each research team was also responsible for filling out a form that described the physical characteristics of the polling place they visited. This form is based on the Barreto et al. (2009) study of polling places with additions based on other research about polling place characteristics (Alvarez et al. 2013; Berger et al. 2008; Brady and McNulty 2011; Kropf and Kimball 2011; Presidential Commission on Election Administration 2014; Schur and Adya 2013; Spencer and Markovits 2010). The observer's form recorded information about the approach to the polling place (visibility from street, ease of parking, etc.), exterior polling place characteristics (outdoor light, access to parking, accessibility of entrance, etc.), interior polling place characteristics (lighting conditions, waiting area signage, etc.), polling place operations (informational instructions, working machines and scanners, etc.), and a sketch of the polling place layout.

Taking our lead from Barreto et al. (2009), we were interested in knowing how easy it was for the voter to find and access their election day polling place, whether the location was easy to use, and whether there were any barriers and/or enhancements to voting in the polling places. We measure a voter's accessibility to their polling place with five 'check list' items including:

1. The polling place address in clear sight (1 = yes, 0 = no)
2. The polling place was readily visible from the street (1 = yes, 0 = no)
3. Flags, banners, or signs made the polling place visible (1 = yes, 0 = no)
4. The polling location was (very easy = 4, somewhat easy = 3, somewhat difficult = 2, very difficult = 1)
5. The outside lighting was adequate (1 = yes, 0 = no)

The quality of the polling place location was defined in terms of seven characteristics including:

1. Adequate parking nearby (1 = yes, 0 = no)
2. Polling place entrance was handicapped accessible (1 = yes, 0 = no)
3. Restrooms were clearly marked (1 = yes, 0 = no)
4. Interior well lit for reading (1 = yes, 0 = no)
5. How small or large was the inside of the polling place (1 = very small, 2 = somewhat small, 3 = medium, 4 = somewhat large, 5 = very large)
6. What kind of waiting area was present (1 = none, 2 = small standing area, 3 = large standing area, 4 = sofas and chairs)
7. Additional amenities for voters (1 = yes, 0 = no)[2]

---

[2]Barreto et al. (2009) report that some polling places in Los Angeles have couches for waiting voters and serve coffee to waiting voters.

Barriers to voting included whether instructions were posted in the polling location to assist voters to check into vote (0 = yes, 1 = no), to operate voting machines or ballot scanners (0 = yes, 1 = no), and how to complete a ballot (0 = yes, 1 = no) and whether all voting machines and scanners were working (0 = yes, 1 = no).[3]

Findings

We obtained information on the attributes of 528 polling places used on election day in 2016 in 26 jurisdictions and 17 states. The distribution of polling traits that Barreto et al. (2009) identified as measures of accessibility, quality, and barriers to voting are reported in Tables 6.3, 6.4, and 6.5, respectively. We also report the distribution of the same traits for Los Angeles County polling places for the 2004 primary election and for our sample ($N = 38$) of 2016 Los Angeles County polling locations (Table 6.6).[4]

Polling Place Accessibility

Our findings point to a greater degree of accessibility than Barreto et al. (2009) observed in Los Angeles in the 2004 primary election, as measured by the adequacy of outdoor lighting and the overall ease of locating the site. This finding is true when we compare Barreto et al.'s 2004 sample of L.A. County polling places with our 2016 sample of L.A.

---

[3]In addition, Barreto et al. (2009) identified whether poll workers lived nearby the polling place (1 = yes, 0 = no) and whether a photo ID was asked for when checking into vote. We have excluded these two items from our composite score of polling place barriers to voting. We are uncertain how poll workers who live in the neighborhood are either a barrier or enhancement to voting. No discussion of this measure is included Barreto et al. (2009). A portion of our sample of voting jurisdictions is in states that require photographic identification in order to vote. Consequently, this is not a discretionary action on the part of either poll workers or county election officials. Barreto et al. (2009) also report whether a "Voter Bill of Rights" was visibly posted.

[4]The dimensionality of the three sets of indices varies considerably. The Cronbach Alpha scores for accessibility are 0.52, 0.45 for polling place quality and 0.7 for barriers to voting.

Table 6.3 Polling place accessibility

Trait	2016 National Sample		2016 L.A.[a]		2004 L.A.
	Count	%	Count	%	%
Adequate outside lighting					
No	56	11.86	0	0	23.5
Yes	416	88.1	21	100	76.5
Polling place was easy to find					
Very difficult	3	0.6	0	0	3.6
Somewhat difficult	36	7.1	5	19	12.2
Somewhat easy	148	29.4	6	23	36.3
Very easy	320	63	15	57.6	48.0
Clearly marked address					
No	195	40.0	8	32	22.1
Yes	293	60.0	17	68	77.9
Visible from street					
No	57	11.3	4	15.3	11.0
Yes	446	88.7	22	84.6	89.0
Flags, signs visible					
No	69	13.8	3	12	24.5
Yes	430	86.2	22	88	75.8

[a]Total number of precincts vary due to missing data

County polling places. The results of our findings about accessibility are reported in Table 6.3.

Nearly two-thirds (65.5%) of our national sample of polling locations were rated 'very easy' to find and less than 8% were rated as either 'somewhat difficult' or 'difficult to find.' Only 47% of 2004 Los Angeles polling places were rated very easy to find. Twice as many Los Angeles County polling places in 2004 (16%) than observed in our 2016 national sample were rated 'very difficult' or 'somewhat difficult' to find.

Between sixty and nearly ninety percent of our 2016 national sample of polling places were rated clearly visible by their signage, unobstructed street addresses and their proximity to major roadways. These ratings, with the exception of whether the site clearly displayed its street address, closely match those reported in the 2004 Los Angeles primary. Outside lighting was highly rated in 2016, especially in parking lots adjacent to polling places. Nearly 90% of our national sample of polling places were rated as having adequate outside

Table 6.4 Polling place quality

Trait	2016 National Sample		2016 L.A.[a]		2004 L.A.
	Count	%	Count	%	%
Handicapped entrance access					
No	28	5.7	3	12.5	18.2
Yes	459	94.3	21	87.5	81.1
Ease of finding parking					
Very difficult	23	4.8	0	0	32.7
Somewhat difficult	23	4.8	2	9.1	–
Somewhat easy	66	13.8	5	22.7	–
Very easy	365	76.5	15	68.2	–
Restroom clearly marked					
No	219	45.1	15	57.7	34.1
Yes	267	54.9	11	42.3	65.9
Amenities					
No	310	73.1	15	78.9	84.6
Yes	114	26.9	4	21.1	15.4
Interior well lit					
No	25	5.0	13	50	12.2
Yes	476	95.0	13	50	87.8
Interior size					
Very small	34	6.8	4	15.4	17.7
Somewhat small	109	21.8	6	23.1	18.3
Medium	144	28.7	7	26.9	26.6
Somewhat large	137	27.4	7	26.9	18.7
Very large	77	15.4	2	7.7	18.7
Waiting area					
None	60	13.2	8	13.5	16.7
Small standing area	184	40.7	12	35.3	33.4
Large standing area	142	31.4	11	32.4	21.5
Chairs and sofas	66	14.6	3	8.8	28.4

[a]Total precincts in 2016 Los Angeles County vary due to incomplete polling place coding forms

lighting, an important feature for early morning and late evening voters. Only 77% of the 2004 Los Angeles primary polling places were rated as having adequate outside lighting.

Table 6.5 Polling place barriers to voting

Trait	2016 National Sample		2016 L.A.[a]		2004 L.A.
	Count	%	Count	%	%
Voting instructions posted					
No	91	18.6	22	0	25[1]
Yes	398	81.4	0	100	75
Voting machine instructions posted					
No	111	22.9	19	82.6	–
Yes	373	77.1	4	17.4	
Check in instructions posted					
No	112	23.0	3	13.1	–
Yes	374	77.0	20	86.9	
All machines/scanners working					
No	25	5	0	0	3
Yes	469	95	25	100	97

[1]Barretto et al. (2009) report whether a "Voter Bill of Rights" was visibly posted
[a]Total precincts in 2016 Los Angeles County vary due to incomplete polling place coding forms

Table 6.6 Descriptive statistics: polling place scores

Variable	Obs.	Mean	Std.	Min	Max
Access	446	6.7	1.3	2	8
Quality	418	11.2	2.0	5	15
Barriers	469	0.73	1.11	0	4

A composite accessibility score is constructed from the summation of ratings for our five indices of polling place access. The composite measure ranges between 2 and 8, with a mean of 6.7 and a standard deviation of 13. The proportion of polling places scoring at the higher end of the accessibility score is skewed.

Quality of Polling Places

The quality of polling places in 2016 was on par with the accessibility of these voting locations. This is also true for four of six measures of polling place quality when we compare 2004 and 2016 polling locations in L.A. County. In 2016, interior lighting and restroom signage were rated significantly lower than in 2004. Our findings about quality are reported in Table 6.4.

In excess of 90% of 2016 polling places were rated as well lit for reading (95%) and handicapped access (94%). Parking at three-fourths of our national sample of polling places was rated 'very easy' to find. Nearly half (42%) of the interior spaces of polling places in 2016 were rated as 'somewhat large' or 'very large.' Waiting areas in 46% of the sample of 2016 polling places had large standing areas and/or chairs and sofas for voters waiting to vote. A quarter of polling places in 2016 provided amenities to voters while they waited to vote, including water, coffee, cookies, and popcorn. Access to clearly marked restrooms was reported in only 54% of 2016 election day polling places, a lower proportion than reported in the 2004 Los Angeles primary election. The 2016 national sample of polling places exhibited higher scores on all other indices of polling place quality than reported for the 2004 Los Angeles primary.

A composite measure of polling place quality in 2016 has a range of 5–17, with an average polling place quality score of 12 and a standard deviation of 2.2. Missing data for several indices of polling place quality (e.g., restrooms and amenities) significantly reduce the proportion of polling places for which we can construct a composite measure of polling place quality ($N=350$).[5] Unlike accessibility, our composite score for polling place quality is normally distributed with little evidence of any skewness toward either end of the measure.

Barriers to Voting

In excess of 75% of all polling places surveyed in 2016 had posted instructions for voting, checking into vote, and using voting machines or optical scanners; this figure is comparable to what was reported for Los Angeles polling locations in 2004. Only a scant 4% of 2016 polling

---

[5]When we reduce our composite quality score to five indices, dropping restrooms and amenities, we obtain scores for 433 observations which ranges from 5 to 15, with a mean of 11.2 and a standard deviation of 2. We used the indices score for quality in our multivariate analysis.

places were observed to have problems with either polling machines or optical scanners for paper ballots. Polling place barriers to voting in L.A. County were comparably rated in 2004 and 2016. Our findings about barriers to voting are reported in Table 6.5.

Overall, few if any significant barriers to voting were identified in our national sample of voting places. The composite barrier score ranges between zero and five with a mean 0.6 and a standard deviation of 1, indicating voters experienced few if any barriers to voting in our 2016 sample of voting locations.

Accessible, high quality facilities and a lack of barriers to voting characterize polling places in the 2016 presidential election. Is this finding consistent across and within jurisdictions? Barreto, Cohen-Marks, and Woods report that "data .... reveal variation in polling place quality across precincts (2009, 5)." Moreover, the authors go on to conclude that the "quality of polling places varies across the diverse neighborhoods of Los Angeles," where diversity is defined in terms of the racial/ethnic and socioeconomic composition of polling place voters.

The Source of Variation in Polling Place Attributes

Limited to only Los Angeles County, the Barreto et al. (2009) finding cannot reflect differences between jurisdictions. To test whether the variation in polling place attributes in our study is a function of within-county polling place attributes or related to differences among jurisdictions (i.e., counties), we regressed each composite score of polling place attributes on the racial and socioeconomic composition of the electorate in each voting precinct and a dummy variable for the polling place's jurisdiction (i.e., county).[6] If Barreto et al. (2009) are correct, variation in polling place attributes will be significantly related to the

---

[6]Our sample of election day polling places essentially consists of one jurisdiction per state (26 jurisdiction in 17 states). Consequently, the dummy measure for county could also be interpreted as a state effect. Information on the racial and socioeconomic composition of the electorate in each polling place location comes from *Catalist* (2016) and is limited to a subsample ($N=491$) of our full sample of polling places.

racial and socioeconomic makeup of the polling place, independent of jurisdictional effects.

Table 6.7 reports regression models for the composite scores of polling place accessibility, quality, and barriers to voting. The models were estimated with fixed effects for counties. The key variables of interest are the proportion of voters in each polling precinct by race and ethnicity (i.e., Black, Hispanic, and Other). The excluded category for race/ethnicity is White. The coefficients for Black, Hispanic, and Other shares of precinct voters represent the effect of a larger racial/ethnic share of the electorate on the polling place attribute relative to same White share of the precinct's electorate.

There is little support for the Barreto et al. (2009) finding that polling place attributes were related to the racial and/or socioeconomic composition of a polling places voters. Polling place accessibility is unrelated to any racial, ethnic, or socioeconomic measure. Similarly, polling place quality is unrelated to any racial, ethnic, or socioeconomic measure. Only the proportion of Hispanic persons is significantly and positively related to the barriers to voting at polling places relative to the same share of the electorate that is White. Polling places with a higher proportion of voters who are of Hispanic origin than White face more barriers to voting relative to polling places with the same share of White voters. This effect is statistically insignificant in the fixed effects model.

To assess the proportion of variance in polling place attributes explained by unspecified jurisdictional factors, we have estimated the regression models reported in Table 6.7 with and without fixed effects for jurisdiction. The difference in R-squares between the models with and without county fixed effects provides us with a relative measure of how much variance in polling place attributes is explained by unobserved jurisdictional factors. Over 90% of explained variation in accessibility, quality, and barriers to voting is attributable to jurisdictional level factors and not racial or socioeconomic conditions unique to within-county polling places.

Table 6.7 Regression coefficient for 2016 polling place attributes

	Access		Quality		Barriers	
	1	2	3	4	5	6
% Other race[a]	0.592	−0.0690	0.483	0.892	−0.0219	1.317
	(0.976)	(1.256)	(1.267)	(1.707)	(0.721)	(0.995)
% African-American	0.914***	0.337	−0.000471	−0.392	−0.0741	0.314
	(0.302)	(0.379)	(0.468)	(0.584)	(0.254)	(0.314)
% Hispanic	0.316	−0.365	−1.452	−1.052	−1.113**	−0.0483
	(0.612)	(0.882)	(1.008)	(1.413)	(0.499)	(0.744)
% Poverty	0.790	−0.533	0.659	0.0600	6.79e−05	0.535
	(0.557)	(0.763)	(0.883)	(1.321)	(0.448)	(0.617)
% Renter	−0.280	0.0946	−0.945*	−0.582	−0.0273	−0.0344
	(0.344)	(0.372)	(0.552)	(0.594)	(0.285)	(0.303)
% College graduates	1.573***	0.709	0.350	−0.0939	−0.546	0.199
	(0.447)	(0.510)	(0.698)	(0.834)	(0.365)	(0.417)
Constant	5.893***	6.627***	11.35***	10.52***	1.018***	−0.118
	(0.240)	(0.633)	(0.380)	(0.927)	(0.197)	(0.575)
Fixed effects	No	Yes	No	Yes	No	Yes
Observations	399	399	377	377	418	418
R-squared	0.042	0.162	0.019	0.113	0.018	0.150

Standard errors in parentheses
***$p<0.01$, **$p<0.05$, *$p<0.1$
[a]The omitted category for race/ethnicity is white

Discussion

The findings from our national sample of polling place practices show the quality and performance of election polling practices to be on balance strong. Our national sample indicated that polling places were accessible, well managed, and with few barriers to voters. Our descriptive findings match what others have reported for single jurisdiction studies (e.g., Barreto et al. 2009) in other elections. We found no evidence that accessibility to polling places, their quality and practices varied by race, ethnicity or the socioeconomic makeup of the persons who voted at our sample of polling places. Variation in the composition of voters according to polling location does not affect polling place quality or practices. We identified the variation in polling place quality and practices to reside at the level of the county and state. This is not unexpected. State governments are largely responsible for legislating how, when, and where elections are conducted. Counties and other sub-state jurisdictions are responsible for implementing these laws. Counties and their election officials have some statutory and administrative discretion in conducting elections as prescribed by state law. Identifying the source of variation in polling place practices might begin with a comparative analysis of state election laws and procedures and their implementation at the county level.

We have not examined the consequences of polling places quality and practices on voting. There are a host of dependent conditions that should be the subject of future research including waiting in line to vote, checking into vote, time to cast a ballot and voter turnout. Barreto et al. (2009) report that poor polling place access, quality, and operations depress polling place turnout. If this is true, is the effect of polling place attributes on turnout direct or mediated? For example, does the inadequacy of waiting room space at a polling place increase time to check in and vote, increasing the number of voters who leave the polling place without voting? Or does the effect of overall polling place quality deter voters from voting in the future? Answers to these questions are consequential for identifying remedies to poor voter participation.

References

Akteson, Lonna, and Kyle Saunders. "The Effect of Election Administration on Voter Confidence: A Local Matter?" *Political Science and Politics*, 40, no. 4 (2007): 655–660.

Alvarez, R. Michael, Lonna Rae Atkeson, and Thad E. Hall. *Evaluating Elections: A Handbook of Methods and Standards*. Cambridge: Cambridge University Press, 2013.

Alvarez, R. Michael, Thad E. Hall, and Morgan H. Llewellyn. 2008. "Are Americans Confident Their Ballots Are Counted?" *The Journal of Politics*, 70, no. 3 (2008): 754–766.

Barreto, Matt A., M. Cohen-Marks, and Nathan D. Woods. "Are All Precincts Created Equal? The Prevalence of Low-Quality Precincts in Low-Income and Minority Communities." *Political Research Quarterly*, 62, no. 3 (2009): 445–458.

Berger, Jonah, Marc Meredith, and S. Christian Wheeler. "Contextual Priming: Where People Vote Affects How They Votes." *PNAS*, 105, no. 26 (2008): 8846–8849.

Bowler, Shaun, Thomas Brunell, Todd Donovan, and Paul Gronke. "Election Administration and Perceptions of Fair Elections." *Electoral Studies*, 38, no. 1 (2015): 1–9.

Brady, Henry E., and John E. McNulty. "Turning Out to Vote: The Costs of Finding and Getting to the Polling Place." *The American Political Science Review*, 105, no. 1 (2011): 115–134.

Catalist, *CATALIST DATA*. 2016. https://www.catalist.us/data/.

Herron, Michael, and Daniel Smith. "Precinct Resources and Voter Wait Times." *Electoral Studies*, 42, no. 1 (2016): 249–263.

Kropf, Matha, and David C. Kimball. *Helping America Vote: The Limits of Election Reform*. New York: Routledge, 2011.

Mann, C., G. Alberda, N. Birkhead, Y. Ouyang, C. Singer, C. Stewart, … J. Wronski, "Pedagogical Value of Polling-Place Observation by Students." *PS: Political Science & Politics*, 51, no. 4 (2018): 831–837.

Presidential Commission on Election Administration. The American Voting Experience: Report and Recummendations. U.S. Government Printing Office, 2014. https://www.eac.gov/assets/1/6/Amer-Voting-Exper-final-draft-01-09-14-508.pdf.

Schur, Lisa, and Meera Adya. "Sidelined or Mainstreamed? Political Participation and Attitudes of People with Disabilities in the United States." *Social Science Quarterly*, 96, no. 3 (2013): 811–839.

Spencer, Douglas M., and Zachary S. Markovits. "Long Lines at Polling Stations? Observations from an Election Day Field Study." *Election Law Journal*, 9, no. 1 (2010): 3–17.

Stein, Robert M., Charles Stewart III, Christopher Mann, et al. "Waiting to Vote in the 2016 Presidential Election: Evidence from a Multi-County Study." Political Research Quarterly first published March 28, 2019. https://doi.org/10.1177/1065912919832374.

Stewart, Charles III. "Managing Polling Place Resources." Report of the Caltech/MIT Voting Technology Project, 2015. http://web.mit.edu/vtp/Managing%20Polling%20Place%20Resources.pdf.

Stewart, Charles III. "2016 Survey of the Performance of American Elections," Harvard Dataverse, 2017. https://dataverse.harvard.edu/dataset.xhtml?persistentId=doi:10.7910/DVN/Y38VIQ.

Robert Stein is a Professor at Rice University and an expert on urban politics and public policy. He is co-author of *Perpetuating the Pork Barrel: Policy Subsystems and American Democracy* (1995, Cambridge University Press), and author of *Urban Alternatives: Public and Private Markets in the Provision of Local Services* (1990, Pittsburgh Press). His work has also appeared in a wide range of scholarly journals. Dr. Stein's current research has been supported by the National Science Foundation and examines the impact of the federal-aid system on the electoral trajectories of office holders at both the subnational and congressional levels. Other research examines collective action among metropolitan area governments and voting behavior.

Christopher Mann is an Assistant Professor of Political Science at Skidmore College in Saratoga Springs, NY. His research has been published in the *Journal of Politics, Political Analysis, Political Behavior, Public Opinion Quarterly*, and other journals. His research focuses on several aspects of elections, campaigns, and voting. Mann conducts research on election administration, particularly the effects of changes to permit (and occasionally restrict) pre-election day voting alternatives. This research includes partnerships with public election agencies to conduct field experiments and analyses of observation data.

Charles Stewart III is the Kenan Sahin Distinguished Professor of Political Science at MIT. Since 2001, Professor Stewart has been a member of the Caltech/MIT Voting Technology Project, leading research efforts that applies scientific analysis to questions about election technology, election administration, and election reform. He is currently the MIT director of the project. Professor Stewart is an established leader in the analysis of the performance of election systems and the quantitative assessment of election performance. Working with the Pew Charitable Trusts, he helped with the development of Pew's Elections Performance Index. Professor Stewart also provided advice to the Presidential Commission on Election Administration. His research on measuring the performance of elections and polling place operations is funded by Pew, the Democracy Fund, and the Hewlett Foundation. He recently published *The Measure of American Elections* (2014, with Barry C. Burden, Cambridge University Press).

Part II

Meeting the Challenges of Professionalism

7

The Evolution of Professionalism in the Field of Election Administration

Mitchell Brown and Kathleen Hale

The administration of elections in the United States has evolved significantly over time, from a volunteer effort of the willing in early America to the highly coordinated, efficient, and professionalized system that we see in many counties, townships, and state offices across the country today. While taking a similar track as many other professions, the timeline for this path has been slower than most. This is due, most likely, to the seemingly sporadic nature of elections in comparison with many other professions and the subsequent coupling of election duties with other local government functions in most jurisdictions. The nature of this work is changing, however. Elections are more common and receive more attention than likely ever before. These changes have simultaneously accompanied changes to the profession. Myriad factors over the past 30 years have influenced the emergence of election administration

---

M. Brown (✉) · K. Hale
Auburn University, Auburn, AL, USA
e-mail: brown11@auburn.edu

K. Hale
e-mail: halekat@auburn.edu

© The Author(s) 2020
M. Brown et al. (eds.), *The Future of Election Administration*, Elections, Voting, Technology, https://doi.org/10.1007/978-3-030-14947-5_7

as a profession per se, including changes in technology, demand, and law, with resources following this demand (see Hale and Brown 2020 for more detail). This evolution has been rapid, with the most significant increases since the 2000 election (Fischer and Coleman 2008; Hale and Brown 2016; Hale et al. 2015).

In this chapter, we lay out the development and progression of election administration as a field. We discuss the third-party organizations that have developed around election administration as a field, existing in an endogenous relationship; forces inside election offices and in election administration influence factors outside of election offices, outside forces coalesce, respond, and in turn influence election administration, and the cycle continues. We then lay out variance across the US states in professionalization and conclude with a discussion of the critical elements of a professionalized election administration workforce for the future and the implications of this for national, state, and local governments.

The Evolution of Professionalism in Election Administration

Professions formalize and develop systematized standards of conduct and training, and self-regulate in order to develop and evolve, to increase quality and consistency, and ultimately to protect themselves. This process encompasses the professionalization of a field, and with it comes many positives as well as some drawbacks. Most notably, professionalism brings widespread and new information, systems improvements, standardization, and networking, and all of this is disseminated broadly through information sharing (Berman 1999, 2006; Berman and Wang 2000; Hale 2011; Rainey and Steinbauer 1999). When combined with accreditation, the credibility of organizations and the people who work in them also increase (McCabe et al. 2017). Together, these things increase the quality of work and services along with specializations that develop. In turn, organizational capacity increases as do efficiency, accountability, and the likelihood of neutral competence in public service specifically. As a consequence, specialization and increased knowledge combined with the presence of information networks impact public policy. The downside of professionalization is that it tends to shift allegiances, particularly in local government organizations, to the profession and their standards as opposed to the local norms, practices, and values (though arguably in some specific instances this can also be a positive result). And in some cases, professionalism may increase deontological adherence to rules and duties of the broader profession, making the work of the professional potentially rigid and inflexible as well as potentially unresponsive and unaccountable to the public it serves (Wilson 1991).

Government services writ large began professionalizing with the advent of government administration and the civil service (see, e.g., White 1958 for general historic perspective). Election administration as a field began with county generalists, whose jobs included elections as one aspect of a larger scope of work (Harris 1934). The people working in these positions often were hired as a result of political spoils, and an interest in election administration in particular was not a part of the motivation for government service. As the nature of election administration has changed—with a greater number of elections, held at greater frequency, and subject to greater regulation—so has the need for a dedicated public workforce. With this, particularly since the 2000 election, has come exponential growth of the field (Fischer and Coleman 2008; Hale and Brown 2016; Hale et al. 2015).

Early election administrators worked in an environment characterized by no "real control over elections throughout the state, and usually, the local city or county officers in charge have only slight powers of control, supervision, and inspection of the work of the precinct officers" (Harris 1934, 8). There were numerous laws about how elections should be run, and periods of election reform often followed periods in which election laws were written to include or exclude particular groups. Corruption has always been a concern in election administration, and the volume of laws and reforms designed to address this aspect of election administration specifically has not been insignificant.

The approach to civil service decision-making in the nineteenth century and early twentieth century can be characterized as individuals making decisions on the basis of their own moral reasoning. But what we know about power, politics, and human nature is that while many people try to be good and neutral administrators, corruption of government officials is a real threat, as is implicit bias. Indeed, in the first-ever study of election administration, Harris (1934) wrote that "no substantial improvement in elections can be made without improving the character of the election officers, without divorcing the whole machinery from politics" (95). This in particular necessitated a focus on ethics training as an important part of election administration training (Adams 1993). When a field professionalizes, part of the process is an intentional focus on field-based ethics, along with specific competencies and skills, with a set path of education and training to achieve the profession's goals (Berman 2006; Hale and Brown 2016; Hale et al. 2015). Often this includes accreditation of training and educational programs as well.

As discussed in Hale and Brown (2020), the professionalization of US election administration is illustrated by three critical and overlapping eras. These include:

- The nation's founding through the early 1900s, characterized by having ad hoc and short-term administrators.
- The late nineteenth century through the 1970s, in which aspects of election administration were under the purview of other local offices.
- The 1940s to the present, with offices that have stand-alone functions in most states, but some variance with some offices that have election administration as one of many functions and a few others that are decentralized and in which multiple offices perform different, discrete functions.

These eras overlap with stages in the evolution of public administration professionalization, which starts with a period of time in which there were no standards or training per se, a period in which these slowly evolve as a part of public service generally, a stage characterized by the emergence of training and specialization for some offices and administrators, and arrives at the current period characterized by the emergence of and eventual widespread presence of systematic training and the advent of professional degrees in the field.

Systematic training largely began in the 1990s through some state programs, as well as through the involvement of outside interest, or third party, groups, namely the Election Center or National Association of Election Officials (NAEO). The Election Center began as a partnership of election officials and academics who were committed to improving the quality of elections and supporting election officials across the country. They developed state-specific training programs as well as a national certification program that combined knowledge, skills, and abilities related to public administration and service generally, and election law and practice specifically.

The 2000 election brought intense scrutiny of election administration and offices. This scrutiny culminated in The Help America Vote Act of 2002 (HAVA), which increased the functions of state chief election officials and the role of state offices; as a consequence state offices grew, as did state-based training and the emergence of other third-party organizations dedicated to elections and election administration specifically. Scrutiny increased again with media attention focused on election administration related to Russian tampering and cybersecurity from the 2016 presidential election.

National, State, and Local Professionalism Efforts

Although professionalization of election administration is relatively recent, the role of third-party groups is not. The League of Women Voters was essentially the first national third-party group that advocated for reform and improvements in election administration, and the expansion of these groups in American society generally swelled starting in the 1960s (Brown 2016; Loomis and Cigler 2016). The advent of these groups developed largely around get-out-the-vote, or GOTV, efforts, though some like the National Association for the Advancement of Colored People (NAACP) and the LWV worked actively to change unfair election rules and practices.

Today, there is a burgeoning array of these types of organizations attempting to enhance and/or influence election administration rules and practices (see Hale et al. 2015 for more discussion). These groups can be characterized by those attempting to make changes on the behalf of a certain affinity or characteristic, those attempting to advance election practices more generally, and those with a particular political motivation (whether advertised or not). For example, the American Association of People with Disabilities (AADP) began in 1995 and is the largest disability rights group in the country, whose mission is to "promote equal opportunity, economic power, independent living, and political participation for people with disabilities." The National Association of State Election Directors (NASED) is another organization dedicated to a specific group, but in this case, it is to advancing the knowledge and networks of state election directors. Alternatively, Black Box Voting, founded in 2004, purportedly serves as a watchdog group whose purpose is public education and enhancing accountability of election officials.

There is no current census of these organizations. Some are long-term and established; however, newer organizations have been developing rapidly including some as outgrowths of other organizations. An example of this is Center for Election Innovation and Research. The executive director and founder of the organization was previously the director of the elections program at the Pew Charitable Trusts. Pew's elections program worked for years to fund activities to advance election administration, and when they got out of the business, so to speak, their director left to continue these efforts by creating a new organization. Others—former election officials, researchers, lawyers, and so on—have developed other similar or smaller organizations to attempt to advance the field.

Another aspect of this is the development of state associations. The prevalence, sophistication, and purpose of these organizations vary rather significantly. States with unified election offices, meaning that at the local level there is one office that performs all of the election administration functions, need only one state association. However, there are several states with decentralized local election administration, and in these cases, some offices have active state associations related to election administration but others do not. Some of these organizations provide training for their members, some serve as conduits for information exchange, others work to advance policy and practice changes, and a few serve all of these functions.

Formal education has begun to emerge for the field. The University of Minnesota and Auburn University have developed online and in-person certificates and degrees at both the graduate and undergraduate levels. There are many more law schools at which students can specialize or take courses in election law. Familiarity with election law and history is necessary, though not sufficient, as training for a well-rounded election official.

The Network of Schools of Public Policy, Affairs, and Administration (NASPAA) has been working to broaden the opportunities for graduate education beyond two member institutions that have formal education certificates or degrees. Their approach is to develop a common platform that would make available specific content knowledge and skills from degree-granting programs to the students in schools without these programs. The idea is that if students are interested in election administration but enrolled at a school without this expertise, students can use distance classes from schools across the country with this expertise and offerings to create their own degree or concentration, providing their home institution permits it. Under its existing policy, member schools can also choose to accredit specializations by demonstrating their ability to deliver this programming. In the future, academic programs with this expertise may also choose to accredit their formal education in this area.

Variance Across the States

As with all things in election administration, there is great variance across the states in professionalization. To compare states on professionalism, we developed the Election Administration Professionalism Index (EAPI) (see Hale and Brown 2020 for more detail). Briefly, in the first iteration of the index, we compiled information on three preliminary professionalism proxies and used these to develop an equal-weighted index. These proxies include: a count of nationally certified election administrators by state[1]; a state-level indicator of whether or not election officials are on the boards of key national organizations relevant to the field,[2] and whether state training programs in election administration are mandated.[3] (Note, however, that in some states that have fragmented local elections offices, it is harder to score well on this index).

A key question is whether there is a relationship between professionalism and performance. To gauge administrative performance, we have pulled the overall measure from the Pew and Stewart Election Performance Index. We also include a measure of whether or not states have adapted or opted out of the Voluntary Voting System Guidelines (VVSG) as a proxy for administrative capacity (Hale and Brown 2013). We are also curious about the relationship between professionalism and turnout.

Variance in professionalism across the states follows a normal distribution and can be generally grouped into three categories (see Table 7.1). States on the left side of the figure, generally speaking, have fewer administrators who have a significant presence in national bodies and discussions about election administration, have no or minimal state-level training programs, and have fewer administrators who have received election administration certification. The opposite is true for those on the right side of the figure. Indeed, most of these states are seen as the leaders in innovation and many others look to the practices and models that emanate from them. The states in the middle, a preponderance, represent a mix. Most have some kind of state training program and some of their administrators actively seek outside certification and other participate regularly in national conversation and attempts to move the needle for the field.

---

[1]We collapsed the counts into an ordinal variable using quartiles and scaled it to match the other variables.

[2]The iteration we present here includes the Election Center, Democracy Fund, Bipartisan Policy Center, the Election Assistance Commission (EAC), the National Association of State Election Directors (NASED), and the National Association of Secretary of State (NASS). In the case of NASS, the measure reflects designation as the chair and co-chair of its Elections Committee. Relationships between local, state and national organizations through board membership and key committees are linked to professionalism, development of new institutional architecture, and innovation across a variety of substantive areas in public service (Hale 2011; Tolbert et al. 2008).

[3]This variable was generated by Katy Owens Hubler through her work with the National Conference on State Legislatures.

Table 7.1 Distribution of states across Election Administration Professionalism Index v 1.0

Low	Low-Medium	Medium	Medium-High	High
Alabama	Alaska	California	Arizona	Colorado
Idaho	Arkansas	Delaware	North Carolina	Connecticut
Missouri	Hawaii	Florida	Ohio	Maryland
Nevada	Kentucky	Georgia	Tennessee	Minnesota
New Jersey	Maine	Illinois	Wisconsin	Oregon
New York	Mississippi	Indiana		Virginia
North Dakota	Montana	Kansas		Washington
Pennsylvania	New Hampshire	Louisiana		
South Dakota	North Dakota	Massachusetts		
Utah	Oklahoma	Michigan		
Wyoming	Vermont	Nebraska		
	West Virginia	New Mexico		
		South Carolina		
		Rhode Island		
		Texas		

Note The District of Columbia is not included in this index because the unit of comparison in this initial version is different. It is included in future iterations. If it were included it would be in the Medium-High to High range

What, if anything, does this have to do with performance? Public administration canon argues that professionalism ought to augment performance or at least be related to it. To measure this, we use the EPI and find a strong and positive correlation ($r = 0.469$, $p < 0.001$). The pattern between the variables suggests that as professionalism rises so does a state's rating on the EPI, but what is less clear is the causal direction between them. Professionalizing an elections staff ought to lead to enhanced performance and enhanced performance may then provide more interest in enhancing the professionalism of others within the system, leading to more and better training and national attention, and so on. We should expect that a collection of factors would be mutually reinforcing—office leadership, resources, networking opportunities, advanced education, experience with technology—each of these are elements of professionalization and of the institutional infrastructure snapshots that were captured by the EPI. Although the causal relationship is probably impossible to determine given the endogenous nature of these concepts and our inability to measure them with precision, the correlation is not surprising.

Related to performance is the ability to fluidly respond to crises. A recent and important test of this is states' responses to emerging cyber threats following the 2016 election. Using a point-in-time measure one year following the election, we attempt to gauge cybersecurity readiness using an aggregate variable that includes evidence of statewide initiatives or plans and the presence of election administrators from the states in national planning bodies related to election cybersecurity.[4] While we would expect to see cybersecurity readiness and election administration professionalism to be strongly correlated, as measured at this point in time there is only a moderate relationship between evidence of rapid cyber response planning and professionalism ($r = 0.259$, $p < 0.07$).

Additionally, professionalism should be related to advancing policy and policy outcomes. To gauge this, we looked at election administration-related policy introduced in the states. We find a positive relationship between the prevalence of legislation about state election equipment ($r = 0.471$, $p < 0.001$) as measured in Hale and Brown (2013). Note that we cannot establish causality here, but what we know about professionalism from other fields suggests that having a greater number of more highly professionalized election administrators in a state would produce greater communication and information exchanges within the state about election administration related issues, thus influencing the prevalence of legislation.

Less clear is whether there should be a relationship between turnout and professionalism. The logic might go that more professionalized administrators will, through neutral competence and greater efficiencies, enhance local trust in the election system and thereby increase turnout. Alternatively, perhaps states with higher turnout understand that they have a vested interest in developing a cadre of professional administrators who can adroitly handle an active voter pool. As with the EPI, professionalism is similarly related to turnout ($r = 0.368$, $p < 0.001$ using 2016 turnout figures). As currently measured, there is a positive relationship, but there is no data that suggest the direction the causal arrows should run.

---

[4] Our thanks to Lindsey Forson, one of our graduate students, with help collecting this information.

The Critical Elements of a Professionalized Election Administration Workforce

Moving forward, elections will likely only become more complicated and the need for training, education, and networking to continue to professionalize the field will be critical. Knowledge about and within the field needs to increase in both depth and breadth, and part of this requires acknowledging that the people who work in election administration today have unique and important expertise. The cybersecurity arena is an example of the value of increased knowledgeable about the field. Through engaging with election administration officials in the year after the Obama January 2017 designation of elections as critical infrastructure, Department of Homeland Security (DHS) officials quickly came to the realization that election officials are both professional and experts, and possess information well beyond the scope and understanding of DHS staff. To continue toward greater professionalization, the field also needs to develop common standards and approaches in several areas. Key among these is the development of a common set of knowledge, skills, and abilities or KSAs; a common path for training; a common path for education; a common set of ethical norms; and a common set of expectations for practice.

The KSAs required for a professionalized election administration workforce are simultaneously broad and focused. Administrators should understand the architecture of election administration in the US historically and in the present context. They should be able to articulate and actualize their role as public servants and public administrators. They should be familiar with the range of local, state, and federal agencies, nonprofit organizations, and private sector actors who work within the election administration space. And they should be able to identify, collect information about, and analyze information related to current challenges and opportunities with respect to practices and public policy. The implications of these KSAs are that election administrators need formal education, regular training, networking opportunities, a path for advancement in their field, and recognition and respect as experts. This also means they need compensation commensurate with this level of expertise.

Formal education can support this. University-based curricula at the undergraduate and graduate levels delivered by qualified faculty established as experts, researchers, and practitioners with experience in the field, is critical. Through exposure to the content and context of election administration, and through integrating classroom-based and experiential learning, current and prospective election administrators can emerge as leaders in election administration offices. This can happen through a variety of course curricula and covering a range of approaches from public administration, computer, technology or cyber training, accounting, and so on. The current election administration workforce includes people with an array of formal education. While a census has not yet been done, anecdotal evidence from our own work in training in the field suggests that a majority have a high school diploma and perhaps some college, but not more. Some have PhDs or JDs, some have MPAs, MAs, MSs, or MBAs, and many have BAs or BSs. This workforce cannot be replaced overnight, nor should it be, and thus systematized training in a number of areas is a necessity.

Following the model of other professions, continuing education should also be a requirement for election administration. The focus on this education and training could be on law and policy, history, reform, technical issues around equipment or cyber structure, emerging issues, and the opportunity to become more specialized in particular aspects of election administration (e.g., ADA, policy advocacy, budgeting, and so on). Even an entry-level staff member in an election office should have some basic knowledge of the field they are a part of.

A common set of ethical norms began emerging in the 1990s with the Election Center's *Code for Election Officials*. Some states have adopted this code in whole, while others have in part. The field needs to coalesce around a common set of these norms, whether they be the existing ones or some other statement. Such norms should be the guiding principles for all of the work done in the field. Particularly in jurisdictions in which the chief election official is elected, the integrity of the office must be preserved.

Finally, the field should develop expectations for a common set of practice. This has begun to emerge with work like the common data format (CDF) and efforts to build a common glossary of terms across states and stakeholders. This does not mean that all states should have the same laws and practices, but rather that there is some level of stability and continuity of operations and standard operating procedures that will advance the field.

Our observations and recommendations here reflect the evolution of public administration practices over time, from the beginnings of a professionalized public service workforce in the mid-1800s to the present (see, e.g., McMurtry 1976). By embracing these critical dimensions of professionalization, highly trained election professionals and policymakers will be able to insure the public of the integrity of election operations across leadership transitions and the succession of leaders, whether elected or appointed.

References

Adams, Guy B. "Ethics and the Chimera of Professionalism: The Historical Context of an Oxymoronic Relationship." *The American Review of Public Administration*, 23 (1993): 117–139.

Berman, Evan M. "Professionalism Among Public and Nonprofit Managers." *American Review of Public Administration*, 60, no. 5 (1999): 409–420.

———. *Performance and Productivity in Public and Nonprofit Organizations*. New York: M. E. Sharpe, 2006.

Berman, Evan M., and Xiao Hu Wang. "Performance Measurement in U. S. Counties: Capacity for Reform." *Public Administration Review*, 60, no. 5 (2000): 409–420.

Brown, Mitchell. "Mobilization Through Third Party Groups." In *Why Don't Americans Vote: Causes and Consequences*, edited by Bridgett A. King and Kathleen Hale, 184–192. California: ABC-CLIO, 2016.

Fischer, Eric A., and Kevin J. Coleman. *Election Reform and Local Election Officials: Results of Two National Surveys*. Washington, DC: CRS Report for Congress, 2008.

Hale, Kathleen. *How Information Matters: Networks and Public Policy Innovation*. Washington, DC: Georgetown University Press, 2011.

Hale, Kathleen, and Mitchell Brown. "Adopting, Adapting, and Opting Out: State Response to Federal Voting System Guidelines." *Publius*, 43 (2013): 428–451.

———. "Inter-Local Diffusion and Difference: How Networks Are Transforming Public Service." In *Transforming Government Organizations: Fresh Ideas and Examples from the Field*, edited by Floyd Dewey, William Sauser, Sheri Bias, 333–356. North Carolina: North Carolina Information Age Publishing, 2016.

———. *Innovation in Election Administration*. Washington, DC: Georgetown University Press, 2020.

Hale, Kathleen, Robert Montjoy, and Mitchell Brown. *Administering Elections: How American Elections Work*. New York: Palgrave Macmillan, 2015.

Harris, Joseph P. *Election Administration in the United States*. Washington, DC: The Brookings Institution Institute for Government Research, Studies in Administration No. 27, 1934. https://www.nist.gov/sites/default/files/documents/itl/vote/harris_6.pdf.

Loomis, Burdett, and Allan Cigler. "The Changing Nature of Interest Group Politics." In *Interest Group Politics*, edited by Allan Cigler, Burdett Loomis, and Anthony Nownes, 1–63. Washington, DC: CQ Press, 2016.

McCabe, Coyle B., Branco Ponomariov, and Fabyan Estrada. "Professional Cities: Accredited Agencies, Government Structure, and Rational Choice." *Public Administration Review*, 78, no. 2 (2017): 295–304.

McMurtry, Virginia A. *History of Civil Service Merit Systems of The United States and Selected Foreign Countries, Together with Executive Reorganization Studies and Personnel Recommendations*. Washington, DC: Congressional Research Service, 1976.

Rainey, Hal G., and Paula Steinbauer. "Galloping Elephants: Developing Elements of a Theory of Effective Government Organizations." *Journal of Public Administration Research & Theory*, 9 (1999): 1–32.

Tolbert, Caroline J., Karen Mossberger, and Ramona McNeal. "Institutions, Policy Innovation, and eGovernment in the American States." *Public Administration Review*, 68, no. 3 (2008): 549–563.

White, Leonard D. *The Republican Era, 1869–1901: A Study in Administrative History*. New York: Macmillan, 1958.

Wilson, James Q. *Bureaucracy: What Government Agencies Do and Why They Do It*. New York: Basic Books, 1991.

Mitchell Brown Ph.D., is a Professor in the Department of Political Science at Auburn University and is an Associate Editor of the *Journal of Political Science Education* (2016–2020). Her broader research agenda focuses on the empowerment efforts of marginalized communities, which she pursues through applied research. She is the author of numerous books, research articles, and reports, in related areas. In addition to her work at the university, she serves as a researcher, evaluator, trainer, and consultant on applied projects around the country focusing on election administration, community building, and community-based problem solving.

Kathleen Hale JD, Ph.D., is Professor of Political Science at Auburn University where she directs its Graduate Program in Election Administration. She is the Series Editor for Palgrave Macmillan's Elections, Voting, and Technology series. Her research examines how to improve government capacity and particularly in the area of election administration operations. Kathleen serves on the Board of Directors of the Election Center and directs faculty involvement in the Certified Elections/Registration Administrator (CERA) Program. She is an active instructor in the CERA Program and frequent speaker on election matters around the country. She serves as an active reviewer for journals and book manuscripts and is a member of the advisory board for the MIT Election Data and Science Lab.

8

The Elections Performance Index: Past, Present, and Future

Charles Stewart III

In our democratic process, citizens must be assured that if they wish to register to vote they can do so, that everyone who is registered can vote, and that all votes are counted as cast. How much progress have the states made in ensuring this happens for every citizen, in every election? Providing an answer to this question is the starting point for the Elections Performance Index (EPI), which began in 2010 as a project of the Pew Charitable Trusts and was assumed by the MIT Election Data and Science Lab in 2017. While the EPI is not unique in its effort to provide an objective assessment of the electoral environment in the

---

I am grateful for the assistance that Claire DeSoi, Cameron Wimpy, and Kathryn Treder provided in the drafting of this chapter, and to the rest of the research team at the MIT Election Data and Science Lab (MEDSL) for work undertaken for the release of the 2016 EPI. This chapter was written when I was an Andrew Carnegie Fellow, and I thank the Carnegie Corporation of New York for supporting my work. I also acknowledge the Pew Charitable Trusts, the William and Flora Hewlett Foundation, and the provost of MIT for supporting the work of MEDSL as the 2016 edition of the EPI was prepared. None of the institutions that supported this work are responsible for its content. All errors are solely my own.

C. Stewart III (✉)
Massachusetts Institute of Technology, Cambridge, MA, USA
e-mail: cstewart@mit.edu

© The Author(s) 2020
M. Brown et al. (eds.), *The Future of Election Administration*, Elections, Voting, Technology, https://doi.org/10.1007/978-3-030-14947-5_8

United States, it is the only one that focuses on the nuts-and-bolts of elections, and the only one that attempts to harness administrative statistics to that purpose.

The EPI is based on seventeen metrics that are designed to provide a comprehensive view of election administration and policy in each of the states and the District of Columbia. The EPI is primarily derived from the Election Administration and Voting Survey (EAVS), which is administered by the US Election Assistance Commission. In addition, the index also includes measures constructed from survey research and reported by state and local election departments.

The impetus for the EPI stretches back to 2000, and the response of the academic community to the deficiencies revealed in the American voting process during the recount of the presidential vote in Florida. Part of this response manifests itself as increased attention to scientific research into the effects of election administration on voting, which in turn led to increased attention on the issue of measuring the salient parameters of the electoral process. The summer 2001 report *Voting: What Is/What Could Be*, from the Caltech/MIT Voting Technology Project, introduced several measures that attempted to quantify the number of "lost votes" in the 2000 election (Caltech/MIT Voting Technology Project 2001). A few years later, Heather Gerken's *Democracy Index* argued that policy improvements were generally spurred on when policymakers and the public had a clear set of metrics in front of them, and that US election administration in particular could advance if an index of election policy outcomes existed (Gerken 2009).

The EPI first took shape in the guiding hand of the Pew Charitable Trusts, which from the mid-2000s to the mid-2010s was the most important institutional player in US election reform. Pew's involvement in the issue began with Make Voting Work, an initiative that helped jump-start a wave of research into the landscape of American election administration and encouraged an explosion of scientific analysis into how Americans voted.[1] Its efforts eventually morphed into a

---

[1] Pew was joined by the JEHT Foundation in sponsoring the Make Voting Work initiative. https://www.pewtrusts.org/en/about/news-room/press-releases-and-statements/2008/01/16/the-pew-center-on-the-states-and-the-jeht-foundation-award-25-million-to-improve-us-elections.

more action-oriented focus as it supported legislative initiatives such as the Military and Overseas Voter Empowerment (MOVE) Act,[2] and administrative efforts to address practical holes in election administration such as the Electronic Registration Information Center (ERIC) and the Voting Information Project (VIP).

The EPI complemented Pew's action-oriented agenda to modernize voting in the United States by documenting and periodically highlighting states' actions to improve elections. Some of the indicators with the biggest influence on the overall index ratings were also directly related to Pew's reform agenda, particularly its drive to encourage states to build a greater online presence to push information to voters and automate routine practices.

The passing of the EPI torch from Pew, a public-interest nonprofit organization, to MIT, an academic institution, represents not only a change in institutional affiliation, but also an opportunity to revisit the indicators and focus of the index. In the decade since its first release, most states have adopted the best practices baked into the EPI and seem unlikely to reverse those changes. As they have done so, new challenges and reform opportunities have arisen. New voting models have emerged. Although the overarching framework of the EPI—with its dedication to encouraging objective, metrics-based assessment of election policy and administration—will likely remain unchanged, the index is at an inflection point in terms of how it appraises the evolving world of American elections.

This essay is a reflection on the EPI as it ends its first decade. I begin with a brief overview of the index itself. From there, I provide an intellectual and organizational history of the project and contrast it with other efforts to assess the quality of democratic practice in the United States. I also discuss the story that the index has told about the evolution of American electoral performance over the past decade. With all of this laid out, I conclude by discussing the challenges of developing and maintaining the index, and suggesting directions the index might evolve in the future.

JEHT was caught up in the Ponzi scheme perpetrated by Bernard Madoff in late 2008 and had to close its doors, leaving Pew alone to support the initiative. Much to Pew's credit, JEHT's departure was experienced as no more than a bump in the road for beneficiaries of the initiative.
[2]HR 2647, Pub. L. 111-84, 123 Stat. 2190.

Index Overview

The Elections Performance Index was first released in 2013 and reported on the federal elections of 2008 and 2010. Since then, it has been updated with new data three times; it now covers federal elections through 2016. It is constructed around the seventeen indicators of election performance listed, along with their data sources, in Table 8.1.

The theory guiding the inclusion of these particular indicators (and the exclusion of others) will be explored further below. For now, it is sufficient to say that these indicators are intended to measure the degree to which registering and voting are convenient, and the degree to which the intentions of voters are secure.

What makes the EPI an *index*, and not just a disjointed collection of metrics, is that the states are ranked according to an aggregation of all the indicators. The details for calculating the index value for each state are reported in the index's methodological report (MIT Election Data and Science Lab 2018). To summarize, every indicator measure for a state is transformed to a 0–100% scale, where a 0% score is typically the worst value possible on that score, either theoretically or empirically, and 100% is the best possible value. The average of all these transformed values is then computed. This yields a state's overall index score for a particular election.

In theory, then, the index score for a state is a measure of how close it has gotten to "perfection" on each of the 17 indicators in a particular federal election.[3] In practice, no state occupies the extreme ends of

---

[3] There are three important details here. First, there are some states in which all 17 indicators are not relevant. North Dakota is the best example of this: Because it does not have voter registration, its index score does not include values for the availability of online registration, provisional ballots cast, provisional ballots rejected, registrations rejected, or registration rate. Thus, North Dakota's index value is based on averaging 12 indicators, not 17. Second, the data needed to calculate an indicator are often missing, due to the fact that some states do not fully report items on the EAVS or other data sources used by the EPI. If a state does not report sufficient information to calculate an indicator, that indicator is set to missing, and the index is calculated using the remaining indicators. For instance, in 2016, Mississippi did not report turnout, making it impossible to calculate the residual vote rate. Thus, its index is calculated by averaging the remaining 16 indicators. Third, the residual vote rate is calculated using votes for the president. Therefore, it does not enter into the index calculations for midterm congressional elections.

Table 8.1 Indicators in the Elections Performance Index

Name	Description	Data source[a]
Data completeness	The degree to which a state's local jurisdictions report critical election statistics to the EAVS	EAVS
Disability- or illness-related voting problems	Percentage of non-voters who cite "illness or disability" as the reason for not voting	CPS
Mail ballots rejected	Number of mail ballots rejected, as a percentage of turnout	EAVS
Mail ballots unreturned	Number of mail ballots unreturned for counting, as a percentage of turnout	EAVS
Military and overseas ballots rejected	Number of Uniformed and Overseas Civilian Absentee Voters Act ballots rejected, as a percentage of UOCAVA ballots returned	EAVS
Military and overseas ballots unreturned	Number of UOCAVA ballots unreturned, as a percentage of ballots distributed	EAVS
Online registration available	Whether a state provides the opportunity for citizens to register online	SED
Postelection audit required	Whether a state requires a post-election audit of election returns	SED
Provisional ballots cast	Number of provisional ballots cast, as a percentage of turnout	EAVS
Provisional ballots rejected	Number of provisional ballots rejected, as a percentage of turnout	EAVS
Registration or absentee ballot problems	Percentage of non-voters who cite "registration problems" as the reason for not voting	CPS
Registrations rejected	Number of registration forms rejected, as a percentage of new registration forms submitted	EAVS
Residual vote rate	Over- and under-votes as a percentage of turnout	SED

(continued)

Table 8.1 (continued)

Name	Description	Data source[a]
Turnout	Number of voters as a percentage of voting-eligible population	USEP
Voter registration rate	Percentage of respondents who voted or stated they were registered	CPS
Voting information lookup tools available	The number of voter information lookup tools on a state's election website, out of a possible five that are tracked	SED
Voting wait time	Average amount of time reported waiting to cast a ballot	SPAE

[a]Data sources
CPS Voting and Registration Supplement of the Current Population Survey
EAVS U.S. Election Assistance Commission, Election Administration and Voting Survey
SED State election departments
SPAE Survey of the Performance of American Elections
USEP United States Elections Project

the indicator scales for all items; the bulk of scores, therefore, have fallen between 60 and 75%. Figure 8.1 displays the index scores for 2017.

To help provide some intuitive understanding about how an index score corresponds with performance, I have chosen three states and reported their overall index values, along with the constituent indicator values (and rankings) in Table 8.2. These three states were chosen because they represent the range of states' index scores from 2008 to 2016. Mississippi received the lowest-ever index value, 40%, in the 2010 election; New Mexico's 69% index value in 2008 was the median for all states across all years; and North Dakota's 88% in 2010 is the maximum value ever given to a state.

The contrast between North Dakota and Mississippi in 2010 showcases the profiles that have been associated with states at the extremes of the index. First, the completeness of the data had a significant impact. North Dakota reported all the required data elements in the EAVS completeness indicator, while Mississippi reported only 78%

8 The Elections Performance Index: Past, Present, and Future 125

Fig. 8.1 Election Performance Index scores for the 2016 election (*Source* Elections Performance Index, https://elections.mit.edu)

Table 8.2 Comparison of three state profiles in the EPI

State	Mississippi	New Mexico	North Dakota
Year	2010	2008	2010
Index value (%)	40	69	88
Data completeness	78.49% (49)	81.18% (38)	100.00% (11)
Disability- or illness-related voting problems	18.51% (50)	16.68% (27)	7.50% (3)
Mail ballots rejected	INC	0.17% (17)	0.08% (13)
Mail ballots unreturned	INC	INC	6.11% (16)
Military and overseas ballots rejected	INC	2.01% (4)	0.55% (2)
Military and overseas ballots unreturned	19.80% (3)	25.46% (20)	33.83% (12)
Online registration available	No	No	NA
Postelection audit required	No	INC	Yes (1)
Provisional ballots cast	INC	0.82% (26)	NA
Provisional ballots rejected	INC	INC	NA
Registration or absentee ballot problems	2.84% (14)	6.04% (22)	1.49% (4)
Registrations rejected	INC	INC	NA
Residual vote rate	NA	0.38% (6)	NA
Turnout	36.98% (45)	61.16% (36)	46.67% (14)
Voter registration rate	82.20% (13)	80.83% (38)	NA
Voting information lookup tools available	1/5 (50)	2/2 (1)	3/3 (1)
Voting wait time	NA	12.3 min. (26)	NA

Note Values represent raw indicator statistics for the indicated states and years. Numbers in parentheses represent that state's rank-order (1 = top) for the indicated year
INC Data "incomplete," that is, too much data is missing to calculate indicator
NA Not applicable to the state

of the data, putting it 49th among all the states. Because Mississippi failed to report many of the items on the EAVS survey, it was impossible to calculate values of EAVS-based indicators related to mail ballots, UOCAVA ballots, provisional ballots, and rejected registrations. Had it been possible to calculate these indicator values, it is likely Mississippi would have gotten a boost in its index score.[4] In addition, Mississippi

---

[4] The value of reporting EAVS statistics was illustrated in 2016 when Mississippi's completeness score rose to 94.12%. This allowed all the EAVS-based indicators to be calculated. Because Mississippi was close to the average on many of these indicators, its index score rose to 67%.

in 2010 had no post-election audit requirement and had virtually no online election information presence—both in contrast to North Dakota. Finally, although Mississippi's estimated registration rate was relatively high, its turnout rate was among the lowest of the states, while North Dakota maintained a high-turnout rate.

Even though Mississippi and North Dakota occupied the two ends of the index spectrum in 2010, this does not mean that North Dakota bested Mississippi on every measure. Notably, Mississippi had one of the highest return rates of UOCAVA ballots, and it was North Dakota that fell to the middle of the pack.

In general, low-scoring states have had profiles like Mississippi's in 2010: They have a lot of missing EAVS data, poor turnout or registration rates, and little, if any, web presence. The profile of a high-ranking state, like North Dakota in 2010, has generally been exactly the opposite. A "typical" state, in terms of overall index rankings, might look most like New Mexico in 2008, which was in the middle of the pack on almost all indicators. Even so, there were exceptions: Notably, New Mexico had one of the lowest rejection rates of UOCAVA ballots, and its residual vote rate was among the lowest, as well.

Overall, the value of the average index score has grown over the years. The average for the 2008 election was 62.8%, rising to 74.1% in 2016. As the scatter plot in Fig. 8.2 shows, values for almost all states have risen. The only exceptions are the few states whose scores in 2016 are less than 2008, mostly because of random fluctuations in indicator values. Below, we discuss in more detail what sets the states that changed the most over the years apart from the rest. For now, we can simply note that the fastest risers were those that did not have a heavy web presence in 2008, but did by 2016.

Also, to presage a discussion below, note that the overall and pervasive rise in index values has caused a scrambling in the resulting state rankings. A state with average performance in 2008 would be a laggard in 2016. For instance, a state with a score of 64% in 2008—the median in that year—would be in the bottom five in 2016. A state with a top-ten score in 2008 would be below average in 2016.

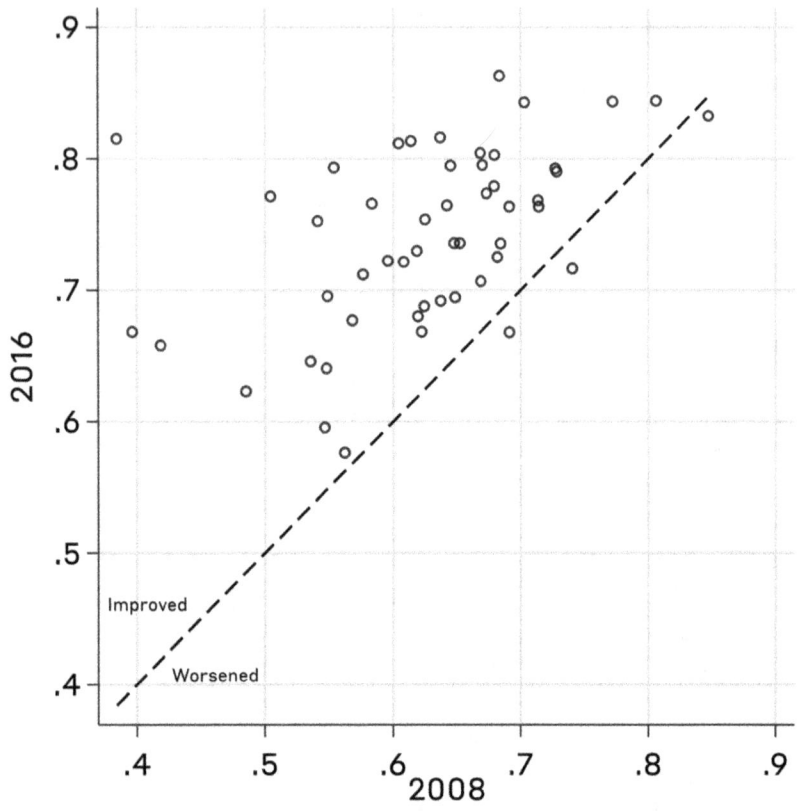

Fig. 8.2 Comparison of index values in 2016 with values in 2008

Intellectual and Organizational History

A goal of the EPI project was to situate an index of elections performance within an intellectually defensible framework that provided objective criteria for separating high performers from laggards. It was clear from the start that there was no single framework to make the development of such a project easy. In the end, the direction taken by the EPI took the individual voter as the lodestone and valued direct measures of experience over perceptions and impressions. This steered the project away from an approach that was predominated by expert opinions, for instance. It also helped steer the enterprise toward elements of election administration and policy that were readily measurable, leaving it to other projects to explore elements that might be less visible, and thus harder to measure directly.

General Background

The first intellectual guide for the EPI was Heather Gerken's[5] book *Democracy Index*, which argued in favor of the creation of a ranking system that helped voters assess how closely jurisdictions reach three goals:

- Every eligible voter who wants to register can do so.
- Every registered voter who wants to cast a ballot can do so.
- Every ballot cast is counted properly (Gerken 2009, p. 27).

Gerken's goal in suggesting a democracy index was to overcome issues—namely, parochialism and partisanship—that hindered the improvement of election administration across the United States. In her view, the existence of a prominent report that ranked states on their electoral performance would create a focal point for voters to begin understanding election administration issues in a hard-nosed, quantitative fashion. By being able to compare one's own state's performance with neighboring states, voters would be drawn to pressuring their election officials to do better.

A second reference point was the work of the Caltech/MIT Voting Technology Project (VTP), which was formed immediately after the 2000 presidential election to study the technological issues that had led to the recount fiasco in Florida, and to suggest the ways to prevent such events from happening again. In framing its 2001 report about the state of voting in America, the VTP proposed thinking about voting as a chain. Like a chain, which is rendered useless if just one link is broken, an individual's efforts to cast a vote that is counted can be rendered null

---

[5]Gerken was an original member of the advisory committee Pew assembled to help it assess the feasibility of what ended up to be the Elections Performance Index.

if just one link in the voting process is broken. For example, a few of the links that could fail and result in a lost vote include:

- A voter fails to find their polling place.
- The polling place has a line so long that the voter leaves before even checking in.
- The voter's name is left off the voting roster.
- The ballot is confusing and misleads the voter into making incorrect choices.
- The technology tabulating the ballot malfunctions, leaving the vote uncounted or misattributed.

Each of these points of failure made an appearance in the saga of the Florida recount, as well as in stories from other states that emerged in the weeks and months after the election. Using a variety of statistical sources, the VTP estimated that problems like this in the 2000 election resulted in the loss of between four and six million votes. The sources of these lost votes were broken down as follows (Caltech/MIT Voting Technology Project 2001, 9):

- 1.5–2 million lost because of faulty equipment and confusing ballots.
- 1.5–3 million lost because of registration mix-ups.
- Up to 1 million lost because of polling place operations.
- Unknown losses because of absentee ballot problems.

Later research into lost votes among absentee ballots suggested that a similar number were lost due to problems with the flow of ballots and ballot requests between voters and local election authorities (Stewart 2010).

With these touchstones as a start, the Pew Center of the States convened a group in the summer of 2010 to help advise Pew about the viability of an Election Performance Index and its possible content. This advisory committee, which was composed of approximately 20 election administrators and academics, met five times between the summer of 2010 and 2013 to consider the matter.

One of the most important results of those deliberations (which are summarized in the methodology document that accompanies the visual presentation of the EPI on its Web site) was the creation of a framework to guide the intellectual direction of the project and assess whether the measures chosen for the index adequately covered the topic. This framework conceived of election performance as existing along two dimensions. The first dimension looked at voting as experienced by the voter, breaking the process down into three sequential tasks: registering, voting, and ballot counting. The second dimension focused in on two perspectives from which registration, voting, and ballot counting could be viewed: the perspective of convenience and that of security.

The idea was that for each of the three functional areas of voting policy, the index should try to help answer questions such as: How convenient is it to vote? How convenient is it to register? How secure is the voting process? How secure is vote counting?

At the same time the issue of the intellectual framework was being hashed out, the committee also pursued the question of measurement. Its examination of possible approaches to measurement was aided by the fact that policy indices in other domains had already been developed, and along with them, the data principles necessary to guide such undertakings.

The world of policy indices can be divided into two broad categories: (1) indices developed using objective measures of policy inputs and outputs, and (2) indices developed using expert ratings. Examples of the former include the Kids Count Data Book of the Annie E. Casey Foundation,[6] the Environmental Performance Index produced at Yale and Columbia universities,[7] County Health Rankings & Roadmaps, produced by the University of Wisconsin Population Health Institute,[8] and the World Bank's Doing Business Index.[9] Examples of

---

[6]Kids Count Data Center, http://datacenter.kidscount.org.
[7]Environmental Performance Index, http://epi.yale.edu.
[8]County Health Rankings & Roadmaps, http://www.countyhealthrankings.org.
[9]http://www.doingbusiness.org/rankings.

the latter include the Freedom House's *Freedom in the World* report,[10] Transparency International's Corruption Perception Index,[11] the Work Justice Project's Rule of Law Index,[12] and the Electoral Integrity Project's reports on perceptions of electoral integrity.[13]

Based on the work underpinning these and other models, Pew adopted the following six principles to guide the selection of indicators into the EPI. In particular, it was decided that any statistical indicator included in the EPI should:

1. be from a reliable source,
2. be available and consistent over time,
3. be available and consistent for all states,
4. reflect a salient outcome or measure of good elections,
5. be easily understood by the public and have a relatively unambiguous interpretation, and
6. be produced in the near future.

These principles helped provide a framework for judging the large number of possible candidate indicators, many of which ended up being eliminated simply because of data limitations. As the project proceeded, on the other hand, some of these principles were also revealed to be aspirational to one degree or another. In particular, while the first, second, fourth, and sixth principles (high data quality, over-time consistency, salient outcomes, and future production) were relatively easy to adhere to on a consistent basis, it was more of a challenge to adhere to the other two one hundred percent of the time.

The work of the advisory board in scrutinizing possible indicators began, as most such exercises do, with a good deal of brainstorming and an attitude of "no bad ideas." Through this process, the committee eventually identified forty candidate indicators; these were subsequently

---

[10]https://freedomhouse.org/report-types/freedom-world.

[11]https://www.transparency.org/research/cpi/overview.

[12]https://worldjusticeproject.org/our-work/wjp-rule-law-index.

[13]https://www.electoralintegrityproject.com/.

investigated more closely for their adherence to the six data principles, as well as for other important attributes, including statistical reliability and validity.[14] In addition to the advisory board's work, Pew also sponsored an academic conference for top scholars of the electoral process, who were commissioned to write papers that addressed the suitability of the candidate indicators for the index in even greater depth. That work was later collected in the book *The Measure of American Elections,* which was edited by Barry C. Burden and Charles Stewart III (Burden and Stewart 2014). All of this work helped to square the possible indicators with the final set of selected indicators. In navigating between theory and practice, a number of difficult choices had to be made, which I now discuss.

Data Principles Meet the Actual Data

The first data principle—that the statistical indicators come from reliable sources—led to a strong preference for using official statistics and for avoiding sources that depended on subjective judgements. This criterion gives the EPI a very different feel from projects that depend on expert opinions, such as the *Freedom in the World* report and the EIP's report on perceptions of electoral integrity. The reason for this was not that expert options were seen as worthless in all circumstances, not by a long shot. Rather, if the idea was to measure outputs of the electoral process, the committee judged that it was better to rely on scientifically valid direct measures, rather than on survey research about what experts think those measures are.

Stating that the EPI would be based on reliable sources and held to high standards of scientific rigor begs the question of whether the sources the EPI relies on actually meet those standards. The EAC's Election Administration and Voting Survey (EAVS), for instance, provides the data for nearly half the indicators in the EPI, but early editions

---

[14]Reliability refers to the ability of a measure to be estimated consistently, either over time or using different methods. Validity refers to the degree to which a measure accurately captures the theoretical construct in question.

of the EAVS data were notoriously difficult to work with and fraught with data-gathering challenges (Stewart 2018). Eventually, the advisory board judged that EAVS data prior to 2008 were in fact of insufficient quality overall, so no data prior to 2008 were included in the index. The inclusion of the EAVS completeness measure in the index is not only a statement that data transparency is a value to be monitored through the EPI; it is also an acknowledgment that the data quality of the EAVS remains variable, and should be monitored across time and states.

The EAVS is not alone in criticism about its data quality. The index utilizes two public opinion surveys—the Voting and Registration Supplement of the US Census Bureau's Current Population Survey (CPS) and the Survey of the Performance of American Elections (SPAE)—each of which is subject to well-known problems of social desirability bias documented in studies of voting (Holbrook and Krosnick 2009). In addition, although election returns are subjected to meticulous checking and double-checking on the way to certification, the EPI still needs to account for the fact that some local jurisdictions report more votes for president than turnout should allow—evidence that election returns themselves are imperfect.

The expectation that the statistical indicators be available and consistent over time is central to a project that intends to track the development of policy over time—particularly one that seeks to help document the effect of policy interventions on policy outcomes. This criterion has probably been easiest to adhere to, but it does mean that information gathered on an ad hoc basis, often by think tanks and citizen groups focused on particular issues, must be excluded.

In contrast, the third criterion (that indicators should be accessible and consistent for all states) may be one of the most difficult to maintain, although there are technical solutions for unavailability.

Cross-state availability is necessary for an index that attempts to highlight interstate differences in policy performance. The challenge of adhering to it shows up in the indicators that are based on the EAVS data, and is most clearly on display in the EAVS completeness indicator, which has never been at the 100% level for all states. The unavailability of EAVS data for all states in all years is also visible when the degree of missing data is so great for a state that one or more indicators that rely on the EAVS data cannot be calculated at all.[15] The biggest culprit on this score has been the rate of rejected voter registration forms, which could not be calculated for 27 states in 2008, or for 12 states in 2016.

Beyond the variability in measures' availability, their interstate consistency is often a challenge. To state the most obvious example, two of the indicators measure the non-return and rejection rates of absentee and mail ballots, and yet the role of the mail is quite different in the three "vote-by-mail"[16] states (Colorado, Oregon, and Washington) when compared to the states that still require a limited set of excuses for voters to cast an absentee ballot. When a traditional "for cause" absentee ballot state such as Massachusetts has an 11% non-return rate, while Indiana's rate is 0.26%, it is reasonable to suspect that Indiana has some absentee ballot practices that Massachusetts might learn from. On the other hand, when Washington mails a ballot to each of its voters and 23% go unreturned, is there anything Washington can learn from Indiana, when mail ballots function so differently in the two states?

Not only are issues of interstate variability implicated in the vote-by-mail example, but *intra*state variability is an issue, too. For instance, in 2012 Colorado had a permanent absentee ballot list; its non-return rate that year was 12.5%. In 2016, the first presidential election after it switched to a vote-by-mail model, the non-return rate rose to 22.2%. Clearly, the rise in the non-return rate was caused by the change in voting models. However, can we say that this 9.7-point increase represented a better or worse performance for Colorado? At best, the interpretation is ambiguous. We return to the problems of interpreting the changing role of mail ballots within the EPI framework below.

The fourth principle, that all indicators should reflect a salient outcome or measure of good elections, played an important role in defining

---

[15] A state is treated as missing for an indicator that relies on the EAVS for data if any of the component parts of the indicator are available for less than 85% of a state's local jurisdictions, weighted by voter registration.

[16] The term "vote-by-mail" increasingly has to be placed in scare quotes because in the three states that distribute ballots by mail to all voters—Colorado, Oregon, and Washington—most voters actually return ballots in person. Thus, terms that are more accurate might be "ballot-distribution by mail" or "vote at home." In this chapter, I use the more familiar term for the sake of clarity.

the scope of indicators included in the EPI. An interesting question that this principle begs is, "salient to whom?" To a majority of voters, indicators related to registering, polling place operations, and mail ballots might be considered most salient. However, a look at policymaking on Capitol Hill over the past two decades seems to indicate that other matters are also salient, such as voting by members of the armed forces and accessibility for people with disabilities. For those reasons, UOCAVA voting forms the foundation of two EAVS-based indicators: the UOCAVA ballot return and rejection rates. To reflect accessibility for people with disabilities, an indicator was constructed from the CPS to measure self-reported problems voting because of illness or disability.

The issue of salience also raises the question of how to weight indicators in the overall index score calculations. While this is not an issue of specific indicator measurement, it is relevant, as an issue of overall index measurement. The EPI is calculated as an unweighted average of the normalized scores of each of the seventeen indicators. An alternative would be to weight each item to reflect an overall view of the importance of the mix of the policy elements reflected by the indicators, or to reflect relative data quality. Different weighting schemes were experimented with during the development of the EPI, but none produced results that were so different from equal weighting that it was worth the effort to provide a justification for one particular set of unequal weights.

That said, the Web site that presents the EPI does permit users to toggle off and on individual indicators. This was a deliberate choice, allowing for a type of crude binary weighting of the indicators, or for the creation of rating based on a subset of indicators that are of interest. The fact that few users appear to use this feature suggests that if differential weighting of indicators should indeed be applied in calculating the overall index, the EPI project cannot depend on its users to provide the weights for it.

The fifth principle—that indicators be easily understood by the public and have relatively unambiguous interpretations—is probably the most challenging of the criteria. The challenge is not so much in explaining what the indicators are, but in mapping between the value of indicators and the valence of "good" and "bad" performance.

Two major hurdles to straightforward interpretation immediately present themselves. The first comes about because some indicators are both a function of an electorate's demographic features or political context, *and* a state's policy and administrative practices. Consider the issue of turnout. On the one hand, a large literature in political science has demonstrated that some policies, such as Election Day registration, have measurable (if disputable) effects on registration and turnout.[17] But on the other hand, so do demographic and political factors. States that are more affluent are likely to have higher turnout and registration rates, as are so-called battleground states. Are Hawaii's abysmal turnout rates (49% in 2008, 44% in 2012, and 43% in 2016) due to the Aloha State's election policies and practices, or because it is a deep-blue state whose voters in presidential years often know the result before they even go to the polls?[18]

Second, it is possible to interpret the high values of some indicators as a sign of both good and bad outcomes. The mail ballot rejection rate is a good example. If mail ballot rejections are mostly caused by administrative pitfalls that prevent legitimate voters from casting ballots—rejecting inconsistent signatures due to aging or illness, for instance—then a state with a higher rejection rate can reasonably be judged as doing worse on this measure than one with a lower rejection rate. If, however, mail ballot usage is prone to fraud due to impersonation, then higher rates may be an indicator of better performance.

The EPI does include some indicators that bear ambiguous relations between the value of the measure and the valence of performance. For these indicators—mail ballot rejections, provisional ballot rejections, and registration rejections—it seemed that the weight of considerations tilted toward high values being problematic, and so they were retained. However, because they are ambiguous, there needs to be further

---

[17]The classic study is Wolfinger and Rosenstone (1980). A more recent update is Leighley and Nagler (2013). On the difficulty of estimating the causal effects of reforms like Election Day registration on turnout, see Keele and Minozzi (2013).
[18]It is interesting that Hawaii's turnout rates in recent midterm years—40% in 2010 and 36% in 2014—are much closer to the national average than its last-in-the-nation on-year rates.

research to understand more precisely whether the "good" reasons for rejections outweigh the "bad."[19]

Indicators that were irredeemably ambiguous or obviously unrelated to good performance were dropped from consideration altogether. One of the most notable of these was a measure of voter confidence that was included among the early candidate indicators. It was originally proposed that voters' answers to the question, "Are you confident that your vote will be counted as cast?" would provide a good overall measure of how they perceived both their voting experience and that of their neighbors. Research has shown that answers to this question were correlated with self-reported voting experiences, such as wait times, poll-worker competence, and voting machine problems. However, other research shows that the strongest factor influencing answers to this question is in fact whether one's favored presidential candidate won the most recent election (Sances and Stewart 2015; Sinclair et al. 2018). Therefore, it is clear that answers to the vote-count-confidence question do not unambiguously measure the quality of the voting experience, and it is correctly excluded from the index.

The final principle—that the indicator be produced in the future—is similar to the second (that it be available and consistent over time), but touches on more practical considerations than the methodological issues related to diachronic analysis. If election administration is an under-funded public service, so too are efforts to collect statistics to measure electoral performance. Data-gathering efforts outside of government have been critical in helping document the state of election administration and policy, but foundations—the principal funding sources for these efforts—by their nature shift their interests, leaving measurement efforts in a fragile state.

This is yet another reason why the EPI relies on official governmental statistics, but even the availability of government data is fragile. The long-standing question of whether Congress might abolish the EAC puts the permanence of the EAVS in peril (Berman 2017). In the end, it may

---

[19]It should be said that upon careful consideration, it is not at all clear that the "good" reasons for large numbers of rejections are in fact reason for celebration. For instance, if a state has a large number of rejected mail ballots because they receive a large number of fraudulent mail ballots, the problem that the indicator measures is not the rejection, but the fraud.

be the EAC's newfound role as intermediary and clearinghouse about cybersecurity threats that saves the EAVS. The Voting and Registration Supplement is a labor of love within the Census Bureau, a fact that places it at risk as a future data source as well. Likewise, the future of the Survey of the Performance of American Elections has grown less certain as Pew, which funded it, withdraws from elections work.

* * *

The diversity of election models has always required users of the EPI to approach it with a grain of salt and an appreciation for nuance. As revealed in this section, however, the index grew directly from and remains firmly planted in a large body of work and prior research. It offers the clearest insights when the question is focused on the experience of the individual voter and the probability that their vote will be included in the final tally. To the degree that the index successfully documents the convenience of voting and the security of the vote count, the fact that it now illustrates change over a full decade of federal elections means that we can stand back and learn about how American elections have been transformed over that time. It is to this topic that I now turn.

What Does the EPI Say About American Elections?

Since its initial release, the Elections Performance Index has been updated three times and now covers the five federal elections from 2008 to 2016. Looking back over the past decade, what does the EPI help us to see in the changing performance of American elections?

One way of answering this question is to calculate the change in the value of each indicator score for each state, comparing 2008–2016. Because the indicators themselves are on different scales, if we are to make the comparison meaningful, we need to look at the difference in scores after they have been normalized to the [0, 1] interval.

That is what I do in Fig. 8.3. To construct this graph, I first calculated the normalized indicator scores for each state in 2008 and 2016 and then subtracted the value in 2008 from the value in 2016. The data tokens in

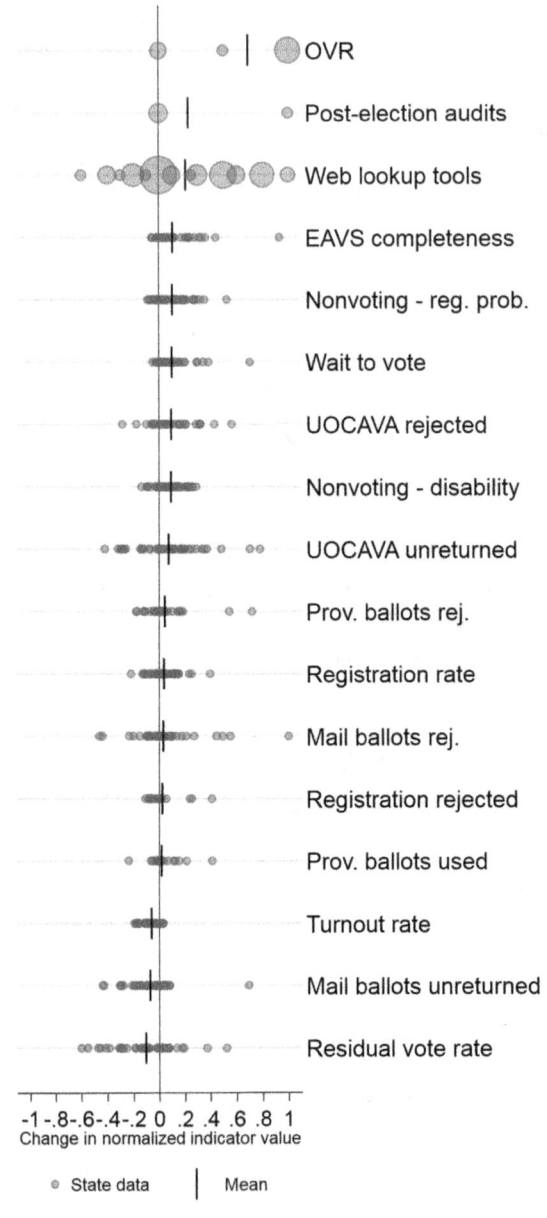

Fig. 8.3 Change in normalized EPI indicator scores for each state, 2008–2016

Fig. 8.3 represent the resulting differences. Positive values represent states that improved their performance from 2008 to 2016; negative values mean that states declined.[20] A state at a value of 1.0 went from being the lowest-ranked state on a given indicator in 2008 to the highest-ranked in 2016. This most often happens with the indicators that are binary, such as the availability of online voter registration—a state can go from worst to best by, for instance, simply adopting online voter registration sometime between 2008 and 2016. A state at zero is one that showed no change in the value of the relevant indicator between 2008 and 2016. States in the negative region saw their performance decline on that indicator.

The black vertical lines in Fig. 8.3 represent the average change from 2008 to 2016. The indicators that saw the biggest improvement since 2008, and for which no state's score declined, measure the presence of online voter registration and post-election audits. The next seven indicators in the figure, ranging from web lookup tools to the non-return rate of UOCAVA ballots, saw average nationwide improvement from 2008 to 2016, with improvement in most, but not all, states. Among the next five indicators, states on average neither rose nor fell. Finally, among the final three indicators—the turnout rate, mail ballot unreturned rate, and residual vote rate—the average indicator score fell a small amount after 2008, with most states under-performing in 2016 compared to 2008.

How do these changes in numerical scores translate into the substance of election performance? First, the widespread improvements in the first two indicators highlight the increasing reliance on the Internet to convey information and provide basic services to voters. In 2008, online voter registration was new on the scene, offered only by Arizona and Washington. By 2016, 33 states and the District of Columbia allowed voters to register online, and five additional states allowed voters to update existing registrations online. In addition to the diffusion of online voter registration over the past decade, states also charged ahead to provide information to voters online. In 2008, there were eleven states without a single lookup tool tracked by this indicator; in

---

[20]The first three items in Fig. 8.3—online voter registration, post-election audits, and web lookup tools—take on a limited number of discrete values, and so it is necessary to vary the size of the data tokens to represent how many states are associated with a specific difference.

2016, every state had at least one. By 2016, every state gave their voters the opportunity to check their polling place location on the state elections Web site, and nearly every state allowed voters to confirm their registration status online.

Growing concern with election security and transparency is also evident in the EPI, indicated by the increasing number of states with post-election audit requirements on the books. In 2008, only 23 states required post-election audits. This number had grown to 34 plus the District of Columbia in 2016.

Many of the other increases in EPI indicator scores since 2008 reflect the steady improvement in administrative practice and professionalism among the states. The improvement in the scope of election data reported to the EAC through the EAVS reflects the increasing value that election officials place on a metrics-based approach to election administration and indicates that information systems are being tuned to make more nuanced performance data readily available to the public. Although states continue to struggle to meet UOCAVA requirements and those for the Military and Overseas Voter Empowerment (MOVE) Act, the EPI shows overall that states are mostly improving in getting ballots back from military and overseas voters on time and including these ballots in the count.

The EPI documents a decline in problems reported with voter registration and an improvement in access to the polls for people with disabilities, at least in most states. Finally, the marked improvement in average wait times is a direct consequence of the coordinated nationwide effort between 2012 and 2016 to better diagnose potential polling place problems and get resources where they are needed to address those issues (Bipartisan Policy Center 2018; Stewart 2017).

The three indicators that show average declines in values from 2008 to 2016 may say as much about limitations of the EPI as they do about changes in policy, practice, and performance. The decline in turnout rate from 2008 to 2016 was undoubtedly due to the failure of the 2008 "Obama turnout bump" to carry over once he was no longer at the top of the ballot. The deterioration in the residual vote rate—the rate of over- and under-votes in the presidential race—was as much due to a spike in abstentions in the 2016 election as it was due to matters of election policy (Alvarez et al. 2018).

Finally, the decline in the indicator gauging the rate of returned mail ballots is undoubtedly due to a mix of factors, with some related to changing performance and others related to the emergence of new election models—most notably, an increase in the number of vote-by-mail (VBM) states and the gradual liberalization of absentee ballot laws in other states.

Mail balloting regimes in the United States can be divided into four types. The first is the traditional excuse-based absentee balloting system, where voters are expected to cast ballots in neighborhood precincts and are allowed to vote absentee only if they have a valid excuse (such as being out of town on election day). The second regime relaxes the criteria for requesting absentee ballots by removing the need for an excuse—anyone can request an absentee ballot without having to justify the request. The third regime pushes the no-excuse system even further, by allowing voters to enter their names onto a permanent absentee ballot list, meaning they do not have to request an absentee ballot every election; it comes automatically. In the final regime, some states have essentially extended the permanent absentee ballot system to all voters by automatically sending a ballot to every registered voter before every election.

Most states still fall into one of the first two regimes, requiring voters to request an absentee ballot before each election. In 2008, nearly every state did—22 required an excuse and another 22 used a no-excuse system. Only six states maintained permanent absentee lists; Oregon alone delivered ballots by mail to all voters. Between 2008 and 2016, though, seven states changed their mail ballot systems, all in a liberalizing direction. Two states that had required an excuse either eliminated the requirement (Illinois) or went so far as to begin a permanent absentee system (Minnesota). Three states (Hawaii, New Jersey, and Utah) that previously had a no-excuse system adopted a permanent absentee list. Finally, two states (Colorado and Washington) that used to operate under a permanent absentee ballot list moved to vote-by-mail.

Overall, the non-return rate of absentee ballots increased from 10.3 to 14.6% from 2008 to 2016, an increase of 4.3 points.[21] Among the 40 states that required voters to at least request an absentee ballot each

---

[21] The absentee ballot non-return rate uses total turnout as the denominator.

election, the non-return rate increased 1.8 points, from 9.4 to 11.2%; among the remaining states that did not require a request—which either had a permanent absentee list or used VBM—the non-return rate increased 11.6 points, from 13.6 to 25.2%.

What should we make of the differences in non-return rates when comparing states with more traditional to more liberalized mail ballot policies? Can we simply conclude that the liberalized states performed more poorly than the traditional states on this measure? Not quite.

First, it must be noted that states of all mail ballot regime types saw an increase in the non-return rate of absentee ballots from 2008 to 2016. This suggests that performance on this indicator declined between 2008 and 2016, regardless of any particular mail ballot regime. But whose performance is implicated? Election administrators? The Postal Service? The EPI cannot answer this question, but it can identify it as an important one to ask and investigate.

Second, to the degree that the non-return rates of the liberalized states are much greater than the rates of traditional states, we can identify specific features of election administration in liberalized states that would cause the non-return rate to rise faster than in traditional states. One obvious factor is the fact that states with both permanent absentee lists and VBM send ballots to lists of voters that by their nature tend to grow over time because of "deadwood." Deadwood in the case of permanent-absentee-list states are those voters who once got on the list but now would prefer to vote in person. In the case of VBM states, deadwood consists of voters who have died or moved, but have yet to be removed from the election rolls. States can take actions to cull their voting lists of deadwood, but to some degree, it will always be a Sisyphean task.

Third, the vote-by-mail states have one more factor working against them on this indicator that is different from all the rest. Before a state adopts VBM, it will have a group of registrants, usually in the range of 10–20% in a presidential election, who fail to vote. These non-voters do not request an absentee ballot; therefore, they do not contribute to the pool of non-returned mail ballots. After a state adopts VBM, ballots will be mailed to those registrants, even if they have no intention to vote. Mailing ballots to these registrants will convert a few of them from non-voters to voters, but most of them will just throw out the ballot. The moment they do so, they contribute to the number of non-returned ballots. Therefore, the adoption of VBM by a state virtually guarantees that its mail non-return rate will grow, because the policy has the effect of sweeping non-voters into the non-return pool.

Working through the different considerations involved in the dynamics of unreturned mail ballots illustrates the risk of interpreting changes to EPI indicator values naively. Even if on the whole the indicator is valid in identifying states that do better and worse jobs of getting mail ballots back to voters, this does not mean that all states can be equally judged by this indicator.

Whither the EPI?

This essay has focused on the original conceptualization of the EPI and what the changing values of its indicators tell us about the performance of elections in America over the past decade. As a way of concluding, I consider what the experience with the EPI tells us more generally about efforts to assess election policy and administration, and speculate about how the EPI might evolve as it enters its second decade.

The most natural thing to mull over is whether some of the current indicators need to be retired, whether others need to be fine-tuned, and whether still others should be added. A more challenging set of speculations opens the EPI up to the possibility that its very approach might change—for instance, de-emphasizing rankings and emphasizing narratives in their place.

Without an anchoring in intellectual and methodological principles, it is always possible to add indicators and follow new ideas about how things might be measured. However, the EPI project is anchored by two sets of core values: one pertaining to the two-dimensional model of election performance and the other to the quality of data. It is within the parameters of this foundation that I offer some ideas.

Putting the current set of indicators up against the principles that guided the development of the EPI, it is possible to argue that they all need to be retained, although the case might be harder to make for some than for others. If retirement is on the table, then two indicators—the residual vote rate and the mail ballot non-return rate—seem especially ripe to consider because their values are driven by a host of factors, not by performance alone. Yet a closer consideration of these two indicators reveals that performance factors can indeed be disentangled from those that are not controlled by administrative policy or practice: the nature of an ongoing political campaign, for example. Thus, perhaps the right response to a suggestion to retire these indicators is instead to provide opportunities to explore their inner workings more thoroughly.

Moving away from the discussion of eliminating some indicators, the idea of refurbishing some of them introduces the idea that social science measurement techniques might be brought to bear to improve the EPI, measuring the concepts behind the indicators with greater validity. Two examples illustrate the opportunities.

The indicator that measures what fraction of non-voters use "disability or illness" as a reason for not voting, for instance, might be improved by taking advantage of new and better data on the subject. When the EPI was created, the CPS did not ask respondents whether they had a disability. The current indicator therefore must gauge the ease of voting for people with disabilities indirectly, by measuring how many people reported they did not vote because of disability or illness.[22] The CPS now asks specifically whether the respondent has a disability, making it possible to base this indicator directly on the voting participation rates of people with disabilities. The EPI methodology document reports that that the new-and-improved indicator will produce similar findings to the old one, but at least it will be based on an even better measurement strategy (MIT Election Data and Science Lab 2018, 22).

A different opportunity is presented by thinking about the best way to construct the turnout indicator. Turnout is a good example of an indicator that is driven by a combination of factors related to administration and policy, on the one hand, and politics on the other. In presidential election years, turnout is correlated with whether a state is a

---

[22]The question also includes disability or illness of a family member, which further muddies the waters.

so-called battleground state. In off-years, turnout is driven by what is at the top of the ballot; if neither a US senator nor governor is at the top, turnout is guaranteed to be depressed. These observations suggest that the turnout indicator could be transformed into something like "competition-corrected turnout," in much the same way that epidemiology now regularly adjusts statistics like death rates for the age of the underlying population.

What difference would it make if the turnout indicator was adjusted for demographics and politics? In some cases, quite a lot; in others, not so much. For instance, if we were to adjust turnout in presidential years to take demographics and political competition into account, high-turnout states that were also well educated and competitive would see their relative scores fall, while low-turnout uncompetitive states with low educational attainment levels would see them rise.

To get a sense about what difference this would make, I conducted a simple adjustment, using linear regression to predict turnout in 2016, using two independent variables: (logged) margin of victory by the victorious presidential candidate and the percent of adults who did not have a high school diploma.[23] The new corrected ranking is just the residual from this regression. Table 8.3 shows the effects of this adjustment for the extremes of states.

With the correction for competition and demographics, two states with traditionally very high-turnout rates, New Hampshire and Wisconsin, fall significantly in the rankings. Both of these were battleground states in 2016, and both were among the top-ten states in terms

---

[23] The results of this regression are summarized in the following table:

Variable	Coeff.	s.e.
Log(Winning margin)	−0.0090	0.0043
% with no h.s. diploma	−1.19	0.19
Constant	0.74	0.03
R^2	0.56	
Adj. R^2	0.54	
N	51	

Table 8.3 Comparison of raw turnout rates in 2016 with normalized rates that take into account political competition and educational attainment

	Uncorrected turn-out rate (%)	Rank, uncorrected rate	Rank, corrected rate
Top-five states			
Minnesota	74.8	1	2
Maine	72.8	2	3
New Hampshire	72.5	3	14
Colorado	72.1	4	1
Wisconsin	69.4	5	21
Bottom-five states			
Oklahoma	52.4	47	49
Texas	51.6	48	40
Tennessee	51.2	49	50
West Virginia	50.1	50	48
Hawaii	43.0	51	51

of educational attainment. Based on these two factors, we would expect turnout to be even higher than it was. In their place among the top five, the adjusted turnout rate would elevate two states that are dominated by one party, rather than battlegrounds: California (whose rank would rise from 37 to 5) and Massachusetts.

The low end of the turnout scale would not be nearly so affected by this correction. The one exception is Texas, which would rise from number 48 to number 40, by "virtue" of its non-competitive status and relatively low educational attainment. Utah would replace Texas in the bottom five, falling from 39 to 47.

Adjusting indicators like this has its virtues, but it comes with risks. First, the adjustment has to be based on sound, simple, and transparent principles. Second, once the adjustment is made, attention must be given as to why it makes some states move so much while others do not. In the end, such adjustments involve trading off at least two of the EPI's data-quality principles: transparency and validity.

Thus, we come to the final question: What needs to be added? From the beginning, the EPI has been heavily weighted toward measures that tap into either the convenience of the voter or the probability that a voter's vote will be counted. This means that relatively few indicators tap the security side of the ledger.

The relative lack of security-related indicators has become even clearer as security and integrity have become bigger concerns in American elections. These concerns are focused in three areas: voting systems, list maintenance, and cybersecurity.

It needs to be mentioned up front that measuring security in any field is problematic, since what is of interest may be unmeasurable. That said, it may be that election security is not as unmeasurable as some imagine—even if it is, it there may be good indirect measures that are worth considering.

For instance, the current EPI entirely avoided the controversy over the use of direct-recording electronic voting machines (DREs) by states. Despite evidence that substantiated cases of malicious attacks on this equipment are virtually non-existent and verified reports of programming errors are relatively uncommon, the fact remains that DREs without voter-verifiable paper audit trails (VVPATs) cannot be independently audited in the event a question arises about the performance of this equipment, nor is there a backup method to count ballots if the machinery fails. The lack of auditability has led to a scientific consensus that DREs without VVPATs should be retired as soon as possible (National Academies of Science 2018). It would be simple enough to include an indicator that reported the percentage of voters who cast ballots on such machines.[24]

The issue of list maintenance became highly salient in 2017, when President Trump appointed the Presidential Advisory Commission on Election Integrity (PACEI).[25] The commission's appointment was rightly criticized for politicizing election administration and for its roots in an assumption that election fraud was more common than it is. However, there is a widespread consensus among the public and election administrators that problems do exist in keeping voting lists clean, and that some states do better than others. There is also a consensus that undertaking certain policy actions, such as joining the Electronic

---

[24]Creating such an indicator would be simple, but not perfectly simple. The complication is that many voters in the states and local jurisdictions that use VVPAT-less DREs vote by mail, and these voters need to be accounted for as voting on independently auditable paper ballots.

[25]https://www.whitehouse.gov/articles/presidential-advisory-commission-election-integrity/.

Registration Information Center (ERIC), would lead to improved list maintenance.

There are a couple of paths that can be followed to account more accurately for list maintenance within the EPI. The first is simply to include membership in ERIC as one of the indicators.[26] The other is to compare list maintenance activities with the need for maintenance. For instance, Pettigrew and Stewart (2018) have conducted research that explores the degree to which local jurisdictions keep up with the deaths of voters by removing them from the rolls. An indicator based on this metric—the divergence between death rates and death removals—is worth exploring.

Finally, the importance of state and local election jurisdictions improving their defenses against cyberattacks was brought to the fore by online interference with the 2016 election. The rising importance of cybersecurity should be met with an indicator to measure the relative responses of the states. But saying that does not make it so. Measuring states' responses to cybersecurity runs up against a host of challenges, ranging from the lack of direct measurability to ethical concerns about working hard to document and publicize states' deficiencies.[27]

Still, all may not be lost. One way of approaching the need to measure the states' responses to the newly realized cybersecurity threat is to make a list of publicly visible best practices and then to report on whether states are following those practices. What are those practices? That is the work to be done. However, this approach is very similar to the one the EPI adopted originally to follow the expanding use of the Internet by election officials to engage with voters and potential voters: Make a list of a small number of achievable but non-trivial actions and then reward states for taking them.

---

[26] An alternative would be to include the Interstate Crosscheck program as well, which was also recommended by President Obama's Presidential Commission on Election Administration. Because Crosscheck is more oriented toward law enforcement than preventive list maintenance, not including Crosscheck membership is probably warranted.

[27] On this latter point, though, it should be said that if a state has a cybersecurity vulnerability that is measurable by a political scientist, it has probably already been exploited by a malicious actor.

Leaving aside the individual indicators, one big question looms as we consider the future of the EPI: ranking the states. There is no doubt that creating a summative measure of election performance draws attention to the index on a regular basis, and there is some evidence that states have taken actions specifically designed to improve their rankings. Once the early lagging states took these actions, almost all states landed in a tight range of scores that makes cross-state comparison very difficult. Only a few points now separate top performers from middling ones, most of whom perform better than the top performers in 2008.

So long as states' performance does not begin deteriorating, there is less to be learned now by comparing states on the overall index score than in 2008. Retaining the current indicators and the method of generating the overall EPI index, then, no longer creates a highly discriminating metric.

This suggests one of two paths. One is to abandon an overall ranked index; the EPI could instead serve as a way to narrate policy change among subsets of states based, for instance, on their overall method of running elections. The other is to explore new indicators that more sharply distinguish between states in their election policy performance. Gerken (2009) argues compellingly that a project such as the EPI is made more relevant by encouraging users to compare across states and time. The task for the future is to revitalize the relevance of those comparisons while at the same time increasing efforts to educate the public about the nuances of the evolving electoral environment.

References

Alvarez, R. Michael et al. "Residual Votes and Abstentions in the 2016 Election." Paper Presented at the Annual Meeting of the Southern Political Science Association: New Orleans, LA, January 2018. https://ssrn.com/abstract=3225197.

Berman, Russel. "The Federal Voting Agency Republicans Want to Kill." *The Atlantic*, 2017. https://www.theatlantic.com/politics/archive/2017/02/election-assistance-commission-republicans-congress/516462/.

Bipartisan Policy Center. "Improving the Voter Experience: Reducing Polling Place Wait Times by Measuring Lines and Managing Polling Place Resources." 2018. https://bipartisanpolicy.org/wp-content/uploads/2018/04/Improving-The-Voter-Experience-Reducing-Polling-Place-Wait-Times-by-Measuring-Lines-and-Managing-Polling-Place-Resources.pdf.

Burden, Barry C., and Charles Stewart III, editors. *The Measure of American Elections*. New York: Cambridge University Press, 2014.

Caltech/MIT Voting Technology Project. *Voting: What Is/What Could Be*, 2001. https://vote.caltech.edu/documents/153/voting_what_is_what_could_be.pdf.

Gerken, Heather K. *The Democracy Index: Why Our Election System Is Failing and How to Fix It*. Princeton: Princeton University Press, 2009.

Holbrook, Allyson L., and Jon A. Krosnick. "Social Desirability Bias in Voter Turnout Reports: Tests Using the Item Count Technique." *Public Opinion Quarterly*, 74, no. 1 (2009): 37–67.

Keele, Luke, and William Minozzi. "How Much Is Minnesota Like Wisconsin? Assumptions and Counterfactuals in Causal Inference with Observational Data." *Political Analysis*, 21, no. 2 (2013): 193–216.

Leighley, Jan E., and Jonathan Nagler. *Who Votes Now? Demographics, Issues, Inequality, and Turnout in the United States*. Princeton: Princeton University Press, 2013.

MIT Election Data and Science Lab. *Elections Performance Index: Methodology Report*, 2018. https://elections.mit.edu/2016-epi-methodology.pdf.

National Academies of Science, Engineering, and Medicine. *Securing the Vote: Protecting American Democracy*. Washington, DC: The National Academies Press, 2018.

Pettigrew, Stephen, and Charles Stewart III. "Moved Out, Moved On: Assessing the Effectiveness of Voter Registration List Maintenance." Paper Presented at the Annual Meeting of the Election Science, Reform, and Administration Conference: Portland, OR, July 27–28, 2018. https://ssrn.com/abstract=3044810.

Sances, Michael W., and Charles Stewart III. "Partisanship and Confidence in the Vote Count: Evidence from US National Elections Since 2000." *Electoral Studies*, 40 (2015): 176–188.

Sinclair, Betsy, Steven S. Smith, and Patrick D. Tucker. "'It's Largely a Rigged System': Voter Confidence and the Winner Effect in 2016." *Political Research Quarterly*, 2018. https://doi.org/10.1177/1065912918768006.

Stewart, Charles III. "Losing Votes by Mail." *NYU Journal of Legislation and Public Policy*, 13 (2010): 573–601.

———. "Waiting to Vote in 2016: Preliminary Evidence About Election Wait-Times in the November Election." Paper Presented at the Annual Meeting of the Southern Political Science Association: New Orleans, LA, January 12–14, 2017.

———. "Is the EAVS a Reliable Guide to Voter List Maintenance?" Paper Presented at the Annual Meeting of the American Political Science Association: Boston, MA, August 30–September 2, 2018. https://ssrn.com/abstract=3238927.

Wolfinger, Raymond E., and Steven J. Rosenstone. *Who Votes?* New Haven: Yale University Press, 1980.

Charles Stewart III is the Kenan Sahin Distinguished Professor of Political Science at MIT and founding director of the MIT Election Day and Science Lab. Since 2001, Professor Stewart has been a member of the Caltech/MIT Voting Technology Project, a leading research effort that applies scientific analysis to questions about election technology, election administration, and election reform. He is currently the MIT director of the project. Professor Stewart is an established leader in the analysis of the performance of election systems and the quantitative assessment of election performance. Working with the Pew Charitable Trusts, he helped with the development of Pew's Elections Performance Index. Professor Stewart also provided advice to the Presidential Commission on Election Administration. His research on measuring the performance of elections and polling place operations is funded by Pew, the Democracy Fund, and the Hewlett Foundation. He recently published *The Measure of American Elections* (2014, with Barry C. Burden).

9

Building Terminology in the Field

Katy Owens Hubler and Tammy Patrick

If you've been involved in election administration for a while, you know that the ways in which elections are run across the country vary greatly. As a result of culture, history, and the quirks of legislators or election officials, each state has developed its own unique way of doing things. But, we're also often struck by the commonalities. At the core, election officials across the country want to do things well and follow the same general blueprint of how to get there.

There have been various efforts over the years of outlining or describing how elections work in different contexts, the most comprehensive of which was close to a century ago, the 1934 tome by Joseph P. Harris, *Election Administration in the United States*. Because there is such diversity in how elections are run across the country, it benefits everyone to have a common understanding of how things work. Harris conducted his research by traveling throughout the country and interviewing

K. O. Hubler (✉)
Democracy Research, Park City, UT, USA
e-mail: katyowenshubler@democracyresearch.com

T. Patrick
Democracy Fund, Washington, DC, USA

© The Author(s) 2020
M. Brown et al. (eds.), *The Future of Election Administration*, Elections, Voting, Technology, https://doi.org/10.1007/978-3-030-14947-5_9

election officials. In this day and age, we have technology to assist with this process—conference calls, screen sharing, process modeling software, and lines of code.

One current effort to outline how elections work in the United States focuses on modeling the election process, concisely defining the terms within the model, and establishing a common data format (CDF) for election systems so that different systems can more efficiently exchange information. Overall, the process model approach accounts for differences between states by recognizing that there are points in the process path where states may diverge along parallel procedures only to reconvene at a later juncture.

Election Process Model

Starting in 2013, a group of election officials and experts across the country began working together to create a comprehensive election process model. The working group was initially formed under the auspices of the Institute of Electrical and Electronic Engineers (IEEE), whose Voting System Standards Committee (P1622) assisted with the development of common data format for election systems. A particular VSSC standard (P1622.1) has been used to support the development of the election model, which will be discussed in detail below; additional uses have become evident as the work progressed.

A process model creates a visualization of a complex system that functions as a sort of road map for the who, when, and how of election administration. Across all election jurisdictions, elections, and the processes and technologies used to facilitate their administration have become more complicated over the years. Gone are the days when election administration was the part-time job of a clerk who accomplished the job with paper and pen. Today's elections are made possible by a web of technological solutions, people, and processes that can be hard to describe to one not familiar with how it all works. From the outside, it is not always evident how much time, effort, and attention to detail is required to successfully run an election, and the nation's election officials are either planning for or running an election almost constantly.

The point of creating an election model for election systems is to visually and succinctly describe how the process works and to create a common basis of understanding among election officials in different states. A common election process model forms the thousand-foot view of election administration in the country, but at the same time can accurately describe the day-to-day process of an individual election official.

Individuals involved in working groups that model the process include election officials from all over the country, in order to establish a broad-based understanding about how elections are actually run. By involving officials from diverse jurisdictions, everyone is forced to test their assumptions about how elections work. You can know your own election process inside and out but not realize that there is an entirely different way of doing things in your neighboring state.

The working groups include election system vendors as well, since they have thought through both how the process works, as well as state variations in the process, in order to develop products for election administrators. Their unique perspective is critical in order to ensure that the representation of the functionality of a system is technically accurate. The fundamental goal of modeling elections is to create a common base of understanding about how everything works, and as such can have several practical applications.

One is to identify opportunities to apply a CDF. The first goal of modeling an election was to see where different components of the process intersect, and therefore where to establish CDFs (discussed in more depth below). Establishing commonalities between the data coming in and out of various election systems can make the process more efficient.

The concept of an election process model and a CDF may also serve as a basis from which to derive requirements for the Voluntary Voting System Guidelines (VVSG) developed under the auspices of the Election Assistance Commission (EAC). The VVSG are voluntary federal standards for voting systems relied upon by vendors and used in one form or another in more than half the states. By looking at the election process as a whole and then drilling down into specific pieces, stakeholders can identify parts of the process that need requirements written as part of the VVSG.

Another application is to provide a learning tool for election officials at the state and county level. Explaining the ins and outs of elections can be tough, and so those new to the field often feel thrown into the deep end. The election model can serve as a training document to help bring those new to the process up to speed. It also assists those who have been in the game a long time to see that there are other ways of doing things and to help identify ways by which they may be able to make the process more efficient.

Election models can also provide a blueprint for elaboration. The high-level election model is meant to show how elections work nationwide, but election officials can also build on it to detail their own internal processes. A model that is representative of the nation as a whole can help individual jurisdictions identify places where they might be able to improve or to see best practices that are already in place elsewhere.

Not least, election process modeling can provide a method for discovering security gaps. Cybersecurity has been at the forefront of the public's attention since the 2016 presidential election. But in fact, security in general—the physical security of election equipment and materials, as well as the cyber aspect—is always on the mind of election officials. Looking at the overall election model can help election officials identify potential security gaps in the process, envision the full scope of their cyber threat-landscape, and therefore aid in developing mitigation, detection, and recovery strategies.

Glossary

Over the course of modeling election processes, one thing that became evident is the inconsistent use of election-related terminology between states. Part of the election modeling work creates a "semantic model" in which terms are scaffolded, so that terms build on other terms. But in order to do this, there has to be a common understanding of what given terms actually mean. A survey of existing glossaries for election terminology as well as definitions prescribed by state statutes and administrative rules showed this variation and also illustrated the need for establishing common terms and definitions in the world of election administration. Often two states (or more) use the same term but use it to mean something entirely different in each state; related, states use different terms to describe the same thing.

A glossary of concise and accurate definitions for election-related terms, and also the consistent usage of these terms, has several advantages. One is simply to define terms for use within the election model. As discussed above, a model of election processes isn't useful unless the terms that it uses are explicitly defined and used consistently. One example of this is the use of the terms "option" and "selection." A ballot contains contest options—a list of candidates or ballot questions under which voters have various options. The voter then makes a "selection" on the ballot, which can be indicated in a variety of ways. For the sake of the election process model, then, the word "option" denotes the opportunity that a voter has, whereas the term "selection" denotes the act and intention of voting for a given option.

A glossary can also enhance academic understanding of the field. It is important for academics who study election administration and its effects to define and refine terms. It's difficult to study the effects of "early voting" without a good, consistent, widely used definition of "early voting." Does in-person absentee voting—a term and process used in many states—qualify as early voting? Does an academic study of early voting contemplate that in-person absentee voting and early voting are different terms used in different states but could apply to the same concept? One-stop absentee voting in North Carolina is the same as advanced voting in Georgia, which both work the same as early voting in Texas (or most anywhere else that uses that term). This becomes especially important for information that is requested as part of the EAC's biannual Election Administration and Voting Survey (EAVS). EAVS data are used extensively by academics, but when election officials receive the EAVS they don't always have a common understanding of what is being asked of them, because they may have a different understanding of a given term. Is a provisional ballot the same as a challenge ballot or an affidavit ballot? The establishment of common terms, definitions, and synonyms would help to streamline this process and improve data collection and analysis of comparative election administration across the states.

A glossary is also useful in interpreting federal forms and requirements. One example is interpretation of the duration of validity of the Federal Postcard Application (FPCA), the form used by military and overseas voters which contains the oath and affirmation that they are an eligible elector entitled to special considerations (reception of their ballot 45 days prior to a federal election, electronic transmission of their ballot to them, extended return periods in some states, etc.). The FPCA is a federal form; however, some states treat their voters differently. The title of the FPCA form states that it is to be used for voter registration and ballot application purposes, yet there are still 5 states that do not actually use the form to register the applicant fully. Instead, voters in these states are placed on a temporary listing, provided a ballot, and allowed to vote. However, these states do not retain a voting history for these voters, and these voters are not deemed to be Active Registered Voters; these voters are removed from the list at the end of each year. In this way, these states do not treat these voters the same as other voters who are covered under the National Voter Registration Act (NVRA). This interpretation and subsequent cancelation of voter access to the franchise requires the voter to register to vote every year in order to participate. Forty-five other states interpret the validity of the application in reference to the request for a ballot. The voter remains on the active voter registration rolls and is protected under the NVRA.[1]

The concept of a glossary also applies outside the English language and beyond purely technical jargon. Hundreds of jurisdictions serve millions of voters in languages other than English and the words that are used can influence translation of materials for voters. As one example, the term "ballot" in Spanish could translate as either "boleta" or "papaleta." The challenges of understanding local vernacular and colloquial usage can be magnified when translating election terminology into other languages.

---

[1] For those states which are covered under the NVRA. The Presidential Commission on Election Administration (PCEA) along with the Council of State Governments (CSG) Overseas Voter Initiative (OVI) have called for the abolition of this practice.

A glossary can also be used to refine the terms used in state legislation. State election law establishes the foundation of election operations in a given state. However, legislators sometimes use election-related terms in their legislation without regard to exact meanings or in different ways than terms are used in different states. Sometimes this may be intentional; divergent usage can also be the result of the lack of a one-stop place to look for election terms and their meanings. For example, legislators might use a term like "risk-limiting audit" or "automatic voter registration" because it is currently *en vogue*, and perhaps without defining or understanding in advance what these terms could mean; this gap can leave election officials in a difficult place when determining how to implement legislation.

Election officials can also use a glossary in interactions with the media. In recent years, election officials have had to become familiar with cybersecurity terms like "phishing" and "scanning for vulnerabilities" and have also discovered that their understanding of these terms does not always match that of the media. The same is true with terms that are more directly related to elections, such as what it means for a voting system or an election to be certified. Having terms that are generally agreed upon by the election community and that are available in a central location also provides the media with the opportunity to use election terminology correctly and consistently.

Common Data Format

In this day and age, data are king (or queen). As with everything else, election administration has become more data-heavy and more device-heavy. It wasn't always this way. Think back to the analog age of giant cumbersome lever voting machines. A lever machine was not electronic and not attached to any other machines that helped it serve its purpose. It allowed electors to cast their vote, and it tabulated the votes without the need to "talk" to anything else. Now, election systems are much more than a big bulky lever machine. Election systems are actually webs of multiple software and hardware systems that need to interact with each other in some way. Data are at the core of each of these systems, from the databases that are used to maintain voter lists, to electronic poll books used to check voters in, to devices used to tabulate votes, and to election night reporting systems that display results.

Sometimes these systems can reflect a sort of United Nations without a translation service. Different devices made by different manufacturers, and for different purposes, all speak different languages. It can take quite a bit of work to translate the data coming out of one device into a language that can be imported into another device. This could mean that software is needed to reformat the file in the middle of a process or even that individuals must manually "key-in" data from one data set into another.

A CDF allows each of these systems to "speak the same language." Having data in the same format across all systems allows for more streamlined exports and imports from one system to another. A CDF advances the goal of interoperable election systems—systems that work together seamlessly no matter who the manufacturer is. A CDF has several advantages. One advantage is efficiency. If different systems "talk" to one another, then officials don't need to re-key the same data across different databases, which is resource-intensive (both time and staff) and often introduces errors. Common formats streamline imports and exports between different systems. A CDF also enhances flexibility for election officials. Eventually, CDFs will allow for easier integration of new components, components from different vendors, and commercial off-the-shelf (COTS) components. Election officials will have more choices in what is available for purchase, which in the long run could save money. Transparency and the enhanced security that accompanies it are also supported by a CDF. Data available in a common format, rather than a proprietary format, increase access by citizens and groups. With more "eyes" on the data in a CDF, it is easier to for citizens and groups to analyze, test for accuracy, and determine whether the data have been changed once they have been exported. Devices that use a CDF will be easier to test, which could potentially speed up the testing and certification process. Once data are in a common format, they can be more easily integrated with other data such as the EAVS and the Voting Information Project (VIP) and used to respond to requests from the media, legislators, campaigns, and others. If election data are easier to consume, more organizations want to use and present data in appealing ways—everyone from Google to MTV can create maps and graphics for presenting voter information and election results.

CDFs for various aspects of the election process are being developed by the National Institute of Standards and Technology (NIST), in collaboration with the EAC and with the help of public working groups. The working groups consist of state and local election officials and their staff, voting equipment manufacturers, and election experts from all over the country. One use of the election model, discussed above, is to identify areas of the election process that might benefit from CDFs.

As of writing, the Election Results Reporting specification (NIST SP 1500-100 Version 1.0) is the most developed of the CDF work. It deals with data formats for unofficial election results, which are often reported on election night. Without a CDF, local jurisdictions have to export results from their systems, translate it in some way (using software or perhaps manually) or even type in result information by hand. Having a CDF allows result information to be automatically downloaded from local jurisdictions and uploaded into the statewide reporting system. It reduces errors from manual entry and makes it possible for candidates, the media, and the public to see results faster and in a more uniform way.

Ohio integrated the use of CDF in its election night reporting system in 2014–2015 and found that both local and national media relied on the system heavily. Results were refreshed every 3 to 5 minutes, giving a real-time view of results as they came in. In November 2016, North Carolina used the election result CDF to send information to Google, which was then able to configure these data into a one-box Google search result and reach a greater number of people.

A CDF also permits states and jurisdictions to form partnerships with other organizations. Using the NIST SP 1500-100 specification permitted the Virginia Department of Elections to work with Google to present results of the 2017 general election, which included a high-profile gubernatorial race. Virginia published result information in the SP 1500-100 format, which allowed Google to directly consume the data and display results on their search page. One advantage that Virginia saw in forming this partnership was the amount of web traffic absorbed by Google, reducing direct web hits on the Department of Elections page. Reducing the traffic load on the state's site can save money on web hosting and can also decrease the risk of the Web site failing on election night. Virginia officials found that the more places that had official access to the data, the better. Official data are getting out to a larger audience and are available through other sources in case of a server outage at the state election office.

Virginia also discovered an unexpected benefit of making changes to their internal data infrastructure to accommodate SP 1500-100. This CDF was also compatible with the VIP specification, permitting the state to implement VIP feeds much more quickly. VIP partners in almost every state will be able to provide official information to voters, such as what is on their ballots and where to vote. The VIP project partners with technology companies and civic engagement groups that then use the data for voter outreach campaigns using the official data that states provide.

Another CDF available for jurisdictions to use is NIST's online Voter Records Interchange (VRI)[2] which deals with data interchange from online voter registration systems, voter registration systems, third-party systems, and motor vehicle agencies. States seeking to replace aging voter registration databases can consider adding language about CDFs into the development of requirements for the new system, a Request for Proposals (RFP), or when contracting with a new vendor.

The VRI CDF has the potential to help election officials more easily consume and integrate data from the department of motor vehicles and other registration agencies. This can be helpful for any state but is especially so for those looking at more automated voter registration system and list maintenance procedures. Having voter registration information in a common format also more easily allows states to adopt integrated voter registration list maintenance processes, both with other agencies within the state and with interstate data sharing programs like the Electronic Registration Information Center (ERIC).

---

[2]The NIST repository for the VRI can be found here. https://github.com/usnistgov/VoterRecordsInterchange.

Another CDF, the Cast Vote Record (CVR) specification, can be used by jurisdictions seeking to purchase new voting systems. It provides for interoperable exports of CVRs produced by vote-capture devices like scanners. A CVR is the archival tabulatable record of all votes produced by a single voter from a given ballot. In other words, it is an electronic record of a voter's selections. The CVR CDF can assist with the performance of post-election audits and provide greater transparency to voting records produced by vote-capture devices.

Voter Records Interchange CDF

The information election officials collect about voters is common in many respects across jurisdictions that manage voter records, however, until the advent of the development of the Voter Records Interchange (VRI), there has not been any commonly accepted data format for the storage or transmission of voter information between parties. While each of the 50 + 1 states has laws, regulations, and practices that govern the information that constitutes a valid voter record and each has processes that are distinct, there are many commonalities across jurisdictional boundaries. The adoption of the VRI by election officials will simplify the implementation of each of these electronic voter record transactions. Additionally, it can provide predictability in the development of technology by entities providing software solutions to election officials.

Paul Stenbjorn has done extensive work to develop cases that illustrate the ways states have made use of record exchanges.[3] His work and that of the Democracy Fund is the basis of the summaries that follow (Stenbjorn 2018; "Democracy Fund").

---

[3] Paul Stenbjorn is a former election official and election technology expert; cases can be found at https://github.com/pstenbjorn/VRIUsecases.

VRI CDF USE CASE 1 Voter Registration Application Programming Interface (API) in Pennsylvania

At the end of 2018, there were 37 states plus the District of Columbia offering online voter registration; one additional state (Oklahoma) passed legislation in 2015 but had not yet implemented the service. Online voter registration is a benefit in and of itself; however, leveraging the platform in the field by use of an API capitalizes on its full potential. Pennsylvania implemented online voter registration in August 2015 and offers an API in order to streamline the integration of data coming in from a multitude of field actors thus reducing the number of paper forms being circulated, improving the speed with which voters' records are updated, and reducing duplication of effort when a voter is already registered. The adoption of the VRI as an API standard can simplify both the technical configuration of the public-facing system and the usability of the API by third-party integrators.

VRI CDF USE CASE 2 Agency Data Sharing in Virginia

Consistency in formatting improves the ability to maintain accurate data and have a more reliable voter registration list. In 2015, the Virginia Department of Elections implemented the receipt of electronic voter record transactions with the Virginia Department of Motor Vehicles (DMV) as its method of receiving NVRA transactions from this agency. The integration of different data sets based on the different statutory and operational parameters of the agencies presented challenges in data alignment. CDF facilitated a more holistic process for integration. The NVRA requires multiple state agencies to inform the registration process and having stability in the association of information is critical.

VRI CDF USE CASE 3 Electronic Poll Books in District of Columbia

In addition to the challenges of data sharing and matching across agencies and jurisdictions, individual offices can also experience impediments due to variation in vendors, service providers, and software. The District of Columbia found that implementing a common data standard in their use of electronic poll books when transferring the voter file to the terminal device negated the need for extensive (and time consuming) manual intervention and resulted in a more accurate representation of the file at the polls. The registration information distributed to electronic poll books is more than a list of voters; it provides the additional needed information to ensure that a voter is provided the right ballot at a polling place. Further, electronic poll book data sets can be used for additional actions, such as Election Day Registration, and provisional ballot disposition. We need to look no further than the headlines to see what happens when voter information is inaccurate.

As with any attempt to use common language and standards, it will take time to see states and jurisdictions begin to adopt CDFs and a shared usage of election terminology. As they begin to do so, though, it will create a domino effect. As states and jurisdictions adopt CDFs and common terms they will test them out, suggest improvements, and increase the value and benefit for those that adopt them later. Using technology in election administration is the new reality; it isn't going anywhere. It benefits everyone if these technologies are more easily interoperable.

References

"Democracy Fund VRI Use Cases and Reference Code Samples." Accessed January 13, 2019. https://github.com/pstenbjorn/VRIUsecases.

Harris, Joseph P. *Election Administration in the United States*. Brooking Institute Press, (1934). Accessible from https://www.nist.gov/itl/election-administration-united-states-1934-joseph-p-harris-phd.

Stenbjorn, Paul. "Executive Summary for Use Cases of the Voter Records Interchange (VRI)." The Democracy Fund, November 2018. https://docs.google.com/document/d/1PNgzhddQpsRgWFy03Kp80-qUHyApJB-4dL6zjqUZAgzc/edit#heading=h.njslixvbokif.

Katy Owens Hubler is a consultant specializing in election administration policy and technology. She previously served as a senior policy specialist in elections at the National Conference of State Legislatures and has also worked for the Denver Elections Division and The Carter Center's Democracy Program. Owens Hubler has a B.A. in international affairs from Lewis and Clark College and an M.A. in political science from the University of Colorado at Denver.

Tammy Patrick is a senior advisor to the elections program at the Democracy Fund where she helps lead their efforts to foster a voter-centric elections system and their work to provide election officials across the country with the tools and knowledge they need to best serve voters. She is a former Federal Compliance Officer from Maricopa County, AZ and served as a Commissioner on the Presidential Commission on Election Administration (PCEA). She has a B.A. in American Studies from Purdue University, is an accredited Certified Elections Registration Administrator (CERA) from Auburn University and an adjunct professor at the University of Minnesota's Humphrey School of Public Affairs.

10

Diversity and Descriptive Representation in Election Administration

Bridgett A. King

In bureaucracies, descriptive representation contributes to minority citizens believing that they belong, are welcome, and their interests supported. Although the role of descriptive representation has been considered in many policy areas where street-level bureaucrats engage the public (elected representatives, policing, schools, etc.), the role of descriptive representation in election administration has received considerably less attention. The role descriptive representation plays in election administration is particularly essential given that historically in the United States, street-level bureaucrats or local election officials used their administrative discretion to systematically disenfranchise minority voters. While over time previously disenfranchised voters have gained access to public spaces and the franchise, most notably due to the 1964 Civil Rights Act and 1965 Voting Right Act, the administration of elections continues to be one dominated by white professionals who are selected through a civil service process, elected, or appointed.

B. A. King (✉)
Auburn University, Auburn, AL, USA
e-mail: bak0020@auburn.edu

© The Author(s) 2020
M. Brown et al. (eds.), *The Future of Election Administration*, Elections, Voting, Technology, https://doi.org/10.1007/978-3-030-14947-5_10

The role of descriptive representation in election administration is not only important because of the history of voting in the United States but also because of the unique way the individuals who manage elections are selected. Beyond the professional public administrators who serve as election officials, elections are managed by poll workers. The almost one million poll workers (Election Assistance Commission 2016) who work on election day and during early in-person voting periods are responsible for checking voters in, distributing and collecting ballots, making decisions about eligibility, and following a wide variety of federal, state, and local policies. In spite of these responsibilities, poll workers are citizens who are appointed to serve as temporary government employees often with limited to no training and minimal qualifications. Although professional election administrators are responsible for registration, voter list maintenance, ballot preparation, identification of appropriate polling locations, maintaining voting machines, and certifying election results, it is the poll workers whom voters encounter on election day and when voting early in person.

Although the administrative discretion of these individuals is limited by federal, state, and local rules, the decisions of election administrators and poll workers have the capacity to affect the voting and registration experiences of citizens. The experiences citizens have with local election officials, and poll workers can shape citizen perception of not only the elections office (the agency) but also confidence in election administration (the process). As confidence in the system is an essential component for a democracy to be perceived as legitimate, confidence in the process and its outcomes and the factors that contribute to legitimacy are something we need to understand to ensure the election administration system is one that creates confidence and trust for all American voters.

Public Administration and Representative Bureaucracy

Kingsley (1944) advocated for a representative government workforce to help ensure responsible decision-making by administrative professionals in public spaces where discretion occurs; he believed that for a bureaucracy to be truly democratic and aware of citizen's desires it needed to demographically reflect classes of citizens it serves. Although Kingsley (1944) primarily focused on class inclusion in bureaucracies, Mosher (1968) expanded notions of descriptive representation by incorporating race, gender, and ethnicity. Beyond these, Mosher (1968) also introduced the notions of active and passive representation in bureaucracies. Passive representative in a bureaucracy occurs when an organization has employees that descriptively represent the constituency that it serves. Active representation in a bureaucracy occurs when an organization has employees that advocate for the interests of the constituencies they represent and serve.

Although Mosher (1968) acknowledges the benefits of active representation, he also was careful to acknowledge the potential pitfalls of the practice. Mosher's primary concern was for active representation run rampant. Under such circumstances, minority interests are given priority over what is in the best interest of the community at large. This, he suggests, is a major threat to democracy. Given this, Mosher (1968) recommended bureaucratic agencies pursue passive representation over active representation. Although passive representation in bureaucracies may provide a smaller substantive advantage or representation for minority groups, it holds symbolic value. Because descriptive representation includes race, sex, class, and creed (Mosher 1968), the value of passive or descriptive representation is that it provides a visible indication to the constituents served by an organization that the organization is open to individuals whatever their station in life and provides equal opportunity for services (17).

Representation and Citizen Participation and Perception

Although early research suggested that the civil service is representative of the American public (Long 1952; Meier 1975), subsequent analyses found that sectors of the civil service do not reflect the demographic composition of the American public. Meier and Nigro (1976) for example find that the demographics of super-grade federal employees (Grades 14, 15, and 16) do not reflect the demographics of the general population as they tend to be predominantly white, male, well-educated professionals from upper-middle-class urban families (462). The authors go on to suggest that having demographic information about bureaucrats explains little about their attitudes and policymaking behavior. They conclude that demographic representation is not useful in the study of civil servant attitudes or behavior. Over time scholars have focused on the relationship between representative bureaucracy and its causes and consequences in settings where bureaucrats are not highly removed from interactions with citizens. As an example, investigating causes and consequences of school board descriptive representation, Stewart et al. (1989) find that the presence of African-American members on school boards and within public school systems increases the likelihood of African-Americans serving as school administrators. While Stewart et al. (1989) do not explore what African-American representation means for constituents' perceptions of the institution, it is possible that in school systems with larger African-American populations, the presence of African-American administrators and board representatives has a positive effect on confidence in the institution and its ability to represent the interests of the children and families served by the school district.

Of the studies that do address the relationship between citizen perceptions of organizations and institutions and representation, they primarily explore this relationship utilizing elected officials and constituents (Gay 2002; Muller 1970; Tate 2001). Although this approach largely ignores the relationships between constituents and public servants who are not elected, it is nonetheless valuable to understand the orientation of constituents toward political action and those who represent them. John Adams argued that a representative legislature, "should be an exact portrait, in miniature, of the people at large, as it should think, feel, reason and act like them" (Adams, Works, Vol. IV, Boston 1852–1865, 284, cited in Pitkin 1967, 60). The most literal interpretation of this exact portrait perspective is a legislative body that mathematically reflects various divisions of the electorate (Grofman 1982, 98). The exact portrait perspective would suggest that representative bodies at the federal, state, and local level should be proportionally identical to the population. It has been suggested that representation by politicians whose reflections mirror their own is a way in which racial/ethnic minorities, women, and individuals who belong to underrepresented socioeconomic groups are more likely to engage and feel a part of the political process.

One explanation that follows this line of reasoning is the empowerment thesis. The empowerment thesis posits that visible political leadership by members of a minority group should enhance trust in government, efficacy, group pride, and participation (Banducci et al. 2004; Gurin et al. 1989; Tate 1991). When representatives and voters share membership in a subordinate group, they can create bonds of trust based specifically on the experience of membership in the subordinate group (Mansbridge 1999). Consequently, when members of the subordinate group see members from that group acting with full legitimacy in the policy process as elected officials, members of underrepresented groups feel as if they are a part of policy decisions, thus legitimizing the electoral process (Mansbridge 1999). Although the empowerment thesis suggests that descriptive representation will result in greater turnout, several scholars have pointed out that there may be several trade-offs associated with descriptive representation. Namely, in supporting descriptive representation (a larger number of elected minorities), the electorate may not reap the benefits of substantive representation (political behavior that may advance minority interests). However, the ability of elected officials to effectively represent the substantive interests of the represented is the primary function of democracy and this, according to Mansbridge (1999), should be the criterion on which descriptive representation is judged.

Evaluating the relationship between empowerment and political participation, Bobo and Gilliam (1990) define political empowerment as "the extent to which a group has received significant influence in political decision making" (378). They identify two reasons why empowerment as they define it should influence participation. First, empowerment should influence participation because people participate because they believe the benefits outweigh the costs. Second, empowerment should influence participation because macro-level aspects of a person's sociopolitical environment affect cost-benefit calculations. They also predict that empowerment will have significant positive effects on political trust, efficacy, and knowledge thereby decreasing the cost of voting and increasing participation. This is a point later reiterated by Gay (2001).

To test the influence of empowerment on turnout, Bobo and Gilliam (1990) focus on the turnout of blacks in large metropolitan cities with black mayors. Using data from the General Social Survey, they find that in cities where blacks hold more positions of political power, blacks participate at rates higher than those of similarly situated whites. Further, black empowerment is an indication of potential political responsiveness that encourages blacks to feel that participation has value. Continuing to focus on the local level, Vanderleeuw and Utter (1993) find that black candidates generate higher levels of political interest and consequently higher levels of participation among black citizens. This finding supports the political interest thesis which asserts that the presence of black candidates generates a greater level of interest in local politics and electoral participation among blacks (Vanderleeuw and Utter 1993).

In addition to issues of empowerment, the literature on descriptive representation has evaluated the importance and effect of the creation of majority-minority districts to secure the representation of blacks in Congress. Similar to the literature that focuses on representation at the local level, the literature on representation at the federal level is also varied. Tate (2003) finds that individuals represented by blacks in the House of Representatives are no more likely to vote than blacks represented by individuals belonging to other racial or ethnic groups. Using an ecological inference model to estimate the turnout of blacks and whites in House districts with and without black representatives, Gay (2001) finds that the election of an African-American to Congress is accompanied by a lower level of political engagement among whites and only rarely contributes to greater political involvement among black constituents. These findings are mirrored by Brace et al. (1995) who find that turnout is not necessarily heightened by the creation of majority-minority districts. Empowerment, defined as having a much greater chance of electing someone from one's group, does not consistently lead to greater participation by blacks. In some instances, the presence of black incumbents, as opposed to black candidates, is associated with lower turnout (Lublin and Tate 1995, 253). Although the research has not presented consistent findings regarding the relationship between participation and descriptive representation, in those elections where descriptive representation is associated with increased voter turnout in congressional districts, thousands of African-Americans who otherwise wouldn't participate, do participate (Gay 2001).

Beyond investigating the relationship between descriptive representation and participation, scholars have also investigated the relationship between racial similarity and dissimilarly between constituents and their elected representatives and constituent attitudes. Tate (2001) identifies a descriptive representation effect between the race of a member of the House of Representatives and constituents' ratings of the representative. Tate (2001) examines the impact of ratings on constituents' attitudes by four interest groups: Americans for Democratic Action (ADA), The American Federation of Labor-Congress of Industrial Organizations (AFL-CIO), and the Chamber of Commerce of the United States (CCUS), and the American Conservative Union (ACU). Taking other factors into consideration including political party, race, ideology, legislative record, committee work, legislative position staff size, and campaign activity, Tate (2001) finds a statistically significant relationship between the representative's race and the ratings of their African-American constituents. On average, African-Americans represented by African-American members of the House rated their representatives higher than African-Americans with white representatives. Tate (2001) concludes that African-Americans rated representatives of the same race higher because they believe that these representatives will act on behalf of their interests. While this assertion aligns with representative bureaucracy theory, Tate (2001) finds that party affiliation congruence had a much greater effect on representative rating than race.

Along a similar line of inquiry, Gay (2001) finds that descriptive representation influences the approval white citizens have of their Congressional representatives more than African-American citizens. Gay (2001) also finds that African-Americans were more likely to reach out to a member of Congress of the same race. Contrary to Tate (2001), Gay (2001) finds that descriptive representation has a direct effect on constituent perceptions; essentially this creates an environment in which individuals are more comfortable contacting their elected representative. Although both Tate (2001) and Gay (2001) identify race as a predictor of citizen orientation toward political institutions, focusing on elected officials who are highly accountable to the public but largely removed from regular interaction with the public does not clearly parse out how unelected officials or street-level bureaucrats influence politically charged environments and citizen perception. Furthermore, those studies that do focus on government agents who are less accountable to the public but interact with them daily tend to focus on the approval of the bureaucrat rather than the bureaucrat's influence on perceptions of government action.

Of the studies that have focused on descriptive representation and citizen interactions with bureaucrats and institutions, they find a positive relationship between descriptive representation and citizen perceptions. Keiser et al. (2004) for example investigate the relationship between race and the treatment that citizens receive from social welfare agencies. Keiser et al. (2004) find that, of the factors included in their analysis, race is the strongest predictor of bureaucratic treatment of constituents in the implementation of social services. Although they do not address the treatment of individuals relative to their race and the race of the bureaucrat that they encounter, the findings demonstrate that race matters and conditions the treatment that individuals receive when interacting with bureaucrats and bureaucratic agencies. Theobald and Haider-Markel (2008) investigate the role of descriptive representation and citizen interactions with their local police force. They find that descriptive representation legitimizes government action in the eyes of minority citizens. When minority citizens reported encountering a minority officer, they viewed the actions of the officer as legitimate more often than when they encountered a non-minority officer. Here, the interaction with a police officer who is of the same race increased the citizen's confidence in the actions of the institution. As is the case with the police force, it is plausible that group identification colors the confidence that citizens have in the electoral process. Whether a poll worker falls in the in-group or out-group in the mind of the voter may shape that citizen's perception of the legitimacy of the voting process. Examining the role of representative bureaucracy among polling locations and workers provides valuable insight into the role of representative bureaucracy in election administration. This inquiry also follows the tradition of scholars who have focused on representation in areas where racial disparities have existed historically.

Polling locations are also an appropriate site for understanding the politics of representation and three reasons illuminate this point. First, polling locations and poll workers play a pivotal role in ensuring citizens can participate in an in-person voting experience that is free and fair. Second, the United States has an extensive history of utilizing administrative discretion to perpetuate racial disparities in voting. Minorities have been disproportionately impacted by voting laws and restrictions in the past and continue to face challenges participating in democratic governance. The Jim Crow laws that dominated the former Confederate states and the continued unequal application of voting requirements (Cobb et al. 2010) are prime examples of these disparities. Lastly, polling locations differ from other sites used in representative bureaucracy studies in that the street-level bureaucrats (poll workers) interact with and provide a service to citizens from many economic, social, and political backgrounds. The focus on the polling location as the point of service delivery is remarkably different from other representative bureaucracy studies which focus on welfare agencies, law enforcement, and educational institutions—institutions that have more homogenous constituent bases. Law enforcement agencies primarily interact with those suspected of deviant behavior. Welfare agencies typically serve women and low-income individuals at a higher rate than males and upper-income citizens. Public school systems often serve young and middle-aged citizens. In contrast, polling locations engage with voters aged 18 and up from various social, ethnic, and economic backgrounds, creating a diverse grouping of citizen voters who differ on demographic characteristics.

In an election, there are nearly one million poll workers assigned to more than 100,000 polling locations across the United States (Election Assistance Commission 2016). Given this, the relationship between poll workers and voter confidence is not unexplored territory in the public administration literature. Election scholars frequently note the importance of poll workers in the election process (Atkeson and Saunders 2007; Hall et al. 2008; Hall and Stewart 2013). However, this research focuses less on voter and poll worker demographics and more on citizen evaluations of poll worker job performance. Atkeson and Saunders (2007), for example, conducted a study on the factors influencing confidence in ballot counts. They find that there was no significant relationship between the race of the voter and confidence but note that the sample did include significantly more Hispanic voters than black voters. Hall et al. (2008) advance similar research on ballot counts but focus on the performance of poll workers as the key explanatory variable. They find that the citizens who rate the quality of poll workers higher have greater confidence in their ballots being counted as intended. While they find that voter race is a statistically significant predictor of turnout, they do not include poll worker race in the model. More recently, Hall and Stewart (2013) address poll worker race. They interact voter and poll worker race and find a significant effect for blacks on election day. Essentially, black voters who had a poll worker of the same race rated the election day voting experience more positively than voters with poll workers of a different race.

Individuals who serve as poll workers do not consistently reflect the demographic composition of the US voting age population across all racial groups. Both white and African-Americans citizens are overrepresented relative to the voting age population (Fig. 10.1). On the contrary, Hispanics, Asians, and Native Americans are underrepresented among the population of poll workers. African-American and white voters are also the most likely to report interacting with a poll worker of the same race, as illustrated in Table 10.1.

Given that race is a clear indicator of shared experiences (Stewart et al. 1989, 288), voters may view the administrative action of poll workers of shared racial identity as more trustworthy than a worker of a different race. In instances where the voter and poll worker are of the same race, shared knowledge of the challenges that minority employees face in the workplace may result in a voter being more empathetic about any shortcomings and give more praise to any achievements. On the other hand, in instances where the voter does not perceive a shared racial/ethnic identity with the poll worker, the failure to identify with the poll worker may result in skepticism of the workers' actions because they lack the shared experiences that aid in forming opinions, values, and beliefs on all things political. Additionally, ensuring that voters have access to a poll worker that is the same race/ethnicity is particularly important for voters who face barriers related to English language proficiency, access to voting and registration information in languages other than English, and hostility

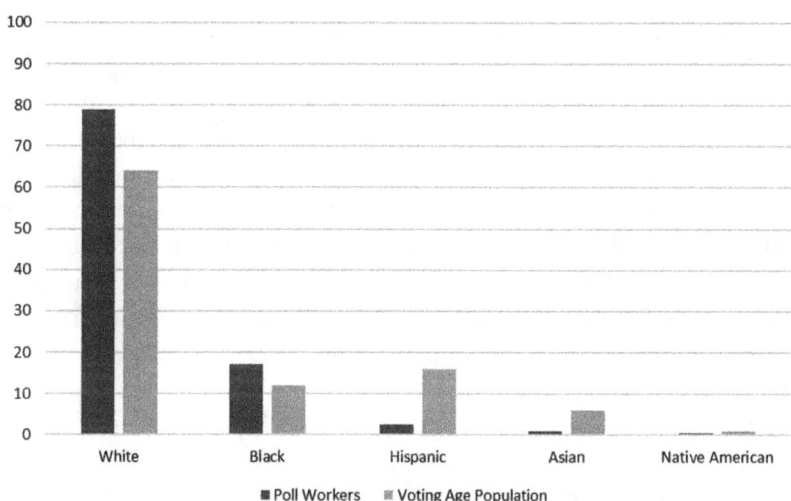

Fig. 10.1 Racial distribution of poll workers and voting age population in the United States (*Source* 2016 Survey on the Performance of American Elections; Population Division, United States Census Bureau)

Table 10.1 Descriptive statistics of poll voter/workers interactions in 2016

	White voter	Black voter	Hispanic voter	Asian voter
White poll worker	86.7	30.0	49.4	66.7
Minority poll worker	13.3	70.0	50.6	33.3
Same race poll worker	86.7	68.7	31.8	23.8

Note Numbers reported as percentages
Source 2016 Survey on the Performance of American Elections

from poll workers (Benson 2007; Hopkins 2011; Parkin and Zlotnick 2011). For these individuals, descriptive representation can not only passively make the polling place appear more open but also actively enhance voter accessibility.

Building on the descriptive representation literature, King and Barnes (2018) investigate the relationship between voter confidence in election administration and voter and poll worker racial congruence using data from the 2008 to 2016 Survey on the Performance of American

Elections (SPAE) for African-American and Hispanic voters. The SPAE is a post-election survey conducted biannually during midterm and presidential election years. The purpose of the survey is to evaluate the quality of the election administration experience from the perspective of citizens who participated in the election. The survey interviews are conducted in all 50 states and the District of Columbia with 200 respondents to represent the nation on several demographic characteristics, including education, income, race, and partisanship (Stewart 2017). Focusing on confidence in election administration is important because it focuses on a specific component of the administrative process as opposed to more general evaluations of government. Utilizing a series of interactive models, they find that for both African-American and Hispanic voters who voted in-person, having an in-person voting interaction with a poll worker who is of the same race increases confidence in election administration.

Although there is limited scholarship on the role of descriptive representation in election administration, the necessity for a racially diverse body of poll workers has been addressed by the courts. In April 1984, Charlie Harris and Mose Batie, black citizens in Pike County, Alabama who were eligible to vote filed suit on behalf of themselves and others similarly situated throughout the state. In the suit, *Harris v Graddick* (later designated *Harris v. Siegelman*), plaintiffs claimed that county officials across the state disproportionality appointed too few black persons as poll workers, which violated Sect. 2 of the Voting Rights Act of 1965. They argued that given the state's history of treating blacks as second-class citizens and the use of intimidation, humiliation, and violence to support white supremacy and segregation, many potential voters still harbored fears about entering all-white public places. Even though there were no longer legal barriers prohibiting them from registering and voting, entering a space that is operated by nothing but white poll workers remained intimidating and created a process that is not open. The suit further suggested that the presence of black poll workers could assuage these fears and create a political process that is more open for black voters in Alabama. In 1984 a preliminary injunction was issued that ordered, "the number of black persons appointed as poll officials at each polling place in the county must reasonably correspond to the percentage of black registered voters assigned to that polling place" in all but two of 67 counties (*Harris v. Graddick*, 593 F. Supp. 128 [M.D. Ala 1984]). In issuing the injunction, US District Judge Myron Thompson stated,

> The open and substantial presence of black poll officials, according to the evidence, is a significant indication to many black persons that voting places are now open to all, that black persons not only have a legal right to come and vote, *they are welcome*. And, of course, the more black poll officials there are, the greater the confidence black persons will have in the election process, and the less fear they will have about participating in that process. (*Harris v. Graddick*, 593 F. Supp. 128 [M.D. Ala 1984])

In response to the injunction, the state created a program that used biracial teams of trainers to train and certify individuals interested in serving as poll workers. Citizens who completed the program were eligible for appointment as poll workers, regardless of whether they had been nominated by political parties, which was the standard procedure before the court order (Montjoy and Brudney 1991).

Representative bureaucracy scholarship suggests that representation serves as a counterbalance to the tension created by our bureaucratic-democratic structure (Kingsley 1944). While bureaucracy is many steps removed from accountability to the public (Mosher 1968), bureaucrats regularly engage citizens in an administrative capacity. In election administration, a diverse body of election officials serves as a symbolic mechanism for racial and ethnic minorities, ensuring that voters are confident in the administrative procedures that produce political outcomes. As the demographic composition of the United States continues to change, becoming increasingly more racially and ethnically diverse, the symbolic role that diversity plays in public institutions will continue to be important. For election administration, this means recruiting a demographically diverse body of poll workers to ensure that voters encounter individuals who are demographically representative when casting a ballot.

References

Atkeson, Lonna Rae, and Kyle L. Saunders. "The Effect of Election Administration on Voter Confidence: A Local Matter?" *PS: Political Science & Politics*, 40, no. 4 (2007): 655–660.

Banducci, Susan, Todd Donovan, and Jeffrey Karp. "Minority Representation, Empowerment, and Participation." *The Journal of Politics*, 66, no. 2 (2004): 534–556.

Benson, Jocelyn Friedrichs. "¡Su voto su voz! Incorporating Voters of Limited English Proficiency into and American Democracy." *Boston College Law Review*, 48 (2007): 251–329.

Bobo, Lawrence, and Franklin Gilliam. "Race, Sociopolitical Participation, and Black Empowerment." *The American Political Science Review*, 84, no. 2 (1990): 337–393.

Brace, Kimball, Lisa Handley, Richard G. Niemi, and Harold W. Stanley. "Minority Turnout and the Creation of Majority-Minority Districts." *American Politics Quarterly*, 23, no. 2 (1995): 190–203.

Cobb, Rachael V., D. James Greiner, and Kevin M. Quinn. "Can Voter ID Laws Be Administered in a Race-Neutral Manner? Evidence from the City of Boston in 2008." *Quarterly Journal of Political Science*, 7 (2010): 1–33.

Election Assistance Commission. "Deep Dive: Poll Workers and Polling Places." 2016. https://www.eac.gov/documents/2017/11/15/eavs-deep-dive-poll-workers-andpolling-places/.

Gay, Claudine. "The Effect of Black Congressional Representation on Political Participation." *American Political Science Review*, 95, no. 3 (2001): 589–602.

———. "Spirals of Trust? The Effect of Descriptive Representation on the Relationship Between Citizens and Their Government." *American Journal of Political Science*, 46, no. 4 (2002): 717–732.

Grofman, Bernard. "Should Representatives Be Typical of Their Constituents?" In *Representation and Redistricting Issues*, edited by Bernard Grofman, Arend Lijphart, Robert B. McKay, and Howard A. Scarrow. Lexington, MA: D. C. Heath, 1982.

Gurin, Patricia, Shirley Hatchett, and James S. Jackson. *Hope and Independence: Blacks' Response to Electoral and Party Politics*. New York, NY: Russell Sage Foundation, 1989.

Hall, Thad E., and Charles Stewart III. "Voter Attitudes Toward Poll Workers in the 2012 Election." Prepared for Presentation at the Annual Meeting of the Midwest Political Science Association: Chicago, IL, 2013. Accessed November 13, 2017. http://ssrn.com/abstract=2245353.

Hall, Thad, J. Quin Monson, and Kelly D. Patterson. "Poll Workers' Job Satisfaction and Confidence." In *Democracy in the States: Experiments in Election Reform*, edited by Bruce E. Cain, Todd Donovan, and Caroline J. Tolbert, 35–51. Washington, DC: Brookings Institution, 2008.

Harris v. Graddick, 593 F. Supp. 128 (M.D. Ala 1984).

Hopkins, Daniel J. "Translating into Votes: The Electoral Impacts of Spanish-Language Ballots." *American Journal of Political Science*, 55, no. 4 (2011): 814–830.

Keiser, Lael R., Peter R. Mueser, and Seung-Whan Choi. "Race, Bureaucratic Discretion, and the Implementation of Welfare Reform." *American Journal of Political Science*, 48, no. 2 (2004): 314–327.

King, Bridgett, and Alicia Barnes. "Descriptive Representation Among Poll Workers and Citizen Confidence in Election Administration." *Election Law Journal* (2018). Early Release. https://doi.org/10.1089/elj.2018.0485.

Kingsley, J. Donald. *Representative Bureaucracy*. Yellow Springs, OH: The Antioch Press, 1944.

Long, Norton. "Bureaucracy and Constitutionalism." *The American Political Science Review*, 46, no. 3 (1952): 808–818.

Lublin, David, and Katherine Tate. "Racial Group Competition in Urban Elections." In *Classifying by Race*, edited by P. E. Peterson, 45–61. Princeton, NJ: Princeton University Press, 1995.

Mansbridge, Jane. "Should Blacks Represent Blacks and Women Represent Women? A Contingent 'Yes'." *The Journal of Politics*, 61, no. 3 (1999): 628–657.

Meier, Kenneth John. "Representative Bureaucracy: An Empirical Analysis." *American Political Science Review*, 69, no. 2 (1975): 526–542.

Meier, Kenneth John, and Lloyd G. Nigro. "Representative Bureaucracy and Policy Preferences: A Study in the Attitudes of Federal Executives." *Public Administration Review*, 36, no. 4 (1976): 458–469.

Montjoy, R. S., and J. L. Brudney. "Volunteers in the Delivery of Public Services: Hidden Costs and Benefits." *The American Review of Public Administration*, 21, no. 4 (1991): 327–344.

Mosher, Frederick Camp. *Democracy and the Public Service*. New York, NY: Oxford University Press, 1968.

Muller, Edward N. "The Representation of Citizens by Political Authorities: Consequences for Regime Support." *American Political Science Review*, 64, no. 4 (1970): 1149–1166.

Parkin, Michael, and Frances Zlotnick. "English Proficiency and Latino Participation in US Elections." *Politics & Policy*, 39, no. 4 (2011): 515–537.

Pitkin, Hanna F. *The Concept of Representation*. Berkeley, CA: University of California Press, 1967.

Stewart, Charles. *2016 Survey of the Performance of American Elections*. Harvard Dataverse, 2017. https://dataverse.harvard.edu/dataset.xhtml?persistentId=doi:10.7910/DVN/Y38VIQ.

Stewart, Joseph, Jr., Robert E. England, and Kenneth J. Meier. "Black Representation in Urban School Districts: From School Board to Office to Classroom." *The Western Political Quarterly*, 42, no. 2 (1989): 287–305.

Tate, Katherine. "Black Political Participation in the 1984 and 1988 Presidential Elections." *The American Political Science Review*, 85, no. 4 (1991): 1159–1176.

———. "The Political Representation of Blacks in Congress: Does Race Matter?" *Legislative Studies Quarterly*, 26, no. 4 (2001): 623–638.

———. *Black Faces in the Mirror*. Princeton, NJ: Princeton University Press, 2003.

Theobald, Nick A., and Donald P. Haider-Markel. "Race, Bureaucracy, and Symbolic Representation: Interactions Between Citizens and Police." *Journal of Public Administration Research and Theory*, 19, no. 2 (2008): 409–426.

Vanderleeuw, James, and Glenn Utter. "Voter Roll-Off and the Electoral Context: A Test of Two Theses." *Social Science Quarterly*, 74, no. 3 (1993): 664–673.

Bridgett A. King Ph.D., is an assistant professor and Director of the Master of Public Administration Program at Auburn University. She teaches graduate and undergraduate courses in state institutions and policy, public policy, and diversity in public administration. Her research focuses on political participation, voter disenfranchisement, and citizen perceptions of the electoral system. Formerly a voting rights researcher in the Democracy Program at the Brennan Center for Justice at New York University, she contributes regularly to the Election Center Certified Election/Registration Administrator Program (CERA).

11

Election Costs: A Study of North Carolina

Martha Kropf and JoEllen V. Pope

Introduction

The Help America Vote Act of 2002 (HAVA) paved the way for more centralized collection of election data in the United States. Every two years, the federal government collects data from every state about as many election jurisdictions (counties or townships) as possible. The Election Administration and Voting Survey (EAVS) collects a variety of data such as voter turnout, voter registration, number of provisional votes cast and counted, early voting, the types of voting equipment used, and even information about the number of poll workers each jurisdiction utilized for the implementation of elections. The survey helped to centralize a process, which at that point had been hyper-decentralized. Yet, the amount that local jurisdictions or states spent administering elections was not a part of the data collection effort and, to a certain extent, remains a mystery to scholars and policymakers. In this chapter, we discuss the challenges inherent in collecting data

---

M. Kropf (✉) · J. V. Pope
University of North Carolina at Charlotte, Charlotte, NC, USA
e-mail: mekropf@uncc.edu

© The Author(s) 2020
M. Brown et al. (eds.), *The Future of Election Administration*, Elections, Voting, Technology, https://doi.org/10.1007/978-3-030-14947-5_11

concerning the costs of election administration as well as efforts that different groups have made to collect these data and focus in particular on research on the 100 North Carolina counties in this regard.

In particular, collecting cost and budgeting data in the United States has been an effort within the "issue network"[1] of those interested in improving elections including nonprofit interest groups, local and state election administrators, government agencies and of course, university professors. Herein, we use that term.

Why Collect Cost Data?

Many consider election cost data potentially valuable because they can help policymakers estimate whether our elections are run consistently with international standards (López-Pintor and Fischer 2005). Further understanding the cost can answer the question, "Are legislative bodies—most particularly local county commissions—providing enough funding for credible elections?" Related, an ongoing problem is the cost of voting equipment, as equipment purchased soon after the 2000 election will need replacement—having a framework for comparison of costs will be vital moving forward (e.g., Gibson 2018). Not only that, such data will provide local election officials with information they can use to advocate for the use of administrative innovations such as vote centers, which research indicates may be less costly under certain conditions (Hall et al. 2012; Stein and Vonnahme 2009). These data might also be used to estimate the costs and benefits of various methods of elections including controversial proposals such as requiring voter identification for voting.[2]

---

[1] Political scientist Hugh Heclo (1978) coined this term to denote sometimes highly complex groups including policymakers of various levels (local, state, and federal) as well as interest groups and scholars who work in given policy area.

[2] The National Conference of State Legislatures published an issue brief detailing some of the costs of implementing photo identification laws, see http://www.ncsl.org/documents/legismgt/elect/Voter_ID_Costs_June2014.pdf, last accessed October 7, 2018 (see NCSL 2018a, b).

Financial data estimating costs to run elections will also allow scholars and policymakers to analyze the extent to which election outputs are related to the amount that is spent on elections in a locality. Voter turnout generally, turnout among specific groups such as voters with disabilities (see Schur et al. 2017), voter registration, residual votes, and provisional votes cast and counted are all examples of visible measures of election outputs.[3] Like all outputs, those related to election administration vary in the degree to which election administrators can affect them.

For example, using North Carolina audited expenditure reports as well as data from the University of North Carolina School of Government reports concerning salaries of local election directors for the period 1994–2012,[4] Kropf and her colleagues examine the question of organizational and management capacity, measured by the total amount spent in each office and election director salary, respectively. Scholars had long suggested that measures of capacity were necessary for a full analysis of such outputs; however, scholars had not been able to put a measurement to capacity other than assuming that the size of the county was its equivalent (Ansolabehere and Stewart 2005; Knack and Kropf 2003; Stewart 2006).

What is the effect of these types of capacity on voter turnout and residual votes using these measures of cost? Kropf and her colleagues found that voter turnout in North Carolina is affected by both the election director's salary and the other expenses reported by county over the time period studied. Residual votes were only affected by the expenses reported in the county.

---

[3]For a more thorough discussion of these various measures, see Burden and Stewart (2014).

[4]In North Carolina, each county has a bipartisan Board of Elections appointed by the Governor as well as a hired election director. The election director has the responsibility for the day-to-day operations of the election office, subject to Board oversight. Note that the composition of the Board during the period of the Kropf et al. (n.d.) study was three members (two of one party, one of the other), but has recently changed to a four-person board (two of each political party, see https://www.newsobserver.com/news/local/article203641864.html, last accessed October 7, 2018).

Challenges in Collecting Financial Data

Following the 2000 election, scholars quickly noted a number of challenges in locating these data—accounting standards, calculations, and tracking for such data inevitably would vary greatly across the more than 10,000 local election jurisdictions (Hale et al. 2015; Kropf 2016).[5] Furthermore, scholarship acknowledged that a number of offices within counties and townships were responsible for various aspects of elections (GAO 2016). For example, in more than a few states the responsibility for various election functions is divided among more than one local office (Kimball and Kropf 2006, 1266; see also Hale et al. 2015).[6]

Another challenge is that those interested in election administration have observed that deciding what counted as "costs" was not entirely clear from a measurement perspective (Mohr et al. 2018; 2019a, b; GAO 2016[7]). Do we need costs of particular inputs, total costs (including, for example, pension and insurance for election employees), or some combination of both? From a cost accounting perspective, the election office may borrow services from other offices in the county such as the use of a server or human resource functions (Mohr 2017; Mohr et al. 2018). Finally, a purely practical problem arises related to tracking costs—from where would one collect these data?—Budget reports? Expenditure reports? Simply asking local or state officials for the information? The hyper-decentralized nature of elections makes the challenge of gathering data a perplexing problem.

Cost is also separate from the question "who ultimately pays the bill for elections?" In 2018, the National Conference of State Legislatures released an important report that identified the responsibilities for

---

[5]Election expert Kimball Brace estimates there are approximately 10,072 election jurisdictions in the United States. For the vast majority of states, the local election jurisdiction is the county (3140). In the Northeast (Connecticut, Maine, Massachusetts, New Hampshire, Rhode Island, and Vermont), the local election jurisdiction is the township (1620). Elections are also operated in more than 5000 townships in the Midwest (Brace 2013).

[6]Other states with more than one office in each election jurisdiction running elections also include Connecticut, Mississippi, and New Jersey, among others (see Kimball and Kropf 2006).

[7]https://www.gao.gov/assets/680/678131.pdf, last accessed September 28, 2018.

payment for elections. Approximately two-thirds of the states reimburse localities for some part of some types of elections; these arrangements are not uniform. Localities, typically counties, may also "charge" smaller subdivisions (municipalities, townships, school districts, etc.) within their jurisdiction for conducting elections, and these charging practices may also be specified by state law. The administration of these arrangements is also likely cataloged through inter-local agreements, which themselves may be incredibly difficult to collect on a nationwide basis.

What Is the Cost of Elections?

While seemingly a simple question, "cost" is actually quite complicated and comprises both direct and indirect expenses; cost may include equipment depreciation and debt servicing as well (Mohr 2017). This complexity also exists in other countries (López-Pintor and Fisher 2005). And, although most local election officials will say that the biggest direct expense of an election is the cost of the poll workers, in an undetermined number of localities, the regular staff and their benefits can cost much more. The regular staff does the work of elections not just on election day, but also between elections. Thus, how one measures the "cost" of elections may depend on what one wants to know about the cost of elections.

Some of the first work to be broadly publicized was the report released shortly after the 2000 election by the Caltech/MIT Voting Technology Project (2001). The Caltech-MIT report considered inputs in calculating how much elections cost: "labor, maintenance, storage, and acquisition of equipment, supplies (such as printing), information systems, and rental space" (2001, 49). Democracy Fund's Tammy Patrick, first as the Federal Compliance Officer for Maricopa County, AZ, contributed to the national conversation. She noted that there are a variety of direct election expenses that many do not consider such as "processing of write-in candidates on ballots, a county deputy on call for potential election security calls, and troubleshooting hotlines and other communications in case of troubles on Election Day" (Kropf 2016, 43).

There have been many other important efforts aimed at understanding how much money we spend on elections. However, much of that effort had been tightly focused on either a small number of jurisdictions[8] (Montjoy 2010) or certain functions such as the cost of election centers or types of convenience voting (Burden et al. 2012; Folz 2014; Hall et al. 2012; Hamilton 1988; Stein and Vonnahme 2009). Nonprofit organizations such as the Brennan Center (2006) have also attempted to help election policymakers (both state and local election officials) by estimating costs of particular inputs, such as voting equipment, done in the aftermath of the 2000 elections when states and localities were making basic decisions about modernizing voting equipment. Other organizations such as the Pew Center on the States have conducted case studies of various states in order to understand costs.[9] Still others such as California Forward and the Accountability in Colorado Elections Project have endeavored to make cost data transparent to the public.[10] For example, the state of Colorado posts many of the county election costs on their Web site. Colorado is able to obtain costs from each of the counties because they reimburse counties when there are state questions on the local ballots—but make a condition of the reimbursement that counties must provide data on their election costs.

However, while the *cost of an election* is an important part of the cost, it is not the *cost of elections*.[11] We define the cost of an election as simply the cost of the personnel, equipment, and supplies needed to conduct an election during the relatively brief period of time when people are voting. By contrast, we define the cost of elections as the cost of

---

[8]It is important to understand that smaller-scale efforts can provide a key understanding of the actual costs of elections, including costs shared, costs of various offices in elections, and other details that larger-scale examinations have not yet been able to tap.

[9]See, for example, http://www.pewtrusts.org/en/research-and-analysis/articles/2013/03/19/the-cost-of-the-2012-general-election-in-wisconsin, last accessed July 12, 2018.

[10]See http://cafwd.org/reporting/entry/website-allows-californians-to-explore-the-costs-of-running-an-election, last accessed July 12, 2018. See also http://www.sos.state.co.us/pubs/elections/ACE/index.html, last accessed July 12, 2018.

[11]Thanks to Judd Choate, Director, Division of Elections, Colorado Department of State (from personal interview with Choate, May 10, 2018).

all election administration that includes the cost of the election and the additional costs of maintaining and securing the voter registration database; updating it with motor vehicle license DMV and military records; updating, testing, and securing the voting equipment; and training election officials throughout the year. In sum, the cost of elections is greater than the cost of an election.

Only recently have scholars uncovered election finance panel data for entire states—all the election jurisdictions within a state over a time period. Previous published work has focused only on California (Hill 2012). Hill (2012) examined the expenditure data within a "public sector cost model" analyzing supply (e.g., voting equipment) and demand factors (e.g., population size and socioeconomic description of county residents) to discover what drove costs of elections. Recently, Mohr et al. (2018) uncovered the same expenditure reports for North Carolina, referred to as Annual Financial Information Reports (AFIRs).[12] The AFIRs are based upon the Comprehensive Annual Financial Reports (CAFRs) that NC counties are required to produce.[13] The audited financial statements vary in their level of detail of expenditures.[14] They often include information about how much "Elections" spends in a county. North Carolina is a relatively "clean" state from a measurement perspective; because one office in each county administers the elections, it is somewhat easier to identify in the reports how much money is spent. Such reports make it possible to estimate the cost of running an election (and associated in-between times) and compare those total costs to the costs of an election (that is to say, the period of time during which people vote).

Budgets and these expense reports measure different concepts, as Mohr and his colleagues were able to show (Mohr et al. 2019a). Mohr and his colleagues compared the audited expenditure data from

---

[12]https://www.nctreasurer.com/slg/lfm/forms-instructions/Pages/Annual-Financial-Information-Report.aspx.

[13]CAFRS are the audited financial statements presented in accordance with generally accepted accounting principles in the United States.

[14]There is currently an effort to collect these statements for other election jurisdictions (counties and townships in the United States) with funding from the MIT Data Science Lab (2017–2019). See Mohr et al. (2018) for a preliminary report of these data.

Table 11.1 Descriptive statistics for election administration expenditures versus Colorado election cost 2013–2015[a]

	N	Mean	Std deviation	Minimum	Maximum
Election administration—source: CAFR	54	274,921	460,544	15,117	2,235,830
Election cost—source: ACE[b]	192	142,493	267,747	3874	1,720,438

[a]Paired $t=4.002$, $p<0.001$
[b]ACE accessed http://www.sos.state.co.us/pubs/elections/ACE/index.html
Table taken from Mohr et al. (2018)

2013 to 2015 with the cost of the election published on the Colorado ACE Web site. They note the two are statistically significantly different—neither are wrong, just different. Table 11.1 displays the range of the data collected in Colorado election jurisdictions for this period, for "Election Administration" and "Election" as reported in the CAFRs and ACE, respectively. The CAFRs reveal an average cost of $274,921, which the ACE Web site reports a cost of $142,493.

The North Carolina team has also generated research showing that there is great variation among counties within the state of North Carolina in terms of spending as reported in the audited CAFRs. Figure 11.1 displays this variation over time within North Carolina.

This spending variation over time raises an important question for local election officials and scholars alike: What is the source of the differences? In North Carolina, county commissions are responsible for the amount budgeted for elections. And, while it is clear that for a variety of reasons, the amount budgeted and the amount spent are often different,[15] Mohr and his colleagues show that politics does affect the amount spent in counties—specifically the politics of the county commission:

---

[15]Mohr et al. (2019b) examined data from five states using the above-mentioned CAFRs data and show that the fiscal environment influences election administration budget, spending, and results in difference between the two.

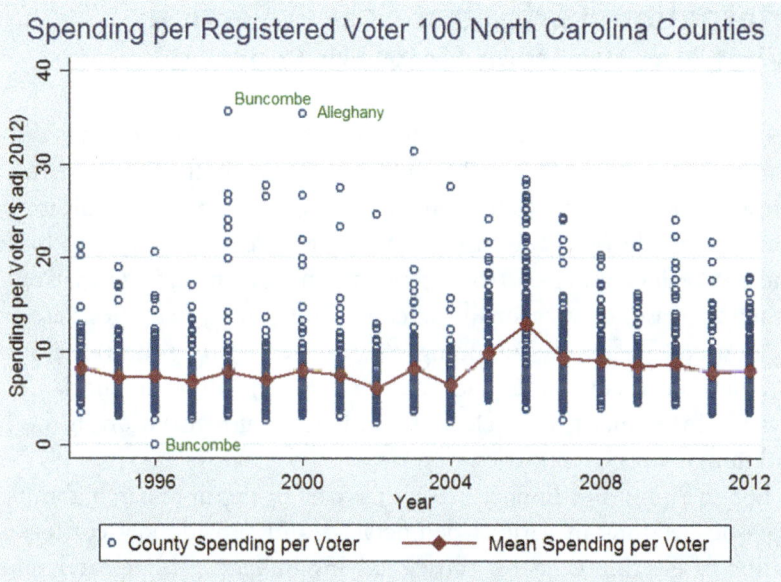

Fig. 11.1 Spending per registered voter in 100 North Carolina counties

We find that Republican county commissions spend significantly less than non-Republican commissions once they have a significant majority of the voters in their county that vote for the Republican presidential candidate. Specifically, when the percentage of the electorate voting for the Republican presidential candidate reaches 57.6%, the interaction is significant and the Republican county commissions are spending more than 10% less than their non-Republican peer county commissions. (Mohr et al. 2019a)

The research does indicate the importance of politics when analyzing spending, which is not factored into previous work using the CAFRs data. Hill (2012) studies the factors in spending as well but examines a public sector cost model—or more specifically, a production model—for which the Mohr et al. (2019a) study finds little support.

International Efforts at Cost Collection: What Has the Issue Network Learned?

Recent interest in the cost of elections is not limited to the United States. James and Jervier (2017) survey local election authorities in Great Britain to discover how much they spend. The data indicate that many local election authorities are under pressure and over budget due to the increasing cost of elections paired with budgets that reflect either decreases or very small increases. Thus, many activities perceived as "non-core" activities including voter outreach and educational activities have been cut. James and Jervier (2017, 7) call for a "fundamental review of the financing of elections and electoral registration in the UK and in many other countries."

López-Pintor and Fischer (2005) provide in-depth research about the costs of elections in various democracies and provide key conceptualization of election costs for those studying budgets. The research shows that there are differing costs depending on the status of the democracy (stable, transitioning, or post-conflict). Other scholars such as Aiyede and Aregbeyen (2012) examine single years in emerging democracies such as Nigeria. Aiyede and Aregbeyen (2012) also examine non-monetary costs such as loss of life due to election administration. Of course, the status of democracy is not an issue about which those studying US election costs must worry.

Conclusion

All in all, scholarship indicates that the greater the amount expended in an election office, the smaller the number of residual votes and the greater the voter turnout. With more funds, local election officials can do more voter education and assist voters with disabilities. Research to date also agrees that when a jurisdiction has a larger population, the cost per voter drops—that is, we have "economies of scale" in elections. Finally, research indicates that county commission politics affect the amount that local election directors are able to spend.

Despite recent data collection efforts and recent scholarship, it appears that there is still much to learn when it comes to the cost of elections, especially in the United States. Yet it is vital that we learn more about costs if only to ensure that local election officials have adequate funds to be able to run a credible and legitimate election.

In terms of collecting these data, and putting them to use to assist local officials, many issues remain a vexing challenge. How can we calculate the cost of elections if there is more than one county or township office that is responsible for different aspects of elections? What if accounting standards vary? Furthermore, while the National Conference of State Legislatures has made progress, we need to learn more about the complex array of intergovernmental agreements used to fund the operations of elections. All of these are important questions as scholars, election officials, and interest groups move ahead. Research will continue to progress on both a small scale and a large scale.

References

Aiyede, E. R., and O. Aregbeyen. "The Cost of the 2011 General Elections in Nigeria." *Journal of African Elections*, 11, no. 1 (2012): 136–152.

Ansolabehere, Stephen and Charles Stewart. "Residual Votes Attributable to Technology." *Journal of Politics*, 67, no. 2 (2005): 365–389.

Brace, Kimball. "Basic Election Administration Facts Powerpoint." 2013. https://www.electiondataservices.com/research-services/. Accessed July 5, 2018.

Brennan Center for Justice at NYU Law School. *The Machinery of Democracy: Voting System Security, Accessibility, Usability, and Cost*. 2006. https://www.brennancenter.org/sites/default/files/publications/Machinery_Democracy.pdf.

Burden, Barry C., and Charles Stewart III. "Introduction to the Measure of American Elections." In *The Measure of American Elections*, edited by Barry C. Burden and Charles Stewart III, 1–39. Cambridge: Cambridge University Press, 2014.

Burden, Barry C., David T. Canon, Kenneth R. Mayer, and Donald P. Moynihan. "The Effect of Administrative Burden on Bureaucratic Perception of Policies: Evidence from Election Administration." *Public Administration Review*, 72, no. 5 (2012): 741–751.

Caltech/MIT Voting Technology Project. *Voting: What Is, What Could Be.* 2001. http://www.vote.caltech.edu/2001report.htm.

Folz, David H. "Vote Centers as a Strategy to Control Election Administration Costs: Findings From a Pilot Project." *SAGE Open*, (January 2014). https://doi.org/10.1177/2158244014525414.

General Accounting Office. "Elections: Issue Related to Registering Voters and Administering Elections." 2016. https://www.gao.gov/assets/680/678131.pdf.

Gibson, Nadine. "Maintaining the Machinery of Democracy: Assessing the Quality of Voting Equipment in the 21st Century." Paper for the 2018 Election Sciences, Reform, and Administration (ESRA) Conference, University of Wisconsin-Madison, July 26–27, 2018.

Hale, Kathleen, Robert Montjoy, and Mitchell Brown. *Administering Elections: How American Elections Work*. New York: Palgrave, 2015.

Hall, Stephen R., Joseph Losco, and Raymond Scheele. "Convenient Turnout: A Case Study of the Indiana Vote Center Pilot Program." *International Journal of Business and Social Science*, 3, no. 8 (2012): 304–312.

Hamilton, Randy H. "American All-Mail Balloting: A Decade's Experience." *Public Administration Review*, 48 (1988): 860–866.

Heclo, Hugh. "Issue Networks and the Executive Establishment." In *The New American Political System*, edited by Anthony King, 87–124. Washington: The American Enterprise Institute, 1978.

Hill, Sarah A. "Election Administration Finance in California Counties." *The American Review of Public Administration*, 1242 (2012): 606–628.

James, Toby S., and Tyrone Jervier. "The Cost of Elections: The Effects of Public Sector Austerity on Electoral Integrity and Voter Engagement." *Public Money & Management*, 37 (2017): 461–468.

Kimball, David C., and Martha Kropf. "The Street-Level Bureaucrats of Elections: Selection Methods for Local Election Officials." *Review of Policy Research*, 23 (2006): 1257–1268.

Knack, Stephen and Martha Kropf. "Invalidated Ballots in the 1996 Presidential Election: A County-Level Analysis." *Journal of Politics*, 65, no. 3 (2003): 881–897.

Kropf, Martha. *Institutions and the Right to Vote in America*. New York: Palgrave, 2016.

Kropf, Martha, Zachary Mohr, JoEllen Pope, and Mary Jo Shepherd. "Capacity to Implement Policy: The Case of Election Administration in North Carolina." Unpublished manuscript, n.d.

López-Pintor, R., and J. Fischer. *Cost of Registration and Elections (CORE) Project*. Center for Transitional and Post-conflict Governance, 2005. http://aceproject.org/ace-en/focus/core/explore_topic_new. Accessed January 21, 2019.

Mohr, Zachary. *Cost Accounting in Government: Theory and Applications*. New York, NY: Taylor & Francis, 2017.

Mohr, Zachary, JoEllen Pope, Martha Kropf, and Mary Jo Shepherd. "Strategic Spending: Does Politics Influence Election Administration Expenditure?" *American Journal of Political Science*, 63 (2019a): 427–438.

Mohr, Zachary, Ahmad Hill, Martha Kropf, JoEllen Pope, and Mary Jo Shepherd. "Evaluating the Recessionary Impact on Election Administration Budgeting and Spending." Paper for the 2019 Southern Political Science Association: Austin, TX, January 16–19, 2019b.

Mohr, Zachary, Martha Kropf, JoEllen Pope, Mary Jo Shepherd, and Madison Esterle. "Election Administration Spending in Local Election Jurisdictions: Results from a Nationwide Data Collection Project." Paper for the 2018 Election Sciences, Reform, and Administration (ESRA) Conference, University of Wisconsin-Madison, July 26–27, 2018.

Montjoy, Robert S. "The Changing Nature … and Costs … of Election Administration." *Public Administration Review*, 70 (2010): 867–875.

NCSL. "The Price of Democracy: Splitting the Bill for Elections." http://www.ncsl.org/research/elections-and-campaigns/the-price-of-democracy-splitting-the-bill-for-elections.aspx. Last Modified February 14, 2018a.

———. "Election Costs: What States Pay." http://www.ncsl.org/research/elections-and-campaigns/election-costs.aspx. Last Modified August 3, 2018b.

Schur, Lisa, Mason Ameri, and Meera Adya. "Disability, Voter Turnout, and Polling Place Accessibility." *Social Science Quarterly*, 98 (2017): 1374–1390.

Stein, Robert, and Greg Vonnahme. "The Cost of Elections." Unpublished manuscript. Houston, TX: Rice University Press, 2009.

Stewart, Charles III. "Residual Vote in the 2004 Election." *Election Law Journal*, 5 (2006): 158–169.

Martha Kropf is a professor of political science and core faculty in the Public Policy Ph.D. program at the University of North Carolina at Charlotte. Kropf is the author of *Institutions and the Right to Vote in America* and co-author of *Helping America Vote: The Limits of Election Reform*. Her current research focuses on local election administration expenditures and how spending affects election outcomes, and is funded by the MIT Election Data and Science Lab.

JoEllen V. Pope is a Ph.D. Candidate in Public Policy at the University of North Carolina at Charlotte. Her dissertation titled, "Flooded with complexity: Do organizational structural complexity, coordination, and managerial discretion impact natural disaster preparedness?" provides research about the effects of organizational structure and coordination on natural disaster preparedness in higher education institutions. She has additional research and teaching interests that focus on election administration and public budgeting and finance.

Part III

Emerging and Future Issues in Election Administration

12

The Role of Election Vendors in Election Administration

Peter Lichtenheld

What, Exactly, Is an "Election Vendor?"

An election vendor is a solution provider in the election system space. That space includes voter registration, election management systems, pollbooks, electronic pollbooks, ballot printing, ballot mail handling and scanning, voting devices, tabulation software, and election night reporting. It is important to note this about election solution providers and their environs:

1. "Election systems" and "voting systems" are not the same thing. The former is comprised, in large part, of the items listed above as well as the related processes created primarily by state and local election officials. The latter is a subset of the former and is limited to ballot design software, ballot and ballot media production software, central ballot scanning software and hardware, in-person voting devices, tabulation software, and the associated processes. "Voting systems" are

P. Lichtenheld (✉)
Hart InterCivic, Austin, TX, USA
e-mail: plichtenheld@hartic.com

© The Author(s) 2020
M. Brown et al. (eds.), *The Future of Election Administration*, Elections, Voting, Technology, https://doi.org/10.1007/978-3-030-14947-5_12

also termed "tabulation systems," "vote capture systems" or even just "voting machines." See Fig. 12.1.
2. Election solution providers are intertwined into the fabric of election administration and how elections are run in the United States of America. It is this topic that this chapter concentrates on.

Election solution providers do what great Americans have done since this country was founded: They identify problems and needs and offer solutions to address those situations and make things better than they were prior to the provided solution. The solutions they offer are focused on the topic of elections, and they offer those solutions as part of a business proposition. For example, Thomas Edison's first patented invention was a vote recorder (US Patent #90,646 issued on June 1, 1869) designed to make the recording of votes in legislative bodies more efficient, because he, apparently, viewed that process as inefficient. He sold some interest in his invention to a partner for $100 and that partner went on the road to sell to legislative bodies (it does not appear that the solution was ever actually purchased by any legislative body) (Daniels 2018). Thomas Edison saw a problem, and he used his inventive genius to provide a solution. What Thomas Edison did not, apparently, consider was the actual need, or demand, for the solution he was providing. A more successful example is the lever voting machine, offered as a solution to the then-prevalent view of manual vote tabulation shenanigans, avoiding the possibility of over-voted contests (voting for more than the

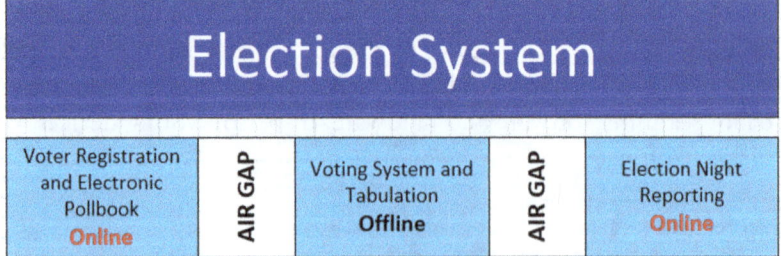

Fig. 12.1 Voting systems as part of the election system. *Note* There are many pieces of an "election system." A "voting system" is one part that deals only with vote capture and tabulation

allowable number of candidates in a contest), and automating tabulation by having the voting machine accomplish that task. The first lever machine was patented in 1889 (US Patent #415,549), and variations of lever machines were used to conduct elections across cities and counties in the United States until the 2002 era (Historical Timeline: Electronic Voting Machines and Related Voting Technology 2013).

Today's election solution provider is driven by a will to make the voting process in America "better." In general, "better" means more efficient, accurate, secure, user-friendly, reliable, and more accessible. To attempt to achieve these goals, companies that provide election solutions must be apolitical and must have the utmost business integrity and respect for the voting franchise. Election solution providers look at the United States as a whole, and each state, county, and city in the United States that conducts elections, and the election companies ask, "What is it that this location needs in the election space, and do I have a solution to fit that need? If I don't have a solution ready, is it worth the investment to build a solution to fit that need? Is there time to build the solution? Is there enough demand for a solution?" Voting systems in the United States have evolved from non-secret (influenced) hand-counted paper ballots (Zarrelli 2016), to Australian/secret hand-counted paper ballots, to lever machines and punch cards that provided voting device technology for over one hundred years with individual voting systems that lasted, in some jurisdictions, up to 40 years "Votomatic" (2019), to optical scanning machines and electronic devices with and without paper records of the voters' choices, to the current combination of much of the above plus digital scanning technologies (Historical Timeline: Electronic Voting Machines and Related Voting Technology 2013). Throughout that evolution election system providers have been supporting state and local election officials with ballot layout, ballot printing, ballot delivery, device media creation, in-person voting, by-mail/absentee voting, tabulation, election night reporting, official canvass, audits, recounts, and challenges.

There are about 3141 counties and county-equivalents in the United States (United States Geological Survey 2019). Most election systems are purchased by counties, though some are purchased on a statewide basis. Additionally, some states have a decentralized form of government where cities and other entities may or must purchase voting systems.

Even with these smaller entities included, the market for election systems, and for voting systems, is small… being a total of around 4000 jurisdictions. In addition to the small market, elections are much more complex than most people realize and that complexity is exacerbated by the myriad number of rules, laws, advisories, and edicts around elections that each state uniquely authors and sets as requirements as well as the ever-changing federal and state certification requirements that election and voting systems must meet (though the certification is mostly around voting systems and not other parts of the election system). Once a need has been identified in one or more of those 4000 jurisdictions that purchase voting systems, the election solution providers' analysis of their ability to meet that need begins. The ability to meet that need starts with the most important questions of all, "Do I know that jurisdiction?" Without knowledge of the jurisdiction and the people in charge of managing elections in the jurisdiction, it is difficult to get the appropriate grasp of the technical, training, and sustaining needs of the jurisdiction. The technical solution offered by an election solution provider needs to either match the existing and future needs of a jurisdiction or the election solution provider needs to have the capacity to build a system that does meet the technical requirements, or adapt an existing system to meet the technical requirements. Election solution providers' costs for designing, building, testing, adapting, and certifying systems are in the millions of dollars, so the targeted jurisdiction and its related market need to be viable enough to be able to have a positive return on investment (ROI) over the life of the installation greater than the election solution providers' costs of research, development, testing, certification, and marketing. Additionally, the targeted jurisdiction needs to be in the market for the same voting system that the election solution provider is designing, building, testing, adapting, and certifying once the system is ready for that market: a process which can take a long time.

Many election administrators, election officials, and election-related professionals realize the complexities, time, and costs that are involved in getting a voting system to market in the United States today, but many do not. It is an inherently challenging process, and it is one that we've arrived at because of the tenacity of election administrators and officials, the general public, and various election advocates, academics, and scholars who see the need for a robust labyrinth to ensure that only well-vetted systems are deployed for use in live elections. Not all election systems go through the rigor that voting systems do, but voting systems are where votes are captured and recorded for reporting, and it is of utmost importance to get that part right. Voting systems are generally designed to the existing or near-future federal Election Assistance Commission (EAC) standards; they take months to ideate and design and many months more to build. Designing and building a voting system includes engineering, real-world testing, customer feedback loops, and quality assurance testing of the software, security features, interfaces, usability, hardware, data input and output, and overall processes and design. When the voting system provider is comfortable that the design and quality goals are met, the system goes for independent lab testing to an EAC-approved Voting System Testing Lab (VSTL), and then with those test result reports in hand, to the EAC for certification. After an EAC approval is earned, the system then goes to states for additional review and approval or formal certification within each state and then to counties in the states where certification was earned for competition with other products for possible purchase. This is the general journey a voting system takes from ideation to the market, and you can see that it is a long journey that can take years. Other election systems, that are not voting systems, take parts of that same journey.

Election solution providers are supportive of the professionalization of election administration. Election solution providers seek to provide systems that result in voters who can vote with confidence and election administrators who can manage a problem-free election. The more competent and professional election administration is, the more likely an election is to be problem-free. Election solution providers spend a lot of time and energy conducting training for election administrators to help ensure that elections are run smoothly. Training happens at every level, from chief election official, to staff, to IT department, to poll workers, and warehouse personnel during an implementation. Training is ongoing through regular user groups, hot topic Webinars, best practices publications, and on-site trainings. Election solution providers' design systems that are meant to be easy to use for election administrators, their staff, their poll workers (the average age of which is about

70 years in the United States (Election Assistance Commission 2017)), and their electorate. Well-managed elections where voters are confident that their votes were counted as they intended and where the processes around the election and the results tabulation are comfortably transparent to all are part of the goal for election solution providers because those end results prove out that the election need was addressed and that the solution provided worked and may be replicated or adapted with other similar jurisdictions. Well-managed elections also validate the fit of the solution and the long-term relationship between the election solution provider and the jurisdiction. Election solution providers do not simply implement systems and walk away. They constantly reach out to their customers to maintain the relationship and to keep their customers' equipment and knowledge levels up to date and ready for continued success.

Election administrators across America are faced with constant challenges. There are changes to election law, rule, and code. There are local, state, and federal politics and political parties to deal with. There is little or no state or federal funding to replace aging equipment or software systems, so there are financial challenges to keeping a system running smoothly and to replacing aging systems with new technologies. There are aging systems in their jurisdictions that need to run effectively so that the election administrator can manage elections. There is often staff turnover, which means finding new people, training them and getting them up to speed on technologies and state and local processes. Part of what election solution providers do is to help election administrators negotiate this maze of challenges, remaining apolitical and keeping existing systems running well for as long as they can. Election solution providers assist election administrators in dealing with these challenges by training (and re-training) staff, assisting with process changes to keep up with new rules and by helping to keep older systems up and running while the jurisdiction works to secure funding for system upgrades. Demands for system security, accessibility, auditability, and transparency have resulted in more technologically complex solutions that require more frequent updates. Gone are the days of punch cards and lever machines, when voting systems sometimes lasted 30 or 40 years.

In recent years, cybersecurity has become a high priority in elections. It will stay as a high priority forevermore. Election system cybersecurity especially impacts those facets of election solutions that are online (Fig. 12.1). Voting systems themselves are not online but are air-gapped from the Internet. Nevertheless, voting systems must be securely built, deployed, implemented, operated, supported, and stored. Election solution providers are consultants with their customers, including on the topic of election security. Of the 3000-plus counties and county-like jurisdictions in the United States that conduct elections, less than 1000 have populations over 50,000. In general, one can estimate the number of registered voters in a county by estimating that 50% of the population falls in the "registered voter" category. Using this logic, over two-thirds of America's jurisdictions that purchase and run election systems have registered voter populations of 25,000 or fewer. One of the things that means for those two-thousand-plus jurisdictions is that they probably have limited resources with which to come up with defenses for election security threats. Many jurisdictions around the country, especially the smaller jurisdictions, simply do not have adequate resources to dedicate to the important topic of election security. The United States Election Assistance Commission (EAC), the Department of Homeland Security (DHS), various Information Sharing and Analysis Centers (ISACs), and individual state Secretary of State (SOS) and other state election official offices make a plethora of information available to local jurisdictions on the topics of election security, but just filtering through that information in itself is a burden and a chore that can be overwhelming for jurisdiction election administrators who are usually already overburdened and who may not even have full time Information Technology assistance available. While the EAC, DHS, ISACs, and SOS offices are aware of this information overload and are working on it, election solution providers work daily to keep their customers informed of the security available in their technologies and best practices for their customers. Additionally, election solution providers keep abreast of the latest cybersecurity news and updates and work to help keep the various state and federal organizations working election security informed of the election solution providers' activities related to ensuring the security of America's election systems.

Another pair of attributes that are important to all election systems are efficiency and speed. Efficiency and speed do not trump accuracy or security by any means, but they are seldom-discussed priorities in election system solutions. Without efficiency voters cannot vote, poll workers cannot function, central scanning of by-mail and absentee ballots cannot get accomplished in a timely manner, people wait in lines, etc. Without speed, the results don't make the evening news. And, making the evening news is important. People lose face, and maybe their jobs, for being the "last in the state to report," for example, but, more importantly, there is simply a great deal of pressure to get election night reports out.[1] That means that there is pressure on poll workers to finish their electronic pollbook and tabulation equipment close out procedures efficiently, on warehouse and support staff to bring equipment in and process it quickly, and on election administrators to tabulate not only accurately, but quickly so that the reports can be posted to whatever Election Night Reporting (ENR) tool the jurisdiction is using (which had also better work efficiently and be user-friendly for media and the general public). So, election solution providers make certain to build systems that are efficient, user-friendly, and fast as they work to design and bring to market new and better technologies.

When a jurisdiction purchases election system technologies, they are not buying a commodity. They are buying a sophisticated technology that is probably expected to last ten years or more and is expected to adapt to changing voting environments within its lifespan. It may be that the jurisdiction buying the technology does not have election day vote centers at the time of purchase, for example, but adopts vote centers within the life of that technology. The technology is expected to be able to adapt, and the solution provider is expected to give sound advice on how to make the adaptations work. The solution provider is expected

---

[1] Sarah Elms. "Lucas Co. Second-Slowest in State to Report Election Results." https://www.toledoblade.com/local/politics/2018/11/07/lucas-county-slow-second-slowest-ohio-report-election-results/stories/20181107120. Last Modified November 7, 2018; "San Diego County was California's Last County to Report Election Results." *News 10*. San Diego. https://www.10news.com/news/san-diego-politics/san-diego-county-was-california-s-last-county-to-report-all-precincts. Last Modified November 7, 2018.

to be, and should be, a consultant on how best to use the solution provided over time as the environment changes. There are constant touches, hand-holding, and working relationships to support and sustain election systems as they age and the voting environment matures. Election solution providers offer that hand-holding and give their customers a one-stop resource for everything related to the system solution. In other words, election solution providers, when they are performing the functions that they should be performing, provide a "one call" solution. This means, for example, that the election solution provider helps election administrators to be efficient and to avoid wasting their time dealing with an overabundance of various commercial-off-the-shelf vendors, sometimes finger-pointing at each other, in order to solve problems.

Purchasing a new election system is a complex process that has to take into account the financial sources available, the purchase processes available or required, the best system type fit for the situation and voting types in place in the jurisdiction, the technologies available, the relative ages of the technologies available, and the relationships or potential for positive relationships with the election solution providers vying for the business. Finances seldom come from federal sources (the 2002 Help America Vote Act being a historical exception), so state and local funds must be used to lease or purchase election systems. Request for Proposal (RFP), Request for Information (RFI), Request for Quote (RFQ), or direct lease or purchase as a sole source must be determined. The current and future voting practices for the state (by-mail, early voting, vote centers, traditional election day precinct polling place voting, or a combination) must be taken into consideration. The voting technologies available must be analyzed and compared: optical scan paper, digital scan paper, electronic voting, electronic voting with paper trail, etc. The relative ages (first introduced to the market, last updated, etc.) of the technologies available must be taken into consideration along with the purchasing jurisdictions' emphasis on innovation and reliability as well as the "freshness" of the technology. A bolt-on solution that is an upgrade of an older election system may not include the most recent technological or security features or may include some newer features and security but also include weaknesses inherent in the old platform, for example. And, finally, the election system providers' depth of knowledge, experience in similar jurisdictions, and reputation must be considered as part of a purchase decision.

Election system providers sustain election systems across America and constantly strive to help to make our nation's voting systems and processes better. Election systems, as technologies go, are long-lived, partly because they are publicly funded and there is not an appetite for constant updating of the solutions, financially, and partly because election system providers plan and build systems that are robust and have actively managed supply chains to enable long-lived products. Election solution providers are not just "vendors" selling commodities to the approximately 4000 jurisdictions in the United States buying election systems, but apolitical partners who value the integrity of the voting franchise and who work hand-in-hand with our nation's dedicated election administrators; helping to run secure, accurate, transparent, accessible elections using modern, sustainable, technologies.

References

Daniels, Patricia. "Thomas Edison One of the World's Most Famous Inventors." *Thought Co.* https://www.thoughtco.com/thomas-edison-1779841. Last Modified January 18, 2018.
Election Assistance Commission. "EAVS Deep Dive: Poll Workers and Polling Places." 2017. https://www.eac.gov/documents/2017/11/15/eavs-deep-dive-poll-workers-and-polling-places/. Accessed January 2, 2019.
"Historical Timeline: Electronic Voting Machines and Related Voting Technology." *ProCon.* https://votingmachines.procon.org/view.timeline.php?timelineID=000021. Last Modified July 22, 2013.
United States Geological Survey. "How Many Counties Are There in the United States?" https://www.usgs.gov/faqs/how-many-counties-are-there-united-states. Accessed January 14, 2019.
"Votomatic" Verified Voting. https://www.verifiedvoting.org/resources/voting-equipment/ess/votamatic/. Accessed January 3, 2019.
Zarrelli, Natalie, "Election Fraud in the 1800s Involved Kidnapping and Forced Drinking." *Atlas Obscura.* https://www.atlasobscura.com/articles/election-fraud-in-the-1800s-involved-kidnapping-and-forced-drinking. Last Modified September 7, 2016.

Peter Lichtenheld is the vice president of customer success for Hart InterCivic. Prior to coming to Hart as a training manager in January 2001, Lichtenheld was a teacher for 19 years. Originally from Wisconsin, Lichtenheld has a bachelor's degree from Beloit College and a master's degree from the University of Texas at Austin. He is a graduate of the Auburn University/Election Center certified elections registration administrator program.

13

Election Integrity in Ensuring Accuracy

Christy McCormick

What is election integrity? There are many views on what it means—a secure electoral process run without corruption and/or irregularities, voting machines that cannot be tampered with or hacked, procedures for verifying either voter eligibility and/or election results—among other expected norms. Indeed, it includes all these views and more. Election integrity is the entire process from voter registration to election certification, and everything in between, which consistently follows recognized best practices and clear standards used to govern the administration of elections.[1] Simply put, it includes everything that election

---

[1]Internationally, the foundation of election standards is in Article 21(3) in the *Universal Declaration of Human Rights* (1948). The declaration states, "[t]he will of the people shall be the basis of the authority of government; this will shall be expressed in periodic and genuine elections which shall be by universal and equal suffrage and shall be held by secret vote or by equivalent free voting procedures." These commitments were further developed in Article 25 of the UN International Covenant for Civil and Political Rights (ICCPR of 1966), namely the need for: periodic elections at regular intervals; universal suffrage that includes all sectors of society; equal

---

C. McCormick (✉)
United States Election Assistance Commission,
Silver Spring, MD, USA
e-mail: cmccormick@eac.gov

© The Author(s) 2020
M. Brown et al. (eds.), *The Future of Election Administration*, Elections, Voting, Technology, https://doi.org/10.1007/978-3-030-14947-5_13

officials do—and almost everything they do is to assure citizens that the vote is free, fair, and honest. This chapter will discuss some of the various procedures and policies that election officials should attend to in order to reinforce and sustain election integrity, and ultimately voter faith and confidence in elections.

The passage of the Help America Vote Act of 2002 (HAVA) was a huge step in the effort to address integrity in American elections. The administrative issues that thrust the presidential election of 2000 into the media limelight caused Congress and the public to acknowledge a national need to modernize and professionalize the election field. Constitutionally, the authority and responsibility to conduct elections is left to the states,[2] and each state had, and still has, its own laws, rules, and procedures that govern qualifications for voting and the electoral process. It wasn't until the second half of the twentieth century, outside of the ratification of the Fifteenth[3] and Nineteenth[4] Amendments to the Constitution in 1870 and 1920, respectively, that the federal government inserted itself into the process of America's elections.[5] Until the National Voter Registration Act of 1993 (NVRA), a little more than 25 years ago, federal intrusion into elections centered on eliminating discrimination in voting and attempting to make it more accessible for certain groups of citizens. With the NVRA, Congress decided to take steps to assure that citizens would have ample opportunity to register to vote and established uniform procedures for maintaining voter

---

suffrage, in the idea of one-person, one-vote; the right to stand for public office and contest elections; the rights of all eligible electors to vote; the use of a secret ballot process; genuine elections; elections that reflect the free expression of the will of the people.

[2]U.S. Constitution Article 1, Sections. 2 and 4.

[3]The 15th Amendment to the Constitution provided that the "right of citizens of the United States to vote shall not be denied or abridged by the United States or by any state on account of race, color, or previous condition of servitude."

[4]The 19th Amendment to the Constitution guaranteed women the right to vote.

[5]The Enforcement Acts during reconstruction attempted to enforce suffrage of African-American men guaranteed by the 15th Amendment, but ultimately failed. See Stephen Cresswell, "Enforcing the Enforcement Acts: The Department of Justice in Northern Mississippi, 1870–1890." *The Journal of Southern History*, 53, no. 3 (August 1987): 421–440.

registration lists.[6] Less than ten years later, the need for more effective election administration and support from the federal government was recognized through the passage of HAVA, which in addition to authorizing the appropriation of funding to help improve elections, established the Election Assistance Commission (EAC), and required states to adopt minimum standards for voting systems, provisional ballots, voter information, statewide interactive computerized voter registration databases, verification information for voter registration applicants, and identification procedures for first-time voters who register to vote by mail. HAVA was intended to bolster election integrity in the United States, and it has been somewhat successful in achieving it, but much work remains.

It is not an overstatement to say that election integrity is the foundation of a legitimate government. The co-chairs of the Commission on Federal Election Reform, former president Jimmy Carter and former White House Chief of Staff and Secretary James A. Baker, stated in their letter prefacing the Commission's report:

> Elections are the heart of democracy. They are the instrument for the people to choose leaders and hold them accountable. At the same time, elections are a core public function upon which all other government responsibilities depend. If elections are defective, the entire democratic system is at risk (Commission on Federal Election Reform 2005, ii).

Without trust and faith in the process that connects the people with its governing officials, elections fail and democracy fails. So how do we achieve election integrity and maintain it?

First and foremost, election officials must conduct elections transparently, with appropriate measures for security and privacy.

---

[6]The NVRA exempted some states on the basis of either not having voter registration, or having same-day registration: North Dakota (no voter registration), Idaho, Maine, Minnesota, New Hampshire, Wisconsin, and Wyoming. Maine lost its exemption when it ended same-day registration in 2011, though it subsequently reenacted same-day registration by referendum later that year.

The availability of timely information and clarity about the implementation of laws, rules, and procedures along with open decision-making are the keys to assuring citizens that they can trust that the election process is genuine and fair and that nothing is being hidden from view. To have confidence in elections, voters must believe that the administrators are not engaging in any unfair dealing or that decisions are being made on an arbitrary or partisan basis. Transparency serves as a safeguard and deterrent to corruption and is essential to election integrity.

Election officials wear many hats, but one of the most important is to be a good communicator and public relations manager. Voter education is vital and election information must be readily available and accurate with regard to qualifications, dates, locations, instructions, the processes used, security of the systems, data privacy standards, and much more. Citizens must be afforded an opportunity to ask questions and be provided the answers they seek. Positive interactions with elections officials, especially at the local level, go far in establishing trust and confidence.

Voter registration and list maintenance has been called "the backbone of elections,"[7] and is the foundation of election integrity (Ansolabehere and Hersh 2014). Unfortunately, it has been the subject of extensive litigation from both the political left and right, especially over the past decade (see Table 13.1). The NVRA, attempted to provide a clear standard for voter list maintenance practices, but is in desperate need of being updated to reflect the vast changes in technology that have occurred since the Act was passed. Questions and varying interpretations on how the NVRA should be applied currently leave local registrars and state election officials unsure of the steps they are allowed

---

[7]"Voter registration is the backbone of election administration in the United States. Registration lists are used to establish eligibility to vote, to determine the offices for which one can vote, to communicate to citizens when elections occur and where and how to vote, to validate people at the polls, and to audit elections after the fact. ... Election administrators and the public as a whole place a premium on accuracy of the lists. Poorly maintained lists can make it difficult for administrators to communicate with voters or to run the election at the polls. Errors in the lists used by the local election offices can prevent some legitimate voters from participating and may be abused by those seeking to perpetrate voter fraud. Election administrators devote considerable effort to continual management of the voter lists. This is a difficult task, especially in less well-staffed offices, and errors do occur. Any effort to improve the quality of lists can be greatly informed by data about the accuracy of the voter files" (Ansolabehere and Hersh 2014).

to take and when they may take them. Alarmingly, some jurisdictions completely neglect compliance with the law, leaving lists sloppy and out-of-date. Clean lists equal clean elections.

HAVA predicated the use of federal funds by states to improve elections, including implementing a computerized statewide voter registration system. The systems funded by HAVA are now ten to fifteen years old,[8] which is ancient in terms of technology. While some states have made improvements to their systems, most of the systems across the country need to be updated.

HAVA also incorporated list maintenance procedures from the NVRA and required that, "[t]he State election system shall include provisions to ensure that voter registration records in the State are accurate and are updated regularly" (Help America Vote Act of 2002).

Even with the establishment of statewide registration systems, problems with the accuracy of voter lists such as incorrect voter information (Pew Center on the States 2012), jurisdictions with inflated voter rolls (Election Assistance Commission 2016),[9] duplicate registrations and voting (Government Accountability Institute 2017),[10] and ineffective list maintenance persist and create numerous issues. Inaccurate voting lists undermine the faith that the process is being fairly administered. When voters hear or read that a jurisdiction retains a voter registration list that well exceeds the citizen voting population,[11] or that voter rolls

---

[8]One exception is California, which only complied with the requirement to develop its HAVA-compliant statewide voter registration system six months before the 2016 general election.

[9]California, Colorado, the District of Columbia, Indiana, Kentucky, Maine, Michigan, and New York all reported more than 100% of Citizen Voting Age Population (CVAP) Election Assistance Commission (2016).

[10]The Government Accountability Institute asserts, "Extending GAI's conservative matching method to include all 50 states would indicate an expected minimum of 45,000 high-confidence duplicate voting matches." And, "GAI was unable to obtain voter roll data from all 50 states, but nevertheless identified 8471 potential cases of illegal duplicate voting across 21 states. These instances should be investigated to determine whether two votes were cast by the same person or if identity theft occurred" (Government Accountability Institute 2017).

[11]See, e.g., *Judicial Watch, Inc.*, et al. *v. Dean C. Logan*, et al., 2:17cv08948 (D.C.Cal. 2017), complaining that in 2017 Los Angeles County, the largest voting jurisdiction in the United States, had registered voters totaling 112% of CVAP, including 1,515,330 inactive registrations, as reported to the EAC, found at http://www.judicialwatch.org/wp-content/uploads/2017/12/JW-v-CA-NVRA-complaint-08948.pdf.

Table 13.1 Select list of NVRA cases from the most recent decade

Case name	State
A. Philip Randolph Institute v. Husted, 584 U.S. ___ (2018)	Ohio
League of Women Voters v. Ashcroft, 2:18cv04073 (W.D.Mo. 2018)	Missouri
League of Women Voters of Arizona v. Reagan, 2:18cv02620 (D.Ariz. 2018)	Arizona
PILF v. Harris Bennett, 4:18cv00981 (S.D. Tex. 2018)	Texas
PILF v. Torres, 1:18cv00463 (M.D. Pa. 2018)	Pennsylvania
Georgia State Conference of the NAACP v. Georgia et al., 1:20cv01427 (N.D.Ga. 2017)	Georgia
North Carolina State Conference of the NAACP v. The North Carolina State Board of Elections, 1:16cv1274 (M.D.N.C. 2017)	North Carolina
Common Cause Indiana v. Lawson, 1:17cv03936 (S.D. Ind. 2017)	Indiana
Judicial Watch, Inc., et al. v. Dean C. Logan, et al., 2:17cv08948 (C.D.Cal. 2017)	California
Judicial Watch, Inc. v. Alison Lundergan Grimes, et al., 3:17cv00094 (E.D.Ky. 2017)	Kentucky
Judicial Watch, Inc. v. Linda Lamone, et al., 1:17cv02006 (D.Md. 2017)	Maryland
League of Women Voters, et al. v. Brian D. Newby, et al., 838 F.3d 1 (D.D.C. 2016)	District of Columbia
Fish v. Kobach, 840 F.3d 710 (10th Cir. 2016)	Kansas
Common Cause v. Kemp, 841 F.Supp.2d 1320 (N.D.Ga. 2016)	Georgia
Voter Integrity Project NC v. Wake County Board of Elections, 5:2016cv00683 (E.D.N.C. 2016)	North Carolina
ACLRU, et al. v. Snipes, 16cv61474 (S.D.Fla. 2016)	Florida
U.S. v. New York City Board of Elections, 1:16cv06122 (E.D.N.Y. 2016)	New York
Scott v. Schedler, 771 F.3d 831 (5th Cir. 2014)	Louisiana
Arcia v. Fla. Sec'y of State, 746 F.3d 1273 (11th Cir. 2014)	Florida
True the Vote, Inc. v. Stewart, 1:13cv03369 (D.Colo. 2013)	Colorado
Judicial Watch, Inc. v. Husted, 2:12cv00792 (S.D.Ohio 2012)	Ohio
Voting for America v. Steen, 732F.3d 382 (5th Cir. 2013)	Texas
U.S. v. Florida, 4:12cv00285 (N.D.Fla. 2012)	Florida
Project Vote v. Long, 682 F.3d 331 (4th Cir. 2012)	Virginia
League of Women Voters of Florida v. Browning, 863 F.Supp. 1155 (N.D.Fla. 2012)	Florida
National Council of La Raza v. Miller, 914 F.Supp. 2d 1201 (D.Nev. 2012)	Nevada

(continued)

Table 13.1 (continued)

Case name	State
Valdez v. Squier, 676 F.3d 935 (10th Cir. 2012)	New Mexico
U.S. v. Louisiana, 3:11cv00470 (M.D.La. 2011)	Louisiana
U.S. v. State of Rhode Island, 1:11cv 00113 (D.R.I. 2011)	Rhode Island
Common Cause v. Coffman, 730 F.Supp.2d 1259 (D.Colo. 2010)	Colorado
Colorado, et al. v. Buescher, 750 F.Supp. 1259 (D. Colo. 2010)	Colorado
NAACP v. Murphy, 1:09cv00849 (S.D.Ind. 2009)	Indiana
Morales v. Handel, 1:08cv03172 (N.D.Ga. 2008)	Georfia
USSAF v. Land, 585 F.Supp.2d 925 (E.D. Mich. 2008), 546F.3d 373 (6th Cir. 2008) (denying stay)	Michigan
ACORN v. Scott, 08-4084-cv (W.D.Mo. 2008)	Missouri
U.S. v. Missouri, 535 F.3d 844 (8th Cir. 2008	Missouri
Montana Democratic Party v. Eaton, 581 F.Supp.2d 1077 (D.Mont. 2008)	Montana

still contain the names of voters who were born over a hundred years ago (Civitas 2010; Fessler 2012; Knight 2016),[12] or discover that a dead parent is still listed, they get suspicious and concerned about the opportunity for fraud.

Polling firms have shown that Americans are concerned about election fraud and believe it happens (Adona 2016; Rasmussen 2018a) even if the prescribed political narrative is that "voter fraud is a myth" (Brennan Center for Justice 2017; Heritage Foundation 2017). But, of course, voter fraud can take many forms including registration or vote buying, providing false information in registering or voting, multiple voting, intimidation, aggressive assistance, registration and/or voting by persons who are ineligible, malfeasance by election officials, destruction or spoiling of valid registrations or ballots, falsification of vote tallies,

---

[12]Sometimes these dates are "legacy" voters for whom the elections office does not have a correct birthdate, therefore they insert a fake date, often January 1, 1900, into the database. However, that fact does not help that there are many cases of dead voters not being removed from the rolls or that voters read and hear these stories, which can increase suspicion of fraud, or at least opportunity for fraud. Also, these types of numbers indicate that the voting rolls are not being kept up-to-date (Civitas 2010), found at https://wwwcache.wral.com/asset/news/state/nccapitol/2012/10/31/11722418/SBOE_Response_to_Civitas_Report.pdf.

and voter suppression (Vandermaas-Peeler et al. 2018).[13] Even a whiff or suspicion of opportunity for any of these activities undermines voter confidence in the integrity of elections. These crimes need to be prosecuted whenever they are discovered and taken more seriously so that the public knows that there are consequences for those who dare to dilute legitimate votes and corrupt the system. Prosecutors too often decline to prosecute these cases because they are hard to prove and take resources from what they consider to be more serious crimes. But, while these crimes are not violent, they are against the social order and failure to prosecute cultivates an attitude that there are no consequences for interfering in elections and that voting isn't a serious matter. This leads to thinking such as, "My vote doesn't matter," or, "Voting is a waste of my time, because the chips are already in," or "Everyone knows the elections are already fixed." Political participation comes down to interest and a belief that one's vote does count and will be counted fairly.

Voter verification is a common-sense tool that when appropriately implemented may increase voter turnout (McCaffrey 2012), and can increase trust in election integrity, as a significant majority of voters support voter ID (Rasmussen 2017).[14] The Commission on Federal Election Reform (also known as the Carter Baker Commission) supported appropriate voter identification and President Carter and Secretary Baker later published an op-ed reiterating their ID proposal. The Carter Baker Report provided some important commentary about voter ID:

> A good registration list will ensure that citizens are only registered in one place, but election officials still need to make sure that the person arriving at a polling site is the same one that is named on the registration list. In the old days and in small towns where everyone knows each other, voters

---

[13] 60% of Hispanics, 62% of African-Americans, and 27% of white voters express concerns about eligible voters being denied the right to vote (Vandermaas-Peeler et al. 2018). These numbers are in spite of the fact that HAVA requires the use of provisional ballots in cases where an eligible voter's name does not appear on the voter registration list. That so many believe that there is rampant denial of the vote in the United States should be of great concern and the source of that belief or evidence of it should be investigated and addressed.

[14] A recent survey showed that 67% of likely US voters think voters should be required to show identification such as a driver's license before being allowed to vote (Rasmussen 2018b).

did not need to identify themselves. But in the United States, where 40 million people move each year, and in urban areas where some people do not even know the people living in their own apartment building let alone their precinct, some form of identification is needed.

There is no evidence of extensive fraud in U. S. elections or of multiple voting, but both occur, and it could affect the outcome of a close election. The electoral system cannot inspire public confidence if no safeguards exist to deter or detect fraud or to confirm the identity of voters. Photo identification cards currently are needed to board a plane, enter federal buildings, and cash a check. Voting is equally important (Commission on Election Reform 2005, 18).

Numerous states already have voter ID laws, most with an affidavit option if a voter does not possess a required form of identification, and the Department of Justice has approved many of those ID laws if they have not been shown to be intentionally discriminatory. Every eligible citizen must be able to register and vote and we need to protect that right—illegitimate interference of any kind, foreign or domestic needs to be prevented. This should not be a partisan issue (McDonald 2018). The US Supreme Court in *Crawford v. Marion County* (2008) noted what the Carter Baker Commission said that Congress passed both the NVRA and HAVA to "protect the integrity of the electoral process." The Court further stated, "… they do indicate that Congress believes that photo identification is one effective method of establishing a voter's qualification to vote and that the integrity of elections is enhanced through improved technology" (Rasmussen 2018b, 1618). The Court went on to say, "…public confidence in the integrity of the electoral process has independent significance, because it encourages citizen participation in the democratic process" (Rasmussen 2018b, 1620).

Inaccurate lists are also a cause for lines at the polls and can create the need for provisional ballots.[15] High provisional ballot rates are a sign that a jurisdiction needs to review the accuracy of its lists

---

[15]Report of the Commission on Federal Election Reform, Commission Letter to the President, found at https://www.eac.gov/assets/1/6/Amer-Voting-Exper-final-draft-01-09-14-508.pdf.

(Election Assistance Commission 2016). Long lines and overuse of provisional ballots cause confusion and frustration at the polls and contribute to unease over election integrity.

It is now possible for registration systems (including those run by motor vehicle departments) to automatically compare data to numerous sources of both government and commercial data. This is done to maintain the integrity of the lists on a regular and consistent basis.[16] Auditing the voter registration system and list is also as important as doing accuracy testing on the voting machines and auditing election results. Full-scale audits should be done at least every four years, and a best practice would be to do it the year before each presidential general election.

Another best practice is for state election officials to do annual statewide mailings to identify voters who have moved, not just to another state, but to another precinct.[17] This should be part of the larger voter registration audit process. Local registrars and officials should also make use of confirmation notices[18] whenever they have reason to believe that a voter has moved, has not voted, or has not recently interacted with the election office.[19] In addition to doing targeted mailings, jurisdictions should do jurisdiction-wide mailings often. This will help voters believe in the efforts of the officials to keep and maintain clean and uncluttered

---

[16]Sources include the Social Security Administration's master death index, the US Postal Service's National Change of Address dataset, several databases maintained by the US Department of Homeland Security, state and local tax agencies, federal and state courts, vital records departments, the corrections divisions, voter registration data sharing groups such the Electronic Registration Information Center (ERIC), of which 24 states and the District of Columbia are members, and the Interstate Voter Registration Crosscheck (IVRC) program (now under politically motivated criticism, but which was started by the secretaries of Kansas, Iowa, Missouri, and Nebraska in 2005), which approximately 25 states utilize. Some jurisdictions such as Orange County, California, also employ commercial credit bureau data (Experian) and ancestry databases, found at http://www.ocvote.com/election-library/docs/2012%20Voter%20List%20Maintenance.pdf.

[17]States should also consider legislation to require state and local election officials to report on their voter registration and list maintenance activities. This would help motivate and identify jurisdictions that are not currently doing effective list maintenance.

[18]The EAC's EAVS survey reported that the 47 states and territories that responded to this inquiry on the survey sent a total of 19,058,066 confirmation notices to registrants during the 2016 election cycle. The response rate by voter registrants to confirmation notices nationwide was just 12.8% (Election Assistance Commission 2016).

[19]See generally, *A. Philip Randolph Institute v. Husted*, 584 U.S. ___ (2018).

rolls. Infrequent use of confirmation notices is not adequate to keep voter records efficient and up-to-date.

More than half of the states have implemented online voter registration, which has made the process more convenient and simple for voters, increased the accuracy of the registration data, and decreased costs to elections offices, although online registration comes with some cybersecurity risks.[20] As a part of an online voter registration system, states should provide voters, upon a showing of confirmable identifying information, the ability to cancel their registration. Currently, there is no simple way for voters to easily remove themselves after moving out of state or for other reasons unless they send written confirmation that they have moved. Obviously, given concerns with hacking and the stealing of personally identifying information, such an online tool must be properly secured (Latek 2018).[21] Removal from previous registration ought to be an automatic part of the new registration process; registrants should be required to provide their previous locality or address so that the new election office can automatically notify the old registration office to remove the voter. The current system of written confirmation by a voter or use of a return card has not been an efficient or sufficient system. Use of online resources and technology would greatly improve this process and give voters the satisfaction of knowing that they are only registered in one place.

Voter confusion also undermines trust in election administration. The way ballots are designed and handled is important to the integrity of the process. Bad ballot design may consist of questionable typefaces, small font sizes, missing headers, not enough white space, poor placement, ambiguously written questions (or inartfully translated questions on minority language ballots), incomprehensible instructions (which many voters don't even attempt to read anyway), and the clutter

---

[20]The United States Computer Emergency Readiness Team (US-CERT) has outlined some of the cyber risks to online voter registration systems and recommends ways to protect them. See US-CERT Security Tip (ST16-001) Securing Voter Registration Data (September 30, 2016), found at https://www.us-cert.gov/ncas/tips/ST16-001.

[21]Bad actors seem very interested in selling voter information, even when not obtained for purposes of interfering in elections (Latek 2018).

of unnecessary additional information.[22] Voters may not notice these issues, but they instinctively register suspicion of the process when it's not clear. This issue takes on even more significance as greater numbers of voters vote by mail-in ballot. If a voter goes to a polling place, at least he or she has an opportunity to ask an election official for assistance when the ballot is not clear. Sometimes ballot design is bound by legislation that requires a particular format or design element (see Table 13.2). Other times, election officials just make bad decisions (Atkinson 2018). Mail-in ballots, utilized in several Western US states, seem to have produced an uptick in voter participation, at least after initial implementation (Edelman and Glastris 2018). Mail-in voting is convenient for voters, allows election officials more control over access to their systems, requires fewer and yet more professional poll workers, but also comes at a cost of accessibility for some voters. Whether the mail-in ballots are the single way to cast a vote, or used for absentee ballots, advanced voting (early voting), or overseas absentee ballots, they do come with some integrity issues that have to be addressed, for example, intimidation, signature verification, and postal issues to mention just a few.

Voting on paper in places other than at polling places or vote centers may precipitate questions of possible intimidation. Federal law states that anyone may assist a voter with the exception of the voter's employer or labor representative.[23] However, intimidation or coercion is a federal criminal violation.[24] There have been reports of "vote farming" or "vote

---

[22]See Designing Usable Ballots, The Center for Civic Design, found at https://civicdesign.org/fieldguides/designing-usable-ballots/.

[23]Voting Rights Act, Section 208 codified as 52 US Code § 10508: Any voter who requires assistance to vote by reason of blindness, disability, or inability to read or write may be given assistance by a person of the voter's choice, other than the voter's employer or agent of that employer or officer or agent of the voter's union.

[24]Voting Rights Act, Section 11 (b) codified in 18 US Code § 594: "Whoever intimidates, threatens, coerces, or attempts to intimidate, threaten, or coerce, any other person for the purpose of interfering with the right of such other person to vote or to vote as he may choose, or of causing such other person to vote for, or not to vote for, any candidate for the office of President, Vice President, Presidential elector, Member of the Senate, Member of the House of Representatives, Delegate from the District of Columbia, or Resident Commissioner, at any election held solely or in part for the purpose of electing such candidate, shall be fined under this title or imprisoned not more than one year, or both."

Table 13.2 Ballot design requirements

State	Description	Code
Alabama	"All ballots shall be printed in black ink on clear book paper. At the bottom of each ballot and at a point an equal distance from the sides thereof there shall be printed a one-inch square in which the number of the ballot shall be placed by the inspector when the ballot is cast"	Ala. Code § 11-46-25(c) (2013)
California	California elections code allows a candidate to add a designation such as his or her current office or occupation "immediately under the name of each candidate, and not separated from the name by any line"	Cal. Elec. Code § 920(2) (13107) (1994)
Georgia	"Each ballot shall have printed thereon the following: 'I understand that the offer or acceptance of money or any other object of value to vote for any particular candidate, list of candidates, issue, or list of issues included in this election constitutes an act of voter fraud and is a felony under Georgia law'"	Ga. Code Ann. § 21-2-285(h) (2010)
Kansas	Kansas law includes the following: "To the name of each candidate for a state office shall be added the name of the city in which the candidate resides"	Kan. Stat. Ann. § 25-613 (2017)
Louisiana	Louisiana provides, "The names of the candidates for each office shall be arranged alphabetically by surname and shall be listed below the title of the office, in smaller capital letters"	La. Rev. Stat. Ann. § 18:552 C(1)(c)(i) (2011)
Massachusetts	Massachusetts prints the candidates "the name of the city or town where he resides, with the name of the street and number"	Mass. Gen. Laws ch. 54 § 41 (2018)
New York	New York State requires, "the image of a closed fist with index finger extended pointing to the party or independent row"	N.Y. Elec. Law § 7-104 (7) (2010)
Oklahoma	Oklahoma allows emblems to be printed on ballots	Okla. Stat. tit. 26 § 6-106 (2011)

(continued)

Table 13.2 (continued)

State	Description	Code
Utah	Utah has very precise instructions for its ballots including the use of "heavy parallel lines," and "the names of candidates are printed in capital letters, not less than one-eighth nor more than one-fourth of an inch high in heavy-faced type not smaller than 10 point, between lines or rules three-eighths of an inch apart"	Utah Code Ann. § 20A-6-301(1)(e) and (g) (2018)

harvesting,"[25] which means that political operatives submit absentee ballot requests on behalf of voters and then vote the ballots themselves after getting the voter to sign the un-voted ballot. Nursing homes and other similar institutions, and low-income housing developments are ripe for these kinds of fraudulent activities. Voters with disabilities have an especially difficult time with paper ballots due to the need to rely on others for assistance in filling out the ballot and confirmation of their choices before casting it. Aggressive assistance outside a polling place cannot be monitored and opens the process to unscrupulous individuals taking advantage of vulnerable voters.

The process of signature comparison must be well defined and those doing the comparison need to be properly trained. As the Colorado Secretary of State's Signature Verification Guide says, "Signature verification plays an important role in our elections because it ensures that only those individuals eligible to vote have their vote counted."[26] Signature verification by persons who are not trained handwriting experts raises questions about the accuracy of the process. Additionally, as some schools have ceased to teach cursive handwriting, the

---

[25]See, e.g., https://www.masslive.com/news/index.ssf/2017/10/voter_fraud_alleged_in_bostons.html; https://www.texasattorneygeneral.gov/news/releases/work-ag-paxtons-election-fraud-unit-results-arrests-4-members-organized-voter-fraud-ring-north-fort.

[26]See *Signature Verification Guide*, Colorado Secretary of State, Overview (September 13, 2018), found at https://www.sos.state.co.us/pubs/elections/docs/SignatureVerificationGuide.pdf.

verification process may get even more difficult in the future (Balmert 2018a; Bill to Include 2018; Shapiro 2013).

Dependence on the US Postal Service (USPS) also comes with challenges. Now that there are fewer processing centers and mail is not being processed on the weekends[27] it is important for voters to know that their ballots need to be mailed earlier, especially in jurisdictions where the deadline for the receipt of ballots is election day. Ballot security in the USPS is also a concern, as elections officials have anecdotally reported finding ballots on floors at post offices and even on unsecured loading docks (Bergin 2018; Curran 2017). The USPS takes mail ballot issues very seriously and is working with the EAC and other organizations to address them. But beyond the current attention being given to postal issues, the future of the postal system itself is in question. Election officials need to be concerned about whether they can count on the longevity of the USPS—at least as a government entity. In April 2018, President Trump issued an Executive Order establishing a task force to evaluate the USPS.[28] It is widely expected that the task force will recommend that the USPS be privatized based on an Executive Order the President signed in March 2017,[29] and a reorganization plan the Executive Office of the White House released in June 2018.[30] The affect this will have on mail-in ballots is currently unknown.

Voting machine security has received a lot of attention, especially in the wake of the reports of attempted interference in the 2016 Election, and faith in the reliability of the machines is integral to voters' trust in the entire system. When HAVA was passed in 2002, cybersecurity issues

---

[27]Area Mail Processing Consolidations, Report Number: NO-AR-15-007, United States Postal Service Office of the Inspector General (June 5, 2015), found at https://www.uspsoig.gov/document/area-mail-processing-consolidations.

[28]https://www.whitehouse.gov/presidential-actions/executive-order-task-force-united-states-postal-system/.

[29]https://www.federalregister.gov/documents/2017/03/16/2017-05399/comprehensive-plan-for-reorganizing-the-executive-branch; https://www.kansascity.com/news/politics-government/article214080449.html.

[30]https://www.whitehouse.gov/wp-content/uploads/2018/06/Government-Reform-and-Reorg-Plan.pdf.

were hardly contemplated, if at all. Issues with lever or punch card voting systems and other outmoded practices such as "butterfly ballots"[31] were the focus at that time, and images of election judges holding magnifying glasses up to indented ballots in order to adjudicate the voter's intent remain with us.[32] To avoid a recurrence of the causes that created chaos in the 2000 presidential election, Congress required jurisdictions accepting HAVA funding to purchase voting systems that permitted the voter to verify their selections in an independent and private manner before the vote was cast and counted, as that would work to eliminate the ballot adjudication controversies over voter intent. The EAC was tasked with developing Voluntary Voting Systems Guidelines (VVSG) and to establish a testing and certification program through accredited laboratories.

Before the EAC established the VVSG, many jurisdictions newly purchased direct-recording electronic voting machines (DREs). DREs allow a voter to vote on a digital ballot and receive immediate feedback for over-voting or under-voting, so the voter may correct the ballot before casting. DREs outfitted with headphones provide accessibility for voters with disabilities so they may vote independently and privately, and they can be programmed in different languages so voters with limited-proficiency English can read the ballot, or hear it read to them in their own languages. Other jurisdictions purchased optical scan voting systems, which have voters fill out ovals on a paper ballot to make their selections and insert that ballot into an optical scanner. If the voter has over-voted or under-voted, the scanner rejects the ballot, giving the voter a chance to correct his or her ballot before the scanner accepts and retains the ballot. Most voters in the country currently vote on these types of systems (Election Assistance Commission 2017, 15).

The integrity issue with voting systems is the belief that they can never be fully secured from either inside or outside tampering. While

---

[31]A butterfly ballot shows names down both sides of a ballot with a row of holes in the center where a voter is to punch his or her selection in the corresponding hole. The design is confusing to many voters, especially because the second name on the left side of the ballot corresponds to the third hole in the center of the ballot (the second hole corresponds to the first name on the right side of the ballot).

[32]See http://americanhistory.si.edu/vote/florida.html.

virtually none of these systems are connected to the Internet, some researchers and election advocacy organizations insist that the systems are not safe and can be "hacked" by inserting infected parts from foreign sources during the manufacturing process, altering configuration codes, or by using corrupted memory cards or thumb drives which are used to transfer vote counts, among other things (Kaplan 2018).

Security of voting systems must always be taken very seriously, but we need to be careful not to allow the theoretical to be the enemy of reality.[33] Everything reasonable that can be done should be done to prove the machines are trustworthy and accurate. How do we assure voters that the equipment they are voting on can be trusted, given the concerns that bad actors will unceasingly attempt to hack the vote and continually look for new ways to do so? And that issue advocacy groups will continue to loudly scare the public into thinking they cannot trust our systems?

Vendors must do their absolute best to assure election officials that the systems they sell are free of corruption and that they have a robust and resilient security program—both cyber and physical. Federal legislation has been introduced to require that a vendor who "provides, supports, or maintains, or seeks to provide, support, or maintain, a voting system used in the administration of an election for Federal office … is solely owned and controlled by a citizen or citizens of the United States" (unless provided a waiver by the Secretary of Homeland Security) and that the vendor discloses any sourcing outside the United States for any parts of the voting system to the EAC, the DHS, and chief election official in the state where the vendor is doing business.[34] Such requirements would, of course, make it incredibly difficult, if not impossible, to do business as an election vendor. This legislative proposal illustrates all the more reason for vendors to do whatever they can to demonstrate that they and their products are trustworthy.

---

[33]See comments of West Virginia Secretary of State Mac Warner at the EAC Election Readiness Summit, Washington, DC (October 3, 2018), see transcript, 30, found at https://www.eac.gov/events/2018/10/03/eac-election-readiness-summit/.

[34]See, for example, H.R. 6449, found at https://www.congress.gov/bill/115th-congress/house-bill/6449/text. Several similar bills have been proposed in Congress.

On the state level, there must be vigorous standards for testing and certifying the systems. The state may decide to use the EAC's testing and certification program, or utilize the EAC's accredited laboratories, or conduct its own program. Currently, approximately 47 states use the EAC program in some manner (Election Assistance Commission 2017). The EAC also provides comprehensive IT training for election officials (Hancock 2017). State and local election officials may now also take advantage of the technical assistance provided by DHS which can conduct cybersecurity risk, vulnerability, and resilience assessments of various types to help secure systems.[35] It is important to realize that the first responders on security issues are at the state and local level. The federal government does not own or operate the voting systems and can only provide assistance if the states invite them to do so.

Local election officials can also do a lot to assure voting system accuracy. They can test systems rigorously before purchasing—making sure that each requirement of the Request for Proposal (RFP) is met. Logic and Accuracy (L&A) testing on each machine just prior to the election assures that it is ready to be used, has been properly configured, and is producing an accurate vote and count for each ballot style that will be used during the election. L&A testing must be conducted by at least two people and ought to be done in public to prove that the machine is indeed working and recording correctly. Machines should then be physically sealed and secured in advance of the election to insure that no tampering has occurred before they go into use on election day.

All systems must be inspected very carefully and especially at each access point. Officials should utilize whatever resources they can and employ redundancy where appropriate. They must communicate with the public that they are securing the systems—not the specific details, of course—and that they are taking all necessary steps and to the greatest degree possible to assure the security of the elections.

---

[35]See DHS Cybersecurity Services Catalog for Election Infrastructure, U.S. Department of Homeland Security (undated), found at https://www.eac.gov/assets/1/6/DHS_Cybersecurity_Services_Catalog_for_Election_Infrastructure.pdf.

Another measure that election officials can take to increase voter trust and confidence is to have well-trained poll workers and election judges, as they are the first and sometimes only point of contact voters have with election officials. Poll workers are often the greatest point of failure in an election. Officials who appear not to know what they are doing, can't provide answers, or furnish erroneous information give voters the idea that the election is not being run competently—and in actuality, untrained poll workers may indicate that it may not be. Bad attitudes and insensitive comments turn voters off and sometimes personally offend them. Thorough preparation and good training is critical, because election day workers are usually recruited for just a few days a year and are not skilled or experienced election professionals. As well, the polling place itself can convey integrity in the election process through sensible room configuration, accessible and logical flow, and appropriate and clear signage. Positive experiences at polling places or in interactions with election officials go a very long way to reassure voters that the process is fair, legitimate, and properly well run.

Post-election activities are also vital for the trustworthiness of the process. By whatever method results are tabulated,[36] election officials must take great pains to secure the data from the possibility of manipulation. The same is true for election night reporting, even though the results aren't yet official. Imagine the hit to voter confidence if the reported results on election night were erroneous for whatever reason (e.g., machine or human error, manipulation, or hacking) and had to be changed a few days later upon discovery that the opposing candidate had actually won (National Constitution Center 2017).[37]

---

[36]The most common forms of tabulation are by mechanical counting (similar to an odometer), where the voting machine records each vote and totals are taken from the machine at the end of the day and written on paper documentation, by memory cards or thumb drives that track the votes on each machine over the day, or by manually counting the actual physical ballots, or a combination of these. Totals, whether on paper, memory card, thumb drive, or ballot, are transferred to election headquarters for either central tabulation or manual counting.

[37]Incorrect reporting of election results has happened before, the most famous being the Truman v. Dewey Presidential contest in 1948. That was, of course, a much less technologically and informationally connected time (National Constitution Center 2017).

Canvassing and post-election audits are also essential for establishing trust in the results of elections. While the media wants to announce winners and losers as quickly as possible after polls close—and we all depend on election night reports for results—those results are not official until the state and/or local jurisdiction officially compiles the election returns and validates them. The official canvass should not be underestimated as a valuable tool as a form of audit to insure accuracy of the count and to increase confidence in the election outcome.

> The purpose of the canvass is to account for every ballot cast and to ensure that each valid vote is included in the official results. For an election official, the canvass means aggregating or confirming every valid ballot cast and counted—absentee, early voting, election day, provisional, challenged, and uniformed and overseas citizen. The canvass enables an election official to resolve discrepancies, correct errors, and take any remedial actions necessary to ensure completeness and accuracy before certifying the election.[38]

There are different methods for conducting canvass activities, depending on the jurisdiction, but the elections results must go through a reconciliation process before the election can be certified.[39] Most jurisdictions have a canvass board or an issues and exceptions board that is governed by state and local laws and procedures, including open meetings acts. The public may and should attend meetings of these boards and election officials should welcome the public in order to support transparency.

Auditing, from voter registration rolls through all management procedures to machines and contest totals, should be a priority for election officials. Post-election audits are particularly beneficial for several reasons, including revealing whether there has been an error in the counting and recording of the results, protecting against fraud, or reinforcing

---

[38]Election Management Guidelines, EAC, 133 (2010), found at https://www.eac.gov/assets/1/6/EMG_chapt_13_august_26_2010.pdf.

[39]Election certification usually includes documentation of reconciled precinct, vote center, and write-in ballot totals, including provisional and challenged ballots, UOCAVA ballots, any duplicated ballots, and an accounting for spoiled and rejected ballots.

that results are accurate and credible. There are several post-election audit models that may work for a jurisdiction depending on how its elections are conducted. Most post-election audits consist of a comparing a paper record against the voting system results for a particular number of precincts or machines, or perhaps a "tiered" number depending on the margin of victory in the contest being reviewed. Typically, a percentage of the ballots or the paper records are hand counted and compared to the electronic machine count. Some jurisdictions use a fully electronic audit process by using a computer or different tabulation system than the original one used. Some states use procedural audits to evaluate the integrity of election day processes and activities.[40] These types of audits may also be used in conjunction with a post-election audit or as a part of the canvassing process. Risk-limiting audits, which use a statistical method to determine the probability of the correctness of the outcome, are becoming more popular. This type of audit depends on manually checking paper ballots or verified paper trails and comparing them to the voting system records or against the outcome (Lovato 2018). Even if state laws or election procedures do not require post-election audits, election officials should consider instituting them as a best practice. If the results of elections are in any way suspect, voters will not have confidence that the elections were fair and members of one party or the other may reject them as illegitimate.

> When close elections trigger automatic recounts, or when challenges are initiated, elections officials need to already have detailed rules and procedures in place to avoid divisive fights – either out of or in court. Publicly laundered accusations of irregularities or shenanigans that include situations such as suddenly "finding" uncounted ballots (Dixon et al. 2010; Ferguson 2018; Jones 2018; Noble 2017; Thompson 2010), machines that for some inconceivable reason were not included in the

---

[40]Procedural audits should include a review and reconciliation of ballot accounting logs, voting system zero tapes from the beginning of election day and the results tapes from the end of the day, number of ballots cast, number of voters who signed in, number of provisional ballots, absentee and UOCAVA ballots, etc. All unusual incidents should be documented (such as spoiled ballots, challenged ballots, or voters signing in, but leaving without casting a ballot). All ballots should be accounted for and any discrepancies reconciled.

result totals,[41] that ballots were destroyed by "mistake," undermine trust in the system and in the people who conduct elections (Balmert 2018b; Barszewski 2018; Bryan 2018).

The media, which, of course, is not in the control of election officials, has a responsibility to report honestly. However, media can have a deleterious effect on the voters' level of confidence in elections by sensationalizing election issues. Too often, members of the media use their platform to try to sway the public to a particular agenda, and that not only hurts the credibility of the media itself as an institution but has a divisive politicizing effect on the country. A recent NPR/Marist poll found that almost a third of Americans believe that a foreign country will tamper with the votes cast to change the results,[42] even though there has been zero evidence that any foreign country has done so (Kelly 2018). The survey also showed that even more respondents believe that many votes will not actually be counted, that people who show up to vote will be told they aren't eligible, and that election officials in the United States will tamper with the votes to change the results.[43] A University of Chicago/Harris/AP-NORC poll found that more than 40% of Americans are very concerned about voter registration information, voting equipment, and that final election results will be hacked.[44] A majority in that poll lacked confidence that votes will be counted accurately and did not change their views about the accuracy of the vote counting even when presented with messages about measures being taken on election security.[45] And, both a recent Ipsos/University of Virginia Center for Politics poll and a recent Rasmussen poll showed that almost half of Americans believe that elections in the United States are not fair and open (Rasmussen 2018c).

---

[41] Sarah Bloom, "Uncounted Richmond Voting Machine Flips Attorney General's Race." *NBC12.com*., November 11, 2013, found at http://www.nbc12.com/story/23938466/uncounted-richmond-voting-machine-flips-attorney-generals-race/.

[42] NPR/Marist Poll Results September (2018): Election Security, 25, found at http://maristpoll.marist.edu/?page_id=42883.

[43] NPR/Marist Poll, 21.

[44] Concerns about the vulnerability of election system ahead of the 2018 Midterms, Associated Press and NORC, 2 (October 2018), found at http://www.apnorc.org/PDFs/Harris%20Poll%20Survey%201/UChicago%20Harris%20APNORC%20Poll%201%20Final.pdf.

[45] Ibid., 7.

These polling outcomes are extremely worrying for election officials. While it is fairly normal for persons whose favored candidates lose their races to question results, it is of great concern that Americans believe that votes or tallies will be changed, that votes cast won't be counted, that eligible voters will be turned away, or that American elections are not fair and open. It seems the basis of these voter concerns is rooted in sensationalized reporting in the media rather than on actual information from election officials. The (poll) results give credence to what election officials have been worried about since at least the summer of 2016: that the intense focus by the media and the federal government on Russia's election interference efforts could be eroding voters' confidence in democratic institutions.

It is imperative that accurate information be reported. And, if there is a concern or report over some kind of interference, it should be presented along with the facts of how the process works and the efforts that are being taken to protect the accuracy, fairness, and security of the elections. Elections officials have a responsibility to educate the media and provide it with truthful information, and to administer the elections as transparently and openly without compromising security.

While turnout in elections mostly depends on the voters' knowledge and interest in what is on the ballot, it is troublesome to hear citizens say that they don't vote because their vote doesn't matter or that the elections are "rigged" anyway (López and Flores 2017). An election administrator's job is incredibly complex—much more so than the general public knows—and in many ways it is becoming more complex all the time. A great deal has changed in elections since the 2000 general election, and it is continuing to change as technology, threats, and partisanship evolve. Election administration is being challenged more often both in and out of the courts, which in and of itself can undermine voter confidence, officials need to be sure that they are careful to comply with election laws and procedures and document that compliance.[46]

---

[46]While the federal government requires election materials to be retained for 22 months (42 U.S.C. § 1974), election officials need to have good retention policies to be able to recreate what has occurred to address any errors, or assuage and suspicion that something was awry.

Sustaining election integrity and thereby voter confidence is an ongoing challenge and officials must take all reasonable measures in everything they do to assure voters they can trust the system, that their votes matter, and that they will be accurately counted and reported. The future of our republic depends on it.

References

Adona, Natalie. "Election Security and the 2016 Voter Experience." *The Democracy Fund* (Blog), December 2, 2016. https://www.democracyfund.org/blog/entry/election-security-and-the-2016-voter-experience.

Ansolabehere, Stephen, and Eitan Hersh. "Voter Registration: The Process and Quality of Lists." In *The Measure of American Elections*, edited by Barry Burden and Charles Stewart III, 61–90. Cambridge, UK: Cambridge University Press, 2014.

Atkinson, Bill. "Petitions Filed Tuesday to Remove Hopewell Electoral Board Members." *The Progress Index*, October 1, 2018. http://www.progress-index.com/news/20181010/petitions-filed-tuesday-to-remove-hopewell-electoral-board-members.

Balmert, Jessie. "Ohio Student Could Learn Cursive Handwriting Again." *Cincinnati Enquirer*, June 20, 2018a. https://www.cincinnati.com/story/news/politics/2018/06/20/ohio-cursive-writing-common-core/717810002/.

———. "Ohio Race Just Got Closer as County Finds Hundreds of Uncounted Votes." *Cincinnati Enquirer*, August 9, 2018b. https://www.cincinnati.com/story/news/politics/2018/08/08/ohio-midterm-uncounted-votes-danny-oconnor-troy-balderson/941603002/.

Barszewski, Larry. "Broward Elections Supervisor Illegally Destroyed Ballots in Wasserman-Schultz Race, Judge Rules." *South Florida Sun-Sentinel*, May 14, 2018. http://www.sun-sentinel.com/local/broward/fl-sb-broward-elections-supervisor-broke-law-snipes-canova-20180514-story.html.

Bergin, Brigid. "Absentee Ballots Left Stranded at Brooklyn Post Office After Election." *WNYC News*, May 31, 2018. https://www.wnyc.org/story/absentee-ballots-left-stranded-brooklyn-post-office-after-election/.

"Bill to Include Cursive Writing in Indiana Schools' Curriculum Moves from Senate to House." *The Indy Channel.com*, January 23, 2018. https://www.theindychannel.com/news/local-news/indianapolis/bill-to-include-cursive-writing-in-indiana-schools-curriculum-moves-from-senate-to-house.

Brennan Center for Justice. "The Myth of Voter Fraud." 2017. https://www.brennancenter.org/issues/voter-fraud.

Bryan, Susannah. "Uncounted Votes: Ballot Woes Still Haunt Broward Supervisor of Elections Office." *South Florida Sun-Sentinel*, August 29, 2018. http://www.sun-sentinel.com/local/broward/fl-sb-ballots-snafu-primary-election-20180829-story.html.

Civitas (Team). "110 Year Olds Vote Strong in NC." *Civitas Review*, October 28, 2010. http://civitasreview.com/elections-campaigns/110-year-olds-vote-.

Commission on Federal Election Reform. "Building Confidence in American Elections." 2005. https://www.eac.gov/assets/1/6/Amer-Voting-Exper-final-draft-01-09-14-508.pdf.

Crawford v. Marion County Election Bd., 128 S. Ct. 1610, 1617 (2008).

Curran, Phillip Sean. "Mercer County: Uncounted Ballots Found at Post Office." *Central Jersey.com*, August 11, 2017. http://www.centraljersey.com/news/mercer-county-uncounted-ballots-found-at-post-office/article_1cc-0ce74-7ebe-11e7-894f-7fccfe483cd4.html.

Dixon, Ken, Timothy Loh, and Brittany Lyte. "Bag of Uncounted Ballots Found in Bridgeport." *Greenwich Time*, November 4, 2010. https://www.greenwichtime.com/local/article/Bag-of-uncounted-ballots-discovered-in-Bridgeport-799081.php.

Edelman, Gilad, and Paul Glastris. "Letting People Vote at Home Increases Voter Turnout: Here's Proof." *The New York Times*, January 26, 2018. https://www.washingtonpost.com/outlook/letting-people-vote-at-home-increases-voter-turnout-heres-proof/2018/01/26/d637b9d2-017a-11e8-bb03-722769454f82_story.html?utm_term=.9e816fb6e06d.

Election Assistance Commission. "EAVS Deep Dive: Provisional Ballots." 2018. https://www.eac.gov/documents/2018/06/07/eavs-deep-dive-provisional-ballots/.

———. "Election Administration and Voting Survey 2016 Comprehensive Report." https://www.eac.gov/assets/1/6/2016_EAVS_Comprehensive_Report.pdf. Accessed January 14, 2018.

Ferguson, Dan. "'Simple Math Mistakes' Left 164 Ballot Uncounted After South Dakota Primary Election." *Argus Leader*, June 12, 2018. https://www.argusleader.com/story/news/politics/2018/06/11/south-dakota-election-164-uncounted-ballots-found-minnehaha-county-bob-litz-primary-2018/690257002/.

Fessler, Pam. "Study: 1.8 Million Dead People Still Registered to Vote." *National Public Radio*, February 14, 2012. https://www.npr.org/2012/02/14/146827471/study-1-8-million-dead-people-still-registered-to-vote.

Government Accountability Institute. "America the Vulnerable: The Problem of Duplicate Voting." 2017. https://www.g-a-i.org/wp-content/uploads/2017/07/Voter-Fraud-Final-with-Appendix-1.pdf.

Hancock, Brian. "U.S. EAC Offers Election Technology Training Course." March 2, 2017. https://www.eac.gov/us-eac-offers-election-technology-training-course/.

Heritage Foundation. "Election Fraud Cases from Across the United States." January 31, 2017. https://www.heritage.org/voterfraud.

Jackson, Chris, and Anne Marie Moran. "Only Half of the American Population Believes Elections Are Fair and Open." *IPSOS*, July 17, 2018. https://www.ipsos.com/en-us/news-polls/half-of-Americans-believe-elections-are-fair.

Jones, Brittany. "300 Uncounted Mail-In Ballots Found in Volusia County." *Spectrum News 13*, August 30, 2018. https://www.mynews13.com/fl/orlando/politics/2018/08/30/300-uncounted-mail-in-ballots-found-in-volusia-county.

Kaplan, Fred. "America's Voting Systems Are Still Dangerously Vulnerable to Hacking." *Slate*, February 22, 2018. https://slate.com/news-and-politics/2018/02/americas-voting-systems-are-still-dangerously-vulnerable-to-hacking.html.

Kelly, Erin. "Senate Report: No Evidence That Russians Changed Vote Tallies in 2016." *USA Today*, May 8, 2018. https://www.usatoday.com/story/news/politics/2018/05/08/senate-report-no-evidence-russians-changed-vote-tallies-2016/592978002/.

Knight, Robert. "More Than 100 Years Old and Still Voting, Pennsylvania's Ancient Voters Raise Disturbing Questions." *The Washington Times*, October 30, 2016. https://www.washingtontimes.com/news/2016/oct/30/pennsylvanias-ancient-voters-raise-questions/.

Latek, Tom. "Report: Ky. Among 19 States Whose Voter Info Being Sold on Dark Web." *Kentucky Today*, October 15, 2018. http://kentuckytoday.com/stories/kentucky-among-19-states-whose-voter-info-being-sold-on-dark-web-report-says,15694.

López, Gustavo, and Antonio Flores. *Dislike of Candidates or Campaign Issues Was Most Common Reason for Not Voting in 2016*. Pew Research Center, June 1, 2017. http://www.pewresearch.org/fact-tank/2017/06/01/dislike-of-candidates-or-campaign-issues-was-most-common-reason-for-not-voting-in-2016/.

Lovato, Jerome. *Risk Limiting Audits—Practical Application*. U.S. Election Assistance Commission, June 25, 2018. https://www.eac.gov/assets/1/6/Risk-Limiting_Audits_-_Practical_Application_Jerome_Lovato.pdf.

McCaffrey, Shannon. "Despite Voter ID Law, Minority Turnout Up in Georgia." *The Atlanta Journal-Constitution*, September 3, 2012. https://www.ajc.com/news/despite-voter-law-minority-turnout-georgia/3wOfD2SkXmTgRwbySd2ZiK/.

McDonald, Michael P. "I Agree with Donald Trump, We Should Have Voter ID: Here's How and Why." *USA Today*, January 15, 2018. https://www.usatoday.com/story/opinion/2018/01/15/national-id-card-voter-registration-system-we-could-love-michael-mcdonald-column/1025903001/.

National Constitution Center. "Looking Back at the Truman Beats Dewey Upset." November 3, 2017. https://constitutioncenter.org/blog/behind-the-biggest-upset-in-presidential-history-truman-beats-dewey/.

Noble, Jason. "Dallas County Failed to Report 5,842 Votes Cast in 2016 Election." *Des Moines Register*, February 8, 2017. https://www.desmoinesregister.com/story/news/politics/2017/02/08/dallas-county-failed-report-5842-votes-cast-2016-election/97665238/.

Parks, Miles. "NPR/Marist Poll: 1 in 3 Americans Thinks a Foreign Country Will Change Midterm Votes." *NPR*, September 17, 2018. Heard at *All Things Considered*. https://www.npr.org/2018/09/17/647420970/npr-marist-poll-1-in-3-americans-think-foreign-country-will-change-midterm-votes.

Rasmussen. "Most Still See Voter Fraud as a Serious Problem." *Rasmussen Reports*, August 10, 2017. http://www.rasmussenreports.com/public_content/politics/general_politics/august_2017/most_still_see_voter_fraud_as_serious_problem/.

———. "See Voters Want IDs at the Polls, Don't See Them as Discriminatory." *Rasmussen Reports*, October 3, 2018a. http://www.rasmussenreports.com/public_content/politics/general_politics/september_2018/voters_want_ids_at_the_polls_don_t_see_them_as_discriminatory.

———. "Voters Have More Faith in U.S. Elections These Days." *Rasmussen Reports*, October 12, 2018b. http://www.rasmussenreports.com/public_content/politics/general_politics/october_2018/voters_have_more_faith_in_u_s_elections_these_days.

———. "Voters Still See Fraud as a Problem." *Rasmussen Reports*, June 14, 2018c. http://www.rasmussenreports.com/public_content/politics/general_politics/june_2018/voters_still_see_voter_fraud_as_a_problem.

Shapiro, T. Rees. "Cursive Handwriting Is Disappearing from Schools." *The Washington Post*, April 4, 2013. https://www.washingtonpost.com/local/education/cursive-handwriting-disappearing-from-public-schools/2013/04/04/215862e0-7d23-11e2-a044-676856536b40_story.html?utm_term=.3b6387471402.

The PEW Center on the States. "Election Initiatives, Issues Brief, Inaccurate, Costly, and Inefficient, Evidence That America's Voter Registration System Needs and Upgrade." February 2012. https://Www.Pewtrusts.Org/~/Media/Legacy/Uploadedfiles/pcs_assets/2012/pewupgradingvoterregistrationpdf.pdf.

Thompson, Kevin. "Box of 500 Uncounted Absentee Ballots Found; Could Skew 3 Races." *Palm Beach Post*, November 11, 2010. https://www.palmbeachpost.com/news/box-500-uncounted-absentee-ballots-found-could-skew-races/UAnGXajZ1aCXcdcAgJi55H/.

U.S. Election Assistance Commission. "Election Administration and Voting Survey, 2016 Comprehensive Report, a Report to the 115th Congress, 54–67." 2016. https://www.eac.gov/assets/1/6/2016_EAVS_Comprehensive_Report.pdf.

———. "Voting System Testing and Certification Program." 2017. https://www.eac.gov/news/2017/03/07/fact-sheet-the-us-election-assistance-commissions-voting-system-testing-and-certification-program-voting-systems-certification-communications-fact-sheet/.

Vandermaas-Peeler, Alex, Daniel Cox, Molly Fisch-Friedman, Rob Griffin, and Robert Jones. *American Democracy in Crisis: The Challenges of Voter Knowledge, Participation, and Polarization*. Public Religion Research Institute (PRRI), 2018. https://www.prri.org/research/american-democracy-in-crisis-voters-midterms-trump-election-2018/.

Christy McCormick was appointed to the US Election Assistance Commission (EAC) in 2014. As its first chairperson in four years, she re-established its operation, including its three advisory boards. She executed a new management policy, secured a long-overdue update to the Voluntary Voting Systems Guidelines, obtained accreditation of a new Voting System Testing Laboratory, oversaw hiring of Executive Director and General Counsel, and led reaffirmation of accessibility in voting as a top priority. She instituted the EAC's first Language Accessibility Summit and its first Election Data Summit. McCormick also launched a continuing effort to improve the Election Administration and Voting Survey as well as addressing postal issues in elections. Previously, she served as Senior Trial Attorney in the Voting Section of the Civil Rights Division at the Department of Justice. She has observed numerous elections and served at the US Embassy in Baghdad, Iraq, as US elections expert on Iraq national elections. Her extensive public law experience includes assistant attorney general and assistant to the solicitor general in the Office of the Virginia Attorney General and service as a judicial clerk. McCormick received her B.A. from University of Buffalo and a JD with honors from George Mason University School of Law.

14

Election Security: Increasing Election Integrity by Improving Cybersecurity

Marian K. Schneider

The term "election integrity" has come into widespread use in recent years. Yet, it seems that a universally accepted definition is elusive. The Global Commission on Elections (GCE) defines election integrity as "any election that is based on the democratic principles of universal suffrage and political equality as reflected in international standards and agreements, and is professional, impartial, and transparent in its preparation and administration throughout the electoral cycle."[1]

---

[1] "Deepening Democracy: A Strategy for Improving the Integrity of Elections Worldwide." Report of the Global Commission on Elections, Democracy and Security, September 2012. Retrieved from https://www.idea.int/publications/catalogue/deepening-democracy-strategy-improving-integrity-elections-worldwide.

President, Verified Voting Foundation. Formerly, Deputy Secretary for Elections and Administration, Pennsylvania Department of State, and Special Advisor to Governor Tom Wolf on Election Policy.

M. K. Schneider (✉)
Verified Voting, Philadelphia, PA, USA
e-mail: marian@verifiedvoting.org

© The Author(s) 2020
M. Brown et al. (eds.), *The Future of Election Administration*, Elections, Voting, Technology, https://doi.org/10.1007/978-3-030-14947-5_14

The "electoral cycle" is an important concept in the definition of electoral integrity. It is not enough that the vote counting and reconciliation process follow international democratic standards. The entire electoral ecosystem must adhere to these standards. The electoral cycle includes the following elements: the design and drafting of legislation, the recruitment and training of electoral staff, electoral planning, voter registration, the registration of political parties, the nomination of parties and candidates, the electoral campaign, polling, counting, the tabulation of results, the declaration of results, the resolution of electoral disputes, reporting, auditing, and archiving.[2] The Electoral Integrity Project has measured the perceptions of electoral integrity in the United States across these elements of the election cycle.[3] Not surprisingly, the United States exhibits wide variation in perceptions of electoral integrity across the 50 states and 5 territories.[4]

According to the GCE, certain critical factors[5] determine whether electoral processes have the indicia of integrity. First is the observance of the rule of law which guarantees human rights and democratic principles. The rule of law means that government is accountable, citizens enjoy equal rights under the law, the judiciary is independent and can enforce the rule of law, and the law is not enforced in arbitrary ways or contrary to human rights.[6] Applied to elections, neither governments nor political interests should be able to manipulate the electoral process with impunity.

---

[2]"Electoral Cycle." The ACE Electoral Knowledge Network. Retrieved from http://aceproject.org/ero-en/topics/electoral-management/electoral%20cycle.JPG/view.

[3]Pippa Norris, Holly Garnett, and Max Grömping. 2017. *The 2016 American Presidential Election—Perceptions of Electoral Integrity, US 2016 Subnational Study, Release 1.0, (PEI_US_1.0)*. The Electoral Integrity Project, University of Sydney. The PEI survey gathers evaluations and survey data from experts in all 50 states and the District of Columbia. the PEI survey asks experts to evaluate elections using 49 indicators, grouped into eleven categories reflecting the whole electoral cycle. The data set also includes a summary 100-point PEI Index based on summing all 49 indicators. Data were gathered from 3 questionnaires sent two weeks after the 2016 US election. 726 experts participated in this survey.

[4]Ibid., at 14. Retrieved from https://www.electoralintegrityproject.com/pei-us-2016/.

[5]The Global Commission on Elections identifies five major challenges to electoral integrity. This paper discusses only three of those five factors.

[6]Deepening Democracy: A Strategy for Improving the Integrity of Elections Worldwide, at 21. Report of the Global Commission on Elections, Democracy and Security, September 2012. Retrieved from https://www.idea.int/publications/catalogue/deepening-democracy-strategy-improving-integrity-elections-worldwide.

Second, elections must be administered by professional independent election administrators. This means that election administrators must conduct elections competently in a professional nonpartisan manner and that the citizenry must perceive that is the case.[7] In the United States, election administrators are responsible for every aspect of the process in the electoral cycle, whether at the local or the state level. Election administrators determine voter eligibility, register voters, create and maintain the voter registration rolls, prepare and set up the voting process for early voting and election day voting, process and handle absentee ballots, are responsible for proper tabulation of and accounting for voting materials, reporting results accurately, and certifying those results. Election administrators also manage candidates by overseeing the process for candidates to get on the ballot, regulate the candidate positions on the ballot, and enforce campaign finance laws. The breadth of their duties offers ample opportunity for skepticism if those duties are not carried out in a professional, transparent, nonpartisan, and credible fashion.

Third, laws and governmental institutions must not erect barriers whether legal, administrative, political, economic, or social, to "universal and equal political participation."[8] Barriers that attempt to exclude certain groups from registering or voting or that limit the ability of certain groups to appear on the ballot as candidates can significantly reduce the representation and political influence of women, minorities, or people with disabilities, among others.

Some election observers have noted that the United States' electoral process compares less favorably to other Western democracies when measured by the above criteria.[9] The reasons for this failure are a matter of debate, but a consensus seems to be growing that the increasing

---

[7]Ibid.

[8]"Deepening Democracy: A Strategy for Improving the Integrity of Elections Worldwide." Report of the Global Commission on Elections, Democracy and Security at 6 September 2012. Retrieved from https://www.idea.int/sites/default/files/publications/deepening-democracy.pdf.

[9]Pippa Norris, Ferran Martínez i Coma, Alessandro Nai, and Max Grömping. February 2016. The Year in Elections, 2015. Sydney, University of Sydney at 86; Pippa Norris. "American Elections Ranked Worst Among Western Democracies. Here's Why." *The Conversation*, March 22, 2016 (The United States scores 62 out of 100 points, the lowest among Western democracies).

partisanship and polarization of American political discourse coupled with decentralized election administration contributes to the perception that US elections lack integrity. The two major parties in America are split ideologically about the steps that make aspects of the electoral process more convenient and about the steps that attempt to ensure that only eligible citizens register, are included on voter registration rolls, and actually vote.

The polarization of the political parties and their ideological differences on election integrity have narrowed the discussion around election integrity to two primary areas of focus: first, the security and vulnerability of the computer assets that comprise our electoral process, and second, the integrity of the voter registration system and the ability to ensure that only eligible US citizens are able to register and vote in elections.[10] In the latter instance, claims of certain groups and politicians that ineligible voters are registered and voting in such numbers that they can sway election results have been discredited over the years. This type of voter fraud, namely, that an ineligible person (e.g., a non-US citizen) registers and votes, as well as allegations that voters are able to impersonate others at polling places and vote more than once has not been proven with any reliability.[11] Further, no credible evidence exists that such activities have occurred at a level to alter the outcome of any election contest or race.

The risk of programming error or tampering with computerized components of US elections that could undetectably alter the outcome of the election is, however, a non-theoretical risk.[12] During the 2016

---

[10]Ideological polarities exist regarding many other reforms centered on voting rights, civic participation and election administration, but those topics are beyond the scope of this chapter.

[11]See "Resources on Voter Fraud Claims." Brennan Center for Justice, a compendium of studies of voter impersonation fraud and non-citizen voting that catalogues the documented rarity of those events available here https://www.brennancenter.org/analysis/resources-voter-fraud-claims.

[12]The public statements during the presidential election cycle centered on tampering. But paperless DREs are also more susceptible to undetected errors, failures, and crashes because of their age. Lawrence Norden, and Ian Vandewalker. "Securing Elections from Foreign Interference." Brennan Center for Justice, June 29, 2017, at 9. Retrieved from https://www.brennancenter.org/publication/securing-elections-foreign-interference. Regardless of the cause of such failures, DREs lack the capability of demonstrating that electronic vote tallies are correct or incorrect.

election cycle, a nation-state conducted systematic, coordinated attacks on America's election infrastructure with the apparent aim of disrupting the election and undermining faith in America's democratic institutions.

The reports of interference in the 2016 election came after remarks of then-candidate Donald Trump. Trump's carefully chosen words—that the election was rigged—unleashed a storm of controversy on both sides of the political spectrum.[13] The "rigged" theme converted into hacking allegations. The hacking narrative alternated with the "voter fraud" narrative that stirred up fears of large numbers of ineligible voters voting and altering the outcome of the election. The "rigging" narrative, coupled with actual reports of interference, created a crisis of confidence in American election integrity during the 2016 election cycle.

Beginning in the summer of 2016, Americans began to learn of Russian interference with the 2016 election. The first indications of that interference related to a breach of the email servers of the Hillary Clinton campaign and the Democratic National Committee (DNC). Pilfered emails were publicly released through Wikileaks first in June 2016 and at other intervals during the year.[14]

The hacks against the DNC email servers were not the only activities. During the 2016 election cycle, Arizona and Illinois state election networks were attacked.[15] Intelligence reports published in 2017 demonstrate

---

[13]David G. Savage. "Pennsylvania's Aging Voting Machines Could Be 'Nightmare Scenario' in the Event of a Disputed Election." *Los Angeles Times*, October 20, 2016. Retrieved from http://www.latimes.com/politics/la-na-pol-pennsylvania-voting-paperless-20161020-snap-story.html; Christian Alexandersen. "Is Donald Trump Right? Can Pennsylvania's Election Results Be Hacked?" *pennlive.com*, September 9, 2016. Retrieved from http://www.pennlive.com/news/2016/09/is_donald_trump_right_can_penn.html.

[14]Greg Miller, Ellen Nakashima, and Adam Entous. "Obama's Secret Struggle to Retaliate Against Putin's Election Interference." *Washington Post*, June 23, 2017. Retrieved from https://www.washingtonpost.com/graphics/2017/world/national-security/obama-putin-election-hacking/?utm_term=.2a86d79dfd60.

[15]Rick Pearson. "Illinois Election Officials Say Hack Yielded Information on 200,000 Voters." *Chicago Tribune*, August 29, 2016. Retrieved from http://www.chicagotribune.com/news/local/politics/ct-illinois-state-board-of-elections-hack-update-met-0830-20160829-story.html; Ellen Nakashima. "Russian Hackers Targeted Arizona Election System." *The Washington Post*, August 29, 2016. https://www.washingtonpost.com/world/national-security/fbi-is-investigating-foreign-hacks-of-state-election-systems/2016/08/29/6e758ff4-6e00-11e6-8365-b19e428a975e_story.html?utm_term=.de487f1d4b90.

that state databases and third-party vendors were not only targeted for attack, but were breached. In June 2017, the media reported that hackers attempted to infiltrate 39 jurisdictions[16] and DHS officials testified before Congressional Intelligence Committees that "Russian government cyber actors" targeted "internet-connected election-related networks" in 21 states.[17] It is unclear whether and to what extent these jurisdictions were actually breached. In its written testimony, DHS noted that a small number of states were actually breached and that attempts to compromise networks occurred in a larger number of states, although these attacks were not successful.[18] Although security agencies and election officials have stated that no vote totals were changed,[19] in fact, no investigation occurred that would uncover whether vote totals were changed.[20] In reality, no evidence exists that vote totals were changed, but for certain kinds of electronic voting systems, that evidence is likely not available. On July 13, 2018, Robert Mueller, Special Counsel, issued indictments of 12 co-conspirator Russian nationals for interfering with the 2016 elections.[21] These indictments demonstrated that prosecutors believe they have enough evidence of such hacking to convict the defendants of criminal conduct.

Regardless of the success of hacking attempts in 2016, the consensus among the intelligence community is that future attacks on American

---

[16]Matthew Cole, Richard Esposito, Sam Biddle, and Ryan Grim. "Top-Secret NSA Report Details Russian Hacking Effort Days Before 2016 Election." *The Intercept*, June 5, 2017. Retrieved from https://theintercept.com/2017/06/05/top-secret-nsa-report-details-russian-hacking-effort-days-before-2016-election.

[17]Written testimony of I & A Cyber Division Acting Director Dr. Samuel Liles, and NPPD Acting Deputy Under Secretary for Cybersecurity and Communications Jeanette Manfra for a Senate Select Committee on Intelligence hearing titled "Russian Interference in the 2016 U.S. Elections," at 4, June 21, 2017. Retrieved from https://www.dhs.gov/news/2017/06/21/written-testimony-ia-cyber-division-acting-director-dr-samuel-liles-and-nppd-acting.

[18]Ibid., DHS has not identified the 21 jurisdictions to date.

[19]Ibid., at 6.

[20]Sam Thielman. "Were Voting Machines Actually Breached? DHS Would Rather Not Know." *TPM Muckraker*, June 30, 2017. Retrieved from http://talkingpointsmemo.com/muckraker/dhs-doesnt-want-to-know-about-vote-hacks.

[21]*U.S. v. Viktor Borisovich Netyksho* et al., Indictment, No. 1:18-cr-00032-DLF (July 13, 2018 D.D.C). Retrieved from https://www.justice.gov/file/1035477/download.

elections are inevitable.[22] The inevitability of attacks is a key concept in cybersecurity; the question is not whether a system will be attacked, but when. Therefore, security teams use a multilayered approach to security and take steps to detect, mitigate, respond, and recover from an attack. The general cybersecurity challenge is to ensure that organizational processes are in place that allow jurisdictions to detect the fact of an attack, respond to a breach, minimize the harm, and restore normal operations as quickly as possible. This concept holds especially true for elections. Only when such processes are uniformly in place and routinely applied will confidence in the process increase.

The narrative of hacking, either of voter registration databases or of precinct voting devices, is extremely destructive to democracy. A healthy democracy can survive when all constituencies have confidence that the candidate chosen by the voters, in reality, won the election. This chapter will summarize the concepts and best practices necessary to establish integrity and security around the voter registration process and the setup and conduct of elections, including the tabulation of voting results and the verification of tabulation results. Implementing these procedures and best practices, thoughtfully and with transparency, creates resilient systems that can recover from cyber events, bolsters confidence in our electoral process, and contributes, at least partially, to "election integrity."

Election Integrity: Ensuring that Computer Processes Are Secure, Trustworthy and Verifiable

Integrity in the Voter Registration Process

Election integrity, defined as it relates to voter registration databases, means that every eligible voter who desired to register was able to register easily and confirm their registration; that all eligible and registered voters were properly and accurately recorded in the poll books, and that none were deleted, either inadvertently or intentionally. For voters to have confidence

---

[22]"Assessing Russian Activities and Intentions in Recent U.S. Elections." ICA 2017-01D, Office of the Director of National Intelligence, 2017 at iii; Lawrence Norden, and Ian Vandewalker. "Securing Elections from Foreign Interference." Brennan Center for Justice, June 29, 2017 at 4.

in the electoral process, they must have confidence that they are properly registered so that they have the ability to vote. Voters in 49 states and the District of Columbia are required to register in advance of an election.[23] Election integrity requires that voter registration lists be as complete and as accurate as possible, because they are a mandatory prerequisite to the constitutional right to vote. The process of registration itself must not be fraught with barriers, and list maintenance procedures must be reasonable and transparent to meet the dual goals of accuracy and completeness.[24]

Voters have options in choosing the method of registration. Filling out and submitting a paper form is uniformly available. After the passage of the National Voter Registration Act (NVRA), also known as "Motor-Voter," voters may register or update their registration when they obtain or renew their license at their state's driver's licensing agency. In approximately 35 states, voter registration records from the driver's licensing agency are transmitted electronically.[25] As of October 10, 2018, voters in 37 states may apply to register or change a registration electronically through an online portal.[26] A relatively newer tool, automatic voter registration, converts the opportunity to register to vote at the driver's licensing agency from an "opt in" choice to an "opt out" choice. In other words, an eligible voter is "automatically" added to the voter rolls unless the voter notifies the state that he or she does not wish

---

[23]"Voter Registration." Nat'l Conference of State Legislatures, September 27, 2016. Retrieved from http://www.ncsl.org/research/elections-and-campaigns/voter-registration.aspx.

[24]This chapter focuses on election technology and best practices for safeguarding it to ensure voter confidence. Barriers to voter registration, strict voter ID laws and aggressive purging of registrations from voter rolls also contribute to the perception of integrity in the electoral process. In 2018, voting rights organizations were challenging via litigation strict voter ID laws in 7 states and voter registration restrictions in 5 states. Wendy R. Weiser, and Max Feldman. "The State of Voting 2018." Brennan Center for Justice, June 5, 2018. Retrieved from https://www.brennancenter.org/publication/state-voting-2018, Historically, aggressive purges of voter lists results in eligible voters caught within a too wide net. Jonathan Brater, Kevin Morris, Myrna Perez, and Chris Deluzio. "Purges: A Growing Threat to the Right to Vote." Brennan Center for Justice, at 5–6, July 20, 2018 (collecting historical examples). Retrieved from https://www.brennancenter.org/publication/purges-growing-threat-right-vote.

[25]"VRM in the States: Electronic Registration." Brennan Center for Justice, February 3, 2017. Retrieved from https://www.brennancenter.org/analysis/vrm-states-electronic-registration.

[26]"Online Voter Registration." Nat'l Conference of State Legislatures, October 10, 2018. Retrieved from http://www.ncsl.org/research/elections-and-campaigns/electronic-or-online-voter-registration.aspx.

to register.[27] Many states also offer tools for voters to check their voter registration status online or find their polling location. These features and other tools for voter information are typically delivered via a web platform over the Internet.

Under the Help America Vote Act, states were required to adopt "a single, uniform, official, centralized, interactive computerized statewide voter registration list defined, maintained, and administered at the State level that contains the name and registration information of every legally registered voter in the State and assigns a unique identifier to each legally registered voter in the State."[28] The statewide voter registration mandate recognized that, in the past, voter registration lists were a patchwork of locally developed solutions that did not communicate either with each other or to any central authority. HAVA intended to remedy that problem while at the same time requiring identification verification through a state's department of motor vehicles and the US Social Security Administration.[29]

Statewide voter registration databases implemented as a result of HAVA receive records in one of three ways: (1) The state maintains a central database and local jurisdictions connect directly to it for the purpose of adding, modifying, or canceling registrations, also known as "top-down" system[30]; (2) the statewide voter registration database collects and aggregates data stored locally at all of the state's the voter registration agencies, also known as a "bottom up" system; and (3) some states have features of both top-down and bottom-up systems, also known as "hybrid" systems.[31]

---

[27]Sixteen states and the District of Columbia currently offer an automatic voter registration option. "Automatic Voter Registration." National Conference of State Legislatures, April 22, 2019. Retrieved from http://www.ncsl.org/research/elections-and-campaigns/automatic-voter-registration.aspx.

[28]Help America Vote Act, 52 U.S. Code § 21083.

[29]52 U.S. Code § 21083(a)(5).

[30]Best practice would dictate that local jurisdictions only have the ability to modify registrations in their own jurisdiction while retaining the ability to search statewide. Similarly, best practice requires that state election authorities should have no ability to modify, alter or delete voter registration records.

[31]Sean Greene. "Statewide Voter Registration Systems." Election Assistance Commission, August 31, 2017. Retrieved from https://www.eac.gov/statewide-voter-registration-systems/.

Regardless of the characterization of the type of system in use, statewide voter registration databases are connected to localities and other agencies via networks. Likewise, Internet-facing applications and tools that touch voter registration present their own set of risks to the integrity of the voter registration rolls because they are connected to the Internet. Finally, complete and accurate voter registration lists must be available at the polling place regardless of whether the pollbooks are paper lists or the jurisdiction signs voters in through electronic pollbooks.[32]

The cybersecurity risks presented by network-connected voter registration databases are no different than similar risks presented by other databases that contain mission-critical data and personally identifying information. According to DHS, voter registration databases are vulnerable to a variety of attacks using an equal variety of methods. These can include direct web-based attacks that seek to inject or send commands to enable the attacker to gain unauthorized access to information; denial of service (DoS) attacks that prevent legitimate users from being able to use election information or services; ransomware attacks that block legitimate users' access to a system until a ransom is paid, and more. Phishing attacks involve forged emails or other messages designed to get the recipient to click on malicious links or otherwise provide an entry point for stealing credentials such as passwords, spread malware or disrupt voting operations.[33] Foreign adversaries successfully used some of these methods in 2016.[34]

---

[32]"Securing the Vote, Protecting American Democracy." The National Academies of Sciences, Engineering and Medicine, Consensus Study Report, September, 2018, appropriately noted that cyber attacks on electronic poll books could alter voter registration data, cause voter disenfranchisement, result in long lines, and/or force greater use of provisional ballots. These events would certainly undermine faith in electoral processes. NASEM recommended that national standards for testing and certifying epollbooks, including national security standards be adopted. NASEM report at 72.

[33]"Securing Voter Registration Data." National Protections and Programs Directorate, Department of Homeland Security, June 26, 2018. Retrieved from https://www.dhs.gov/sites/default/files/publications/Securing%20Voter%20Registration%20Data_0.pdf; see also Pamela Smith. "Verified Voting Testimony submitted to the Milton Marks 'Little Hoover' Commission on California State Government Organization and Economy," July 26, 2018. Retrieved from https://www.verifiedvoting.org/wp-content/uploads/2018/07/CALHC-Testimony-Smith-July2018.pdf.

[34]"Securing the Vote, Protecting American Democracy." The National Academies of Sciences, Engineering and Medicine, Consensus Study Report, September, 2018 at 24–29.

Thus, to preserve electoral integrity, jurisdictions that administer elections must adhere to those cybersecurity best practices to reduce the risk of a cybersecurity intrusion by using recommended multilayered approaches to system security, such as patching applications and operating systems, application whitelisting, and appropriate deployment of firewalls. Election jurisdictions must also permit monitoring of the system to detect any such intrusions, limit the level of network connectivity to protect and isolate data, restrict administrative privileges and permit periodic audits of the voter registration data to detect any problems. Election jurisdictions must also implement strong disaster recovery plans and practice response to an event in real time, including an event within the statewide database and an event discovered on election day. Not least, election administrators must establish and enforce good cyber hygiene practices throughout the entire supply chain. Specifically, for voter registration databases, jurisdictions should have frequent backups and secure storage of those backups. In planning to recover from an error or cybersecurity event, jurisdictions should implement procedures to restore operations to a "clean" database within a reasonable amount of time from discovery of an intrusion.[35]

Setup and Conduct of Elections—Election Integrity of Voting Systems

There are two basic kinds of electronic voting systems in use in the United States—direct-recording electronic (DRE) systems and optical scan systems. Both types of systems use computers. The primary

---

[35]Several organizations have researched and published guidelines for securing election computer assets. See, e.g. "Securing Voter Registration Data." National Protections and Programs Directorate, Department of Homeland Security, June 26, 2018. Retrieved from https://www.dhs.gov/sites/default/files/publications/Securing%20Voter%20Registration%20Data_0.pdf; "A Handbook for Elections Infrastructure Security, Version 1.0." The Center for Internet Security, February 2018. Retrieved from https://www.cisecurity.org/elections-resources/; "The State and Local Election Cybersecurity Playbook." Belfer Center for Science and International Affairs, Harvard Kennedy School, February 2018. Retrieved from https://www.belfercenter.org/publication/state-and-local-election-cybersecurity-playbook#practices. The extent to which jurisdictions adhere to these recommendations will determine the level of integrity they are perceived to have. This chapter does not attempt to duplicate information found in these reports but rather desires to place the need for cyber security around voter registration databases in the context of election integrity.

difference is that an optical scan system incorporates a voter-marked paper ballot, marked either with a pen or pencil or with a ballot marking device, the ballots are counted by scanners and then those ballots are retained for recounts or audits.

DRE systems directly record the voter's choices to computer memory. The voter may interface with the voting machine in one of several ways, such as a touchscreen or push buttons; regardless, the voter's selections are recorded directly to memory stored in the machine. There is no "software-independent"[36] record of voter intent provided with a DRE system. Some DREs are capable of producing a voter-verified paper audit trail that is shown to the voter before the voter submits her ballot.

DRE systems are inherently insecure and lack a way to recover in the event of an intrusion or software error. A printout of election results from the memory card after the fact or a printout of "cast vote records" does not provide any additional verification of the election results. Those printouts simply call up the data that is stored on the computer's memory. If the data were not stored correctly, whether because of malware or malfunction in the voting system, a printout of incorrect data is meaningless. Without a contemporaneous software-independent record of voter intent, there is no way to verify, audit, or recount DREs.

In an optical scan electronic voting system, voters mark their choices on a paper ballot and feed the ballot through a scanner that electronically tabulates the votes. The voter-marked paper ballot serves as evidence of the voter's intent and may be recounted or audited to confirm the results of the electronic tabulation.

DREs and optical scanners are portions of the electronic voting system that are deployed to the polling place on election day. Some jurisdictions may also use accessible ballot marking devices. Those devices provide accessible features and print either a ballot identical to the ballot marked with a pen or pencil, or a summary of the voter's choices which can also

---

[36]Software independence in voting systems was described by Ron Rivest (MIT) and John Wack (NIST) as follows: "A voting system is software-independent if an undetected change or error in its software cannot cause an undetectable change or error in an election outcome." See Rivest, R. and Wack, J. "On the Notion of Software Independence in Voting Systems." Retrieved from https://people.csail.mit.edu/rivest/RivestWackOnTheNotionOfSoftwareIndependenceInVotingSystems.pdf.

be scanned and retained for recounts and audits. Election officials must securely store, maintain, prepare, and test their voting systems in preparation for each election, ensuring that unauthorized access is prevented, and that security protocols are followed for the physical process of uploading new ballot definitions and preparing systems for deployment.

Election systems include not only the systems used for marking our ballots and for tallying the votes but also the systems used to set up the computer files that instruct the voting devices how to interpret voter inputs, how to correlate that input with the correct candidate names and ballot measures, and properly add that input to the tally of votes. Consequently, another aspect of election integrity is assurance that the electronic voting systems were properly programmed in a secure manner, adequately tested and securely deployed to the polling locations, that the voting devices are functioning and available to be used and the correct ballot was presented to the voter, who was able to mark the ballot, check or verify it and cast it securely and privately. Each step in this process has an important role to play in the overall integrity of our electoral system.

Typically, commercially available voting systems in the US market include several different hardware and software components. The software that runs the entire system is the election management system (EMS), which defines, develops and maintains election databases, performs election definitions and setup functions, formats ballots, counts votes, consolidates and report results, and maintains audit trails.[37] The EMS runs on either Windows or Linux operating systems and uses typical laptop or desktop computers. Although jurisdictions "should" not connect those computers to a network or the Internet, no systematic efforts exist to ensure compliance with recommended security configurations. Many jurisdictions contract with third-party vendors to do the work of setting up the election. Those externally developed program files are frequently transmitted to jurisdictions via the Internet, or via removable media. Unless jurisdictions are scrupulous in their attention to best practices, these transmissions present another method of possible intrusion. All voting systems use removable media to transfer files from the EMS

---

[37]Voluntary Voting System Guidelines, Version 1.1. 2015, United States Election Assistance Commission, available here https://www.eac.gov/assets/1/28/VVSG.1.1.VOL.1.FINAL1.pdf.

computer to the precinct devices. The use of removable media is itself a security vulnerability and provides a vector for attack. Access ports for peripheral devices and memory cards present opportunities to attack the system either by connecting a malicious device to the system or by inserting fraudulent code via an unauthorized memory card. These risks and vulnerabilities exist for all types of computerized voting used in America.

While it may be the case that precinct devices are not connected to the internet, other pathways for tampering with the software exist and can be exploited.[38] Because electronic voting systems may be connected directly or indirectly to a network during some part of the election process, they are vulnerable to most, if not all, of the risks that affect network-connected voter registration databases. The Center for Internet Security, in fact, categorizes its recommended best practices according to the potential degree and type of network connectivity presented by each election infrastructure component.[39] Accordingly, election integrity depends upon robust implementation of the same cybersecurity best practices described in the previous section on voter registration databases.

However, pre-election testing, sometimes referred to as Logic and Accuracy testing, is critically important for several purposes, including to confirm that the ballot styles are complete and correct, and that voting systems are functioning as they are prepared for deployment to polling places. Pre-election testing is necessary for supporting secure election practices, but it is not sufficient on its own to confirm outcomes because of the need to observe security protocols throughout the entirety of the electoral process.

Once deployed to a polling place, poll workers oversee physical security of the voting system until the system is returned to the local office. Threats to voting systems can include insider tampering via injection of

---

[38]On September 12, 2017, the Presidential Advisory Commission on Election Integrity ("Pence Commission") held a hearing during which three respected computer scientist and security advisors testified: Dr. Andrew Appel, Professor of Computer Science, Princeton University; Dr. Ronald Rivest, Professor of Computer Science, Massachusetts Institute of Technology; and Harri Hursti, Co-Founder of Nordic Innovation Labs. Their presentations are available here https://www.whitehouse.gov/presidential-advisory-commission-election-integrity-resources and a summary of the materials is available here https://medium.com/@max.hailperin/presidential-advisory-commission-on-election-integrity-september-12-2017-meeting-materials-4512dd139ee6.

[39]"A Handbook for Elections Infrastructure Security, Version 1.0." at 8, the Center for Internet Security, February 2018. Retrieved from https://www.cisecurity.org/elections-resources/.

malware through a tampered memory device or other communication method, tampering or damage to a voting system en route to or at a polling location. Any of these could result in voter disenfranchisement if the voting system is not functioning or if results are altered. To ensure integrity, the voter-marked paper ballot is counted via a scanner, separate from the device through which it is marked, the ballot is retained for recounts and audits, the ballot is counted accurately along with all the other ballots, and the jurisdiction includes all validly cast ballots submitted by eligible voters in the universe of ballots. Because there is no absolute guarantee that prevents tampering with voting systems, routine and rigorous post-election audits must be conducted to ensure that the electronic system reported the results accurately.

Verification of Tabulation Results

Probably the most critical component of election integrity of the tabulation system involves the ability to demonstrate that the outcome reported by the electronic voting system is the correct outcome. According to the findings of the National Academies of Sciences, Engineering, and Medicine (NASEM), no realistic mechanism exists to fully secure the vote casting and tabulation processes from cyber threats.[40] Even if the risk of a hacking or error in the voting machine never materializes, the existence of the risk coupled with the destructive narrative that the outcomes could be compromised serves to undermine faith on our electoral processes.

Currently, the best practice requires trustworthy evidence of voter intent in the form of voter-marked paper ballots and a method of checking that the electronic vote tally matches those paper records. A contemporaneous voter-marked paper ballot prevents an undetected change in system software from producing an undetectable change in the voting results. The presence of such a record renders the system

---

[40] "Securing the Vote, Protecting American Democracy." The National Academies of Sciences, Engineering and Medicine, Consensus Study Report, September, 2018.

"software independent."[41] When a voting system retains a voter-marked paper ballot for recounts and audits, the election administrator has the ability to demonstrate that the ballots were counted correctly through a post-election tabulation audit, such as a risk-limiting audit. This audit occurs before the official certification of results to allow for correction of any errors detected via the audit.

Risk-limiting audits examine individual randomly selected ballots until sufficient statistical assurance in the election outcome is obtained. The statistical assurance means that the chance of an incorrect reported outcome escapes detection is less than the predetermined risk limit. Sampling of ballots continues until the risk limit is achieved or a hand recount is deemed necessary because of the closeness of the race or anomalies in the counting.

Risk-limiting audits depend on two critically important characteristics. First, the electoral processes must observe procedures to maintain rigorous chain of custody of the paper ballots from the time the ballots were deployed, through voting and finally when returned to the jurisdiction after voting. Second, an audit designed to check whether the software operated correctly must involve manual processes, namely, observation by humans of the human readable text, or marks on the voter-marked paper ballot and that such a process is independent of the system that counted the votes originally.[42]

Conclusion

The seeds of doubt sown by the hacking narrative cause distrust in our democracy and skepticism about the correctness of the election outcome. Defusing that destructive narrative is the most effective way to

---

[41] See Rivest, R. and Wack, J. "On the Notion of Software Independence in Voting Systems." Retrieved from https://people.csail.mit.edu/rivest/RivestWackOnTheNotionOfSoftwareIndependenceInVotingSystems.pdf.

[42] For more complete description of the characteristics of risk-limiting audits, see "Securing the Vote, Protecting American Democracy." The National Academies of Sciences, Engineering and Medicine, Consensus Study Report, September, 2018; See also "Principles and Best Practices for Post-Election Audits," December 2018. Retrieved from https://electionaudits.org/files/Audit%20Principles%20and%20Best%20Practices%202018.pdf.

instill confidence in the election result. Today, given the known vulnerabilities and inability to perfectly safeguard any computer system from attack, the best evidence of the voter's choices is evidence from voter-marked paper ballots. Jurisdictions can leverage technology to tally those paper ballots, but they can also use them to conduct an audit, or a spot check of the results and they provide the ability for candidates in close races, to have a meaningful recount of the contest.

Prevention of cyber-attacks is necessary to reduce the risk that one will occur. However, prevention is never 100% effective, leaving jurisdictions to adopt practices that allow them to detect interference, respond to it, and restore operations as quickly as possible. When those procedures are uniformly adopted, rigorously applied and reported to the public and press, our electoral processes will come that much closer to having integrity. Perhaps more importantly, confidence in American elections will increase.

Marian K. Schneider is the President of Verified Voting, a leading national not-for-profit, nonpartisan organization focused exclusively on the critical role technology plays in election administration. She formerly served as the deputy secretary for elections and administration in the Pennsylvania Department of State and as special advisor to Pennsylvania Governor Tom Wolf on election policy. She oversaw implementation of Pennsylvania's online voter registration application and introduced significant improvements to election administration. In 2016, she invited assistance from the US Department of Homeland Security and convened a cross-agency working group to secure Pennsylvania's election infrastructure. Schneider has advocated to remove barriers to voting especially for voters of color and for the use of secure, verifiable voting systems that permit meaningful recounts and audits.

15

Election Audits

Jennifer Morrell

Auditing and Risk-Limiting Audits

As a society, we accept and rely on federal testing to ensure the integrity of our food and drugs. We feel at ease taking a flight because we trust the strict standards for aircraft design, maintenance, and flight practices. We look to other ratings and standards to identify high-quality goods like running shoes or coffee. We accept that local government institutions must have their financial records audited on a regular basis, in part to establish a bond rating. None of us would deposit money in a financial institution or invest in a corporation if we didn't trust that audits are performed to ensure their solvency. Why should we expect less from the institution at the heart of our democracy?

Audits have played a role in US companies since the creation of the Securities and Exchange Act of 1934. The Securities and Exchange Commission established audits as a way to ensure financial records and transactions were reported accurately and a system of internal controls

J. Morrell (✉)
Democracy Fund, Washington, DC, USA

was established and followed. Historically, audits provided a backward-looking view of the financial health of a company by relying on a manual process of collecting, processing, and reporting information. Today, audits evaluate processes and internal controls by providing real-time information. They can also alert companies to errors and fraudulent activity and highlight areas for process improvement (Byrnes et al. 2012).

Similar auditing standards can be applied to elections.[1] The components of an audit are relatively simple. At its essence, an audit is a check that the ballots cast are the ballots correctly counted. They center on a documented process for obtaining relevant and verifiable evidence, then evaluating that evidence against a set of audit criteria. How much evidence to collect is a central question in a risk-limiting audit (RLA). The standards of the Public Company Accounting Oversight Board (PCAOB) state, "as the risk increases, the amount of evidence that the auditor should obtain also increases." PCAOB standards also highlight the need for quality evidence. They state, "obtaining more of the same type of audit evidence…cannot compensate for the poor quality of that evidence" (Public Company Accounting Oversight Board, n.d.).

This chapter discusses the relationship among the components in a risk-limiting audit, and how they relate to the sample size, or the amount of evidence you need to collect. I also summarizes key definitions related to auditing and voting technology. It makes sense to rely on standard, national definitions, even though the logistics and process will vary somewhat state to state depending on the election model and voting equipment. The chapter does not address best practices for ballot security, chain of custody, or ballot reconciliation. Those are all practices that determine the quality of the evidence. Having a trustworthy audit trail is critical to the validity of the audit.

Finally, by looking at auditing literature we can establish that audits are meant to detect errors, provide accountability, deter fraud, limit risk, determine accuracy, and provide feedback. When we extend this idea to elections, an audit can provide the same benefits including:

---

[1] This chapter is not meant to address how to create election audit standards but a good starting point for exploring this idea can be found in a project conducted by the Maryland State Board of Elections, "Development of a Pilot Election Audit Program."

- Detecting errors in the voting equipment and other elements of the election system
- Providing accountability to voters
- Deterring fraudulent activity (hacking or altering voting equipment)
- Limiting the risk of certifying an incorrect outcome
- Providing assurance that votes were counted and reported accurately
- Providing feedback to the election official for process improvement

As we work to incorporate auditing practices into election administration it helps to understand the common types of audits, phases of an audit, and who performs the audit.

Types of Audits

1. A **product audit** is an examination of a particular product (voting system) to evaluate whether it conforms to requirements and performance standards.
2. A **process audit** evaluates an operation against predetermined instructions or standards and asks the questions:

    - Did it conform to the standards?
    - Are the instructions effective?

    The process audit examines:

    - Resources (equipment, materials, people)
    - Environment
    - Methods (procedures and instructions)

3. A **system audit** verifies that applicable elements of the system are appropriate and effective and have been developed, documented, and implemented in accordance with specified requirements.

For example, an election system audit would determine if the election system conforms to state and federal policies and requirements.

Phases of an Audit

1. Preparation: Audit preparation consists of everything that is done in advance by interested parties, such as the auditor, the lead auditor, the client, and the audit program manager, to ensure that the audit complies with the client's objective. The preparation stage of an audit begins with the decision to conduct the audit. Preparation ends when the audit itself begins.
2. Conducting the Audit.
3. Reporting and Feedback: The purpose of the audit report is to communicate the results of the investigation. The report should provide correct and clear data that will be effective as a management aid in addressing important organizational issues. The audit process may end when the report is issued by the lead auditor or after follow-up actions are completed.
4. Closure: The audit is completed when all the planned audit activities have been carried out and there is verification of follow-up actions.

Internal and External Audits

First-party audit—when an organization measures its strengths and weaknesses against its own procedures or against external standards.

Third-party audit—performed by an independent audit organization and free of any conflict of interest.

Risk-Limiting Audits

A RLA[2] is a post-election tabulation audit in which a random sample of voted ballots is manually examined for evidence that the originally reported outcome of the election is correct. If the originally reported outcome is

---

[2]The RLA definition provided here is a heuristic, based on the author's interpretation from the sources listed and numerous discussions on the topic.

incorrect, there is a pre-specified minimum chance that the audit will correct the result. The correction is made by performing a full manual tally.

A risk-limiting audit does not verify that every vote was counted correctly. It verifies "that the reported results of the contest are correct; that is, they agree with the results that a full hand-count would reveal" (Sridhar and Rivest, n.d.). Stated another way, it is "an 'intelligent' incremental recount that stops when the audit provides sufficiently strong evidence that a full hand-count would confirm the original (voting system) outcome" (Lindeman and Stark 2012, 42).

An appropriate initial sample size for the audit is determined based on the contest margins, the total number of votes cast, and the desired confidence in the outcome of the audit. This allows election officials to retrieve and examine the fewest ballots possible[3] while still achieving strong statistical evidence that the outcome is correct. If the sample does not provide strong enough evidence that the outcomes under audit are correct, more ballots are inspected, with the possibility that the audit could ultimately lead to all ballots being manually examined.

Traditional Audits

RLAs are meant to be a more efficient and statistically sound process than traditional post-election audits that rely on hand tallying a fixed number or fixed percentage of voted ballots. Both RLAs and traditional audits require some type of voter-verifiable paper record, such as paper ballots, that voters have the opportunity to inspect and correct before casting.

The ballots selected for a traditional post-election audit normally come from several randomly selected batches, precincts, or voting machines. While RLAs can also be based on such sampling this is not an efficient approach to ensuring that the outcome will be corrected if it is wrong. Traditional audits may sample more or fewer ballots than required to confirm the outcome of a race of interest, but they will not,

---

[3]It is perfectly fine to audit more ballots than the initial sample size requires.

in general, correct tabulation errors, even if they altered the reported outcome.

RLA Concepts and Terms

A good starting point for understanding how RLAs work is to become familiar with some of the common terms and definitions. To ensure you are using the terminology in a consistent manner it is helpful to discuss the terms with a group; connect them with tangible forms, reports, and outcomes from prior elections; and practice communicating the meaning of the terms.

Risk-Limiting Audit

An RLA is a post-election tabulation audit in which a random sample of voted ballots is manually examined for evidence that the originally reported outcome of the election is correct. If the originally reported outcome is incorrect, there is a pre-specified minimum chance that the audit will correct the result. It corrects the result by performing a full manual tally. As its name suggests, an RLA limits the risk of certifying a contest with the wrong winner.

This means that if the originally reported outcome is incorrect, there is a pre-specified minimum chance that the audit will reveal a problem. Then a full manual tally can be conducted to determine the correct outcome.

Risk Limit

The risk limit is the largest chance that an incorrect reported tabulation outcome is not detected and corrected in RLA. For example, a 5% risk limit provides at most a 5% chance that the audit will not correct the outcome if the outcome is incorrect. In other words, there is at least a 95% chance that the audit will discover an error and correct the outcome if the outcome is wrong.

Table 15.1 Example calculation of diluted margin

Candidate A	2175	
Candidate B	1766	(Candidate A votes − Candidate B votes) ÷ Total ballots cast
Total Votes	*3941*	(2175 − 1766) ÷ 4098 = .0998, which is 10%
Over- and Under-Votes	157	
Total Ballots Cast	4098	Diluted Margin is 10%

Outcome

The outcome means the winner(s), not the tabulated vote totals. A wrong outcome is when the originally reported outcome disagrees with what a full hand count would show.

Diluted Margin

The diluted margin is the measure used to determine the closeness of the election, for the purpose of determining how many ballots need to be examined in some RLA methods. The diluted margin of the target contest is calculated by dividing the smallest reported margin (in votes) by the total number of ballots cast in the collection of ballots from which the sample is drawn. This measure accounts for the possibility that the vote tabulation system mistook an undervote or over-vote for a valid vote or vice versa. As an example, see Table 15.1.

Target Contest

A target contest is the contest selected for a risk-limiting audit. The target contest determines the number of ballots that must be examined during the RLA and is used to determine if the audit has met the risk limit. It should not preclude the opportunity to audit other contests on ballots already selected for audit. There can be one or more target contests.

Cast Vote Record

A cast vote record (CVR) is the electronic record of a voter's selections in every contest for a given ballot. This record is generated by the voting system and needs to provide enough information to pair the CVR with the physical ballot from which it was created. The CVR is the digital representation of each individual ballot that has been scanned and tabulated. It represents the votes cast in each contest after adjudication for voter intent or any other tabulation rules have been applied, e.g., write-in candidates.

Ballot-Level Comparison Audit

A ballot-level comparison audit is a type of RLA in which individual paper ballots are randomly selected, the voter markings are examined and interpreted manually, and the human interpretation of voter intent is compared to the voting system's interpretation as reflected in the corresponding CVRs. This type of RLA requires the voting system to create and export individual CVRs in a way that the corresponding physical ballot can be identified and retrieved for manual inspection, and vice versa. Methods to link CVRs to the corresponding ballot generally rely either on the order in which the ballots were scanned, or on imprinting ballots with identifiers after they have been separated from the voter (to preserve anonymity). Currently, central-count optical scan systems make this easier than precinct-count systems do, because the ballots have already been separated from the voters' identities before the scan occurs. However, most currently fielded voting systems in the United States cannot export CVRs in a way that links them to the corresponding paper ballot. Some do not even create CVRs internally.

Ballot-Polling Audit

A ballot-polling audit is a type of RLA in which individual paper ballots are randomly selected, the voter markings are examined and interpreted manually. If a large enough sample shows a large enough majority for the reported winner, the audit stops. A ballot-polling audit cannot identify whether a specific ballot was mistabulated, but it can provide convincing evidence about whether the reported outcome is correct. This type of RLA does not require a CVR or other data export from the voting system, nor does it involve comparing human interpretation of voter intent to the machine interpretation of voter intent. It is an RLA method that can be used with any voting system that produces voter-verifiable paper records. While the setup costs and equipment requirements for ballot-polling audits are less than they are for ballot-level comparison audits, ballot-polling audits generally require manually inspecting more ballots (when the outcome is correct). It is a good option when ballots are scanned in polling locations or when the voting system cannot report how it interpreted individual ballots—which is the situation with most voting systems currently deployed in the United States.

Batch-Level Comparison Audit

A batch-level comparison audit is a type of RLA that most resembles a "traditional" audit. In a batch-level comparison audit, the voting system must export subtotals for identifiable physical batches of ballots, such as all ballots cast in a precinct or all mail ballots scanned together as a batch by a particular machine. The auditors add up those batch-level results to verify that they produce the reported contest outcomes. If so, some physical batches are selected at random. The votes in each selected batch are examined manually and tabulated, and the audit counts are compared to the voting system's reported subtotals. Depending on the number and type of discrepancies the audit finds in the sample, the audit either stops or examines more batches manually. This type of RLA does check the tabulation where ballot polling audits only check the outcome. Like ballot polling audits, batch-level comparison audits generally require manually inspecting more ballots (when the outcome is correct) than ballot-level comparison audits do.

Workload/Sample Size

The sample size or workload is the number of ballots required to be inspected before the audit can stop. For ballot-level comparison audits, the total sample size depends on the diluted margin of the contest being audited, the risk limit that has been established for the audit, the sampling scheme and the discrepancies the audit uncovers as it progresses. For ballot-polling audits, the workload depends on the true vote shares of each candidate, on the number of ballots that do not contain a valid vote for any candidate in the contest, and on the sampling scheme.

Ballot Manifest

A record that documents where and how physical ballots are stored. A ballot manifest is critical for conducting any type of RLA. It is unique to the jurisdiction conducting the audit based on how ballots are organized, scanned, and stored and may include:

- An identifier for each scanner used
- A unique batch number
- The total number of ballots scanned in a batch
- The container ID where the batch of ballots is stored

The information in the manifest should never come from the voting system. It should be created and maintained by the local election official. The log can be as simple as a paper form or spreadsheet completed by whomever is handling a batch of ballots.

Policy Considerations

When developing and establishing RLA policy, lawmakers and administrators should focus on the central goal of strengthening voter confidence and election transparency. By establishing a policy framework that is both easy to understand and implement, while not being overly prescriptive, policymakers can provide the foundation for solid post-election tabulation audit procedures that generate voter confidence in election administration and operations. Outlined below are considerations for effective RLA policy.

Statute

The statutory requirements for RLAs should not prescribe the process or the calculations involved in conducting an RLA, such as setting a specific risk limit. At a minimum, it should establish RLAs as the method for conducting a post-election tabulation audit, provide any necessary definitions, an implementation date, and how further rules, regulations and procedures will be established. This allows for innovation as new methods of auditing are developed and voting system technology advances.

Two good examples come from Washington and Colorado.

> The secretary of state shall…establish procedures for implementation of risk-limiting audits, including random selection of the audit sample, determination of audit size, and procedures for a comparison risk-limiting audit and ballot polling risk-limiting audit as defined (Washington 29A.60.185 (1)(c)(iii).
>
> The secretary of state shall promulgate rules… as may be necessary to implement and administer the requirements of this section. In connection with the promulgation of the rules, the secretary shall consult recognized statistical experts, equipment vendors, and county clerk and recorders, and shall consider best practices for conducting risk-limiting audits (Colorado 1-7-515 (4)).

The timeframe for implementing the audit is another important consideration. For example, Colorado accelerated the conversation about RLAs once the majority of counties purchased new voting equipment that provided a CVR (2016–2017). Throughout 2017, various stakeholders spent an intensive year writing and passing election rules, regularly meeting with the state's RLA advisory group to decide on how the audit would be implemented, working to develop an RLA software tool, creating a training program, and conducting mock audits. After a multiyear process, the first statewide RLA happened in November 2017. Administering a pilot program over several elections prior to implementing an official RLA allows states to establish solid procedures for performing the audit. This process includes understanding and exploring various methods for conducting an RLA and working through the technology requirements to assist in conducting the audit. Ensuring the RLA can be performed prior to certification of the election is another policy change that needs to be considered. In addition, there should be a way to change the outcome of the election if the audit escalates to a full manual tally that concludes that the originally announced outcome was incorrect.

Definitions as They Appear in State Laws

Some of the terms used to describe the risk-limiting audit process are unique enough that they will require drafting definitions for clarity. The challenge is drafting language that can be interpreted and understood by the non-RLA expert while still being precise enough to ensure good auditing practice. It will be helpful to review the definitions used by other states as well as the definitions found in this chapter.

Listed below are three examples of how a RLA has been defined in election statute:

- **Rhode Island Election Law** (§ 17-19-37.4) for post-election audits defines a RLA as "a manual tally employing a statistical method that ensures a large, predetermined minimum chance of requiring a full manual tally whenever a full manual tally would show an electoral outcome that differs from the outcome reported by the vote-tabulating system for the audited contest. A RLA shall begin with a hand tally of the votes in one or more audit units and shall continue to hand tally votes in additional audit units until there is strong statistical evidence that the electoral outcome is correct. In the event that counting additional audit units does not provide strong statistical evidence that the electoral outcome is correct, the audit shall continue

until there has been a full manual tally to determine the correct electoral outcome of the audited contest."
- **Colorado Revised Statutes** (C.R.S. 1-7-515) for RLAs defines an RLA as "an audit protocol that makes use of statistical methods and is designed to limit to acceptable levels the risk of certifying a preliminary election outcome that constitutes an incorrect outcome."
- **Washington Election Laws** (RCW 29A.60.185) for the audit of results defines a RLA as "an audit protocol that makes use of statistical principles and methods and is designed to limit the risk of certifying an incorrect election outcome."

Voting Equipment and Technology

The voting equipment plays a major role in determining the type of audit that can be conducted. This includes the ability to produce a paper ballot that can be retrieved and examined as well as a CVR that will allow you to compare how the voting system interpreted each and every ballot.

Pilot RLAs

Any jurisdiction considering implementing RLAs should first conduct a pilot. It provides a great opportunity to help officials become familiar with the terms and procedures. The best way to learn how an RLA works is through hands-on experience. To make the pilot as effective as possible, limit the number of ballots that will be subject to audit to just a few precincts or a handful of scanned batches. Anywhere from 1000 to 4000 ballots (depending on the size of staff and estimated sample size) should be enough. The goal of the pilot is for staff to perform as many of the audit functions as possible including the role of the audit team in retrieving and examining ballots. Ideally, the pilot should be conducted immediately after an election has been certified and the period to request a recount has passed. This ensures the processes involved in handling, scanning, and accounting for ballots are still fresh on everyone's mind. It will also provide everyone involved an opportunity to reflect on the way ballots are organized and stored after scanning.

Post-audit Reporting and Feedback

Feedback and data gathered from post-election audits should be analyzed and used to continuously improve all elements of the election process—including the RLA process. This can be done in formal and informal feedback sessions after the audit is complete. It is important to document the thoughts and lessons learned from everyone that participated.

Communication

Communicating the RLA process to voters, candidates, election officials, and policymakers in a way that is both meaningful and understandable is a challenge. It is a complex idea that even subject matter experts struggle to clearly communicate what it is and how it works. The definitions are technical and the formulas for calculating the sample size or when the risk-limit has been satisfied, for instance, are grounded in math and statistics which can be difficult to explain.

Are there creative ways to inform voters of the process through information guides, infographics, social media posts, or other methods? Or is it enough for election officials to state that "there is strong statistical evidence that all votes cast were counted and reported accurately"? While we tackle better ways to communicate the RLA process we need to also think about transparency. Making audit information available on a public Web site is a good start. Some things to consider posting:

- Notice of the public meeting to establish the RLA random seed
- Established random seed
- Target contests selected for audit
- Ballot manifests

- Ballots selected for audit
- Total number of discrepancies.

The communication issues are not just as simple as putting the math into words or creating graphics to illustrate the process of retrieving ballots. One major hurdle will be a collaborative effort among RLA stakeholders to create standard terms and definitions that are used consistently when discussing policy and practices.

Conclusion

Election management problems seem to increase as the margin of victory decreases and public perception outweighs the assurances of experts and election officials. We must find a way to change this. Audits, standards, and testing are not the only remedy, but they are one way that election administrators can provide "the American electorate with a modern, voter-centric election system that runs efficiently and inspires trust in the electoral outcome" (Democracy Fund, n.d.).

The theories and application of post-election tabulation audits continue to evolve. In addition to more efficient ways to select ballots in a polling audit, there continues to be discussion and research about other methods for conducting post-election audits. This includes formulas for hybrid audits, combining ballot comparison and ballot polling, along with other forms of stratified sampling. Several jurisdictions have run pilot RLAs using a transitive audit method, where ballots have been completely rescanned and retabulated on different voting equipment.

There is also much debate and discussion about the role of ballot images in election audits. Auditing ballot images alone provides no evidence that ballots were not omitted from scanning, scanned twice, misinterpreted by the voting system, or altogether recorded incorrectly. However, they are being used in many states to improve tabulation accuracy by allowing for electronic adjudication and have the potential to help augment, but not replace, the human examination of voted ballots.

All these developments make it a fascinating time to be working in elections and working in the area of election audits. Administering elections and inspiring public confidence in election results requires more skill and expertise than ever before. Adding auditing expertise is one more element that puts election administration into a professional and technical field of its own and provides greater transparency that can help write the future of voting.

Elections Must Be Audited End-to-End

Auditing how votes are tabulated plays an important role in validating the outcome of an election. However, it is only one of several elements in the election system that need to be examined. An RLA only provides a modest benefit if you cannot provide evidence of a solid chain of custody from the beginning of an election to end, for both ballots and voting equipment. As you start to think about incorporating audit principles into election administration, consider other critical components in your election system that can be audited:

- Voter registration databases
- Voter district and precinct assignments
- Security procedures (physical and cybersecurity)
- Voting equipment testing (focused on paper ballots)
- Ballot reconciliation and chain of custody
- Ballot layout and design
- Resource planning and allocation (enough equipment, supplies, and people to meet demand).

Steps on the Path

Conducting an RLA does not need to be an immediate destination but can be viewed more as a path with steps along it. Here are some suggested steps that will help ease the transition toward RLAs:

- Maintaining strong collaboration among election officials
- Making the RLA terms and definitions a regular part of your vocabulary

- Creating documented voter intent guidelines
- Developing a well-crafted plan for ballot storage and organization
- Requiring precise ballot reconciliation
- Implementing dates and deadlines to accommodate time for a post-election audit prior to certification
- Basing the number of ballots selected for audit on the contest margins[4]
- Using dice or similar methods to randomly select the ballots, precincts, voting machines, etc. that will be audited
- Purchasing a voting system that produces a voter-verifiable paper ballot and CVR

References

Byrnes, Paul Eric, Abdullah Al-Awadhi, Benita Gullvist, Helen Brown Liburd, Ryan Teeter, J. Donald Warren Jr., and Miklos Vasarhelyi, "Evolution of Auditing: From the Traditional Approach to the Future Audit." *American Institute of Certified Public Accountants*, 2012. Accessed January 9, 2019. https://www.aicpa.org/interestareas/frc/assuranceadvisoryservices/downloadabledocuments/whitepaper_evolution-of-auditing.pdf.

Democracy Fund. "*Election Administration & Voting.*" Accessed January 9, 2019. https://www.democracyfund.org/electionsmap.

Lindeman, Mark, and Philip B. Stark. "A Gentle Introduction to Risk-Limiting Audits." *IEEE Security and Privacy, Special Issue on Electronic Voting*, 10, no. 5 (2012) 42–49.

Public Company Accounting Oversight Board. "AS 1105: Audit Evidence." Accessed January 9, 2019. https://pcaobus.org/Standards/Auditing/Pages/AS1105.aspx.

Sridhar, Mayuri, and Ronald Rivest. "k-Cut: A Simple Approximately-Uniform Method for Sampling Ballots in Post-election Audits". Massachusetts Institute of Technology. Accessed January 9, 2019. http://people.csail.mit.edu/rivest/pubs/SR18b.pdf.

---

[4]Similar to the way post-election audits are conducted in New Mexico.

Jennifer Morrell works as a consultant with Democracy Fund leading the Election Validation Project, aimed at increasing trust in elections through rigorous audits, standards, and testing. As the Deputy of Elections in Arapahoe County, Colorado, Jennifer was instrumental in Colorado's successful implementation of the first statewide risk-limiting audit. She has a vision of creating uniform audit and testing standards for all critical components of the election system. Jennifer worked as an election official for nine years (2009–2018) in Utah and Colorado. She is an Election Center CERA graduate and holds a Master of Arts in Management from Webster University. Additional information on risk-limiting audits can be found in the author's two-part guide, Risk-Limiting Audits: A Practical Guide for State and Local Officials. Knowing It's Right Part 1: A Practical Guide to Risk-Limiting Audits - http://electionline.org/resources/rla-practical-guide and Knowing It's Right Part 2: Risk-Limiting Audit Implementation Workbook - http://electionline.org/resources/rla-implementation-workbook.

16

Election Cybersecurity

Judd Choate and Robert Smith

As the industrial age is transforming into the information age, cybersecurity has become a major concern. Reliance on machines that depend on intricate electronics and often unfathomable amounts of data to enhance productivity, production, and make our daily lives more manageable has opened a Pandora's box of potential vulnerabilities. Some can be mere annoyances or minor inconveniences, like when your home network won't sync and you have to reboot your computer, router, and modem because the problem could be in any of the three. The same issue at a nuclear power plant, in a control system for water purity and/or distribution, or in a military command and control system is a concern of a completely different magnitude.

During the early days of the information age transition, people accepted that these things happened occasionally and, while often inconvenienced for a while, would wait out the issue or find alternatives. Now,

J. Choate (✉)
Colorado Department of State, Denver, CO, USA

R. Smith
National Intelligence University, Bethesda, MD, USA

© The Author(s) 2020
M. Brown et al. (eds.), *The Future of Election Administration*, Elections, Voting, Technology, https://doi.org/10.1007/978-3-030-14947-5_16

there is more and more reliance on what are becoming essential tools for which there are few (or no) alternatives and which others are actively looking to exploit and even create vulnerabilities for personal advantage or for the advantage of a (their) country, waiting it out is not a viable strategy. This is the existing cybersecurity world.

In this chapter, we present general information on the cyber threat, discuss the federal infrastructure dedicated to protecting our critical infrastructure from malicious cyber actors, and then take a deep dive into what is being done specifically with respect to election administration. This deep dive includes discussion of how the federal government, the Department of Homeland Security specifically, and states coordinate to protect election security, and provides a more in-depth examination of how one state, Colorado, is responding to this important and evolving threat.

Context

Cybersecurity is not a wholly new problem. The Government Accountability Office (GAO) recognized federal cybersecurity (then known as information security) as a high-risk problem in 1997, expanded the problem to include cyber infrastructure in 2003, and added personally identifiable information in 2015 (Government Accountability Office 2018). For elections, however, the concern came of age in 2017, when the US intelligence community reported in an unclassified Intelligence Community Assessment, one of the more formal documents produced by the community, that malicious actors operating for a foreign government conducted cyber operations in an apparent effort to affect the 2016 presidential election and that they were expected to continue their attempts (ICA 2017-001D).

There is no question that elections are vulnerable to disruption based on cyber activity. Any activity that relies on digital information and/or Internet connectivity is vulnerable to interference. This disruption could be unintentional or intentional, and could range from natural disaster, to coding errors, to attacks by hackers, disgruntled employees, or foreign nations (Government Accountability Office 2018). The potential for cyber interference with the voting process becomes a significant concern because between one-quarter and one-third of voters are in jurisdictions that use DRE voting machines that do not create a paper tally or trail of votes (DeSilver 2016). Under these conditions, if the electronic record is lost, there is no way to recover the vote totals.

One of the primary challenges when addressing cybersecurity is identifying the nature of the threat or even defining the term itself. Cybersecurity encompasses a wide range of concepts, concerns, and activities. These range from cyber operations, which could include equipment tampering, hacking, or distributed denial of service attacks to information operations, which include attempts to influence voters, to manipulating post-election information.[1] Agawu (2018) focuses only on hacking, but breaks that down into: manipulating voters, manipulating votes, and causing disruption.

Even when the concepts are defined, in the diverse and decentralized field of election administration accountability for cybersecurity transcends traditional boundaries of responsibility and expertise. American elections require inputs from every level of government—federal, state, and local—in a web of dynamic interactions (Hale et al. 2015; Hale and Slaton 2008). In addition, there are numerous non-governmental entities—vendors, political parties, political action groups, and volunteers—who must be considered (Brown et al. forthcoming). As a result of this complexity, it is evident that no one person or entity can be held entirely responsible for securing the entire system.

The elections process is a complex and interconnected ecosystem (Alvarez et al. 2013). The failure or degradation of a single entity produces effects that ripple into other elements of the system, and in fact across multiple systems that are integrated across jurisdictions, office responsibilities, and layers of government (Hale et al. 2015). Vulnerable election systems include electronic and paper voter

---

[1] To explicate some of the complexity of identifying the cyber threat, in The State and Local Election Cybersecurity Playbook, the Belfer Center puts denial of service attacks in both cyber operations and information operations depending on if the goal was to prevent user access or to undermined trust in the electoral systems or process (Mook et al. 2018).

registration processes, voting machines, and the tabulation and reporting process. In many locations, vendors and volunteers develop, store, maintain, and operate much of the equipment, which raises a concern of insider threat. Some parts of the election system are the responsibility of the state; others belong to local jurisdictional authorities which vary between, and sometimes within, states. A final challenge is that the cyber environment, and threat, will change as technology evolves; practices and tools which are effective today may not be tomorrow.

The diversity of the system does have its advantages. It is unlikely that any single cyber action can have broad effect, the interconnectivity of the system notwithstanding. However, given the relative closeness of the 2016 presidential election, malicious actors can have significant impact with success in a small number of strategically selected locations.

The 2016 Election

Democratic National Committee e-mails damaging to Hillary Clinton's presidential campaign and Democratic Party leadership surfaced in the summer of 2016. As it turns out, this was one of several activities Russia undertook to sabotage the United States 2016 presidential election. Later that fall, e-mails from John Podesta, the national chairman of Clinton's campaign, also found their way to the Internet and were damaging to the Clinton campaign. In addition, Russian operatives created thousands of Facebook, Twitter, and Instagram accounts to create petty disputes and sow discord in the country. While potentially relevant to the eventual election outcome, the Russian efforts appeared to have very little, if anything, to do with the actual administration of US elections. That perception changed in July 2016.

The first inkling that an organized, state-sponsored attack on US election infrastructure was underway came on July 12, 2016, when an information technology (IT) employee in the Illinois state election office noticed that an unauthorized user was downloading the personal data of tens of thousands of Illinois voters. It was quickly apparent that a sophisticated hacker had gained access to the Illinois voter registration system. Within days, the Department of Homeland Security (DHS) understood the nature and severity of the threat. The Illinois hack was not merely an individual blackhat hacker who found a backdoor; it was a state-sponsored effort by one of the US's strongest antagonists—Russia. And, Illinois likely was not the only state Russia was targeting.

The Illinois Incident

Unbeknownst to Illinois election officials, Russian hackers infiltrated the Illinois voter registration database (IVRS) on June 23, 2016. They did so by typing Structured Query Language (SQL) code into a less-well-protected driver license entry field on the application status page of the Paperless Online Voter Application site. This is the page where Illinois voters can check the status of their voter registration application by providing a driver license number and additional information. The SQL injection originally generated little or no discernable activity and election, and IT staff at the Illinois State Board of Elections (SBE) were unaware of the breach for nearly three weeks. Only on July 12, when hackers dramatically increased their activity, did staff recognize that the site had been hacked.

The official incident report issued by the Illinois SBE described what happened. First, "processor usage had spiked to 100% with no explanation" ("Illinois Voter Registration", n.d., 1). IT staff informed election administrators and an investigation commenced. "Analysis of server logs revealed that the heavy load was a result of rapidly repeated database queries on the application status page of the Paperless Online Voter Application (POVA) web site" ("Illinois Voter Registration" n.d., 1). They then applied input validation to the vulnerable form field so no new bad actors could use it as a point of entry. This also stopped the queries from executing against the database. Shortly thereafter, the Illinois team began blocking the attacking IPs at the firewall level so the traffic could not reach the web servers. The attack was mitigated within an hour of discovery. By blocking the IPs at the firewall, Illinois created an additional security step to protect the web servers and reduce the load on the POVA.

Illinois continued to see the same pattern of traffic from these IPs for a month after discovery and termination of the session. Therefore, the mitigation of the attack did not affect the ongoing nature of the attack itself. Given the rapid nature of the queries, it is nearly certain that the attack was automated.

Illinois' original "analysis concluded that in addition to viewing multiple database tables, attackers accessed approximately 90,000 voter registration records" ("Illinois Voter Registration" n.d., 1). That number jumped after the initial incident report was published. Federal indictments a year later stated that the number was much higher. Illinois Senator Richard Durbin characterized the Illinois incident this way: "Today's indictment stated that the individuals 'hacked the website of a state board of elections… and stole information related to approximately 500,000 voters, including names, addresses, partial social security numbers, dates of birth, and driver's license numbers." Despite this, extensive analyses by Illinois officials found the true number of individuals affected by the breach was closer to 76,000 (Personal communication with Matt Emmons, IT Director for the Illinois State Board of Elections, November 27, 2018). This determination has been reviewed by federal law enforcement, which does not dispute its veracity (Personal communication with Matt Emmons, IT Director for the Illinois State Board of Elections, November 27, 2018).

Illinois' voter registration database was the only database the Russians successfully breached, but not for a lack of trying. DHS communicated with election officials from each US state on September 22, 2017, to inform them whether there was evidence that Russians targeted their state. Twenty-one states had been determined by DHS to have been contacted, as presented in Fig. 16.1. The DHS list was based on a review of the IP addresses that the hackers appeared to use in the Illinois and past non-election hacking efforts. In at least one case, Colorado, Department of State IT security officials tracked down the IP address and effectively "self-reported" without DHS assistance.

This original determination that only 21 states were targeted gradually fell out of favor by early 2018. By April that year, DHS had concluded that likely all US state was targeted by Russian hackers—it

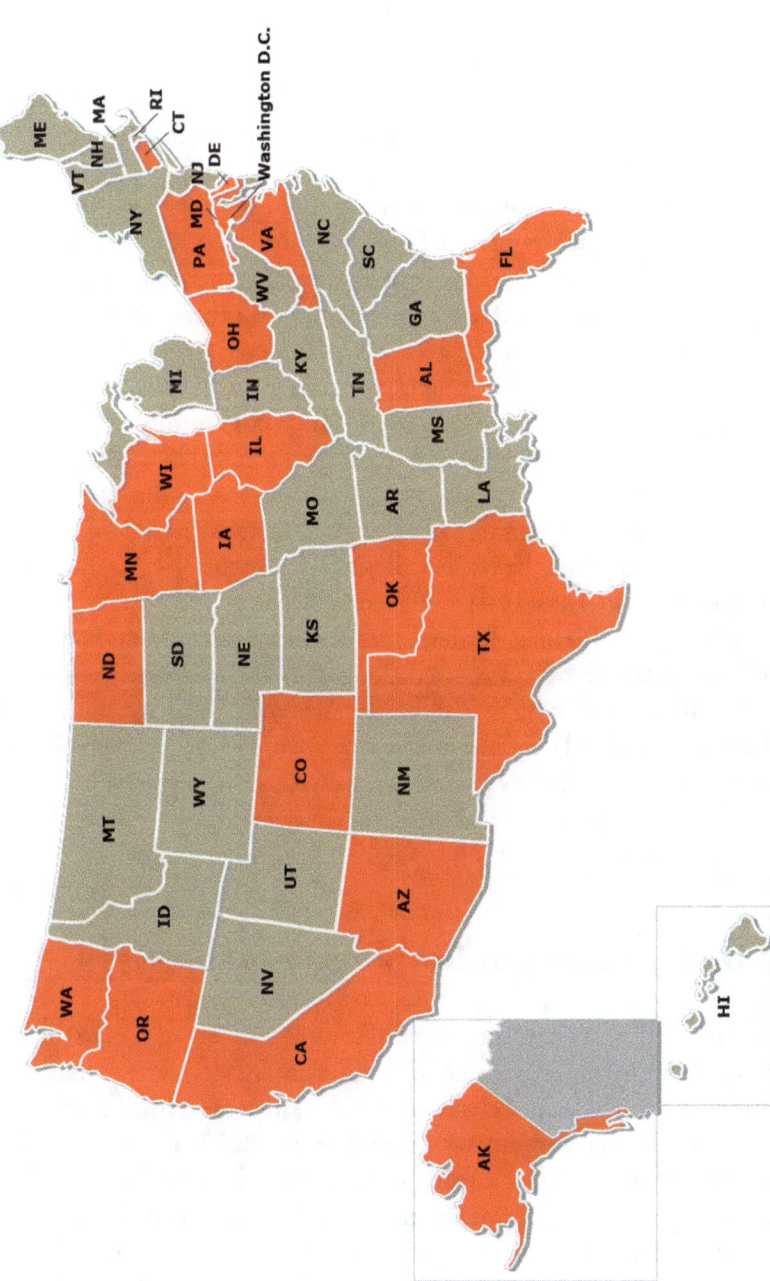

Fig. 16.1 The 21 states who learned they were targeted by Russian hackers during the 2016 general election

was only in the original 21 where evidence was strong enough to formally accuse the Russians of direct intrusive efforts. DHS Head of Cybersecurity, Jeanette Manfra and later DHS Secretary Kirstjen Nielsen, stated that the Russians likely did not target any particular state (Levine 2018).

In the weeks and months following the 2016 general election, post-incident assessments of the Illinois intrusion by election officials, the FBI, and DHS among others concluded that the hackers made no changes to the database, altered no voter files, or otherwise effected the 2016 or future elections.

So, why did the Russians do it? Reporting from *The Washington Post* and other sources concluded that the security community believes the Russians had no grand plan in attempting to access US voter registration databases. Instead, it was a part of a coordinated effort to sow distrust in the American election system, so that if an individual voter's preferred candidate lost, he or she might feel that the election had been stolen (Goudie and Tressel 2018; Hawkins 2018).

For their part, Russian leaders and spokespersons denied involvement. One example of many such denials sheds light on the Russian administration's thinking. *The New Yorker* cited an unnamed, pro-Kremlin Russian lawmaker who at first denied Russian involvement but then tried to justify any hypothetical Russian interference by accusing past US administrations of engaging in generations of interference in Russian politics (Yaffa 2017).

The US Government Response—Framework

When faced with an amorphous and complex threat to a part of the US critical infrastructure, the federal government develops a response. In a process detailed below, elections were classified as critical infrastructure by the Obama administration in January 2017 and that process began. Different parts of the federal government have different responsibilities, and, as noted previously, any actions must be coordinated with state and local officials and new requirements must be implementable by potentially thousands of jurisdictions. This section will provide an overview of the cybersecurity roles and responsibilities of the two major federal players, DHS and the Department of Defense (DOD).

There are 16 critical infrastructure sectors each with a Sector-Specific Agency charged with providing expertise and day-to-day engagement under the guidance and direction of the DHS, the federal agency with primary responsibility for critical infrastructure protection (PPD 21). While elections were only designated as critical infrastructure in 2017, cybersecurity has been a concern for much longer; Executive Order (EO) 13636, Improving Critical Infrastructure Cybersecurity, was issued in February 2013. EO 13636 is relevant to elections because it directed the Director of the National Institute of Standards and Technology (NIST) to create a framework to help organizations mitigate threats and improve the security of critical infrastructure, which, with the 2017 update, has become the required standard for cybersecurity implementation (Framework 2014).

Through its responsibility for oversight of critical infrastructure, DHS provides the oversight role for cybersecurity of elections. Because it has the ability to regulate election processes based on the critical infrastructure designation, DHS can improve on the work done by the Election Assistance Commission (EAC), which can only advocate for voluntary action. EAC has had great success with programs like the Voluntary Voting Systems Guidelines (VVSG), which focus on voting data security, but is restricted from "issuing any rule, promulgating any regulation, or taking any other action" (Pub. L. No. 107-252, 209, 116 Stat. 1678). As of 2018, DHS concentrates its attention on risk mitigation overall, not against specific threats. The agency focuses on offering election administrators advisement on, and assessment of, cybersecurity practices. The department provides cybersecurity training, much of which is developed by NIST, and limited incident response services. DHS has taken on the task of cybersecurity information and best-practice clearinghouse through coordinating councils comprised of officials at all levels of government as well as private sector actors (Brown et al., forthcoming, 17).

The Department of Defense (DOD) is often considered the other major federal player when it comes to election cybersecurity. This is in part because, should a response be needed, DOD possesses the nation's offensive cyber capability. DOD and DHS look at different parts of the issue. DOD has an external view and focuses on threats, warning, and potentially responses. In contrast, DHS has an internal, domestic view and focuses on risk mitigation. DOD senior cyber officials say that the DOD role is one of support, providing information to DHS to share with state and local officials based on the large scale and scope of DOD cyber and intelligence activities. Under the Defense Support to Civil Authorities mission, DOD has developed scalable response options should they be needed. Generally, when it comes to cybersecurity and elections, DOD works under the authority and leadership of DHS.

In 2018, one specific capability DOD provides directly to local jurisdictions is cybersecurity trained National Guard troops. This is not technically a federal effort. The guard troops receive federal training while working for the state. This is a good way to get capability without raising concerns about federal interference in what is seen as a state function. Often these troops have little election specific training and have served in roles that pertain to DHS risk management rather than in roles related to DOD threat awareness and countering.

Overall, in 2018 senior cyber officials from DHS and DOD said they believe the agencies' alignment of activities and roles regarding cybersecurity for critical infrastructure was breaking new ground in federal government interaction and support. These officials emphasize that the federal agencies worked together to provide information so that state and local election officials could better understand the risks in, and threats to, election infrastructure. They reinforce that the common essential element in mitigating risk and defending against threats is communication between and among all the stakeholders at every level. An emphasis on communication is what drives federal support to election cybersecurity.

US Government Response—Action

The US government's response to the events of 2016 was multifaceted. It included a new and coordinated focus through DHS, the formation of Government and Sector Coordinating Councils, and election security funding.

Critical Infrastructure Designation

Illinois election officials became aware of the hack on July 12, 2016. Ironically, the National Association of Secretaries of State (NASS) and the National Association of State Election Directors (NASED) along with election directors from nearly 40 US states held a joint meeting in Nashville, Tennessee from July 15–18, 2016—a perfect opportunity for Illinois election officials or DHS to inform the other states of the intrusion and potential of further attack. There were rumors that something had happened in Illinois, but neither Illinois election officials nor DHS representatives attended the meeting. Instead, the conference's central theme was increasing registration and turnout in the lead up to the 2016 presidential election.

After the NASS/NASED conference, in late July 2016, NASS Executive Director Leslie Reynolds contacted DHS, asking that the Secretaries be briefed on the rumor that the Russians had hacked a voter registration system and were generally attempting to influence US elections. Two weeks later, on August 15, 2016, DHS Secretary Jeh Johnson joined Secretaries of State and state election directors on a conference call where Secretary Johnson asked states to accept a federal role in protecting election systems. He made this ask without acknowledging the hack or any discussion about it, nor the Russian's role in that attack.

The conference call devolved into a battle over states' rights. Secretary Johnson began by briefly explaining DHS concerns regarding voter registration database vulnerability, without specifically naming Illinois. Secretary Johnson then noted the availability of various DHS offerings that state officials might find helpful in managing risks to voter registration systems (Jeh 2016). He congratulated officials on the work already undertaken by states to ensure election integrity and security, but also noted that DHS could offer specialized assistance. These offers were largely met with silence.

Secretary Johnson then pivoted to the call's main objective. The DHS was exploring various ways to deliver more support to election officials, and the Secretary would be considering whether designating certain electoral systems as critical infrastructure would be an effective way to offer such support. This brought an immediate and robust reaction.

Republican Secretaries of State Brian Kemp of Georgia and Tom Schedler of Louisiana, among others, voiced their vehement opposition to federal intrusion in a purely state function. Kemp, in particular, expressed his concern that this was the beginning of federal control over elections. Other Secretaries, Republican Wayne Williams of Colorado and Democrat Alex Padilla of California, voiced their interest in receiving some of the more sophisticated DHS offerings, such as risk and vulnerability assessments, so long as this cooperation did not lead to a formal federal role. It was a contentious call. Several Secretaries were opposed to a federal role in state election management. Furthermore, and more importantly, the states still knew very little about the Illinois hack and how to prepare for similar, future attacks on their state voter registration systems.

In the end, Secretary Johnson promised to set up a working group to assess the wisdom of designating elections as critical infrastructure. Secretaries volunteered to be members of the working group and NASS began efforts to convert its cybersecurity committee into a formal organization to work with DHS. But DHS never followed up and no working group was formed. Another, similarly contentious call occurred later that fall in which very little additional information on the Illinois hack was provided. Fortunately, the 2016 election passed without additional cybersecurity incidents.

Then, on January 6, 2017—14 days prior to leaving office—Secretary Johnson formally designated elections as critical infrastructure as a subsector of the Government Facilities Sector. President Trump took office two weeks later. His first Secretary of the Department Homeland Security was General John Kelly was confirmed that same day. In one of his first acts as Secretary, Kelly announced he would retain the elections' infrastructure designation.

The Governmental Coordinating Council Formation

Under the critical infrastructure designation, the National Protection and Programs Directorate (NPPD)—an agency within DHS that houses each of the 16 critical infrastructure sectors—took the lead in creating the organizational framework of the election subsector. It typically takes years to create a fully operational functional subsector. But, DHS had only months before the next major election cycle was in full swing, with the possibility of more Russian efforts to hack voter registration or other systems. And, the new administration brought completely new leadership, including new office directors and deputy secretaries. Relevant to the election subsector was the leadership, or lack thereof, at the NPPD. When no discernible activity had commenced by middle of March, the NASED president and incoming NASS president set up a series of meetings, first with low-ranking holdovers from the Obama DHS, then with NASS leadership, to discuss the lack of movement.

These talks eventually led to a July 25–26, 2017, meeting in Albany, New York with the dual purpose of creating a Governmental Coordinating Council (GCC), which is the first formal measure taken in creating a critical infrastructure subsector, and introducing election officials to the Multi-State Information Sharing and Analysis Center (MS-ISAC), which is housed in a facility outside Albany. A compromise was forged about the GCC membership. There would be nine local election officials representing the International Association of Government Officials and Election Center, eight secretaries of state representing NASS, and seven election directors representing NASED. Three federal representatives, one from DHS, and both the chair and vice chair of the Election Assistance Commission, brought the final number to 27. An Executive Committee was also created, to be led by the President of NASED, President of NASS, Chair of the EAC, and the DHS representatives.

At an October 2017 meeting in Atlanta, Georgia, the GCC was formally created and plans set in motion to create a special ISAC to deal exclusively with elections security. The Elections Infrastructure ISAC (EI-ISAC) was established and officially endorsed by the GCC and funded by DHS in March 2018. The EI-ISAC set about deploying intrusion detection sensors, called Alberts, on voter registration web facilities in all 50 US states, or at least those states that permitted their installation. By the 2018 midterm election, 45 states and the District of Columbia had Alberts and 1400 of the 8800 local election offices were EI-ISAC members. Of the five states without Alberts, four were due to technical delays; one state, South Dakota, rejected the EI-ISAC offer.

The open-source Albert sensors provide automated alerts on both traditional and advanced network threats. The Albert project grew out

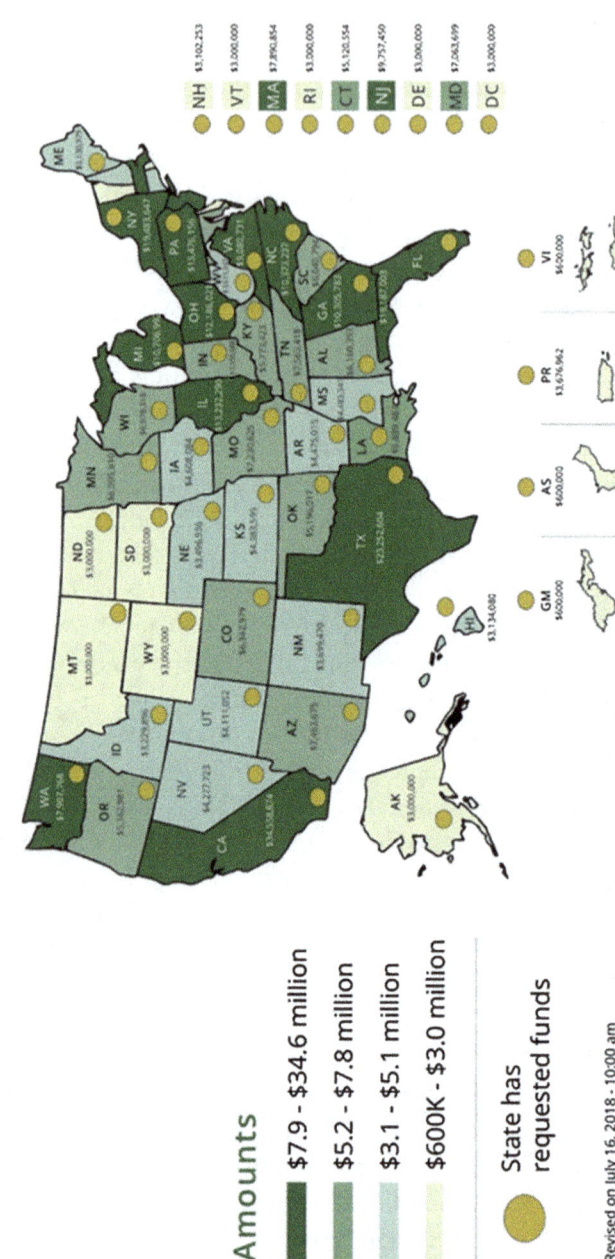

Fig. 16.2 Distribution of 2018 Help America Vote Act (HAVA) funds (*Source* Consolidated Appropriations Act of 2018, Title V, Section 501, Election Assistance Commission, Election Reform Program)

of DHS's Einstein project, which was designed to detect and block cyberattacks within federal agencies. DHS approached the Center for Information Security (CIS), which runs the MS-ISAC, about creating similar capability for states and localities; with the name Einstein already taken, CIS called the sensors Albert instead.

Parallel to the GCC, DHS worked with private election companies and nonprofits to create a Sector Coordinating Council (SCC). The SCC's mandate was similar to the GCC's, to improve election security. The SCC represents almost fifty for-profit and nonprofit corporations that produce voting systems or other elections-related technology. In addition, projects like the Electronic Registration Information Center (ERIC), the Voter Information Project (VIP) are also represented. The GCC and SCC held their first joint meeting in Philadelphia at the NASS/NASED meeting in the summer of 2018.

Election Security Funding

The 2016 Russian attack on US elections had many short- and long-term consequences. One was not additional money for the states to combat cyber intrusions, however. That is, until March 23, 2018, when President Trump signed into law the 2018 Consolidated Appropriations Act. Early in Title V, Section 501, nearly a third of the way through the legislation, one paragraph appropriated a $380,000,000 addition to HAVA funding. Figure 16.2 presents the distribution of these funds to each state.

States received several HAVA appropriations beginning in 2002, following the Florida election equipment problems in 2000 and subsequent recount. The 2018 funding was merely a new authorization of money under the HAVA law.[2]

The EAC came to call this batch of HAVA funding the "2018 HAVA Election Security Funds." The legislation gave states two years to match the funds at 5% with a deadline of five years to use the entire authorized amount before the money would be refunded to the US Treasury. The funds were allotted based on state population, with California

---

[2] 52 U.S.C. §§ 20901–21145.

receiving the largest amount at $34.6 million. Another 41 states fell between $23 million and just over $3 million, eight US states and the District of Columbia received the minimum of $3 million, and four US territories or protectorates received $600,000 apiece.[3]

The EAC requested that each state submit a detailed plan for the use of the money; however, a handful of states balked. The Consolidated Appropriations Act specified that the funds should be used for "election security improvements." However, funds authorized under HAVA could be used for the general purpose of improving federal elections; these states contended that the original HAVA language gave them broad authority to use the money for any purpose that fell under Title 1 HAVA authorization. In the end, all states that requested funds submitted budgets that specified security-related improvements.

Jurisdictions receiving the funds opted to prioritize different security objectives. At the time of the authorization, five US states cast all non-absentee ballots via voting equipment that did not produce a paper trail. These states considered using the HAVA funds as a down payment on the purchase of newer equipment that could produce a paper trail. A change of this type could also help these states conduct a post-election audit, which are difficult without a paper trail. In Colorado, for example, election administrators decided to use HAVA funds across several security-related areas, including technological improvements, auditing, and training for both state and local election officials, as well as IT staff at the state and local level.

Colorado Case Study: One State's Plans for the HAVA Money

Every US state, the District of Columbia, and four US territories or protectorates received a new tranche of HAVA funds in the summer of 2018. Different jurisdictions have prioritized this money in different ways. A handful set it aside for the purchase of new voting equipment that uses auditable paper trails. Others will overhaul or purchase completely new

---

[3]This includes American Samoa, Guam, Puerto Rico, and the US Virgin Islands. See: https://www.eac.gov/assets/1/6/FY2018HAVAGrantsExpenditureReport.pdf.

voter registration databases. Finally, there are states that lack a big-ticket-item and are instead focusing on smaller improvements across several election systems. Colorado falls into that latter category. Below is a list of HAVA funding objectives Colorado has planned before March 2023.

Improved Technology and Software for Both State and County Election Officials

- Expansion of secure portal for sensitive information exchange.
- Smart, secure removable media for elections data exchanges.
- Development team for modernization of core SCORE application.
- Software/Service to track social media and dark web for threats and compromise indicators.
- Security automation and orchestration platform.
- Emergency/Critical communications capability.

Improved Risk-Limiting Audits and Audits of Elections-Related Systems

- Improvements to risk-limiting audits (RLA) systems.
- Security audits of all elections-related systems.

Improved Incident Preparedness Exercises and Certification Program Integration

- Table Top Exercises on incident response and preparedness.
- Vulnerability/Penetration tests of elections-related systems.
- Attacker/Defender exercises.
- Integration of white hat hacking into SDLC (software development life cycle).

The Future of Election Security

US elections have progressed in epochs. There was the time before the 1965 Voting Rights Act (VRA) when states exercised essentially complete control over-voter registration and election administration.

The years from 1965 until the 2000 presidential election witnessed the expansion of the vote to previously disenfranchised segments of the population, including racial and ethnic minorities, younger adults (26th Amendment), and those largely without resources through the National Voter Registration Act (NVRA). Following the Florida recount in the year 2000, elections became much more legalistic, with a focus on challenges to expanded voting rights. The US Supreme Court's decision in *Shelby County v. Holder*[4] eliminated prior federal review and approval of all substantive state and local election changes that had been required for more than 50 years under Section 5 of the VRA. The most recent epoch began with Russian efforts to hack the 2016 election, thus pushing election security to the forefront.

This brief history of the past 55 years of US elections demonstrates the changing demands on election officials but also illustrates the changing demands on those agencies that help the administration of elections, and the increased support that has been provided. The Department of Justice, state departments of motor vehicles, and other agencies have stepped in, with varying success, to assist in election administration when called upon.

As a consequence of the most recent changes, DHS, the GCC, and EAC have each made cybersecurity their post-2016 general election focus, with an emphasis on training. Noteworthy among those was development of nontraditional training options. For instance, representatives from a majority of US states attended presentations at Harvard's Belfer Center, which brought the familiar military training method table top exercises (TTXs) to elections. These have helped state and local election officials game-out possible scenarios and work with IT professionals to devise mitigation strategies. Many state representatives took these lessons home to develop TTXs specific to local laws and policies. DHS, as well as the EI-ISAC, expanded training options including both introductory and advanced cybersecurity options.

In this post-2016 environment, DHS and the EAC are the election community's most important partners. DHS was unprepared to assist states in 2016. The agency had no established relationships with

---

[4]570 U.S. 623, 133 S. Ct. 2612; 186 L. Ed. 2d 651.

election administrators prior to the Illinois breach and made no effort to create them during the lead up to the 2016 election. Fortunately, the personnel changes and reoriented focus that followed the administration turnover boosted the prominence of election operations within the agency, leading in turn to the increased prominence of election critical infrastructure. In particular, elections received a noticeable boost when Chris Krebs was appointed Director of the NPPD; Krebs was later named the first director of the DHS Cybersecurity and Infrastructure Security Agency (CISA).

DHS also added Robert Kolasky to lead the NPPD National Risk Management Center and Juan Figueroa as the lead for Election Infrastructure, both of whom prioritized election infrastructure. Many states, notably those with Republican secretaries, remained skeptical of federal assistance, which from their perspective was more like election intrusion. Finally, when DHS added an elections cybersecurity specialist, former EAC Commissioner and Chairman, Matthew Masterson, the states were largely appeased. Masterson's addition was widely hailed by the election community as a sure sign that DHS understood that elections are complicated and that specialized knowledge was necessary for DHS to assist the states in a meaningful way.

The EAC underwent a less dramatic evolution in response to the new cybersecurity environment, largely because the EAC was already election-focused. But many of the agency objectives pivoted as a result of the Russian hacking efforts. Most notable was the assistance the EAC provided to states regarding proper use of the new HAVA funds. This included support for fund accounting procedures as well as preparation for the inevitable audit that will follow the five-year usage window.

On the DOD side, the National Guard hopes to expand cyber units to 38 states by 2019. In summer of 2018, Senators Maria Cantwell (D-WA) and Joe Manchin (D-WV) introduced legislation "to provide for the establishment and operations of reserve component cyber civil support teams" to advance that goal.

Finally, DHS and other intelligence agencies prioritized review of security clearance applications. This allowed most of the nation's state election directors and many secretaries and their staff members to receive clearance-level briefings on possible intrusive activity on the part of the Russians and other counties/entities. The speed and efficiency with which DHS met this need was a heavy lift and substantial deviation from procedure on the part of DHS.

References

Agawu, Emefa Addo. "How to Think About Election Cybersecurity: A Guide for Policymakers." April 3, 2018. https://www.newamerica.org/cybersecurity-initiative/policy-papers/how-to-think-about-election-cybersecurity/.

Alvarez, R. Michael, Lonna Rae Atkeson, and Thad E. Hall. *Evaluating Elections: A Handbook of Methods and Standards*. New York: Cambridge University Press, 2013.

DeSilver, Drew. "On Election Day, Most Voters Use Electronic or Optical-Scan Ballots." *Pew Research Center*, November 8, 2016. http://www.pewresearch.org/fact-tank/2016/11/08/on-election-day-most-voters-use-electronic-or-optical-scan-ballots/.

Goudie, Chuck, and Christine Tressel. "How the Russians Penetrated Illinois Election Computers." *ABC 7 Live Chicago*, July 19, 2018. https://abc7chicago.com/politics/how-the-russians-penetrated-illinois-election-computers/3778816/.

Government Accountability Office. "Critical Infrastructure Protection: Additional Actions Are Essential for Assessing Cybersecurity Framework Adoption." February 2018. https://www.gao.gov/assets/700/690112.pdf.

Hale, Kathleen, and Christa Daryl Slaton. "Building Capacity in Election Administration: Responding to Complexity and Interdependence." *Public Administration Review*, 68, no. 5 (2008): 839–849.

Hale, Kathleen, Mitchell Brown, and Robert Montjoy. *Administering Elections: How American Elections Work*. New York: Palgrave, 2015.

Hawkins, Derek, "The Cybersecurity 202: Voters' Distrust of Election Security Is Just as Powerful as an Actual Hack, Officials Worry." *Washington Post*, June 5, 2018. https://www.washingtonpost.com/news/powerpost/paloma/the-cybersecurity-202/2018/06/05/the-cybersecurity-202-voters-distrust-of-election-security-is-just-as-powerful-as-an-actual-hack-officials-worry/5b1567091b326b08e883912f/?utm_term=.7a03e7805651.

"Illinois Voter Registration System Database Breach Report." n.d. https://www.intelligence.senate.gov/sites/default/files/documents/os-ssandvoss-062117_0.pdf.

Jeh, Johnson. "Readout of Secretary Johnson's Call with State Election Officials on Cybersecurity." *Department of Homeland Security*, August 15, 2016. https://www.dhs.gov/news/2016/08/15/readout-secretary-johnsons-call-state-election-officials-cybersecurity.

Levine, Mike. "Russia Likely Targeted All 50 States in 2016, but Has Yet to Try Again, DHS Cyber Chief Says." *ABC News*, April 24, 2018. https://abcnews.go.com/US/russia-targeted-50-states-2016-dhs-cyber-chief/story?id=54695520.

Mook, Robby, Matt Rhoades, and Eric Rosenbach. "The State and Local Election Cybersecurity Playbook." *Belfer Center for Science and International Affairs, Harvard Kennedy School*, February 2018. https://www.belfercenter.org/publication/state-and-local-election-cybersecurity-playbook.

Yaffa, Joshua. "Russia's View of the Election Hacks: Denials, Amusement, Comeuppance." *The New Yorker*, December 20, 2017. https://www.newyorker.com/news/news-desk/russias-view-of-the-election-hacks-denials-amusement-comeuppance.

Judd Choate is the state election director for Colorado and past president of the National Association of State Election Directors. Prior to joining the Secretary of State's office, he was an attorney at Kelly Garnsey Hubbell + Lass in Denver, and before that a professor of political science at the University of Nebraska. In a previous life, Choate was a scout for the Kansas City Royals. He is a graduate of the Auburn University/Election Center certified election registration administrator program.

Robert Smith is associate vice president of the Office of Research at National Intelligence University in Bethesda, Maryland. He oversees the Center for Strategic Intelligence Research, the university's Research Fellows Program, the National Intelligence Press, and the John T. Hughes Library. Prior to his current position, Smith served in the United States Air Force for 35 years in a wide variety of policy and academic jobs. The views expressed in this chapter are the author's own and do not reflect the official policy or position of the National Intelligence University, the Department of Defense or the US Government.

17

Special Elections Costs: Filling Legislative and Congressional Vacancies

Dean C. Logan

For over a decade now, California has experienced increasing issues with legislative and congressional vacancies. Stakeholders were tasked with understanding the impacts this would have on the adoption of a ranked choice voting (RCV) model. This chapter details the cost analysis in Los Angeles County, California that was performed. The review for Los Angeles County considered specific issues concerning the frequency and costs of rolling vacancies and the limitations of the county's voting system to adapt to new models of election administration.

A cost analysis of special vacancy elections in Los Angeles County was performed on behalf of the Registrar-Recorder/County Clerk and the Los Angeles County Board of Supervisors. There were three objectives:

1. Review options for reducing costs.
2. Reduce voter fatigue.
3. Increase voter participation.

D. C. Logan (✉)
Los Angeles County Registrar-Recorder/County Clerk,
Los Angeles County, CA, USA

Background

The Governor of California, according to law, must call special vacancy elections by issuing a proclamation. This requires a special election to be held between 112 and 126 days from the issuance of the proclamation. Currently, the law does not provide recourse for appointing temporary officeholders by the Governor, except in filling vacancies for US Senator.

In 1990, voters approved legislative term limits that resulted in more special elections to fill vacancies, but did not guarantee reimbursement costs to cover the special elections. Impacted counties could get reimbursement from the state, however, the formulas to calculate reimbursement were outdated and the legislative authority subject to expiration or suspension. This caused counties a significant financial burden when charged with conducting special vacancy elections.

Los Angeles County conducted special elections to fill 10 vacancies from 2000 to 2009. Five of these elections were special runoff elections that determined the winning candidate and over a dozen more individual elections were conducted to fill vacancies during this time.

The county's special vacancy elections cost $10.7 million between 2000 and 2009. California state reimbursement for these costs totaled less than half, at $4.3 million. Net reimbursement to the county totaled $7.9 million including funds from other sources. The Registrar-Recorder/County Clerk was burdened to pay all this cost. As election costs have increased over the years, the reimbursement rates applied by the state have not. This simply is not sustainable going forward. Figure 17.1 provides detailed cost breakdowns for each of the elections analyzed.

An important factor to consider as part of the analysis was the impact that consolidating special vacancy elections with larger county or statewide elections had on costs. Looking at the vacancy elections for the 32nd State Senate District in 2000 and the 55th Assembly District in 2007 and 2008, it was possible to discern the actual cost savings produced by consolidating these vacancy elections (see Fig. 17.1). In both instances, the special primary was conducted as a stand-alone election, while the special runoff election for each was consolidated with a larger election, producing significant cost savings.

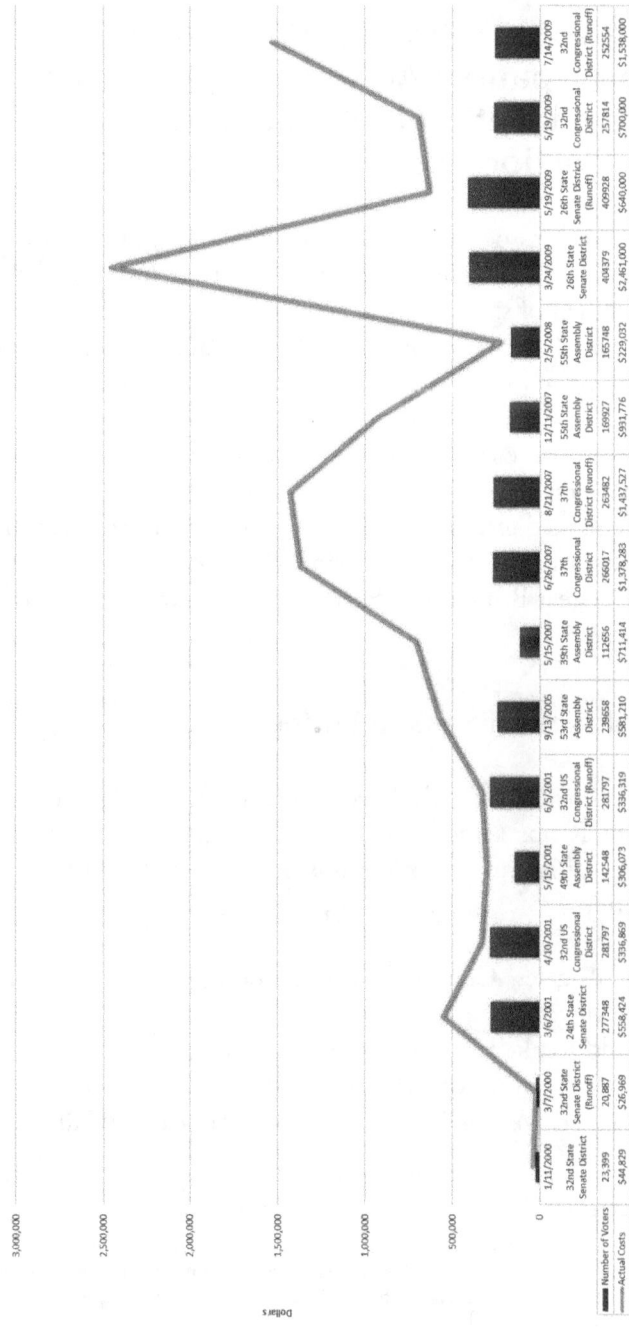

Fig. 17.1 Election costs compared to voter turnout for special vacancy elections, 2000–2009

Reducing Voter Fatigue and Increasing Voter Participation: An Analysis of Ranked Voting as an Option to Reduce Special Vacancy Election Costs

Several factors associated with Ranked Voting (RV) models were researched and considered along with the impact of such models on the conduct of special vacancy elections.

RV[1] is a method of voting that allows voters in an election to cast their vote for qualified candidates by ranking them in order of preference—first, second, and third. In elections requiring a 50% + 1 majority vote to be elected, ranked voting models provide the ability to determine a majority winner without the need to conduct a runoff election. The ranked choices of every voter are used to conduct multiple tallies of votes cast until a majority winner is determined. Countries like Australia and Great Britain use RV, as well as certain jurisdictions in the United States.

Implementation of Ranked Voting

This chapter provides an early look into Los Angeles County's capacity to implement RV as a method for conducting special elections to fill vacancies for legislative and congressional offices. It also answers the following questions:

- Can Los Angeles County's current voting system accommodate Ranked Voting?
- What would Ranked Voting cost to implement?
- Could Ranked Voting save money?
- Could Ranked Voting increase voter participation while reducing voter fatigue?

---

[1] Ranked Voting (RV) is also referred to as ranked choice voting or Instant RunOff Voting (IRV). For purposes of this chapter, the method is referred to as RV to maintain consistency with language in recent legislative proposals considered by the California State Legislature.

Implementing RV for use in special vacancy elections would place Los Angeles County's 5.2 million registered voters at the forefront in the United States. Los Angeles County would also be the largest and most diverse jurisdiction using RV, with 4000 polling locations spanning 4082 square miles serving 88 cities and more than 500 sub-units of local government.

Overview of Jurisdictions Use of Ranked Voting Systems

At the time of the study, 17 different jurisdictions across the country had either implemented or were in the process of definitively implementing RV.[2] Of these, the largest included: San Francisco, CA (477,651 registered voters); Pierce County, WA (468,656 registered voters); and the city of Memphis, TN (460,000). It is important to note that of the 17 jurisdictions, only nine used RV in a live election. In addition, only two or three of those jurisdictions used RV for electing partisan federal or State officials. Those that did so (Arkansas and South Carolina) used the method exclusively for military and overseas voting and not for the general voter population.

Is It Possible to Implement Ranked Voting Using the County's Current Voting System?

There is only one voting system approved for use in California that has been tested and conditionally approved by the Secretary of State for processing RV ballots. The possibility of implementing RV using Los Angeles County's current voting system was evaluated by considering the system's technical environment, procedural functions, and state approval requirements. Voting system transparency, security, and integrity were also given due consideration in evaluating this option. Based

---

[2]New America Foundation, "Instant Run-Off Voting: Use in U.S. Jurisdictions." 2009. http://www.newamerica.net/files/jurisdiction_summary_irv__apr__2009.pdf.

on the evaluation, we concluded that implementation of a RV methodology using the County's existing system would prove difficult without a significant overhaul of the voting system. Further, the county would need to further research comparable systems to inquire about audit procedures and state or federal certification of systems in place for RV.

The county's legacy paper-based voting system is comprised of precinct-based InkaVote Plus components and the county's centralized Microcomputer Tally System (MTS) operated on a DOS-based PC platform. Voters cast their ballots using the InkaVote Vote Recorder, an adaptation of the county's pre-Bush vs. Gore traditional punch card voting system. Voters utilize an ink pen to mark their ballots, and votes are recorded on IBM 312 format paper ballot cards. In compliance with Help America Vote Act (HAVA) requirements for second-chance voting, the InkaVote Plus Precinct Ballot Readers are deployed at every polling place to check ballots for *overvotes* and *blank* ballots. Voted ballots are then processed, inspected, and counted centrally at the Registrar-Recorder/County Clerk's headquarters in Norwalk, CA.

The tally of the votes is then executed using LR 3000 card readers that scan the entire voted ballots and detect ink marks in specified ballot positions associated with contests and candidates. The votes detected are then pushed to an MTS terminal and tabulated for the corresponding position/contest. The precinct tally results from each individual terminal are sent over a Token Ring Network to a server that cumulates the precinct totals into a summary total for the entire election. This process is the voting system architecture, as approved for use by the California Secretary of State.

It is important to emphasize that the state of Los Angeles County's current voting system is one requiring serious consideration and attention. As the description of the system and the findings of this assessment suggest, the county's voting system is complex and relies on dated and inflexible technology. The system has served, and continues to serve, the voters of Los Angeles County with accuracy and integrity, but the design of the system and the age of the platform upon which it was built offer very little technical and functional elasticity for making the major changes that RV would entail.

To implement RV, the county's MTS tally system's programming code would need to be rewritten to support multiple reads of a single ballot. Currently, every ballot that is run through MTS in a live election is read and counted only once. The system cannot discern whether a ballot was run once before—a necessary component of RV models. Furthermore, if a second reading were possible, the system would need to be altered to ignore all contests except for the RV contest.

Programming changes of this magnitude would require review and approval through the California Secretary of State's Office of Voting Systems Testing. Because the county is both the vendor and client of the MTS system, all costs involved in recertification would be borne by the county. In practical terms, this finding identifies a broader need for a new voting system (further addressed in our recommendations) as it is unlikely that modification to the county's existing, legacy voting system would meet new and developing standards for state approval and federal certification.

Without further analysis of the re-programming required to implement RV, at present, is not possible to provide a clear assessment of the new measures of transparency and auditability that would be required to preserve the integrity of tally processes and results using the potential fixes. This matter requires further consideration of the detailed technical requirements that would need to be developed to implement RV.

Would RV Cost Anything to Implement and Would It Produce Cost Savings?

It is difficult to provide a fixed figure for RV cost and cost savings at this time. The following general consideration will apply:

Costs:

- Staffing costs would be incurred in the re-programming of the county's voting system; although as previously stated, this option may not be cost-effective given the assessment that the voting system needs replacement.

- Added costs would also be expected for the voting systems certification process. In order to conduct legislative and congressional vacancy elections using RV, the voting system would first need to obtain independent test lab review/clearance and then approval by the Secretary of State.
- Potential costs would be incurred for any new hardware or software equipment needed for implementation.
- As part of implementing any new voting system, the strong recommendation is that the county expect significant costs associated with voter education and outreach. This is necessary to ensure voters fully understand the alternate method of voting and ranking their choices. Using even a conservative estimate of about $.55 per voter, a countywide education campaign could cost $2.2 million. District-specific education costs could be around $200,000 for any given district. These figures represent voter education costs for a single election cycle. It is unknown the degree to which these specific costs would become ongoing election expenses beyond the first election with RV, especially if the system were used intermittently for special vacancy elections only.

Cost Savings:

- In the case of RV for special vacancy elections for legislative and congressional offices, the system could yield cost avoidance by eliminating the need for runoff elections. Again, the cost avoidance would vary based on whether the election was consolidated with other scheduled elections or conducted as a stand-alone election. The cost of a single election can also vary depending on the district size. Using the 37th Congressional District runoff in 2007 as an example, the cost avoidance potential is estimated to be around $1.4 million for a single election.
- The election of nonpartisan county offices occurs during even-year statewide elections in March (previously June) and, if necessary, in November. As such, county office elections fall on regularly

scheduled election dates. In this case, the county would be faced with conducting a countywide election on each date whether a runoff was required for a vacancy or not. Under these circumstances, it is unclear whether using RV would result in a cost savings; although in some forms of implementation it would provide for cost avoidance.

Would RV Help Reduce Voter Fatigue?

Voter fatigue is understood to mean the growing disinterest of voters to participate in elections as a result of successive and frequent elections. While there is limited empirical data on voter fatigue, it is rational to assume that participating in elections takes a physical and emotional investment on the part of voters. Election-related transactions such as registering to vote, reviewing the sample ballot, requesting a vote by mail ballot, or taking time to go to the polls certainly require the investment of time on the part of the voter. Additionally, election schedules have a significant impact on the ability of communities to mobilize the necessary resources to conduct voter education and get-out-the-vote activities. With all these factors considered, it is safe to say that rolling elections can have a significant impact on participation and contribute to voter fatigue.

Given that RV would eliminate the need to conduct runoff elections, there is definite cause for concluding that RV could have a positive impact on reducing some form of voter fatigue. It is important to note, however, that to what extent this would result in greater voter participation in unscheduled, stand-alone special vacancy elections is unclear. Research cited by RV advocates suggests exponential increases in voter turnout; however, this conclusion is based on data from regularly scheduled contests as part of a city or countywide consolidated election and not with stand-alone, unscheduled special vacancy elections (see Table 17.1 for ranked choice voting impact).

Table 17.1 Summary of ranked choice voting impact

Option	Upfront cost impacts	Potential savings	Impact on voter fatigue	Impact of voter participation	Intervention required
Ranked choice voting (RCV)	High Voting system modification; voter education and outreach	Significant cost avoidance	Favorable	Assumed favorable for scheduled elections Less conclusive for special vacancy elections	Legislation; voting system modification; voting system certification, testing and approval; voter education and outreach

Other Options

What follows is a summary of additional options or approaches that could impact the costs of special vacancy elections and issues of voter fatigue and voter participation. As with RV, further consideration of any of these options would warrant more comprehensive analysis and recommendation.

Expand the Election Calendar to Include Odd Year Elections for Consolidation

The state could establish an expanded regular election calendar that would provide for even and odd year March (or June) and November election schedules. These could provide greater opportunities to amend the State Elections Code to require that vacancy elections be consolidated with regularly scheduled elections, while at the same time avoiding the problem of extended vacancies. In theory, this option would also allow for greater consolidation of special district and municipal elections and, therefore, has the potential to favorably address issues of voter fatigue by limiting the frequency of elections and reducing election costs.

Institute Limited Appointments to Fill Vacancy Period

This proposal would require a change to the California State Constitution to allow vacancies in congressional, state assembly, and state senate offices to be filled by appointment until the next regularly scheduled election at which time a successor to complete the full unexpired term would be elected by voters of the district. This act would greatly reduce the number of special elections occurring in California, generating significant cost avoidances for the state and counties. Reducing the number of special vacancy elections would also help reduce voter fatigue in the state.

Special primary and general elections have cost Los Angeles County at least $2 million in addition to the regular costs to be incurred for statewide primary and general elections. Since 2007, special vacancy elections have cost the state and county more than $16 million, with a substantial share of this cost not reimbursed to the county.[3]

With markedly low voter turnout rates for special vacancy elections generally averaging around 11%, it is apparent that Los Angeles County voters suffer from voter fatigue. Amending the California State Constitution to allow for an appointment to vacated congressional or legislative seats until the next scheduled election would garner a greater voter turnout ratio in addition to the cost savings.

A similar model is currently in place in the Los Angeles County Charter for filling vacancies in county offices. This option achieves the objectives of reduced election costs and reduced voter fatigue; however, it presents a new variable in the direct democracy model of representative governance by seating appointees in positions designated as voter-nominated representatives.

---

[3]In the interests of fiscal responsibility, Los Angeles County seeks to reduce the number of special vacancy elections while preserving the interests of California voters.

Establish Plurality Winners for Special Vacancy Elections

The legislative and congressional vacancy election rules could be amended to allow for plurality winners in special vacancy elections. This proposal would eliminate the need for runoff elections under the current 50% + 1 majority requirement. This option would achieve the same cost avoidance benefit as identified under RV without the costs associated with procuring and certifying a voting system with ranked choice capability.

Like the option of instituting limited appointments, this option achieves the objectives of reduced election costs and reduced voter fatigue; however, it does result in filling vacancies through an election where a majority vote may not be established.

All Vote by Mail Special Vacancy Elections

The State Elections Code could be amended to authorize counties to conduct special vacancy elections entirely by mail. Statistically, based on a limited sampling of vote by mail elections conducted in the county, this option would both reduce election costs and would increase voter participation. An anecdotal illustration of this is a comparison between voter turnout in the March 24, 2009 special vacancy primary election for the 26th District State Senate seat, which was 7.91% and the all vote by mail election conducted in 2010 for the San Marino Unified School District, which exceeded 50%.

This option would require serious consideration regarding its implementation in traditionally underserved communities where vote by mail has been less effective in increasing voter access and turnout.

Make State Reimbursement for Special Vacancy Elections Permanent and Amend Payment Formulas

Since the passage of the first reimbursement bill in 1993, vacancy elections have persisted and increased in frequency. Historically, reimbursement had been based on "per voter" rates established in 1993. These reimbursement rates have remained unchanged despite the increasing

Table 17.2 Comparison of alternatives and impact

Option	Upfront cost impacts	Potential savings	Impact on voter fatigue	Impact of voter participation	Intervention required
Ranked choice voting (RCV)	High	Significant	Favorable	Assumed favorable	Legislation; voting system modification; voter education
Expanded election calendar	None	Significant	Favorable	Assumed favorable	Legislation
Limited appointments	None	Significant	Favorable	Assumed neutral	Legislation; direct democracy implications
Plurality/ eliminate run-offs	None	Significant	Favorable	Assumed neutral	Legislation; majority vote implications
All vote by mail	Low	Moderate	Moderate	Favorable	Legislation; voter education; special consideration for under-served communities
State reimbursement	None	Cost shift local → state	N/A	N/A	Legislation; appropriation

cost of conducting elections. Amending state reimbursement provisions to authorize reimbursement of the true costs of conducting vacancy elections for legislative and congressional offices would benefit the county. This option alone, however, only shifts the economic burden associated with the current system for filling vacancies to the state and does not address the overall costs of conducting vacancy elections or the issues of voter participation and fatigue (see Table 17.2 for comparison of alternatives and potential impact).

Other Considerations and Recommendations

Given the fiscal environment as well as the dynamics of the electoral process in California and throughout the nation, the analysis and options highlighted in this chapter are timely.

In addition to county capacity, cost, and the consequences of RV for voters in special elections, three additional broad areas were recommended for consideration before advancing policy initiatives or structural changes more narrowly focused on special vacancy elections. The three areas of focus were addressing the future needs of Los Angeles County's voting systems, continued commitment to voter outreach and engagement, and engaging with and anticipating the expectations of future generations of voters.

Addressing the Future Needs of Los Angeles County's Voting System(s)

The current voting system has served Los Angeles County voters well. The county acted with caution in evaluating a new voting system and we focused on identifying the long-term needs for a system that adheres to the federal certification requirements. The system is captive to aging ballot layout and a central tallying system that are increasingly difficult to support and operate.

The voting system certification process at the state and federal level have experienced rapid change since the establishment of the US Election Assistance Commission (EAC) in 2002. The requirements for certifying voting systems have continually expanded and become more complex. This has created uncertainty in the industry and slowed the testing and certification process for any new advancement or development of voting systems.

This situation created a particularly challenging environment for Los Angeles County. On the one hand, there are no certified commercial off-the-shelf (COTS) voting systems on the market that will meet the specific needs of the county. And, new as-yet-uncertified COTS systems proposed by the major vendors do not seem sufficient either. On the other hand, the process of developing or purchasing a custom voting system solution especially for Los Angeles County can be costly and risky in terms of certification, maintenance, and implementation.

With that in mind, Los Angeles County embarked on a Voting System Assessment Project in 2009 led by the Registrar-Recorder/County Clerk to discuss, analyze, and document the issues and factors central to the implementation of a new voting system, and the options available for design, development, and procurement. The assessment project set priorities and made recommendations. By the end of the assessment, the Registrar-Recorder/County Clerk developed and committed to a workable strategy and a formal project plan for implementing a new voting system by 2020.

The Voting System Assessment Project brought together a team of managers from within the county to identify, discuss, prioritize, and document the issues, factors, and options involved in implementing a new voting system. The project has documented the analysis and provided a recommendation to the Los Angeles County Board of Supervisors and Chief Executive Officer that commits the county to a concrete and specific solution and a detailed project plan for implementing a new voting system by 2020.

A vital part of this assessment process is input and consent from community stakeholders representing important constituencies such as city officials, diverse communities, disability rights advocates, voting integrity activists, and representative samples of the electorate itself. At the time of the study, the county's assessment project had actively engaged more than 3800 stakeholders throughout the process.

Continued Commitment to Voter Outreach and Engagement: Modernization of the Voter Registration Process

Following the successful administration of the 2008 presidential election cycle, much of the national policy focus on elections shifted toward a review and analysis of voter register and voter engagement in the electoral process. The Registrar-Recorder/County Clerk participated in this dialogue and played an active role in a collaborative working group with advocates and researchers considering alternative approaches. As with voting system dynamics, the focus of these efforts was two-fold—(1) increased access and participation and (2) modernization and cost-effectiveness.

The county needs to build on the successful partnerships that were formed with the media and community organizations committed to providing voter education and information. Communities see increased confidence in the electoral process when information is readily available and easily accessible. This approach is viable in Los Angeles County but also other jurisdictions across the United States that work toward improving voter registration and engagement.

Engaging with and Anticipating the Expectations of Future Generations of Voters

In the last decade, the county experienced a noticeable increase in registered voters between the ages of 18 and 29; a demographic often disproportionately underrepresented among eligible voters. The county should focus on the expectations that future voters will have and ensure that efforts or initiatives for identifying and selecting new systems and voting models cultivate a process that encourages and accommodates the newest generation of voters.

This information, along with the factors identified in Table 17.2 (costs, savings, voter fatigue, and voter participation), can be used as a framework for evaluating RV and for evaluating other policy options now and in the future.

Dean C. Logan is the Registrar-Recorder/County Clerk for Los Angeles County, California. Logan has over 25 years experience in election administration, records management, and public service. Prior to moving to Southern California, Logan served as the Director of Records, Elections and Licensing Services for King County, Washington, as State Elections Director for the Washington Secretary of State; and as the elected County Clerk and Chief Deputy County Auditor in Kitsap County, Washington.

Currently, Logan serves as the President for the California Association of Clerks and Election Officials (CACEO) and on the Pew Center on the States' Voter Registration Modernization, Voter Information Project and Performance Index for Elections working groups. He is an active participant in the Future of California Elections collaborative, an initiative sponsored and funded by the James T. Irvine Foundation. Past work includes serving on the California Statewide Voter Registration System Advisory Committee and on the National Election Center's Task Forces on Education & Training and Election Reform.

18

Increasing Confidence in International Elections

Kelly Ann Krawczyk and Avery Davis-Roberts

Although only one element of democratic governance, elections lay at the heart of the democratic process. The degree to which the people of a nation have confidence in the outcomes and accuracy of the voting process is essential to overall confidence in democracy. While the majority of US voters had confidence in the accuracy of the vote count in 2016, a startling 34% did not (Gallup, n.d.). The statistics from the same poll regarding the public's confidence in the honesty of elections were even more concerning. Almost 70% of Americans polled stated that they did not have confidence in the honesty of the 2016 elections.

Elections that are free and fair provide legitimacy and credibility that helps build confidence in elections. Free and fair elections also reduce the use of non-democratic and/or violent methods of attaining

---

K. A. Krawczyk (✉)
Auburn University, Auburn, AL, USA
e-mail: kak0037@auburn.edu

A. Davis-Roberts
The Carter Center, Atlanta, GA, USA

power. In this chapter, we discuss five different processes and tools that can impact electoral integrity, thereby boosting, or in some cases even diminishing, confidence in elections.

Election Observation and Improved Electoral Outcomes

One mechanism that can help safeguard elections is the practice of election observation. Election observation is the "purposeful gathering of information on the electoral process, and the making of informed judgements on the conduct of an election based on the information that is gathered" (West Africa Civil Society Institute 2009).[1] Election observation assesses an election in accordance with established international principles for democratic elections, yet also recognizes the sovereignty of a country in determining the credibility and legitimacy of their own electoral process.

Election observation offers several key benefits. First and foremost, election observation is used to help detect and deter electoral fraud. This can lead to additional benefits, such as increased confidence in the credibility of elections, increased confidence and trust in election results, improved compliance with legal requirements and enforcement of electoral law, and increased transparency and accountability of election administrators and personnel.

There are several ways to conceptualize and categorize election observation. First, observation can be carried out by either domestic or international observers. Domestic observers can be partisan (such as political parties) or nonpartisan (nongovernmental organizations). International observers are often members of international bodies such as the European Union, the African Union, and the Organization of American States, as well as international nongovernmental organizations. Second, election observation can be either short term or long term. Short-term

---

[1] It is important to differentiate election observation from election monitoring. Both processes involve gathering and assessing information and then making an informed judgement on the accuracy and quality of the electoral process. The key difference is that monitors can intervene in the electoral process, while observers cannot.

observation focuses primarily on voting day and the vote-counting process and assesses only some phases and/or aspects of the electoral cycle. The duration of short-term observation is usually around a week, typically beginning during the final campaign period and ending with the post-election statement. While irregularities (e.g., fraud, malpractice, or incompetence) can occur at various points in the electoral cycle (e.g., during voter registration), and at different points on election day (such as when votes are tabulated at aggregation centers), short-term observers focus on irregularities at polling places.

Long-term observation is more comprehensive and encompasses the entire electoral cycle: the formation and installation of electoral management bodies, creation and conformation of electoral boundaries, voter registration, voter education, political party registration, candidate nomination, campaigning, media coverage, voting, vote counting, and electoral dispute resolution. Long-term observers must be in-country long enough to gather information on all parts of the electoral cycle (or as many parts as can be observed) and make judgments for assessment. This means that long-term observers become very familiar with the electoral system and process in the country where they are observing, as well as with the political and legal environment of the election. It often makes sense for domestic citizen observers to conduct long-term observation work, because they reside in the country and know the language and political culture.

Unfortunately, electoral fraud is a common event, and it is often serious enough to impact election outcomes. According to the Database of Political Institutions (DPI), 20% of recent executive elections experienced such a degree of fraud or intimidation that outcomes were affected (Keefer 2002). An alternate DPI data set that identifies fraud only in cases where international election observers were present reports "moderate or major problems of election integrity" in one-quarter of countries where elections took place between 1980 and 2004. The deployment of election observers is meant to enhance the integrity of elections in both developing and developed countries, due to the belief that this can prevent or reduce electoral irregularities (Kelley 2012). This is in part why approximately 80% of elections that took place around the world in 2006, for example, were monitored by observers.

Research supports the contention that international election observers are successful in reducing election fraud (Enikolopov et al. 2013; Hyde 2007, 2010, 2011; Ichino and Schündeln 2012; Kelley 2012; Sjoberg 2012). One recent study by Asunka et al. (2013) offers particularly valuable insight into the use of election observation to deter electoral fraud. Using the 2012 Ghanaian national election as a case study, they explore whether domestic election observation deters electoral fraud, by examining the effect of domestic observers on two specific markers of fraud: (1) over-voting (more votes cast than registered voters in a polling location) and (2) unnaturally high levels of turnout. The researchers worked in partnership with Ghana's largest and most well-established organization of domestic election observers, the Coalition of Domestic Elections Observers (CODEO), in order to randomly assign election observers to just over 1000 of Ghana's 26,000 polling places. In addition, data were also collected from an additional randomly selected 1000 polling stations at which no observers were deployed. Through this rigorous randomized experimental research design, they extracted two major findings. First, observers significantly reduced over-voting and suspicious turnout at polling stations where they were deployed, by up to 60%. This is an encouraging outcome and offers support for the idea that election observation can reduce fraud. However, they also found that Ghana's two major political parties were actually able to "relocate" fraud from observed to unobserved polling places in their historical strongholds, where they enjoy social penetration and where political competition is low. The parties were not able to do this among politically competitive constituencies. Thus, while research supports the use of election observers in order to deter fraud, the potential positive effect of observers does not appear to be limitless and may come with some important caveats.

Using Civic Education to Enhance Confidence in Elections

When we think of civic education initiatives, we tend to think about voter registration drives or citizen instructions for voting. However, there is emerging evidence from around the globe that new, innovative civic education campaigns can contribute to positive electoral outcomes, with the potential to increase electoral credibility and legitimacy, increase voter turnout, and even reduce the threat of electoral violence. In addition, emerging evidence indicates that citizens are capable of processing complex civic education messaging and that this messaging influences their voting behavior.

One example of this sort of innovative civic education initiative was implemented in Nigeria prior to the 2007 national election. This election was seriously marred by violence, and 300 people were killed in election-related violence. Collier and Vincente (2014) designed and conducted a nationwide field experiment during the run-up period, in which they implemented a randomized, grassroots, anti-violence civic education campaign. Their research examined how the anti-violence messaging changed citizens' perceptions and attitudes about electoral violence, how it impacted voter behavior, and how the intervention impacted actual incidences of electoral violence.

Collier and Vincente's (2014) civic education campaign was randomized across neighborhoods and villages in six Nigerian states. The campaign was conducted in half of the locations by a major international NGO called ActionAid, which specializes in community participatory development. Interventions included town hall meetings, popular theater, and the distribution of campaign material and were standardized across all locations. The interventions were aimed at empowering citizens to counteract local violence and at reducing the costs of citizen "protest" and collective action. The campaign also appealed to citizens to vote against violent politicians. Collier and Vincente's (2014) empirical results indicate the anti-violence campaign was effective in providing an increased sense of local safety and security to the treatment population and in boosting citizens' sense of empowerment to counteract electoral violence. In addition, the intervention increased voter turnout by 7% and illustrated that candidates who were perceived to be violent were penalized by voters.

We can look to India for another example of a unique civic education initiative. In this environment, a population with lower levels of formal education, coupled with weak state institutions, leads to rampant vote buying. The Banerjee et al. (2011) field experiment examined how providing performance information for elected officials impacted not only vote buying, but also voter turnout and incumbent vote share. During the run-up to the 2008 elections, residents in a random sample of Delhi's slum communities received door-to-door delivery of newspapers containing report cards on politicians. The report card presented information on performance of the incumbent legislator, as well as qualifications of the incumbent and the two main challengers. Communities that received the civic education intervention had higher turnout, reduced vote buying, and higher vote share for better performing and more qualified incumbents. In addition, the field experiment shows that voters demonstrated sophistication in how they used the report card to judge performance and qualifications: They evaluated jurisdiction-level information on the incumbent's public goods spending and used challenger qualifications to judge qualifications of the incumbent. Both the Nigerian and Indian field experiments provide thought-provoking evidence that indicates researchers and practitioners should be considering how new and innovative civic education campaigns can positively influence elections.

Does Biometric Technology Enhance Electoral Integrity?

Biometric technology is increasingly employed to promote the integrity of elections. Biometrics are defined as "any automatically measurable, robust and distinctive physical characteristic or personal trait that can be used to identify an individual or verify the claimed identity of an individual" (Woodward et al. 2003). Fingerprints, face prints, and iris scans are the most common features used for biometric identification.[2] Biometrics can be used both (1) to identify an individual within a larger population (i.e., who are you?) and (2) to authenticate an individual against a record (i.e., are you who you say you are?).

---

[2]Recently, however, voice prints, retinal scans, vein patterns, tongue prints, lip movements, ear patterns, gait, dynamic signature, DNA, brain waves (EEG), and even butt prints have all been used for biometric identification, with the latter two still at an experimental stage (Woodward et al. 2003).

There has been rapid growth in use of biometrics, in part because of the variety of ways the technology can be utilized. In resource-rich countries, biometrics are employed mainly for forensics and security purposes. In low- to middle-income countries, biometrics are used for a wide variety of non-security applications such as civil registries, voter rolls, health records, social transfers, public payrolls, and pension payments (Gelb and Clark 2013). One of the largest applications of biometrics, in both developing and developed countries, is in elections. The total number of countries that have adopted biometrics in elections has increased to over 50, and as of 2016, 35% of 130 surveyed electoral management bodies (EMBs) across the globe were capturing biometric data as part of their voter registration process (IDEA ICTs in Elections Database 2014). At least 34 low- to middle-income countries have incorporated or are planning to incorporate biometric technology into their electoral processes (Gelb and Clark 2013).

There are significant variations in usage of biometrics between regions, however. While there are virtually no users in Europe, about half of the countries in Africa and Latin America use this technology in elections (IDEA ICTs in Elections Database 2014). There is also variation in the extent to which biometric capability is employed. For example, while biometric information may be used to identify voters at polling stations, in many cases this does not involve electronic biometric identification, but simply a manual check of each voter's photograph on the voter list. Only 9% of surveyed countries utilize an electronic biometric voter identification system, and, in some of these cases, fingerprint scans are only conducted in selected precincts and not the entire country (IDEA ICTs in Elections Database 2014).

Potential Benefits of Biometrics

The primary motivation for using biometrics is to reduce fraud. Biometrics are typically employed at two points in the electoral cycle. During voter registration, biometrics can ensure that individuals only register once, through de-duplication. On Election Day, biometric voter verification has the potential to prevent multiple voting or impersonation of another voter by an individual and can also be used retroactively to detect fraud. If the number of verified voters at a polling station is compared to the number of ballots cast, biometric authentication can also help prevent ballot stuffing, one of the most common forms of electoral fraud in developing countries. Biometric authentication is less common at polling stations, however, in part due to resource constraints. Large-scale voter biometric registration exercises can be accomplished with a relatively low equipment to citizen ratio. Elections, however, require a mass, simultaneous mobilization of staff and citizens within a short-time period and require widespread distribution of technology and connectivity. There are less-expensive, lower-tech ways to prevent multiple voting such as checking photos and cards against voter lists and using indelible ink to mark voters; these may be sufficient in many scenarios (Gelb and Clark 2013).

Despite their resource-intensive nature, biometric elections have produced positive outcomes in some countries. Bolivia's biometric registration effort helped dispel concerns about the quality of the electoral roll and expanded the number of registered voters from 3 million to 5 million by enrolling previously undocumented citizens from indigenous communities. Constraints on connectivity hampered efforts to fully de-duplicate Bolivia's electoral roll, however (Gelb and Clark 2013; The Carter Center 2009). Pakistan implemented a massive clean-up and updating of its voter roll in 2012 using a biometrically based ID system, and almost half the entries in the existing roll were struck off and replaced by a similar number of new enrollees (Malik 2014). Venezuela, which has used biometrics in elections since 2004, broke new ground in October 2012 by using biometric voter authentication with electronic voting for the first time (Mayhew 2012).

In some instances, the potential benefits of biometrics may outweigh its high costs. For example, biometric technology can increase voters' trust in the electoral process and contribute to perceived reductions in electoral fraud. After Ghana's 2012 voter registration, over three-quarters of registered Ghanaian voters agreed that biometric registration was an improvement over the old system, and 87% believed it promoted credible and peaceful elections (Piccolino 2016). Similarly, a 2014 Gallup poll in Pakistan found that 52% of Pakistanis believed the introduction of electronic voting machines and a biometric system were the most effective reforms for free and fair elections (Gallup 2014). In Nigeria, the highly polarized 2015 election prompted widespread concern that disputes could turn violent. Instead, the election resulted in a peaceful transition of power, and biometric permanent voter cards and card readers were credited with curbing multiple voting and ballot stuffing, despite reports of technical difficulties in authenticating voters at the polls (Nwangwu 2015).

The "Unintended Consequences" of Biometrics

As discussed above, there has been a huge increase in the use of technology in elections. This is because we view technology as a solution that automatically leads to higher performing electoral management bodies, reduced election irregularities, and increased confidence in election results (Cheeseman et al. 2018). Yet using sophisticated technology does not in and of itself increase the credibility and fairness of elections. Biometrics can only address certain types of electoral fraud, so whether they can contribute to cleaner elections depends on whether these types of threats are present. In addition, in environments where fraud is common, new kinds of electoral manipulation can occur.

We also need to bear in mind that technology is not infallible, and biometric failures are common. Biometric failures can be technological (such as failure to read fingerprints) or due to poor implementation and logistics (e.g., biometric kits distributed without power or time for a charge). They may be unintended or result from deliberate actions. During Ghana's 2012 elections, for example, biometric machines failed at 19% of polling stations (CODEO 2013). In Kenya's 2013 elections, the electronic polling book malfunctioned or failed at 55% of the polling stations at some point during the day (ELOG 2013).

Biometric technology also does not guarantee a comprehensive, inclusive, error-free voter registration. For example, while biometrics can be used to verify voter identity, they cannot be used to verify voter eligibility. Whether a registrant is underage or is eligible to vote in a certain constituency cannot be checked biometrically. In addition, when a new registration system—including a biometric system—is introduced, it is always a challenge to reach all eligible citizens. This presents the risk of exclusion.

Existing evidence strongly suggests that biometric technology may not always be the most cost-effective solution (Gelb and Diofasi 2016; Wolf 2017). Elections involve the entire population and operate according to a strict schedule. These logistical and time constraints can strain the capability of biometrics. In addition, while there is popular support for biometrics from international donors, this support often lacks sufficient lead time or adequate resources. Many countries start voter registration (biometric or otherwise) less than a year before an election. This allows little time for proper training on new, highly technical biometric systems. These complex systems may also be perceived as "black boxes" that voters cannot observe or evaluate for fairness, which can perpetuate an atmosphere of suspicion and mistrust (Evrensel 2010). Without an understanding of how the biometric technology works, there is no basis for increased trust and greater legitimacy among voters.

Another potential drawback is that not all biometric systems are created equally. Countries can get locked into systems with unfavorable features or even substandard technology. In addition, many developing countries do not have the capability to implement biometrics without assistance. Contracting with foreign technology companies to deliver the biometric equipment, and also to manage and clean the voting database, may weaken ownership of the electoral process and raise further concerns about its independence. Overall, despite the early promise and continued reliance on biometric technology in elections, it may not always be the most effective tool for increasing the fairness and legitimacy of elections.

Ensuring the Accuracy of the Vote Count

Confidence in elections can suffer if constituents do not trust the accuracy of the vote count. Inaccuracy in the vote count can stem from multiple issues including fraud, malpractice, or problems or errors in the technological solutions employed. In each of these cases, steps can be taken to identify and determine whether the vote count is correct, and if not, what may have happened.

In this section, we explore some of the measures taken internationally to promote the accuracy of the vote-counting process. Specifically, we examine the role that audits and the practice of nonpartisan statistically based observation can play as a means of promoting accuracy, transparency, and confidence in the vote-counting processes, and how these tools can impact continuous improvement and confidence in election administration.

Audits

Post-election audits are increasingly the subject of interest and debate within the election administration field in the United States. According to the National Conference of State Legislatures, 30 states and Washington, DC have a requirement to conduct a "traditional" audit, while a further three states (Colorado, Virginia, and Rhode Island) are required to conduct a risk-limiting audit (NCSL 2019).[3] Audits are conducted to ensure that the count is correct, and implicit in this is recognition that fraud, malpractice, or system errors could have impacted the vote count.

---

[3] A traditional audit here means a recount of ballots from a fixed percentage of polling stations, districts, or voting machines, regardless of the margin of victory in the election. A risk-limiting audit, on the other hand, uses statistical models and protocols to determine whether the election count is correct. The exact number of ballots recounted may vary depending on factors such as the margin of victory in the election and/or whether early ballot counts in the audit are presenting evidence that the count was correct.

In Venezuela and the Philippines, audits are used to verify that the votes as cast by the voter using electronic voting technologies are counted, though they use quite different auditing methods. In Venezuela, large-scale "hot audits" of cast ballots have taken place since the turn of the century (Rosnick and Weisbrot 2013).[4] In conducting these hot audits, Venezuela uses advanced technology to identify voters and to count and cast ballots. After casting their ballots, voters take the ballot receipt produced by the voting machine and place it in a physical ballot box. At the end of the election day, ballots are manually recounted in 52% of polling places (Martinez 2013). In 2006, the Carter Center's international mission noted that these measures can help to promote transparency and confidence, but their utility is limited if the manual counts are not compared to the machine counts and if subsequent analysis and learning does not take place to improve future elections (The Carter Center 2006).

Since 2010, voters across the 7000 plus islands of the Philippines have used optical scanning technologies to have their votes counted. Given a troubled history of electoral fraud and election violence, as part of the standard election procedures the Commission of Elections (COMELEC) undertakes a random manual audit (RMA), in which the paper ballots from a small percentage of polling stations are manually recounted. In 2010, the introduction of these audits was an important trust-building measure; there was a high level of public distrust in the voting machines because of the haste with which the vendor was selected and the lack of transparency in COMELEC practices (Carter Center 2010). Despite procedural difficulties, the RMAs in 2010 produced results that largely corresponded to the official tally. Since 2010, the RMA has indicated that the vote count is over 99% accurate (UNTV News 2016). Importantly, in 2016, nonpartisan election watchdog NAMFREL collaborated with the COMELEC to oversee the RMA process, bolstering the credibility of the process (Bueza, n.d.).

Audits were conducted in both the 2014 elections in Afghanistan and the 2010 elections in Haiti. Not only were these audits conducted with the aim of determining whether the vote count was accurate, they were also conducted to bolster the legitimacy of results of highly contested

---

[4]A "hot audit" is an audit that takes place on election day. Sometimes the term is also used in reference to other forms of parallel, election day testing of electronic election systems.

elections that were seen to lack legitimacy and for which there was a lack of trust in the election commission itself.

Following troubled elections in 2009, the political parties in Afghanistan agreed that a comprehensive audit of the 2014 elections should take place. The audit reviewed 100% of the second-round presidential votes and was facilitated by the United Nations along with input from the election commission and the political parties. The goal of the audit was to move the political process forward and have objective clarity about the winner of the election. This was an incredibly costly and time-consuming process. Ultimately, although both parties agreed to the audit, when the audit failed to uncover evidence of fraud that would have changed the result of the election, one party boycotted the audit and political negotiations were necessary to ensure a government could be put in place. In this case, the mechanics of the election and audit procedure had to bow to the political forces in the country (Byrd 2015).

During the 2010 election in Haiti, an audit of the results of the first round of voting in the presidential election was conducted. The Organization of American States participated in this audit process and was ultimately unable to confirm that the results of the election, as released, were accurate given the scale of the irregularities that their audit of a small number of polling stations uncovered. The audit process was particularly challenging because the team was working without predetermined audit procedures in place (Organization of American States 2011).

Despite the differing scope of the audits in the examples above, they illustrate some important points about the principles and approaches to audits, many of which have been captured in the literature. First, agreement on the goal of the audit prior to embarkation is important. As Norden et al. (2007) point out, there can be many different goals for an audit including "creating an appropriate level of public confidence in the results of an election; deterring fraud against the voting system; detecting and providing information about large-scale, systemic errors; providing feedback that will allow jurisdictions to improve voting technology and election administration in future years; providing additional incentives and benchmarks for elections staff to reach higher standards of accuracy; and confirming, to a high level of confidence, that a complete manual recount would not change the outcome of the race."

Second, transparency throughout the process, including the provision of information to the public, is critical to ensuring that audits really are confidence-boosting measures. This means that the process should be accessible to the public, and it places a burden on election administrators to explain in clear and easy-to-understand language what an audit is, what it can do, and its limitations.

Third and finally, as Darnolf et al. (2015) highlight, ownership of the audit process by election administrators is important. This means not only ensuring that they are active participants in the audit process itself, but also taking steps to mitigate risk in advance of the election. These pre-election actions, when combined with audits, can help to identify vulnerabilities and discrepancies in the vote-counting system and can also create a continuous learning loop that supports the improvement of future election administration processes. Norden et al. (2007) note that in 2007, only one state, North Carolina, had collected and made public the outcomes of their audit for the purposes of improving future elections.

Statistically Based Observation

As outlined above, election observation has proven to be an important means of providing impartial information about an electoral process to the public and is an important method of promoting continuous improvement of election processes. In many parts of the world, not only are international election observers deployed, but domestic, nonpartisan, citizen observers deploy to polling stations on election day to verify the integrity of the election process.

One tool in the toolkit of election observers around the world is statistically based observation (SBO), which is also known as a Parallel Vote Tabulation or a Quick Count. In the context of transitional elections the use of these vote verification techniques can have multiple goals and outcomes that include: exposing attempted fraud; verifying opposition victory and convincing incumbents to accept defeat; and verifying incumbent victory and convincing opposition to accept defeat. In more developed and stable democracies, the methods described below, when executed appropriately, can help to promote confidence in counting processes that are increasingly opaque in the age of electronic voting (Bjornlund and Cowan 2011; Estok et al. 2002).

Citizen observers regularly deploy large numbers of volunteers on election day. In teams of two, they will deploy to a polling station as election officials are beginning poll opening procedures and they will remain in the polling station all day long. This ensures that they will have witnessed any attempts to tamper with the voting materials and/or any disruptions that may take place throughout the day or at vote counting. At the end of the day, observers in a random sample of polling stations, who have been in the polling station all day and observed the counting process, will be asked to collect polling station level results. These results, collected by the observers at polling stations across the country, can then be compared to the official results released by the polling officials as part of the vote tabulation and aggregation process. Using this method, citizen observation groups can help provide an independent check on the accuracy of the vote count (Estok et al. 2002).

This method was first developed and used by the National Citizens Movement for Free Elections (NAMFREL) in the Philippines during the 1986 elections. In the end, NAMFREL collected results from some 70% of the Philippines 85,000 polling stations (Bjornlund and Cowan 2011). NAMFREL's parallel vote count exposed widescale fraud by then-President Ferdinand Marcos and was an igniting spark to the People Power Revolution that ultimately led to his ouster. In 1988, a similar method was used to shed light on the fraudulent vote count of the Chilean Pinochet regime and in 1989, former US President Jimmy Carter used the results of a SBO exercise to denounce fraud in the Panama elections. Since 1986, SBO has been used to verify vote counts in Albania, Bangladesh, Belarus, Burundi, Indonesia, Georgia, Kenya, Macedonia, Slovakia, Mozambique, Peru, and Ukraine and more recently in the 2018 elections in Zimbabwe (Bjornlund and Cowan 2011).

The use of SBO as means of verifying vote counts is not without controversy or concern. If implemented poorly, it can undermine voter confidence in the process and in election administration institutions. These concerns have been exacerbated by lack of agreement among experts and practitioners about the best methods to use, although best practice is emerging (Bjornlund and Cowan 2011). These practices include using statistically significant sampling and ensuring that organizations have the statistical know-how and expertise to adequately collect and analyze data.

Social Media and Elections

The role of the Internet and social media in elections has been an issue at the fore, particularly since the 2016 elections in the United States. However, social media is also impacting elections internationally. Much of the debate has focused on the role of social media in influencing social movements (e.g., during the so-called Arab Spring), its impacts on elections from the perspective of political campaigns, and more recently its use to spread disinformation and negatively influence public opinion. However, there has been less emphasis on policy and research to examine (and address) the impact of social media on the practice of election administration. Looking forward, we anticipate that social media will continue to play an important role in the overall conduct of elections. Social media will increasingly influence election administration and either bolster or significantly undermine public confidence in election processes. In the following sections, we outline four areas where international practice could illuminate challenges and paths forward for the field of election administration.

Social Media for Outreach

Government bodies are increasingly using social media to provide the public with up-to-date information and even asking the public to help them co-design new programs (Hofmann et al. 2013; Kavanaugh et al. 2012). In the context of elections, election administration bodies around the world are increasingly using social media to communicate voter information to the public, to facilitate participation through voter registration drives, and increasingly to learn more about potential election irregularities (see below for more information). In 2013, International IDEA found that of 172 countries and territories only 55 election management bodies (or 31%) had Facebook pages, not all of which were active. On Twitter, a mere 27% of election management bodies were active (International IDEA 2014). This number has undoubtedly increased in the last five years.

There are many potential benefits to election administration bodies using social media for voter outreach including provision of up-to-date information, increasing transparency and accessibility in the electoral process, inclusion of diverse groups of voters, and also receiving feedback as part of two-way communication with the electorate. The National Electoral Institute of Mexico (INE), for example, uses Twitter to share information about its activities, voter education videos, and other relevant information to its 778 thousand followers. The Independent Nigerian Election Commission (INEC) tweets not only about ongoing outreach activities, but also provides updates on the actions it is taking in response to reports of election irregularities and has 1.02 million followers in a country with limited Internet penetration.

However, use of social media as part of an election administration outreach campaign does require a different skill set from that required for more traditional public relations (Hofmann et al. 2013). As some election administrators have noted, social media requires that offices be able to inform, educate, and entertain the public (Chapin 2017). This is supported by the research of Hofmann et al. (2013) which found that the public in their sample preferred Facebook posts that were not announcements or reports; they were less interested in posts that advertised government services; and interactive videos and photo posts gained four to five times as many likes as static or text-based posts. Going forward, election administrators are going to have to continue to think innovatively to capture the attention of a distracted public.

Election Administration and the Rise of Disinformation

The Internet and social media, in particular, are increasingly being used by foreign and domestic actors as means of influencing public opinion using false or misleading information (Frenkel 2018). The messages spread by disinformation purveyors on Facebook, Twitter, blogs, and other Internet sites fall across the political spectrum are generally negative and are usually intended to sow distrust and discord. These messages are then amplified by bots and human users, some of them influential, that comment on, retweet, like, and share them (Howard et al. 2018). Sometimes these efforts are state-sponsored and well organized (Bradshaw and Howard 2017; Nyst and Monaco 2018). Experts are split in their predictions about whether we will see a more truthful future or one in which disinformation is the norm (Anderson and Rainie 2017).

Widespread disinformation campaigns about the technical aspects of election administration (e.g., misleading posts or tweets about when polls open, reports of violence or intimidation that might keep voters away from the polls, etc.) have the potential to radically shake voter confidence in a specific election and in election administration more generally and should not be underestimated (Roose 2018).

Globally, states are taking significant measures to address the impact of disinformation on public opinion. Given the scale, scope, and complexity of the issues, as well as the work required to identify who is behind the campaigns, these efforts are a laborious and challenging task (Bradshaw and Howard 2017). Concerned about foreign influence on their elections, the Swedish government is taking a multipronged approach to addressing the issue that not only includes the creation of a new Psychological Defense Agency whose principal task will be to build the resilience of the public to disinformation, but also widescale training of local government officials on how to identify and respond to false or misleading information online (Cederberg 2018).

While the budgets and resources of those using social media to manipulate and influence public opinion are unknown, it is likely that the resource needs for a response at the local level may be high. As the Swedish case illustrates, a response to these campaigns requires a coordinated and well-planned response at the national, state, and local levels, that includes training for local officials, and awareness-raising among the public. It will also require that already limited resources (both financial and human) be allocated to focusing on these issues.

Our collective understanding of the influence of social media and of disinformation on political participation remains quite limited. While it is a burgeoning area of inter-disciplinary research, there are few established theoretical models and a dearth of reliable data sets on which to rely (Dimitrova and Matthes 2018). Learning will continue to unfold over the coming years, and election administrators have an opportunity to influence the conversation and research in this area by actively engaging with scholars, researchers, and other practitioners.

Use of Social Media for Learning and Improvement of Election Administration

Finally, social media is being used by election administration bodies as a means of collecting information in real time about unfolding election processes so that they can respond and address current issues as well as learn for the improvement of future elections. While there are many benefits to such learning processes, they are not without their own challenges.

Nigeria has a relatively long history of social activism and engagement through social media. Building on this momentum, the Independent Electoral Commission of Nigeria established a situation room for the 2011 elections that allowed them to receive to information about electoral irregularities directly from the public. During the 2011 presidential election, the INEC received about 4000 tweets over the course of three days (Bartlett et al. 2015). These efforts were supported by civil society efforts to collect information on incidents and irregularities in parallel. At the end of the election, Attahiru Jega, Chairman of the INEC, stated that, through the use of social media, the INEC had been made more accountable to the people for the conduct of the elections.

During the 2015 elections in Nigeria, Bartlett et al. (2015) collected 13.6 million tweets regarding the election that were shared by 1.38 million unique users. In addition, they collected information from Facebook pages associated with candidates, news outlets, and informal news outlets (e.g., bloggers). Through various means of analysis, including network analysis, user analysis, and type analysis, the research team determined that monitoring and analyzing social media around elections can be a useful means of understanding who may be influencing public opinion about an election process; detecting and responding to irregularities and events as they occur; responding to rumors and misinformation; and supplementing existing learning and evaluation tools for election administration.

Using social media information in this way is not without its challenges. It requires resources (time, money, and qualified people) to be able to sift through large amounts of data. Analysis of this information can also be challenge—as the Bartlett et al. study (2015) points out, social media data have a number of weaknesses including the unpredictability of the scale and quality of the data, the lack of demographic variables that might provide a more robust understanding of users, and the general reliability of the data which is user-generated. That being said, social media can be a useful source of additional information when evaluating election administration performance, and collaboration between scholars and election administrators will no doubt yield important insights in the future.

Conclusions and Implications

In this chapter, we have presented and discussed five different mechanisms and tools that can be used to increase, or in some cases may even decrease, electoral integrity. Evidence indicates that election observation and civic education initiatives have the potential to help reduce election irregularities, influence voter behavior, and help increase electoral confidence through free and fair elections. While election observation is already regularly employed across the globe in the hopes of reducing voting irregularities, until recently, there has been a lack of rigorous empirical evidence that supports this contention. The research discussed above offers rationale for the continued deployment of observers in elections. Furthermore, the use of innovative and comprehensive civic education campaigns, even in developing environments, appears to impact voter knowledge and behavior and help strengthen elections. These new types of civic education interventions appear to have underutilized and untapped potential.

The evidence presented here on biometrics leads us to several conclusions. Cheeseman et al. (2018) suggest instead of simply assuming that technology can enhance and improve electoral outcomes, we must instead engage in a much more thorough and careful assessment of the potential risks and gains associated with use of election technology. If, after this analysis, we decide the gains outweigh the costs and risks, we must do a better job in planning for and implementing this technology.

In the context of the future of election administration, both the use of audits and SBO raise important points about the need for inclusive and transparent processes that not only identify discrepancies in the vote count, but also allow for their correction in a way that is accessible and understandable to the public. Ideally, these processes can feed into longer-term learning and improvement processes for election administrators. Recently, social media has taken on a negative role when it comes to creating electoral legitimacy, due to the use of social media to spread disinformation and negatively influence public opinion. It is clear, however, that social media is here to stay. Stakeholders must work together to overcome the weaknesses of social media, as well as to leverage its strengths in a way that makes a positive contribution to election integrity.

This chapter outlines innovative opportunities for strengthening elections worldwide, as well as identifies critical challenges that must be addressed in order to leverage these opportunities. It is imperative that, when implementing these tools and mechanisms, election officials, scholars, and policymakers collaborate to identify, select, fund, and monitor these tools in a manner that ensures they are strengthening electoral integrity, versus weakening it.

References

Anderson, Janna, and Lee Rainie. "The Future of Truth and Misinformation Online." *Pew Research Center*, October 19, 2017. http://www.pewinternet.org/2017/10/19/the-future-of-truth-and-misinformation-online/.

Asunka, Joseph, Sarah Brierley, Miriam Golden, Eric Kramon, and George Ofosu. "Protecting the Polls: The Effect of Observers on Election Fraud." Unpublished manuscript, 2013. http://cega.berkeley.edu/assets/miscellaneous_files/Asunka_etal_Protecting_the_Polls.pdf.

Banerjee, Abhijit Vinayak, and Rohini Pande Selvan Kumar. "Do Informed Voters Make Better Choices? Experimental Evidence from Urban India." 2011. https://scholar.harvard.edu/files/rpande/files/do_informed_voters_make_better_choices.pdf.

Bartlett, Jamie, Alex Krasodomski-Jones, Nengak Daniel, Ali Fisher, and Sasha Jesperson. "Social Media for Election Communication and Monitoring in Nigeria." *Demos*, 2015. https://www.demos.co.uk/wp-content/uploads/2015/11/Social-Media-in-Nigerian-Election.pdf.

Bjornlund, Eric, and Glenn Cowan. "Vote Count Verification: A User's Guide for Funders, Implementers and Stakeholders." *Democracy International*, 2011. http://democracyinternational.com/resources/vote-count-verification-a-users-guide-for-funders-implementers-and-stakeholders/.

Bradshaw, Samantha, and Philip N. Howard. "Troops, Trolls and Troublemakers: A Global Inventory of Organized Social Media Manipulation." *Computational Propaganda Project: Oxford Internet Institute*, 2017. http://comprop.oii.ox.ac.uk/wp-content/uploads/sites/89/2017/07/Troops-Trolls-and-Troublemakers.pdf.

Bueza, Michael. n.d. "2016 Elections Random Manual Audit Report Out Soon." *Rappler*. http://www.rappler.com//nation/politics/elections/2016/133261-preliminary-random-manual-audit-report-target-release.

Byrd, William A. "Understanding Afghanistan's 2014 Presidential Election." *United States Institute of Peace*, 2015. https://www.usip.org/sites/default/files/SR370-Understanding-Afghanistan's-2014-Presidential-Election.pdf.

Carter Center. "Carter Center Limited Mission to the May 2010 Elections in the Philippines: Final Report." 2010. https://www.cartercenter.org/resources/pdfs/news/peace_publications/election_reports/philippines-may%202010-elections-finalrpt.pdf.

Cederberg, Gabriel. "Catching Swedish Phish: How Sweden is Protecting its 2018 Elections." *Belfer Center for Science and International Affairs*, 2018. https://www.belfercenter.org/sites/default/files/files/publication/Swedish%20Phish%20-%20final2.pdf.

Chapin, Doug. "The Rise of Social Media in Election Administration." *Election Online Weekly* (Blog), October 20, 2017. http://editions.lib.umn.edu/electionacademy/2017/10/20/electionlineweekly-on-the-rise-of-social-media-in-election-administration/.

Cheeseman, Nic, Gabrielle Lynch, and Justin Willis. "Digital Dilemmas: The Unintended Consequences of Election Technology." *Democratization*, 25, no. 8 (2018): 1397–1418.

CODEO. "Preliminary Statement on Ghana's December 7 to 8, 2012 Presidential and General Elections." 2013. http://www.codeoghana.org/images/CODEO_Preliminary_statement-2012_1.pdf.

Collier, Paul, and Pedro C. Vicente. "Votes and Violence: Evidence from a Field Experiment in Nigeria." *The Economic Journal*, 124, no. 574 (2014): F327–F355.

"COMELEC Records 99.884% Overall Accuracy Rate Based on the Ongoing Random Manual Audit." *UNTV News*, June 10, 2016. https://www.untvweb.com/news/comelec-records-99-884-overall-accuracy-rate-based-ongoing-random-manual-audit/.

Darnolf, Steffan, Katherine Ellena, Emily Lippolis, Erica Shein, Chad Vickery, Dan Murphy, Jed Ober, and Naomi Rasmussen. *Election Audits: International Principles That Protect Election Integrity*. Washington, DC: Democracy International and IFES, 2015. https://www.ifes.org/sites/default/files/2015_ifes_di_election_audit_white_paper_0.pdf.

Dimitrova, Daniela V., and Jörg Matthes. *Social Media in Political Campaigning Around the World: Theoretical and Methodological Challenges*. Los Angeles, CA: Sage, 2018.

ELOG. "ELOG's Observation of the Voting Process." 2013. http://www.elog.or.ke/index.php/104-voting2013.

Enikolopov, Ruben, Vasily Korovkin, Maria Petrova, Konstantin Sonin, and Alexei Zakharov. "Field Experiment Estimate of Electoral Fraud in Russian Parliamentary Elections." *Proceedings of the National Academy of Sciences*, 110, no. 2 (2013): 448–452. https://www.pnas.org/content/110/2/448.

Estok, Melissa, Neil Nevitte, and Glenn Cowan. *The Quick Count and Election Observation: An NDI Handbook for Civic Organizations and Political Parties*. Washington, DC: National Democratic Institute for International Affairs, 2002. https://www.ndi.org/node/24021.

Evrensel, Astrid. (Ed.). *Voter Registration in Africa: A Comparative Analysis*. Johannesburg: Electoral Institute for the Sustainability of Democracy in Africa, 2010. https://www.eisa.org.za/pdf/vrafrica.pdf.

"Final Report Expert Verification Mission of the Vote Tabulation of the November 28, 2010 Presidential Election in the Republic of Haiti." *Organization of American States*, 2011. http://scm.oas.org/pdfs/2011/CP25512E.pdf.

Frenkel, Shereen. "Made and Distributed in the U.S.A.: Online Disinformation—The New York Times." *New York Times*. https://www.nytimes.com/2018/10/11/technology/fake-news-online-disinformation.html. Accessed October 11, 2018.

Gallup. "Electronic Voting Machines/Biometric System Considered Most Effective For Free and Fair Elections." *Gallup Pakistan Website*, 2014. Retrieved from http://gallup.com.pk/wp-content/uploads/2015/02/241014.pdf.

Gallup. n.d. "Update: Americans' Confidence in Voting, Election." *Gallup.com*.. Accessed October 10, 2018. https://news.gallup.com/poll/196976/update-americans-confidence-voting-election.aspx.

Gelb, Alan, and Julia Clark. "Identification for Development: The Biometrics Revolution." *The Center for Global Development*, Working Paper 315, January 2013. https://www.files.ethz.ch/isn/159149/1426862_file_Biometric_ID_for_Development.pdf.

Gelb, Alan, and Anna Diofasi. "Biometric Elections in Poor Countries: Wasteful or a Worthwhile Investment." *The Center for Global Development*, Working Paper 435, August 2016. https://www.cgdev.org/sites/default/files/biometric-elections-poor-countries-wasteful-or-worthwhile-investment.pdf.

Hofmann, Sara, Daniel Beverungen, Michael Räckers, and Jörg Becker. "What Makes Local Governments' Online Communications Successful? Insights from a Multi-method Analysis of Facebook." *Government Information Quarterly*, 30, no. 4 (2013): 387–396.

Howard, Philip N., Samuel Woolley, and Ryan Calo. "Algorithms, Bots, and Political Communication in the US 2016 Election: The Challenge of Automated Political Communication for Election Law and Administration." *Journal of Information Technology & Politics*, 15, no. 2 (2018): 81–93.

Hyde, Susan D. "The Observer Effect in International Politics: Evidence From a Natural Experiment." *World Politics*, 60, no. 1 (2007): 37–63.

———. "Experimenting in Democracy: International Observers and the 2004 Presidential Elections in Indonesia." *Perspectives on Politics*, 8, no. 2 (2010): 511–527.

———. *The Pseudo-Democrat's Dilemma: Why Election Observation Became an International Norm*. New York: Cornell University Press, 2011.

Ichino, Naomi, and Matthias Schündeln. "Deterring or Displacing Electoral Irregularities? Spillover Effects of Observers in a Randomized Field Experiment in Ghana." *Journal of Politics*, 74, no. 1 (2012): 292–307.

"ICTs in Elections Database." *International Institute for Democracy and Electoral Assistance*, 2014. http://www.idea.int/elections/ict/.

Kaiser, Shana. "Social Media: A Practical Guide for Electoral Management Bodies." *International IDEA*, 2014. https://www.idea.int/sites/default/files/publications/social-media-guide-for-electoral-management-bodies.pdf.

Kavanaugh, Andrea L., Edward A. Fox, Steven D. Sheetz, Seungwon Yang, Lin Tzy Li, Donald J. Shoemaker, Apostol Natsev, and Lexing Xie. "Social Media Use by Government: From the Routine to the Critical." *Government Information Quarterly*, 29, no. 4 (2012): 480–491.

Keefer, Philip. "DPI2000: Database of Political Institutions: Changes and Variable Definitions." *The World Bank*, 2002. http://siteresources.worldbank.org/INTRES/Resources/DPI2004_variable-definitions.pdf.

Kelley, Judith G. *Monitoring Democracy: When International Election Observation Works, and Why It Often Fails*. Princeton, NJ: Princeton University Press, 2012.

Malik, Tariq. "Technology in the Service of Development: The NADRA Story." *Center for Global Development*, 2014. https://www.cgdev.org/publication/ft/technology-service-development-nadra-story.

Martinez, Eugenio. 2013. "Venezuela's Election System Holds Up as a Model for the World." *Forbes Leadership Forum*, 2013. https://www.forbes.com/sites/forbesleadershipforum/2013/05/14/venezuelas-election-system-holds-up-as-a-model-for-the-world/#6c701f671e23.

Mayhew, S. "Smartmatic Assists Venezuela [to] Conduct National Election." *BiometricUpdate.com*, October 10, 2012. Retrieved from www.biometricupdate.com/201210/smartmaticassists-venezuela-conduct-national-election/.

Norden, Lawrence, Aaron Burstein, Joseph Lorenzo Hall, and Margaret Chen. *Post-election Audits: Restoring Trust in Elections*. New York: Brennan Center for Justice, 2007. https://www.brennancenter.org/sites/default/files/legacy/d/download_file_50228.pdf.

Nwangu, Chikordiri. "Biometric Voting Technology and the 2015 General Elections in Nigeria." *National Conference on the 2015 General Election in Nigeria: The Real Issues*. The Electoral Institute, July 27–28, 2015. http://www.inecnigeria.org/wp-content/uploads/2015/07/Conference-Paper-by-Chikodiri-Nwangwu.pdf.

Nyst, Carly, and Nick Monaco. *State-Sponsored Trolling: How Governments Are Deploying Disinformation as Part of Broader Digital Harassment Campaigns*. Institute for the Future, 2018. http://www.iftf.org/fileadmin/user_upload/images/DigIntel/IFTF_State_sponsored_trolling_report.pdf.

"Observation Mission of the Bolivia Voter Registration 2009: Final Report." Atlanta, GA: The Carter Center, 2009. https://www.cartercenter.org/resources/pdfs/news/peace_publications/election_reports/finalreportboliviavoterregistration2009.pdf.

"Observing the 2006 Presidential Elections in Venezuela Final Report of the Technical Mission." n.d. *The Carter Center*, November 2017. https://www.cartercenter.org/resources/pdfs/news/peace_publications/democracy/venezuela_2006_eng.pdf.

Piccolino, G. "Infrastructural State Capacity for Democratization? Voter Registration and Identification in Cote d'Ivoire and Ghana Compared." *Democratization*, 23, no. 3 (2016): 498–519.

"Post-election Audits." *National Conference of State Legislatures*, January 3, 2019. http://www.ncsl.org/research/elections-and-campaigns/post-election-audits635926066.aspx.

"Preliminary Statement: Observation Mission to the 2014 Presidential and Provincial Council Elections in Afghanistan." *Democracy International*. http://democracyinternational.com/resources/preliminary-statement-observation-mission-to-the-2014-presidential-and-provincial-council-elections-in-afghanistan/. Accessed October 10, 2018.

Roose, Kevin. "6 Types of Misinformation to Beware of on Election Day (and What to Do If You Spot Them)—The New York Times." *New York Times*, November 5, 2018. https://www.nytimes.com/2018/11/05/us/politics/misinformation-election-day.html.

Rosnick, David, and Mark Weisbrot. "A Statistical Note on the April 14 Venezuelan Presidential Election and Audit of Results." *Center for Economic and Policy Research*, 2013. Retrieved from http://cepr.net/documents/publications/venezuela-election-audit-05-2013.pdf.

Sjoberg, Fredrik M. "Making Voters Count: Evidence from Field Experiments About the Efficacy of Domestic Election Observation." Unpublished paper, 2012. https://papers.ssrn.com/sol3/papers.cfm?abstract_id=2133592.

West Africa Civil Society Institute. "Conflict Prevention Resource Pack for Civilian Actors in West Africa. Module 1: Elections and Election Observation." 2009. (WACSI), Kofi Annan International Peacekeeping and Training Centre (KAIPTC), and German Technical Cooperation (GTZ).

Wolf, Peter. "Introducing Biometric Technology in Elections." *International Institute for Democracy and Electoral Assistance*, 2014. https://www.idea.int/publications/catalogue/introducing-biometric-technology-elections.

Wolf, Peter. "Introducing Biometric Technology in Elections." *International Institute for Democracy & Electoral Assistance (IDEA)*, 2017.

Woodward, John, Nicholas Orlans, and Peter Higgins. *Biometrics: Identity Assurance in the Information Age*. McGraw-Hill Osborne Media, 2003. https://dzapoytvj.updog.co/ZHphcG95dHZqMDA3MjIyMjI3MQ.pdf.

Kelly Ann Krawczyk is an associate professor of political science at Auburn University, where she directs the Ph.D. program in Public Administration and Policy. She teaches nonprofit and public administration courses in Auburn's MPA and Ph.D. programs. Her research focuses on the relationship between civil society and democracy. Her research is published in journals such as *Nonprofit & Voluntary Sector Quarterly, Voluntas*, and *International Review of Administrative Sciences*. She has authored book chapters and professional publications for the Governance Commission of Liberia and the World Bank.

Avery Davis-Roberts is associate director of the Democracy Program of The Carter Center, where she manages the center's projects on election standards, human rights and elections and inclusive and participatory political processes. She has managed election observation missions in Asia, Africa, South America, and the Middle East. Davis-Roberts has also worked as a human rights research consultant in the UK. She gained her undergraduate and master of laws degrees from the School of Oriental and African Studies at the University of London.

19

Conclusion

Kathleen Hale, Mitchell Brown and Bridgett A. King

The chapters in this volume identify several key themes for election officials in their work to execute elections, for policymakers in their reform efforts, and for researchers as they continue their examinations of the work of election administrators and related outcomes. The authors suggest areas of continuing research as well as new topics that warrant systematic study. As the nation moves into the 2020 election cycle, several large questions loom. One is how best to equip the election administration profession with the necessary knowledge and skills to operate effectively in a rapidly changing legal and technological environment. Another is how to equip election offices with voting systems and operating procedures that inspire voter confidence about the integrity of

K. Hale (✉) · M. Brown · B. A. King
Auburn University, Auburn, AL, USA
e-mail: halekat@auburn.edu

M. Brown
e-mail: brown11@auburn.edu

B. A. King
e-mail: bak0020@auburn.edu

© The Author(s) 2020
M. Brown et al. (eds.), *The Future of Election Administration*, Elections, Voting, Technology, https://doi.org/10.1007/978-3-030-14947-5_19

election administration broadly. Not least, another is how to sustain access to registration and voting for all eligible voters, which has been hard-won and which is still contestable in some locations.

Underlying all of these concerns is a clear intergovernmental mismatch between resources and authority. Long the province of local governments and funded by local commissions, election offices are strapped for the resources needed to enhance their operations, either through personnel capacity development or technology upgrades. State offices may be relatively more resource-rich in terms of technology, but are utterly without the personnel to conduct elections in almost every state. The federal government is perceived to be the "cash cow" in this dynamic, but lacks direct administrative authority outside the constitutional mandate of equal protection for voting rights (nor do we want this to read that we, or any of the authors in this volume, are advocating for such). The road forward may take many directions, but any productive policy or practice changes will require resources and cooperation across the intergovernmental system. With these, vendors will adapt to the changing environment, and nonprofit professional associations will meet the needs for training, professional development, and advocacy.

In the section that follows, we lift up the implications for practice, policy, and research from the chapters in this volume. We use these to craft a discussion about the key issues that policymakers, administrators, researchers, and the general public should be paying attention to in upcoming elections.

Implications from the Chapters in This Volume

Local control in election administration predates the formation of American states. Post *Shelby*, the role of the federal government in assuring equal protection in the exercise of voting rights has been less obvious. House Bill 1, the first piece of legislation introduced in January 2019 by the new Democratic-controlled House of Representatives, and redistricting cases across the country illustrate renewed Congressional interest and continuing judicial involvement in access (although the latter now requires voters to return to the courts on an ad hoc basis). Together these may suggest new pressures for centralization in principle in American federalism.

The hyper-partisanship that exists in early 2019 and the longest federal government shutdown in American history starting in 2018 and lasting into 2019 also brought some federal operations to a halt. A call for common ground has not been issued, and it remains to be seen whether common ground can be found on election issues. The continuing divide between the security canon (Republicans) and the access canon (Democrats) has perhaps stymied real progress toward practical solutions. The most recent federal judicial decision about the US Census illustrates the broader point. The country needs nonpartisan, or at least, well-intentioned, and reasoned bipartisan, discussions about how to support American elections best. This will take policy leadership from advocacy groups, election officials, and politicians and needs to be supported by unbiased research and media coverage.

The pressures for nationalization emanate from activities across the election administration system including access to registration and access to voting. Although the states retain great prerogative in the area, pressures for nationalization can arise from the inconsistent application of election administration practices. Different procedures for voter registration, voter file maintenance, and the administration of fail-safe provisional ballots fuel that conversation. While the success of reforms such as provisional ballots also suggests the need for nationalization, there are other reasons not to nationalize. The field also needs an unbiased, reasoned discussion about this.

Administrative capacity is an issue across government which, as a result of devolution, has worked permanent structural change into the relationships between subnational governments and the federal government, and between the private sector (public and nonprofit) and government at all levels. Public sector dependence on technology and the pressures of technological change are evident in relationships across the election administration system. Election administration capacity is critical and yet a great deal of this capacity comes from non-governmental sources.

Professionalization of the field has contributed to capacity. This has occurred at the institutional level through instruments like the Election Administration and Voting Survey (EAVS) and state-level comparative tools such as the Election Performance Index and the Election Administration Professionalism Index. Professionalization is also necessary at the individual level, and through training and identification of key competencies for the field, additional gains will continue. As these chapters illustrate, the local aspects of professionalism and capacity cannot be ignored. State level measures of election performance obscure local variation, which is itself not well-understood and has emerged only recently as a field of systematic study. These measures are important in any federal system, and yet state-to-state comparisons are challenging in this particular policy field due to historically localized implementation. Performance measurement in general also creates difficulties for local election officials if the measures that are used or the outcomes that are evaluated reflect factors outside their control. The local character of election administration is unlikely to change significantly given the constitutional imperatives that bifurcate responsibility between the federal government and the states. The human and financial resources required to shift any significant portion of local election office operations from counties and townships to the states are prohibitive. This means that researchers in the field must engage in a concerted effort to conduct coordinated and responsible studies of the work in localities both within and across states and by jurisdiction size and demographics.

Building capacity in a federal system also requires the development of common language across subnational units and subsystems, and the ability to communicate across election offices, nonprofit organizations, branches of government, and across election functions. These efforts have been enhanced significantly in recent years through the pursuit of a common data format and process maps for particular aspects of election operations. This work also needs to continue.

Several areas of the field remain understudied and should be the focus of additional systematic research. These include diversity of the election sector workforce and the cost of election administration. Diversity is a well-established principle of public administration and the public workforce in local and state election offices should be engaged in that conversation. No census exists of election office personnel at either the local or state level; anecdotal data suggests that the field can make great strides in this area. The costs of election administration remain illusive; the development of common terminology will also contribute to this aspect of the field.

Voting system integrity and security are essential to public trust in the election process. Vendor involvement with election offices is critical in sustaining the electronic technology that supports virtually all voting machines. Experts offer different opinions about the extent to which particular elements of America's voting systems are vulnerable to physical attacks (including cyber attacks) and natural disasters. What experts can agree on, however, is that all systems have vulnerabilities, and that election officials and vendors must be vigilant in monitoring and other preventive activities to be best situated to take appropriate action when (not if) threats occur. We add a note of caution to all of the related fields: vilifying vendors does not and will not help anyone.

Significant federal and intergovernmental infrastructure now exists to support local election operations. The designation of election systems as critical infrastructure has fostered new collaborative arrangements and new cross-jurisdictional relationships, and through these developments, election officials, vendors, and others related state offices have recognized the need to cooperatively to develop and maintain systems that inspire public confidence. This suggests that the field of election administration is particularly well situated to understand from and contribute to collaborative and information sharing processes.

New methods of post-hoc review or audits of election results are also emerging, such as risk-limiting audits, among others. Election officials can be expected to incorporate these methods into their office operations, increasing the technical pressure on these offices. New methods of addressing voter needs and public resources are also being developed. Together with researchers and advocates, these changes will help us better understand the efficacy of administrative practice and will hopefully feed back into policy, diffusion, and practice improvements, but only if resources are dedicated to this.

Finally, the international arena offers lessons for policy incorporated into American election systems. Outside the United States, trust in election operations is far less robust. But many of the processes used are more streamlined within other countries, and policies exist in these to encourage greater participation. As a field, we should pay more attention to the advances in other places to help forward our own.

Appendix: The Future of Election Administration: Cases and Conversations

Table of Contents
Chapter 1. Introduction
Bridgett A. King, Kathleen Hale, and Mitchell Brown

Section One: Reflections on History and Links to Reform

Chapter 2. Inter-Organizational Implementation: Carrying Out a Federal Court Order in Alabama
Robert Montjoy

Chapter 3. Reflections on the Creation and Implementation of Voting System Guidelines
Donetta Davidson and Tom Wilkey

Chapter 4. Improving Voting for Overseas Citizens, Military Personnel, and their Dependents
Kamanzi Kalisa

Chapter 5. Assisting Voters, Language Access, and the Role of Election Administrators
Jill LaVine and Alice Jarboe

Chapter 6. Accessibility Issues for Poll Sites and Voters
Bruce Adelson

Chapter 7. Protecting Election Infrastructure: A View from the Federal Level
Matthew Masterson

Chapter 8. Diversity in Election Administration: Understanding and Serving Your Voters
Lauri Ealom

Chapter 9. Changing Demographics in Election Administration
Shauna Dozier

Chapter 10. What Is the Role of the Vendor in Modern Elections?
Mindy Perkins

Chapter 11. The Cost of Convenience
Lori Edwards

Chapter 12. Ghana's 2012 General Election: Free, Fair, and Flawed?
Kelly Ann Krawczyk

Section Two: Professionalizing the Field and Building Capacity

Chapter 13. Creating Professionalism in the Field
Ernest Hawkins

Chapter 14. State Support for Local Election Offices
Lori Augino

Chapter 15. State Considerations in Understanding the Costs of Elections
Virginia Vander Roest

Chapter 16. Professional Development and Election Administration Advocacy
Lindsey Forson

Chapter 17. How an Election Administration Student Evolved into an Election Professional
Blake Evans

Chapter 18. Observations and Lessons from Election Administration in Nigeria
Tyler St. Clair and Shaniqua Williams

Chapter 19. The Role of Professional Associations in Supporting Election Administration
Tim Mattice

Chapter 20. The Road to Election Administration Professionalization—Follow the Bottom Line
Doug Chapin

Section Three: Tools for the Field

Chapter 21. A Voter-Centered, Voter First Approach to Elections
Amber McReynolds

Chapter 22. Implementing Wait Time Innovation in Election Administration: The Case of the EV Wait Times APP
Tim Tsujii

Chapter 23. Election Security and Large Counties
Noah Praetz

Chapter 24. Technology Procurement in Election Systems
David A. Bennett

Chapter 25. Using GIS to Improve Accuracy and Efficiency in Election Administration
Kim Brace

Chapter 26. Common Physical Barriers That Limit Access for Voters with Disabilities and Options to Solve Them
Jim Terry, Kaylan Dunlap, Steve Flickinger, and Dan Woosley

Chapter 27. Communication and Etiquette Considerations When Working With Voters Who Have Disabilities
Jim Terry, Kaylan Dunlap, Steve Flickinger, and Dan Woosley

Chapter 28. Operational Solutions That Help Voting Work for Everyone
Jim Terry, Kaylan Dunlap, Steve Flickinger, and Dan Woosley

Chapter 29. The Value of the Election Administration and Voting Survey (EAVS)
Sean Greene

Chapter 30. Local Engagement with the Election Administration and Voting Survey (EAVS)
Susan Gill

Chapter 31. Innovation in Synthesizing Big Data: The Electronic Registration Information Center (ERIC)
David Becker

Index

A

Absentee ballots 20, 59, 123, 126, 130, 135, 143, 144, 208, 224, 226, 245, 294
Absentee voting 2, 159, 203
Accessibility 20–22, 43, 44, 49–52, 57, 58, 84, 88–90, 92, 93, 95, 97, 136, 179, 206, 224, 228, 241, 333
Active duty service members 54
Administrative discretion 97, 169, 170, 177
10th Amendment 17
Auburn University vii, viii, 4, 12, 30, 41, 109, 117, 168, 184, 211, 343
Audit(s) vi, 5, 6, 11, 19, 123, 126, 127, 141, 142, 149, 161, 165, 203, 216, 222, 232, 233, 253–255, 257–259, 262–277, 294, 295, 297, 327–330, 337, 349
Audited expenditure reports 187
Automatic voter registration 2, 37, 60, 62, 63, 161, 250, 251

B

Ballots vii, 2, 6, 7, 11, 20–22, 26, 34, 40, 43, 54–57, 59, 66, 67, 72, 74–78, 94, 122, 123, 126, 127, 130, 135–138, 141–145, 149, 164, 170, 178, 189, 190, 203, 215, 219–221, 223, 224, 226–228, 231–233, 252, 254, 255, 257–259, 264–270, 273,

275–277, 306, 324, 327, 328, 347
Barriers to voting 84, 89, 93–95
Biometrics 322–326, 336
Budgets 10, 51, 191, 194, 294, 334
Bush v. Gore 32

C

Canvassing vii, 232, 233
Capacity 7, 66, 78, 104, 110, 117, 170, 181, 187, 204, 304, 346–348
Certification vi, 41, 45, 107, 110, 134, 162, 204, 205, 213, 228, 230, 232, 258, 272, 277, 295, 307, 308, 314
Civic education initiatives 320, 321, 336
Civil Rights Act (CRA) 18, 40, 169
Collaboration 163, 276, 336
Commission on Federal Election Reform (Carter-Baker) 215, 220, 221
Common Data Format (CDF) 9, 115, 156, 161–167, 348
Cost 5, 10, 11, 18, 26, 44, 45, 78, 173, 186–189, 194, 204, 223, 224, 269, 301, 302, 307, 308, 312, 313, 321, 324, 329, 336, 348
Curbside voting 17, 44
Cybersecurity 11, 19, 107, 112, 113, 139, 149, 150, 158, 161, 207, 223, 227, 230, 248, 249, 252, 253, 256, 279–281, 286–288, 290, 297

D

Democracy Index 120, 129
Democratic principles 243, 244
Department of Defense (DOD) 21, 56, 287, 288, 297
Department of Homeland Security (DHS) 11, 113, 207, 222, 230, 248, 252, 253, 259, 280, 283, 284, 286–291, 296–298
Department of Motor Vehicles 164, 166, 251
Descriptive representation 169–176, 179, 180
Direct Recording Electronic (DRE) 149, 246, 253, 254, 281
Disenfranchisement 12, 30, 184, 252, 257
Disinformation 6, 332–334, 337

E

Education 21, 41, 106, 108, 111, 113, 114, 180, 194, 216, 308, 309, 315, 319–322, 333, 336
Election accuracy 19, 50
Election Administration and Voting Survey (EAVS) 4, 9, 57, 65, 77, 78, 120, 122, 124, 126, 133, 134, 138, 142, 159, 162, 185
Election Assistance Commission (EAC) iv, v, ix, 19, 33, 43, 44, 47, 50, 58, 65, 110, 120, 124, 157, 170, 205, 207, 215, 217, 221, 222, 228, 230, 241, 251, 255, 291, 292, 314
Election costs 186, 190, 192, 194, 302, 311, 312

Index   357

Election day registration 19, 37, 61, 62, 77, 167
Election day voter registration 21, 66
Election fraud 149, 219, 320
Election integrity 10, 32, 213–216, 220, 222, 236, 243, 246, 247, 249, 253, 255–257, 289, 319, 337
Election jurisdictions 2, 3, 10, 32, 44, 84, 85, 150, 156, 185, 188, 191, 192, 253
Election night reporting 162, 163, 201, 203, 208, 231
Election observation 318, 320, 330, 336, 343
Election Performance Index (EPI) 9, 65, 78, 110–112, 119–122, 126, 128–130, 132–139, 142, 144–146, 148, 150, 151
Election security 49, 58, 142, 149, 189, 207, 234, 280, 288, 293, 295, 296
Elections Infrastructure Information Sharing and Analysis Center (EI-ISAC) 291
Election solution provider 10, 201–210
Election systems 2, 9, 19, 49, 58, 100, 153, 156, 157, 161, 162, 201, 203, 205, 207, 209, 210, 255, 281, 289, 295, 349
Electoral cycle 243–245, 319, 323
Electoral integrity 132, 133, 244, 253, 318, 322, 336, 337
Electoral Integrity Project 132, 244
Electronic pollbooks vi, 201, 208, 252

Electronic Registration Information Center (ERIC) 69, 121, 149, 150, 164, 222, 293
Expert ratings 131

F
Federalism 347
Federal Voting Assistance Program (FVAP) 20, 56, 57
Felon disenfranchisement 23
Fraud vi, 3, 35–37, 137, 138, 216, 219, 232, 246, 247, 262, 318–320, 323–325, 327–331

G
Get-out-the-vote (GOTV) 107
Global Commission on Elections 243–245
Glossary 9, 115, 158–161

H
Hacking 6, 223, 231, 247–249, 257, 263, 281, 284, 295, 297
Help America Vote Act (HAVA) 2, 19, 21, 32, 33, 43, 50, 66, 72, 77, 214, 215, 217, 220, 221, 227, 251, 293, 294, 297
Human rights 213, 244, 343

I
ICA 249
Independent election administrators 245
Information Sharing and Analysis Centers (ISACs) 207, 291

Innovation 5, 8, 11, 17, 23, 27, 62, 110, 186, 209, 271
Instant run off voting (IRV) 304, 305
Integrity 5, 10, 11, 33, 35, 39, 40, 50, 58, 59, 114, 115, 149, 203, 210, 214, 215, 220–224, 228, 231, 233, 243–246, 249, 250, 252, 253, 255, 257, 305–307, 315, 319, 322, 330, 345, 349
Interstate Crosscheck 69, 150

J

Jim Crow 50, 177

L

Language assistance 50, 53, 54
League of Women Voters 107, 218
Lever machines 203, 206
Limited English proficiency 52
Lines 1, 6, 24, 44, 87, 141, 156, 208, 221, 252
List maintenance 10, 60, 68, 69, 78, 82, 149, 150, 164, 170, 216, 217, 222, 250
Logic and Accuracy 230

M

Mail ballots 23, 56, 67, 123, 126, 135, 137, 138, 141, 143–145, 227, 309
Manipulation 34, 45, 231, 325
Margin 147, 233, 265, 267, 270, 277, 327
Measurement 5, 131, 136, 138, 146, 187, 188, 191, 348

Media 3–6, 35, 107, 161–163, 201, 203, 208, 214, 232, 234, 235, 248, 255, 274, 295, 315, 319, 332–337, 347
Military and Overseas Voter Empowerment Act (MOVE Act) 20, 55, 121, 142
Military and overseas voters 50, 54, 142, 160
Motor Voter 18

N

National Association of Election Officials (NAEO) 107
National Guard 288, 297
National Voter Registration Act (NVRA) ix, 18, 60–63, 67, 69, 71, 77, 78, 160, 166, 214–218, 221, 250, 296

O

Online registration 2, 122, 123, 126, 223
Online Voter Registration 62, 141, 164, 166, 223, 250, 259
Optical scan 209, 228, 253, 254, 268
Optical scanners 93, 94, 228, 254

P

Participation 3, 5, 7, 8, 12, 17, 18, 21, 22, 24–27, 32, 36, 39, 41, 44, 58, 62, 85, 97, 108, 146, 171, 173–175, 220, 221, 224, 245, 246, 301, 304, 309, 310, 312, 313, 315, 332, 349

Partisanship 31, 32, 42, 129, 180, 235, 246, 347
Pew Charitable Trusts 62, 65, 100, 108, 119, 120, 153
Polarization 246
Political empowerment 173
Political participation 12, 22, 24–26, 30, 108, 173, 220, 245
Pollbooks 201, 252
Polling locations 1, 2, 9, 17, 22, 24, 25, 84, 88–90, 92, 93, 97, 170, 176, 177, 251, 255, 257, 269, 305, 320
Polling places 21–23, 26, 40, 44, 51, 52, 54, 55, 58, 83–95, 97, 130, 136, 142, 167, 179, 180, 209, 224, 226, 231, 246, 252, 254, 256, 306, 319, 320, 328
Poll workers vii, 9, 22, 24, 52, 53, 58, 72, 77, 89, 170, 176–181, 185, 189, 205, 208, 224, 231, 256
Precinct 7, 24, 62, 72, 74, 85, 86, 94, 95, 105, 143, 209, 222, 232, 233, 249, 256, 265, 268, 273, 276, 277, 306, 323
Pre-registration 60, 62, 63
Privacy 21, 43, 215, 216
Process model 9, 156–159
Professionalism 9, 348
Professionalization 5, 8, 42, 45, 104–107, 109–113, 115, 142, 205, 347, 348
Provisional ballots 59, 68, 72, 74–76, 78, 122, 123, 126, 137, 159, 167, 215, 220, 221, 233, 252, 347
Purcell rule 38

R
Rank choice voting 301, 304, 309
Ranked voting 304, 305
Recount 6, 120, 129, 130, 203, 233, 254, 255, 257, 258, 265, 273, 293, 296, 327, 329
Registration 2, 7, 9, 11, 17–23, 37, 40–42, 45, 51, 56, 57, 59–61, 65, 66, 68, 69, 72, 73, 77, 78, 126, 130, 135, 137, 139, 142, 160, 166, 170, 178, 185, 187, 191, 194, 201, 213, 215, 217, 219, 222, 223, 232, 234, 244, 246, 249–251, 253, 282, 284, 289, 291, 295, 319, 324, 347
Resources 5, 7, 10, 18, 19, 23, 24, 34, 44, 45, 51–53, 56, 57, 104, 111, 142, 207, 220, 223, 230, 263, 296, 309, 326, 334, 335, 346, 348, 349
Risk limiting audit 295
Run off voting 304, 305

S
Same day registration 60, 62
Secretary of State 25, 42, 51, 55, 207, 226, 229, 306–308, 316
Section 203 22, 23, 53, 54
Security viii, 5, 10, 19, 34, 49, 50, 58, 131, 139, 148, 158, 162, 205–207, 209, 215, 216, 223, 227, 229, 230, 235, 243–246, 248, 249, 252, 253, 255, 256, 262, 276, 283, 284, 287, 291, 293–297, 305, 321, 323, 347, 349
Special election 302, 304, 311

Index

Stakeholders vi–viii, 51, 115, 157, 275, 288, 315, 337
50-state portability 7
Straight ticket voting 63
Street level bureaucrats 176, 177
Systems/subsystems 2, 3, 5–7, 19, 41, 46, 49, 51, 68, 104, 142, 143, 149, 156, 162, 164, 172, 189, 201, 203–206, 208, 222, 224, 228–230, 248, 253, 256, 268, 290, 291, 293, 295, 307, 308, 314, 316, 326, 345, 348

T

Tabulation 11, 201–203, 206, 208, 231, 233, 244, 245, 249, 254, 257, 258, 264, 266–268, 271, 275, 282, 330, 331
Tampering 107, 228, 230, 246, 256, 257, 281
Third party organizations 21
Threat environment 49
Training 6, 19, 41, 45, 52, 61, 104, 106, 107, 109–111, 113, 114, 158, 170, 191, 204–206, 231, 244, 287, 288, 294, 296, 326, 334, 346, 348
Transparency 3, 78, 134, 142, 148, 162, 165, 206, 216, 232, 249, 270, 274, 305, 307, 318, 327, 328, 330, 333
Trust 25, 26, 34, 36, 112, 170, 173, 215, 216, 220, 223, 227, 229, 231, 232, 236, 281, 318, 324, 326, 328, 349
Trust in government 25, 173

Turnout 6, 18–20, 23, 25, 61, 63, 77, 78, 83, 85, 97, 110, 112, 122, 123, 126, 127, 134, 137, 141–143, 146–148, 173, 174, 178, 185, 187, 194, 220, 235, 289, 309, 311, 312, 320–322

U

Uniformed and Overseas Citizens Absentee Voting Act (UOCAVA) 20, 55–57, 123, 126, 127, 136, 141, 142, 233
United States Postal Service (USPS) vi, 21, 56, 227
United States Supreme Court 32, 38, 221, 296
Universal and equal political participation 245
University of Minnesota 109, 168

V

Vacancy 301, 302, 304, 305, 308–314
Vendor(s) vii, viii, 5–7, 10, 157, 162, 164, 167, 201, 209, 210, 229, 248, 255, 281, 282, 307, 314, 328, 346, 349
Voluntary Voting System Guidelines (VVSG) 110, 157, 228, 255, 287
Vote by mail 2, 37, 67, 149, 215, 224, 309, 312
Voter access 5, 8, 160, 179, 312
Voter confidence 33, 36, 50, 58, 83, 138, 177, 179, 220, 231, 235, 250, 270, 331, 334, 345

Voter fatigue 304, 309–312
Voter fraud 3, 35, 216, 219, 246, 247
Voter identification 36, 186, 220, 323
Voter intimidation 35, 36
Voter participation 3, 17, 62, 85, 97, 224, 301, 304, 309, 310, 312, 313
Voter registration 2, 6, 8, 18–21, 37, 40, 41, 45, 59–63, 65–68, 72, 77, 78, 122, 124, 126, 135, 141, 142, 160, 164, 166, 185, 187, 191, 201, 213–217, 220, 222, 223, 232, 234, 244–246, 249–253, 256, 281–284, 286, 289–291, 294, 295, 315, 316, 319, 320, 323, 324, 326, 332, 347
Voter registration database 68, 164, 252, 253, 276
Voter registration lists 9, 59, 251, 252

Voter suppression 25, 35–37, 220
Voters with disabilities 2, 43, 44, 50, 51, 58, 187, 194, 226, 228
Voting Information Project (VIP) 121, 162, 164, 293
Voting machines 19, 22, 24, 26, 51, 77, 89, 93, 161, 170, 202, 203, 213, 222, 227, 231, 234, 247, 248, 254, 257, 265, 277, 281, 282, 325, 327, 328, 349
Voting Rights Act (VRA) 4, 18, 21, 22, 40, 53, 60, 180, 224, 295
Voting system v, vi, 2, 21, 51, 149, 157, 161, 165, 201–207, 210, 215, 228–230, 233, 241, 248, 253–259, 263, 265, 268–271, 273, 275, 277, 293, 305–308, 312, 314, 315, 329, 349
Voting technology 120, 129, 203, 329

GPSR Compliance

The European Union's (EU) General Product Safety Regulation (GPSR) is a set of rules that requires consumer products to be safe and our obligations to ensure this.

If you have any concerns about our products, you can contact us on

ProductSafety@springernature.com

In case Publisher is established outside the EU, the EU authorized representative is:

Springer Nature Customer Service Center GmbH
Europaplatz 3
69115 Heidelberg, Germany

www.ingramcontent.com/pod-product-compliance
Lightning Source LLC
LaVergne TN
LVHW010334260326
834688LV00036B/708